THE OXFORD

Essential Dictionary
of Legal Words

D1506712

Oxford Titles Available
from Berkley Books

THE OXFORD

Essential Dictionary
of Legal Words

BERKLEY BOOKS, NEW YORK

THE OXFORD ESSENTIAL DICTIONARY OF LEGAL WORDS

A Berkley Book / published by arrangement with
Oxford University Press, Inc.

PRINTING HISTORY
Berkley edition / July 2004

Copyright © 2004 by Oxford University Press, Inc.
Oxford is a registered trademark of Oxford University Press, Inc.

ISBN: 0-425-19706-9

A BERKLEY BOOK®
Berkley Books are published by The Berkley Publishing Group,
a division of Penguin Group (USA) Inc.
375 Hudson Street, New York, New York 10014.
BERKLEY and the "B" design
are trademarks belonging to Penguin Group (USA) Inc.

PRINTED IN THE UNITED STATES OF AMERICA

10 9 8 7 6 5 4 3 2 1

Contents

Staff

Preface

The *Oxford Essential Dictionary of Legal Words* is intended as a comprehensive, easy-to-use guide to the basic language of the law for professionals, students, and anyone who needs to understand our complex legal system. This dictionary includes more than a thousand of the most essential legal terms, defines them precisely, and adds additional information and example sentences to make their meanings crystal-clear for the nonlawyer. Including words relating to criminal justice (great for watchers of lawyer shows), everyday contracts and obligations, powers of attorney, words for those serving on juries or embroiled in divorces or small claims court, and words dealing with inheritance, trust, and estate law, this book will turn fear of "legalese" into competent understanding of important terms. Backmatter includes a list of online resources for legal aid and a bibliography for further reading about the law.

This handy "essential" dictionary, from Oxford, the most trusted name in dictionaries, is an excellent yet economical choice for those who need a quick reference to the language of the law.

Using This Dictionary

The "entry map" below explains the different parts of an entry.

Syllabification

Pronunciation set off with slashes / /

Grammar information in square brackets [ ]

dis•miss /dis'mis/ ▸ v. [trans.] refuse further hearing to (a case): *the judge dismissed the case for lack of evidence.*

■ revoke an order of a court: *the writ of certiorari is dismissed as improvidently granted.*

DERIVATIVES **dis•miss•al** /dis'misəl/ n.; **dis•miss•i•ble** /dis'misəbəl/ **adj.**

ORIGIN late Middle English: from medieval Latin *dismiss-*, variant of Latin *dimiss-* 'sent away,' from the verb *dimittere.*

Derivative section, derivatives in **boldface**

Etymology section

Subsenses signaled by ■

con•sor•ti•um /kən'sôrsH(ē)əm; -'sôrt̬ēəm/ ▸ n. (pl. **con•sor•ti•a** /kən'sôrsH(ē)ə; -'sôrt̬ēə/ or **con•sor•ti•ums**) the right of association and companionship with one's husband or wife.

PHRASES **loss of consortium** damage to a spouse for loss of companionship (often including sexual relations) due to injury to their spouse: *the extent to which a spouse may apply for loss of consortium damages in a wrongful death claim.*

Phrases section, phrases in **boldface**

Examples in *italic*

pub•lic law /'pəblik 'lô/ ▸ n. **1** the law of relationships between individuals and the government, such as constitutional, criminal, and administrative law.

2 another term for PUBLIC ACT.—— Cross references in BOLD SMALL CAPITALS

Main entries and other boldface forms

Main entries appear in boldface type, as do inflected forms, idioms and phrases, and derivatives. The words PHRASES and DERIVATIVES introduce those elements. Main entries and derivatives of two or more syllables show syllabification with centered dots.

Parts of speech

Each new part of speech is introduced by a small right-facing arrow.

Senses and subsenses

The main sense of each word follows the part of speech and any grammatical information (e.g., [trans.] before a verb definition). If there are two or more main senses for a word, these are numbered in boldface. Closely related subsenses of each main sense are introduced by a solid black box. In the entry for **dismiss** above, the main sense of "refuse further hearing to" is followed by a related sense, "revoke an order of a court."

Example sentences

Example sentences are shown in italic typeface; certain common expressions appear in bold italic typeface within examples.

Cross references

Cross references to main entries appear in small capitals. For example, in the entry **public law** seen previously, a cross reference is given in bold small capitals to the entry for PUBLIC ACT.

Pronunciation Key

This dictionary uses a simple respelling system to show how entries are pronounced, using the following symbols:

æ	*as in*	**hat** /hæt/, **fashion** /'fæsHən/, **carry** /'kærē/
a	*as in*	**day** /dā/, **rate** /rāt/, **maid** /mād/, **prey** /prā/
ä	*as in*	**lot** /lät/, **father** /'fäTHər/, **barnyard** /'bärn‚yärd/
b	*as in*	**big** /big/
CH	*as in*	**church** /CHərCH/, **picture** /'pikCHər/
d	*as in*	**dog** /dôg/, **bed** /bed/
e	*as in*	**men** /men/, **bet** /bet/, **ferry** /'ferē/
ē	*as in*	**feet** /fēt/, **receive** /ri'sēv/
er	*as in*	**air** /er/, **care** /ker/
ə	*as in*	**about** /ə'bowt/, **soda** /'sōdə/, **mother** /'məTHər/, **person** /'pərsən/
f	*as in*	**free** /frē/, **graph** /græf/, **tough** /təf/
g	*as in*	**get** /get/, **exist** /ig'zist/, **egg** /eg/
h	*as in*	**her** /hər/, **behave** /bi'hāv/
i	*as in*	**guild** /gild/, **women** /'wimin/
ī	*as in*	**time** /tīm/, **fight** /fīt/, **guide** /gīd/, **hire** /hīr/
ir	*as in*	**ear** /ir/, **beer** /bir/, **pierce** /pirs/
j	*as in*	**judge** /jəj/, **carriage** /'kærij/
k	*as in*	**kettle** /'ketl/, **cut** /kət/
l	*as in*	**lap** /læp/, **cellar** /'selər/, **cradle** /'krādl/
m	*as in*	**main** /mān/, **dam** /dæm/
n	*as in*	**honor** /'änər/, **maiden** /'mādn/
NG	*as in*	**sing** /siNG/, **anger** /'æNGgər/
ō	*as in*	**go** /gō/, **promote** /prə'mōt/
ô	*as in*	**law** /lô/, **thought** /THôt/, **lore** / lôr/
oi	*as in*	**boy** /boi/, **noisy** /'noizē/
o͝o	*as in*	**wood** /wo͝od/, **football** /'fo͝ot‚bôl/, **sure** /sHo͝or/
o͞o	*as in*	**food** /fo͞od/, **music** /'myo͞ozik/

ow	*as in* **mouse** /mows/, **coward** /'kowərd/
p	*as in* **put** /pŏŏt/, **cap** /kæp/
r	*as in* **run** /rən/, **fur** /fər/, **spirit** /'spirit/
s	*as in* **sit** /sit/, **lesson** /'lesən/
SH	*as in* **shut** /SHət/, **social** /'sōSHəl/, **action** /'ækSHən/
t	*as in* **top** /täp/, **seat** /sēt/
t̩	*as in* **butter** /'bət̩ər/, **forty** /'fôrt̩ē/, **bottle** /'bät̩l/
TH	*as in* **thin** /THin/, **truth** /trŏŏTH/
TH	*as in* **then** /THen/, **father** /'fäTHər/
v	*as in* **never** /'nevər/, **very** /'verē/
w	*as in* **wait** /wāt/, **quick** /kwik/
(h)w	*as in* **when** /(h)wen/, **which** /(h)wicH/
y	*as in* **yet** /yet/, **accuse** /ə'kyŏŏz/
z	*as in* **zipper** /'zipər/, **musician** /myŏŏ'zisHən/
ZH	*as in* **measure** /'mezHər/, **vision** /'vizHən/

Foreign Sounds

KH	*as in* **Bach** /bäKH/
N	*as in* **en route** /äN 'rŏŏt/, **Rodin** /rō'dæN/
œ	*as in* **hors d'oeuvre** /ôr 'dœvrə/, **Goethe** /'gœtə/
Y	*as in* **Lully** /lY'lē/, **Utrecht** /'Y,treKHt/

Stress marks

Stress marks are placed before the affected syllable. The primary stress mark is a short vertical line above the letters ['] and signifies greater pronunciation emphasis should be placed on that syllable. The secondary stress mark is a short vertical line below the letters [ˌ] and signifies a weaker pronunciation emphasis.

A

a•bate /əˈbāt/
▸ v. [trans.] lessen, reduce, or remove (esp. a nuisance): *this action would not have been sufficient to abate the odor nuisance.*
ORIGIN Middle English (in the legal sense 'put a stop to (a nuisance)'): from Old French *abatre* 'to fell,' from *a-* (from Latin *ad* 'to, at') + *batre* 'to beat' (from Latin *battere, battuere* 'to beat').

a•bate•ment /əˈbātmənt/
▸ n. the ending, reduction, or lessening of something: *noise abatement* | *an abatement in the purchase price.*
ORIGIN Middle English: from Anglo-Norman French, from Old French *abatre* 'fell, put an end to' (see ABATE).

ab•duc•tion /æbˈdəkSHən/
▸ n. the action or an instance of forcibly taking a person or persons away against their will: *they organized the abduction of Mr. Cordes on his way to the airport* | *abductions by armed men in plain clothes.*
■ the illegal removal from parents or guardians of a child.

a•bet /əˈbet/
▸ v. (**abetted, abetting**) [trans.] encourage or assist (someone) to do something wrong, in particular, to commit a crime or other offense: *he was not guilty of murder but was guilty of **aiding and abetting** others.*
■ encourage or assist someone to commit (a crime): *we are **aiding and abetting** this illegal traffic.*
DERIVATIVES **a•bet•ment** n.; **a•bet•tor** /əˈbetər/ (also **a•bet•ter**) n.
ORIGIN late Middle English (in the sense 'urge to do

something good or bad'): from Old French *abeter*, from *a-* (from Latin *ad* 'to, at') + *beter* 'hound, urge on.'

ab•jure /æb'jŏŏr/

▶ v. [trans.] formal solemnly renounce (a belief, cause, or claim): *the state has abjured the authority to execute custodial arrests for such minor offenses.*
DERIVATIVES **ab•ju•ra•tion** /ˌæbjə'rāsHən/ n.
ORIGIN late Middle English: from Latin *abjurare*, from *ab-* 'away' + *jurare* 'swear.'

a•bridge /ə'brij/ ▶ v. [trans.] (usu. **be abridged**) curtail

(rights or privileges): *even the right to free speech can be abridged.*
ORIGIN Middle English (in the sense 'deprive of'): from Old French *abregier*, from late Latin *abbreviare* 'cut short'.

ab•ro•gate /'æbrəˌgāt/

▶ v. [trans.] formal repeal or do away with (a law, right, or formal agreement): *a proposal to abrogate temporarily the right to strike.*
DERIVATIVES **ab•ro•ga•tion** /ˌæbrə'gāsHən/ n.
ORIGIN early 16th cent.: from Latin *abrogat-* 'repealed,' from the verb *abrogare*, from *ab-* 'away, from' + *rogare* 'propose a law.'

ab•scond /æb'skänd/

▶ v. [intrans.] leave hurriedly and secretly, typically to avoid detection of or arrest for an unlawful action such as theft: *she absconded with the remaining thousand dollars.* ■ (of someone on bail) fail to surrender oneself for custody at the appointed time. ■ (of a person kept in detention or under supervision) escape: *176 detainees absconded.*
DERIVATIVES **ab•scond•er** n.
ORIGIN mid 16th cent. (in the sense 'hide, conceal

(oneself)'): from Latin *abscondere* 'hide,' from *ab-* 'away, from' + *condere* 'stow.'

ab•so•lute ti•tle /'æbsə‚lo͞ot 'tīṯl/
▶ n. guaranteed title to the ownership of a property or lease.

ab•stract of ti•tle /'æbstrækt əv 'tīṯl/
▶ n. a summary giving details of the title deeds and documents that prove an owner's right to dispose of land, together with any encumbrances that relate to the property.

ac•ces•sion /æk'seSHən/
▶ n. **1** the attainment or acquisition of a position of rank or power, typically that of monarch or president: *the queen's **accession to the throne** | lost the vote on the Fortas accession to the chief justiceship.*
■ the action or process of formally joining or being accepted by an association, institution, or group: *the accession of Spain and Portugal into the European Community.*
2 a new item added to an existing collection of books, paintings, or artifacts.
■ an amount added to an existing quantity of something: *did not anticipate any further accession of wealth from the man's estate.*
3 the formal acceptance of a treaty or agreement: *accession to the Treaty of Paris.*
▶ v. [trans.] (usu. **be accessioned**) record the addition of (a new item) to a library, museum, or other collection.
ORIGIN late 16th cent. (in the general sense 'something added'): from Latin *accession-*, from the verb *accedere* 'approach, come to' (see ACCEDE).

ac•ces•so•ry /æk'ses(ə)rē/ (also ac•ces•sa•ry)
▶ n. (pl. **ac•ces•so•ries**) someone who gives assistance to

the perpetrator of a crime, without directly committing it, sometimes without being present: *she was charged as an **accessory** to murder.* Compare with PRINCIPAL.

PHRASES **accessory before** (or **after**) **the fact** dated a person who incites or assists someone to commit a crime (or knowingly aids someone who has committed a crime).

ORIGIN late Middle English: from medieval Latin *accessorius* 'additional thing,' from Latin *access-* 'increased,' from the verb *accedere*.

ac•com•plice /ə'kämplis/
▸ n. a person who helps another commit a crime.
ORIGIN mid 16th cent.: alteration (probably by association with *accompany*) of Middle English *complice* 'an associate,' via Old French from late Latin *complex, complic-* 'allied,' from *com-* 'together' + the root of *plicare* 'to fold.'

ac•cu•sa•to•ri•al /ə,kyo͞ozə'tôrēəl/
▸ adj. [attrib.] (esp. of a trial or legal procedure) involving accusation by a prosecutor and a verdict reached by an impartial judge or jury. Often contrasted with INQUISITORIAL.

ac•quaint•ance rape /ə'kwāntəns ,rāp/
▸ n. rape by a person who is known to the victim.

ac•quit /ə'kwit/
▸ v. (**acquitted, acquitting**) [trans.] (usu. **be acquitted**) free (someone) from a criminal charge by a verdict of not guilty: *she was acquitted on all counts* | *the jury **acquitted** him of murder.*
ORIGIN Middle English (originally in the sense 'pay a debt, discharge a liability'): from Old French *acquiter*, from medieval Latin *acquitare* 'pay a debt,' from *ad-* 'to' + *quitare* 'set free.'

ac•quit•tal /əˈkwitl/
 ▸ **n.** a judgment that a person is not guilty of the crime with which the person has been charged: *the trial resulted in an acquittal* | *the women felt their chances of acquittal were poor.*

act /ækt/
 ▸ **v.** [intrans.] (**act for/on behalf of**) represent (someone) on a contractual, legal, or paid basis: *he chose an attorney to act for him.*
 ▸ **n. 1** (often as **criminal act**) a constituent element of a crime or tort: *they argued over whether the burning of the flag is a criminal act.*
 2 a written ordinance of Congress, or another legislative body; a statute: *the act to abolish slavery.*
 ◼ a document attesting a legal transaction. ◼ (often **acts**) dated the recorded decisions or proceedings of a committee or an academic body.
 PHRASES **act of God** an instance of uncontrollable natural forces in operation (often used in insurance claims).
 read the Riot Act see Riot Act.
 ORIGIN late Middle English: from Latin *actus* 'event, thing done,' *act-* 'done,' from the verb *agere*, reinforced by the French noun *acte.*

ac•tion /ˈækSHən/
 ▸ **n.** a legal process; a lawsuit: *an action for damages.*
 ORIGIN late Middle English: via Old French from Latin *actio(n-)*, from *agere* 'do, act.'

ac•tion•a•ble /ˈækSHənəbəl/
 ▸ **adj.** giving sufficient reason to take legal action: *slanderous remarks are actionable.*

ac•tus re•us /ˌæktəs ˈrēəs; ˈrāəs/
 ▸ **n.** action or conduct that is a constituent element of a crime, as opposed to the mental state of the accused:

[as modifier] *the statutes do not characterize hate and bias as actus reus conditions.* Compare with MENS REA.

ORIGIN early 20th cent.: Latin, literally 'guilty act.'

ad li•tem /æd ˈlītəm/
▸ **adj.** (esp. of a guardian) appointed to act in a lawsuit on behalf of a child or other person who is not considered capable of representing themselves: *you'll have to discuss that with the girls' guardian ad litem.*

ORIGIN mid 18th cent.: Latin, literally 'for the lawsuit.'

ad•min•is•tra•tion /ədˌminəˈstrāsHən/ (abbr.: **admin.**)
▸ **n.** the management and disposal of the property of an intestate, deceased person, debtor, or other individual, or of an insolvent company, by a legally appointed administrator: *the company went into administration* | [as adj.] *an administration order.*

ORIGIN Middle English: from Latin *administratio(n-)*, from the verb *administrare.*

ad•min•is•tra•tor /ədˈminəˌstrātər/
▸ **n.** a person legally appointed to manage and dispose of the estate of an intestate, deceased person, debtor, or other individual, or of an insolvent company.

ad•min•is•tra•trix /ədˈminəˌstrātriks/
▸ **n.** a female administrator of an estate.

ad•mi•ral•ty /ˈædmərəltē/
▸ **n.** (pl. **ad•mi•ral•ties**) the jurisdiction of courts of law over cases concerning ships or the sea and other navigable waters (maritime law).

ORIGIN late Middle English: from Old French *admiralte*, from *admirail* 'emir, leader.'

ADR
▸ **abbr.** alternative dispute resolution.

a•dult /ə'dəlt; 'æd,əlt/
  ▸ n. a person who has reached the age of majority.
  ORIGIN mid 16th cent.: from Latin *adultus*, past participle of *adolescere* 'grow to maturity.'

a•dul•ter•y /ə'dəlt(ə)rē/
  ▸ n. voluntary sexual intercourse between a married person and a person who is not his or her spouse: *she was committing adultery with a much younger man.*
  ORIGIN late 15th cent.: from the obsolete noun *adulter*, from Latin *adulter* 'adulterer,' replacing an earlier form *avoutrie*, from Old French *avouterie*, likewise based on Latin *adulter*.

ad va•lo•rem /,æd və'lôrəm/
  ▸ adv. & adj. (of the levying of tax or customs duties) in proportion to the estimated value of the goods or transaction concerned: [as adj.] *the property owner may be eligible for a reduction in ad valorem taxes.*
  ORIGIN late 17th cent.: Latin, literally 'according to the value.'

ad•vance di•rec•tive /əd'væns də,rektiv/
  ▸ n. a written statement of a person's wishes regarding medical treatment, often including a living will, made to ensure those wishes are carried out should they be unable to communicate them to a doctor.

ad•ver•sar•i•al /,ædvər'serēəl/
  ▸ adj. (of a trial or legal procedure) in which the parties in a dispute have the responsibility for finding and presenting evidence: *equality between prosecution and defense is essential in an adversarial system of justice.* Compare with INQUISITORIAL.

ad•verse pos•ses•sion /'ædvərs pə'zeSHən/
  ▸ n. the acquisition of property by a trespasser whose

occupation of the property is exclusive, open, and continuous for a statutory period.

ad•vo•ca•cy /ˈædvəkəsē/
▸ n. the profession or work of a legal advocate.
ORIGIN late Middle English: via Old French from medieval Latin *advocatia*, from *advocare* 'summon, call to one's aid' (see ADVOCATE).

ad•vo•cate
▸ n. /ˈædvəkit/ a pleader in a court of law; a lawyer: *Marshall was a skilled advocate but a mediocre judge.*
ORIGIN Middle English: from Old French *avocat*, from Latin *advocatus*, past participle (used as a noun) of *advocare* 'call (to one's aid),' from *ad-* 'to' + *vocare* 'to call.'

af•fi•ant /əˈfiənt/
▸ n. a person who swears to an affidavit: *your affiant, Special Agent Perez, has been a sworn police officer for 22 years.*
ORIGIN early 19th cent.: from French, present participle of *afier*, from medieval Latin *affidare* 'declare on oath.'

af•fi•da•vit /ˌæfiˈdāvit/
▸ n. a written statement confirmed by oath or affirmation, for use as evidence in court.
ORIGIN mid 16th cent.: from medieval Latin, literally 'he has stated on oath,' from *affidare*.

af•firm /əˈfərm/
▸ v. [trans.] declare, support, or defend as fact, specifically:
■ accept or confirm the validity of (a judgment or agreement); ratify: *we affirm the judgment of the trial court.* ■ (of a court) uphold (a decision) on appeal: *the committee shall have the power to affirm, modify, or reject the decision.* ■ [intrans.] make a formal declaration rather than taking an oath (e.g., to testify truthfully): *I solemnly affirm.*

ORIGIN Middle English (in the sense 'make firm'): via Old French from Latin *affirmare*, from *ad-* 'to' + *firmus* 'strong.'

af•firm•a•tion /ˌæfərˈmāsHən/
▶ **n.** a formal declaration by a person who declines to take an oath for reasons of conscience.
ORIGIN late Middle English: from Latin *affirmation-*, from the verb *affirmare* (see AFFIRM).

af•fray /əˈfrā/
▶ **n.** dated an instance of group fighting in a public place that disturbs the peace: *Lowe was charged with causing an affray | a person guilty of affray.*
ORIGIN Middle English (in the general sense 'disturbance, fray'): from Anglo-Norman French *afrayer* 'disturb, startle,' based on an element of Germanic origin related to Old English *frithu* 'peace, safety' (compare with German *Friede* 'peace').

a•fore•thought /əˈfôrˌTHôt/
▶ **adj.** see MALICE AFORETHOUGHT.

AG
▶ **abbr.** attorney general.

age of con•sent /ˈāj əv kənˈsent/
▶ **n.** the age at which a person's, typically a girl's, consent to sexual intercourse is valid in law.

ag•gra•vat•ed /ˈægrəˌvātid/
▶ **adj.** [attrib.] (of an offense) made more serious by attendant circumstances (such as frame of mind): *aggravated burglary.*
■ (of a penalty) made more severe in recognition of the seriousness of an offense: *aggravated damages.*
DERIVATIVES **ag•gra•vat•ing adj.**: *aggravating factors in a death penalty case.*

a·gree·ment /əˈgrēmənt/
▸ n. a typically legally binding arrangement between parties as to a course of action: *a trade agreement* | *a verbal agreement to sell.*
ORIGIN late Middle English: from Old French, from *agreer* 'make agreeable to.'

al·ien·a·ble /ˈālēənəbəl; ˈālyən-/
▸ adj. able to be transferred to new ownership: *alienable common stock.*
DERIVATIVES **a·lien·a·bil·i·ty** /ˌālēənəˈbilitē; ˌālyən-/ n.

al·ien·ate /ˈālēəˌnāt; ˈālyə-/
▸ v. [trans.] transfer ownership of (property rights) to another person or group: *he had the right to alienate the property.*
PHRASES **alienate someone's affections** induce someone to transfer their affection from a person (such as a spouse) with legal rights or claims on them: *the plaintiff sued a colleague for alienating the affections of plaintiff's wife.*
ORIGIN early 16th cent.: from Latin *alienat-* 'estranged,' from the verb *alienare*, from *alienus* 'of another.'

al·ien·a·tion /ˌālēəˈnāsHən; ˌālyə-/
▸ n. the transfer of the ownership of property rights.
ORIGIN late Middle English: from Latin *alienatio(n-)*, from the verb *alienare* 'estrange,' from *alienus*.

al·i·mo·ny /ˈæləˌmōnē/
▸ n. a husband's or wife's court-ordered provision for a spouse after separation or divorce.
ORIGIN early 17th cent. (in the sense 'nourishment, means of subsistence'): from Latin *alimonia* 'nutriment,' from *alere* 'nourish.'

al·lo·cu·tion /ˌæləˈkyooSHən/
▸ n. the right of a convicted defendant to speak on their

own behalf before sentencing is pronounced: *the trial court determined Goodwin was not granted allocution at his original sentencing.*

■ an unsworn statement delivered (to the sentencing court) by a convicted defendant in which the defendant attempts to win a lesser sentence by such persuasion as requesting mercy, expressing regret, or giving a reasonable explanation for the criminal conduct: *the sentencing court indicated on the record that the defendant's allocution did not affect its sentencing decision.*

DERIVATIVES **al•lo•cute** /ˌælə'kyo͞ot/ v.; **al•loc•u•tor•y** /ˌælə'kyo͞otərē/ adj.

ORIGIN early 17th cent.: from Latin *allocutio(n-)*, from *alloqui* 'speak to,' from *ad-* 'to' + *loqui* 'speak.'

al•ter•na•tive dis•pute res•o•lu•tion /ôl'tərnətiv dis'pyo͞otrēzəˌlo͞oSHən/ (abbr.: **ADR**)

▸ n. the use of methods such as mediation or arbitration to resolve a dispute instead of litigation.

a•me•na•ble /ə'mēnəbəl; ə'men-/

▸ adj. (**amenable to**) (of a thing) capable of being acted upon in a particular way; susceptible: *the defendant was amenable to suit in the jurisdiction.*

DERIVATIVES **a•me•na•bil•i•ty** /əˌmēnə'bilitē; əˌmen-/ n.; **a•me•na•bly** /ə'mēnəblē; ə'men-/ adv.

ORIGIN late 16th cent. (in the sense 'liable to answer (to a law or tribunal)'): an Anglo-Norman French legal term, from Old French *amener* 'bring to,' from *a-* (from Latin *ad*) 'to' + *mener* 'bring' (from late Latin *minare* 'drive (animals),' from Latin *minari* 'threaten').

a•merce•ment /ə'mərsmənt/

▸ n. historical a fine.

DERIVATIVES **a•merce** v.

ORIGIN late Middle English: from Anglo-Norman French *amerciment*, based on *estre amercie* 'be at the mercy of another' (with respect to the amount of a fine), from *a merci* 'at (the) mercy.'

a•mi•cus /əˈmēkəs; əˈmī-/ (in full **a•mi•cus cu•ri•ae** /ˈkyo͝orēˌī; ˈkyo͞o-rēˌē/)

▶ n. (pl. **a•mi•ci** /əˈmēkē; əˈmīkī/, **amici curiae**) an adviser, often voluntary, to a court of law in a particular case, who is a party to the case: [as adj.] *he was planning to advance this position in an **amicus brief**.*

ORIGIN early 17th cent.: from modern Latin *amicus curiae*, literally 'friend of the court.'

an•swer /ˈænsər/

▶ n. the defendant's reply to the plaintiff's charges: *jury demand is made in defendant's answer.*

▶ v. [trans.] defend oneself against (a charge, accusation, or criticism): *he said he would return to Spain to answer all charges.*

■ [intrans.] (**answer to**) be required to explain or justify oneself to (someone): *you will have the police to answer to.*

PHRASES **answer the description of** correspond to a description, esp. one of a suspect issued by the police: *he answers the description of being slightly taller than his two supposed companions.*

ORIGIN Old English *andswaru* (noun), *andswarian* (verb), of Germanic origin; from a base shared by SWEAR.

an•tic•i•pa•to•ry /ænˈtisəpəˌtôrē/

▶ adj. (of a breach of contract) taking the form of an announcement or indication that a contract will not be honored: *the appellants' commencement of the lawsuit constituted anticipatory breach of the contract.*

an•ti•trust /ˌæntēˈtrəst; ˌæntī-/

▶ adj. of or relating to legislation preventing or controlling trusts or other monopolies, with the intention of promoting competition in business: *West Virginia joins Massachusetts in its ongoing antitrust battle against Microsoft.*

ap•peal /əˈpēl/
▸ **v.** [intrans.] apply to a higher court for a reversal of the decision of a lower court: *he said he would* **appeal against** *the conviction* | [trans.] *they have 48 hours to appeal the decision.*
▸ **n.** an application to a higher court for a decision to be reversed: *he has 28 days in which to* **lodge an appeal** | *the right of appeal.*
DERIVATIVES **ap•peal•a•ble** /əˈpēləbəl/ **adj.**
ORIGIN Middle English (in legal contexts): from Old French *apel* (noun), *apeler* (verb), from Latin *appellare* 'to address,' based on *ad-* 'to' + *pellere* 'to drive.'

ap•peals court /əˈpēlz ˌkôrt/
▸ **n.** a court that hears appeals from a lower court.

ap•pear /əˈpir/
▸ **v.** [intrans.] (of an accused person, witness, or lawyer) make an official appearance in a court of law: *he* **appeared on** *six charges of theft.*
ORIGIN Middle English: from Old French *apareir*, from Latin *apparere*, from *ad-* 'toward' + *parere* 'come into view.'

ap•pel•lant /əˈpelənt/
▸ **n.** a person who applies to a higher court for a reversal of the decision of a lower court.
ORIGIN late Middle English: from French *apelant*, literally 'appealing,' from the verb *apeler* (see APPEAL).

ap•pel•late /əˈpelit/
▸ **adj.** (typically of a court) concerned with or dealing

with applications for decisions to be reversed: *there are two appellate courts in Iowa | rules of appellate procedure.* ORIGIN late Middle English (originally in the sense 'appealed against, accused'): from Latin *appellatus* 'appealed against,' from the verb *appellare* (see APPEAL). The current sense dates from the mid 18th cent.

ap•pel•lee /ˌæpeˈlē/
▶ n. the respondent in a case appealed to a higher court.
ORIGIN mid 16th cent.: from French *appelé,* past participle of *appeler* 'call,' from Latin *appellare* 'to address' (see APPEAL).

ap•point /əˈpoint/
▶ v. [trans.] decide the disposal of (property of which one is not the owner) under powers granted by the owner: *trustees appoint the capital to the beneficiaries.*
DERIVATIVES **ap•point•ee** /əˌpoinˈtē/ n.; **ap•point•er** n.
ORIGIN late Middle English: from Old French *apointer,* from *a point* 'to a point.'

ar•bi•tral /ˈärbitrəl/
▶ adj. relating to or resulting from the use of an arbitrator to settle a dispute: *the tribunal respects the enforcement of international arbitral awards.*
ORIGIN late 15th cent.: from late Latin *arbitralis,* from *arbiter* 'judge, supreme ruler.'

ar•bi•trar•y /ˈärbiˌtrerē/
▶ adj. based on unreasonable or capricious exercise of discretion: *Amnesty International condemns the nationwide arbitrary arrests of forty-two journalists | the applicant has failed to demonstrate the judge's decision is arbitrary.*
DERIVATIVES **ar•bi•trar•i•ly** /ˌärbəˈtrerəlē/ adv.; **ar•bi•trar•i•ness** n.
ORIGIN late Middle English (in the sense 'dependent on one's will or pleasure, discretionary'): from Latin *ar-*

bitrarius, from *arbiter* 'judge, supreme ruler,' perhaps influenced by French *arbitraire.*

ar•bi•trate /'ärbi,trāt/
▸ v. [intrans.] (of an independent person or body) reach an authoritative judgment or settlement: *by agreeing to arbitrate this dispute, parties give up their legal right to bring a court action and to have a jury trial.*
ORIGIN mid 16th cent.: from Latin *arbitrat-* 'judged,' from *arbitrari,* from *arbiter* 'judge, supreme ruler.'

ar•bi•tra•tion /,ärbi'trāsHən/
▸ n. the use of an arbitrator to settle a dispute: *arbitration is generally faster, less expensive, and more informal than going to court.*
PHRASES **go to arbitration** submit a dispute to an arbitrator: *the fifty-seven school districts went to arbitration in sixty-eight separate cases.*

ar•bi•tra•tor /'ärbi,trātər/
▸ n. an independent person or body officially appointed to settle a dispute: *the decision of the arbitrator can be enforced by the courts, if necessary.*

ar•raign /ə'rān/
▸v. [trans.] (often **be arraigned**) call or bring (someone) before a court to answer a criminal charge: *her sister was arraigned on attempted murder charges.*
DERIVATIVES **ar•raign•ment** n.
ORIGIN late Middle English: from Old French *araisnier,* based on Latin *ad-* 'to' + *ration-* 'reason, account.'

ar•ray /ə'rā/
▸n. a list of jurors empaneled.
▸v. [trans.] empanel (a jury).
ORIGIN Middle English (in the senses 'preparedness' and 'place in readiness'): from Old French *arei* (noun),

areer (verb), based on Latin *ad-* 'toward' + a Germanic base meaning 'prepare.'

ar•rears /ə'rirz/

▸ **plural n.** money that is owed and should have been paid earlier: *he was suing the lessee for the arrears of rent.*

PHRASES **in arrears** (also **in arrear**) behind in paying money that is owed: *two out of three tenants are in arrears.*

DERIVATIVES **ar•rear•age** /ə'ririj/ n.

ORIGIN Middle English (first used in the phrase *in arrear*): from *arrear* (adverb) 'behind, overdue,' from Old French *arere*, from medieval Latin *adretro*, from *ad-* 'toward' + *retro* 'backward.'

ar•rest /ə'rest/

▸ **v.** [trans.] seize (someone) by legal authority and take into custody: *the police **arrested** him for possession of marijuana | two youths aged 16 were arrested.*

▸**n.** the action of seizing someone to take into custody: *I have a warrant for your arrest | they **placed** her **under arrest** | at least 69 arrests were made.*

ORIGIN late Middle English: from Old French *arester*, based on Latin *ad-* 'at, to' + *restare* 'remain, stop.'

ar•rest•ee /ə,res'tē/

▸ **n.** a person who has been arrested.

ar•son /'ärsən/

▸ **n.** the criminal act of deliberately setting fire to property: *police are treating the fire as arson | [as adj.] an arson attack.*

DERIVATIVES **ar•son•ist** /'ärsənist/ n.

ORIGIN late 17th cent.: an Anglo-Norman French legal term, from medieval Latin *arsio(n-)*, from Latin *ardere* 'to burn.'

ar•ti•cle /'ärtikəl/

▸ **n.** a separate clause or paragraph of a legal document

or agreement, typically one outlining a single rule or regulation: [as adj.] *it is an offense under Article 7 of the treaty.*

ORIGIN Middle English (denoting a separate clause of the Apostles' Creed): from Old French, from Latin *articulus* 'small connecting part,' diminutive of *artus* 'joint.'

as•por•ta•tion /ˌæspərˈtāsHən/
▸ n. rare the detachment, movement, or carrying away of property, considered an essential component of the crime of larceny.

ORIGIN late 15th cent.: from Latin *asportation-*, from *asportare* 'carry away.'

as•sault /əˈsôlt/
▸ v. [trans.] make a physical attack on: *he pleaded guilty to assaulting a police officer* | *she was sexually assaulted as a child.*
▸ n. a physical attack: *his imprisonment for an **assault on** the film director* | *sexual assaults.*
■ an act, criminal or tortious, that threatens physical harm to a person, whether or not actual harm is done: *he appeared in court charged with assault.*

DERIVATIVES **as•sault•er** n.

ORIGIN Middle English: from Old French *asaut* (noun), *assauter* (verb), based on Latin *ad-* 'to' + *saltare*, frequentative of *salire* 'to leap.'

as•sault and bat•ter•y /əˈsôlt ən(d) ˈbæt(ə)rē/
▸ n. the crime of threatening a person together with the act of making physical contact with them.

as•sign /əˈsīn/
▸ v. [trans.] transfer (legal rights or liabilities): *they will ask you to assign your rights against the airline.*
▸ n. another term for ASSIGNEE.

DERIVATIVES **as•sign•a•ble** adj.; **as•sign•or** /əˈsīnôr/ n.

ORIGIN Middle English: from Old French *asigner*, *assiner*, from Latin *assignare*, from *ad-* 'to' + *signare* 'to sign.'

as•sign•ee /ˌəˌsīˈnē/

▶n. a person to whom a right or liability is legally transferred.

ORIGIN Middle English: from Old French *assigne*, past participle of *assigner* 'allot' (see ASSIGN).

as•sign•ment /əˈsīnmənt/

▶n. an act of making a legal transfer of a right, property, or liability: *an assignment of leasehold property.*
▪ a document effecting such a transfer.

ORIGIN late Middle English: from Old French *assignement*, from medieval Latin *assignamentum*, from Latin *assignare* 'allot' (see ASSIGN).

as•size /əˈsīz/

▶n. (usu. **assizes**) historical a court that formerly sat at intervals in each county of England and Wales to administer the civil and criminal law. In 1972 the civil jurisdiction of assizes was transferred to the High Court, and the criminal jurisdiction to the Crown Court.

ORIGIN Middle English: from Old French *assise*, feminine past participle of *asseeir* 'sit, settle, assess,' from Latin *assidere* (see ASSESS).

at•tach /əˈtæCH/

▶v. [trans.] **1** include (a condition) as part of an agreement: *the Commission can attach appropriate conditions to the operation of the agreement.*
2 seize (a person's property) by legal authority: *the court attached his wages for child support.*

DERIVATIVES **at•tach•a•ble** adj.

ORIGIN Middle English (in the sense 'seize by legal authority'): from Old French *atachier* or *estachier* 'fasten, fix.'

at•tach•ment /əˈtæCHmənt/

▸ n. legal seizure of property.

ORIGIN late Middle English (in the sense 'arrest for contempt of court'): from Old French *attachement*, from *atachier* 'fasten, fix' (see ATTACH).

at•tain•der /əˈtāndər/

▸ n. historical the forfeiture of land and civil rights suffered as a consequence of a sentence of death for treason or felony. See also BILL OF ATTAINDER.

ORIGIN late Middle English: from Anglo-Norman French, variant (used as a noun) of Old French *ateindre* in the sense 'convict, bring to justice.'

at•test /əˈtest/

▸ v. [intrans.] declare that something exists or is the case: [with clause] *the deceased's attorney attested that he had been about to institute divorce proceedings.*

■ be a witness to; certify formally: *the witnesses must attest and sign the will in the testator's presence.*

DERIVATIVES **at•tes•ta•tion** /ˌæteˈstāSHən/ n.

ORIGIN early 16th cent.: from French *attester*, from Latin *attestari*, from *ad-* 'to' + *testari* 'to witness' (from *testis* 'a witness').

at•tor•ney /əˈtərnē/

▸ n. (pl. **at•tor•neys**) **1** a person appointed to act for another in business or legal matters.
2 a lawyer.

DERIVATIVES **at•tor•ney•ship** /əˈtərnēˌSHip/ n.

ORIGIN Middle English: from Old French *atorne*, past participle of *atorner* 'assign,' from *a* 'toward' + *torner* 'turn.'

at•tor•ney gen•er•al /əˈtərnē ˈjen(ə)rəl/ (abbr.: **AG** or **Atty. Gen.**)

▶ n. (pl. **at•tor•neys gen•er•al**) the principal legal officer who represents a country or a state in legal proceedings and gives legal advice to the government.
■ the head of the US Department of Justice.

Atty.

▶ abbr. Attorney.

a•ver /əˈvər/

▶ v. [trans.] (**a•verred, a•ver•ring**) formal allege as a fact in support of a plea: *they aver that they did not receive any compensation.*
ORIGIN late Middle English (in the sense 'declare or confirm to be true'): from Old French *averer*, based on Latin *ad* 'to' (implying 'cause to be') + *verus* 'true.'

a•ver•ment /əˈvərmənt/

▶ n. formal a formal statement by a party in a case of a fact or circumstance that the party offers to prove or substantiate.
ORIGIN late Middle English: from Old French *averrement, averement,* from *averer* 'declare true' (see AVER).

B

bail /bāl/

▶ n. the temporary release of an accused person awaiting trial, on condition that a sum of money be lodged to guarantee their appearance in court: *he has been released on bail*. See also RECOGNIZANCE.

■ money paid by or for such a person as security.

▶ v. [trans.] (usu. **be bailed**) release or secure the release of (a prisoner) on payment of bail: *his son called home to get bailed out of jail*.

PHRASES **jump bail** informal fail to appear for trial after being released on bail: *he jumped bail and was on the run until his arrest*. **go bail** (or **stand bail**) act as surety for an accused person: *before leaving the court, she went bail for four of the strikers* | *Mr. Harvey's father stood bail for his son*. **post bail** pay a sum of money as bail: *I posted bail for him*.

DERIVATIVES **bail•a•ble** adj.

ORIGIN Middle English: from Old French, literally 'custody, jurisdiction,' from Old French *bailler* 'take charge of,' from Latin *bajulare* 'bear a burden.'

bail•ee /bāˈlē/

▶ n. a person or party to whom goods are delivered for a purpose, such as custody or repair, without transfer of ownership.

bail•iff /ˈbālif/

▶ n. an official in a court of law who keeps order, looks after prisoners, etc.

ORIGIN Middle English: from Old French *baillif*, inflected form of *bailli*, based on Latin *bajulus* 'carrier, manager.'

bail•ment /'bālmənt/
> n. an act of delivering goods to a bailee for a particular purpose, without transfer of ownership.

bail•or /'bālər/
> n. a person or party that entrusts goods to a bailee.

bank•rupt /'bæNGkrəpt/
> adj. (of a person or organization) declared in law unable to pay outstanding debts: *the company was declared bankrupt* | *this editorial explains why the airlines are going bankrupt*.
> n. a person judged by a court to be insolvent, whose property is taken and disposed of for the benefit of creditors or whose financial affairs are recognized.
> v. [trans.] reduce (a person or organization) to bankruptcy: *the strike nearly bankrupted the union*.
ORIGIN mid 16th cent.: from Italian *banca rotta* 'broken bench,' from *banca* 'bench' (relating to a money dealer's table) and *rompere* 'to break.' The change in the ending was due to association with Latin *rupt-* 'broken.'

bar /bär/
> n. 1 (**the Bar**) the legal profession.
■ lawyers collectively. ■ Brit. barristers collectively.
2 (**the bar**) a partition in a courtroom, now usually notional, beyond which most persons may not pass and at which an accused person stands: *the prisoner at the bar*.
■ a plea arresting an action or claim in a law case. ■ a particular court of law.
> v. (**barred, barring**) [trans.] prevent or delay (an action) by objection.
ORIGIN Middle English: from Old French *barre* (noun), *barrer* (verb), of unknown origin.

bar•ra•try /'berətrē/
> n. vexatious litigation or incitement to it.

DERIVATIVES **bar•ra•tor** /'berətər/ **n.** (historical); **bar•ra•trous** /'berətrəs/ **adj.**
ORIGIN from Old French *baraterie*, from *barater* 'deceive,' based on Greek *prattein* 'do, perform, manage' (sometimes dishonestly); perhaps influenced by Old Norse *barátta* 'contest.'

bar•ris•ter /'bærəstər; 'ber-/ (also **bar•ris•ter-at-law**)
▸ **n.** chiefly Brit. a lawyer entitled to practice as an advocate, particularly in the higher courts. Compare with ATTORNEY, SOLICITOR.
ORIGIN late Middle English: from the noun BAR, perhaps on the pattern of *minister*.

bat•ter•y /'bætərē/
▸ **n.** the crime or tort of unconsented harmful or offensive physical contact with another person. See also ASSAULT AND BATTERY.
ORIGIN Middle English: from French *batterie*, from *battre* 'to strike,' from Latin *battuere*.

bel•lig•er•ent /bə'lijərənt/
▸ **adj.** engaged in a war or conflict, as recognized by international law: *belligerent military forces are expected to strike by day's end.*
▸ **n.** a nation or person engaged in war or conflict, as recognized by international law: *Oxfam will refuse money from belligerents during any war.*
DERIVATIVES **bel•lig•er•ent•ly** /bə'lijərəntlē/ **adv.**
ORIGIN late 16th cent.: from Latin *belligerant-* 'waging war,' from the verb *belligerare*, from *bellum* 'war.'

bench /bencH/
▸ **n.** (**the bench**) the office of judge or magistrate: *his appointment to the civil bench.*
■ a judge's seat in a court of law: *approach the bench.*
■ judges or magistrates collectively: *rulings from the bench.*

PHRASES **on the bench** appointed as or in the capacity of a judge or magistrate: *he retired after twenty-five years on the bench.*
ORIGIN Old English *benc*, of Germanic origin; related to Dutch *bank* and German *Bank*.

bench•er /'benCHər/
▸ n. (in the UK) a senior member of any of the Inns of Court.

ben•e•fi•cial /ˌbenə'fiSHəl/
▸ adj. of or relating to rights, other than legal title: *the beneficiary will be taxed on the value of his beneficial use of the property.*
DERIVATIVES **ben•e•fi•cial•ly** adv.
ORIGIN late Middle English: from late Latin *beneficialis*, from *beneficium*.

ben•e•fi•ci•ar•y /ˌbenə'fiSHē,erē/
▸ n. (pl. **ben•e•fi•ci•ar•ies**) a person who derives advantage from a trust, will, or life insurance policy.
ORIGIN early 17th cent.: from Latin *beneficiarius*, from *beneficium* 'favor, support,' from *bene* 'well' + *facere* 'do.'

be•queath /bi'kwēTH; -'kwēTH/
▸ v. [trans.] leave (a personal estate or one's body) to a person or other beneficiary by a will: *he bequeathed his art collection to the town.*
DERIVATIVES **be•queath•er** n.
ORIGIN Old English *becwethan*, from *be-* 'about' (expressing transitivity) + *cwethan* 'say.'

bet•ter•ment /'betərmənt/
▸ n. the enhanced value of real property arising from local improvements: [as adj.] *a betterment charge.*

bi•cam•er•al /bī'kæmərəl/
▸ adj. (of a legislative body) having two branches or chambers.

DERIVATIVES **bi•cam•er•al•ism** /bī'kæmərə,lizəm/ n.
ORIGIN mid 19th cent.: from *bi-* 'two' + Latin *camera*
'chamber' + *-al*.

big•a•my /'bigəmē/
▸ n. the act of going through a marriage ceremony or being married while already married to another person.
DERIVATIVES **big•a•mist** /'bigəmist/ n.; **big•a•mous**
/'bigəməs/ **adj.**
ORIGIN Middle English: from Old French *bigamie*, from
bigame 'bigamous,' from late Latin *bigamus*, from *bi-*
'twice' + Greek *-gamos* 'married.'

bill of at•tain•der /'bil əv ə'tāndər/
▸ n. an item of legislation (prohibited by the US Constitution) that inflicts attainder without judicial process:
*during the Revolutionary War, bills of attainder were passed
to a wide extent.*

bill of in•dict•ment /'bil əv in'dītmənt/
▸ n. a written accusation as presented to a grand jury.

Bill of Rights /'bil əv 'rīts/
▸ n. a statement of the rights of a class of people, in particular:
■ the first ten amendments to the US Constitution, ratified in 1791 and guaranteeing such rights as the free-
doms of speech, assembly, and worship. ■ the English
constitutional settlement of 1689, confirming the deposition of James II and the accession of William and
Mary, guaranteeing the Protestant succession, and laying down the principles of parliamentary supremacy.

bind /bīnd/
▸ v. (past and past part. **bound** /bownd/) [trans.] formal impose
a legal or contractual obligation on: *a party who signs a
document will normally be bound by its terms.*
■ (**bind oneself**) formal make a contractual or enforce-

able undertaking: *the government cannot bind itself as to the form of subsequent legislation.* ■ secure (a contract), typically with a sum of money: *I have mailed a check to bind the contract.*

▶ n. formal a statutory constraint: *the moral bind of the law.*

PHRASES **bind someone over** (usu. **be bound over**) (of a court of law) hold for trial: *he was bound over on a felony charge.*

ORIGIN Old English *bindan*, of Germanic origin; related to Dutch and German *binden*, from an Indo-European root shared by Sanskrit *bandh*.

birth cer·tif·i·cate /ˈbərTH sərˌtifikit/

▶ n. an official document issued to record a person's birth, including such identifying data as name, gender, date of birth, place of birth, and parentage.

bod·y cor·po·rate /ˈbädē ˈkôrp(ə)rit/

▶ n. formal term for CORPORATION.

bo·na fide /ˈbōnə ˌfīd; ˈbänə/

▶ adv. sincerely; without intention to deceive: *the court will assume that they have acted bona fide.*

ORIGIN mid 16th cent.: Latin, literally 'with good faith,' ablative singular of BONA FIDES.

bo·na fi·des /ˈbōnə ˌfīdz; ˈfīdēz; ˈbänə/

▶ n. [treated as pl.] informal documentary evidence showing a person's legitimacy; credentials: *are you satisfied with my bona fides?*

ORIGIN mid 20th cent.: Latin, literally 'good faith.'

bond /bänd/

▶ n. an agreement or promise with legal force, in particular:

■ a document by which a person is committed to make payment to another. ■ a promise to pay a sum if a de-

fendant does not appear for trial. ■ a certificate issued by a government or a public company promising to repay borrowed money at a fixed rate of interest at a specified time. ■ (of dutiable goods) a state of storage in a bonded warehouse until the importer pays the duty owing. ■ an insurance policy held by a company, which protects against losses resulting from circumstances such as bankruptcy, failure to perform a contract, or misconduct by employees.
▶v. **1** issue a bond.
2 [usu. as n.] (**bonding**) place (dutiable goods) in bond.
ORIGIN Middle English: variant of *band*.

bond•ed /ˈbändid/
▶ adj. [attrib.] **1** (of a person or company) bound by a legal agreement, in particular:
■ (of a debt) secured by bonds: *there are declines in bonded debt being paid by other agencies.* ■ (of a worker or workforce) obliged to work for a particular employer, often in a condition close to slavery: *the bonded workers are always powerless.*
2 (of dutiable goods) placed in bond.

bonds•man /ˈbändzmən/
▶ n. (pl. **bonds•men**) a person who stands surety for a bond.
ORIGIN early 18th cent.: from BOND + *man*.

breach /brēCH/
▶ n. an act of breaking or failing to observe a law, agreement, or code of conduct: *a breach of confidence* | *I sued for breach of contract.*
▶v. [trans.]
■ break or fail to observe (a law, agreement, or code of conduct): *Australian companies may be breaching the law by deleting business-related e-mail.*
PHRASES **breach of the peace** an act of violent or noisy

behavior that causes a public disturbance and is considered a criminal offense. **breach of promise** the action of breaking a sworn assurance to do something, formerly esp. to marry someone.

ORIGIN Middle English: from Old French *breche*, ultimately of Germanic origin; related to BREAK.

break /brāk/

▶ v. [trans.] (past **broke** /brōk/; past part. **brok•en** /'brōkən/) fail to observe (a law, regulation, or agreement): *the district attorney says she will prosecute retailers who break the law | a legally binding contract that can only be broken by mutual consent.*

▶**break in** force entry to a building: *it sounded like someone trying to break in.*

ORIGIN Old English *brecan* (verb), of Germanic origin; related to Dutch *breken* and German *brechen*, from an Indo-European root shared by Latin *frangere* 'to break.'

break-in /'brāk ˌin/

▶ n. a forced or unconsented entry into a building, car, computer system, etc., typically to steal something.

break•ing and en•ter•ing /'brākiNG ən(d) 'entəriNG/

▶ n. the crime of entering a building by force so as to commit burglary.

brief /brēf/

▶ n. a written summary of the facts and legal points supporting one side of a case, for presentation to a court.

■ a written summary of a judicial opinion, typically prepared by law students.

▶v. [intrans.] prepare a summary of a judicial opinion.

ORIGIN Middle English: from Old French *brief*, from Latin *brevis* 'short.' The noun is via late Latin *breve* 'note, dispatch,' hence 'an official letter.'

bring /briNG/
▸ v. (past and past part. **brought** /brôt/) initiate (legal action) against someone: *riot and conspiracy charges should be brought against* them.
ORIGIN Old English *bringan*, of Germanic origin; related to Dutch *brengen* and German *bringen*.

bro•ker /ˈbrōkər/
▸ n. a person who buys and sells goods or assets for others.
▸ v. [trans.] arrange or negotiate (a settlement, deal, or plan): *the ACLU of Maryland brokered the deal.*
ORIGIN Middle English (denoting a retailer or peddler): from Anglo-Norman French *brocour*, of unknown ultimate origin.

bur•glar /ˈbərglər/
▸ n. a person who commits burglary.
ORIGIN mid 16th cent.: from legal French *burgler* or Anglo-Latin *burgulator, burglator*; related to Old French *burgier* 'pillage.'

bur•glar•ize /ˈbərglə,rīz/
▸ v. [trans.] (often **be burglarized**) enter (a building) illegally with intent to commit a crime, esp. theft: *our summer house has been burglarized.*

bur•gla•ry /ˈbərglərē/
▸ n. (pl. **bur•gla•ries**) entry into a building illegally with intent to commit a crime, esp. theft: *a two-year sentence for burglary | a series of burglaries.*
ORIGIN early 16th cent.: from legal French *burglarie*, from *burgler* (see BURGLAR).

bur•gle /ˈbərgəl/
▸ v. another term for BURGLARIZE.
ORIGIN late 19th cent.: originally a humorous and colloquial back-formation from BURGLAR.

by•law /'bī,lô/ (also **by-law**)

▸ n. **1** a rule made by a company or society to control the actions of its members.

2 a regulation made by a local authority; an ordinance.

ORIGIN Middle English: probably from obsolete *byrlaw* 'local law or custom,' from Old Norse *býjar*, genitive singular of *býr* 'town.'

C

cal•en•dar /ˈkæləndər/
▶ n. a list of people or events connected with particular dates, esp. cases for trial; a court schedule.
▶ v. [trans.] enter (something) in a calendar: *when a case is calendared, the parties are notified by the court.*
ORIGIN Middle English: from Old French *calendier*, from Latin *kalendarium* 'account book,' from *kalendae*.

cam•er•a /ˈkæm(ə)rə/
▶ see IN CAMERA.

can•cel•la•tion /ˌkænsəˈlāsHən/
▶ n. the annulling of a legal document: *the debtor can procure cancellation if satisfied within one month.*

ca•pac•i•ty /kəˈpæsətē/
▶ n. **1** a person's legal competence: *cases where a patient's testamentary capacity is in doubt.*
2 [in sing.] a specified role or position: *I was engaged in a voluntary capacity* | *writing **in his capacity as** legal correspondent.*
ORIGIN late Middle English: from French *capacité*, from Latin *capacitas*, from *capax*, *capac-* 'that can contain,' from *capere* 'take or hold.'

ca•pi•as /ˈkāpēəs/
▶ n. (pl. **ca•pi•as•es**) a writ ordering the arrest of a named person.
ORIGIN late Middle English: from Latin *capias (ad respondendum)*, literally 'you are to seize (until reply is made),' from *capere* 'take.'

cap•tion /ˈkæpsHən/
▶ n. a title or brief explanation appended to a pleading document or judicial opinion.

■ the heading of a legal document.

ORIGIN late Middle English: from Latin *caption-*, from *capere* 'take, seize.' Early senses 'arrest' and 'warrant for arrest' gave rise to 'statement of where, when, and by whose authority a warrant was issued' (late 17th cent.): this was usually appended to a legal document, hence the sense 'heading or appended wording' (late 18th cent.).

car•nal know•ledge /'kärnl 'nälij/
▶ **n.** dated sexual intercourse.

case /kās/
▶ **n. 1** an incident or set of circumstances under police investigation: *a murder case.*
2 a legal action, esp. one to be decided in a court of law: *a libel case* | *a former employee brought the case against the council.*
■ a set of facts or arguments supporting one side in such a legal action: *the case for the defense.* ■ a legal action that has been decided and may be cited as a precedent. ■ a reported judicial opinion.

ORIGIN Middle English: from Old French *cas*, from Latin *casus* 'fall,' related to *cadere* 'to fall'; in sense 4 directly from Latin, translating Greek *ptōsis*, literally 'fall.'

case•book /'kās,bŏŏk/
▶ **n.** a book containing a selection of source materials on a particular subject, esp. one used as a reference work or in teaching.

case law
▶ **n.** (also **case•law**) the law as established by the outcome of former cases. Compare with COMMON LAW, STATUTORY LAW.

cas•u•al•ty /'kæzH(ŏŏ)əltē/
▶ **n.** (pl. **cas•u•al•ties**) a person killed or injured in a war or accident.

■ (chiefly in insurance) an accident, mishap, or disaster. ■ a loss caused by accident or injury.

ORIGIN late Middle English (in the sense 'chance, a chance occurrence'): from medieval Latin *casualitas*, from *casualis*, from *casus* 'fall,' on the pattern of words such as *penalty*.

cau•sa•tion /kô'zāSHən/

▸ n. in tort law, the requirement of factual connection between the defendant's conduct and the plaintiff's harm: *this decision has reaffirmed the need to establish causation in cases where a medical practitioner fails to warn the patient of material risks.*

ORIGIN late 15th cent.: from Latin *causatio(n-)* 'pretext' (in medieval Latin 'the action of causing'), from *causare* 'to cause.'

cause /kôz/

▸ n. **1** a person or thing that gives rise to an action, phenomenon, or condition: *the cause of the accident is not clear.*
2 a matter to be resolved in a court of law.
■ an individual's case offered at law.

PHRASES **cause of action** a fact or facts that enable a person to bring an action against another.

ORIGIN Middle English: from Old French, from Latin *causa* (noun), *causare* (verb).

ca•ve•at /'kævē,ät; 'käv-/

▸ n. a notice, esp. in a probate, that certain actions temporarily may not be taken.

ORIGIN mid 16th cent.: from Latin, literally 'let a person beware.'

ca•ve•at emp•tor /'kævē,æt 'emp,tôr; 'käv-/

▸ n. the principle that the buyer alone is responsible for checking the quality and suitability of goods before a purchase is made.

ORIGIN early 16th cent.: Latin, literally 'let the buyer beware.'

cer•tif•i•cate

▶ n. /sər'tifikit/ an official document attesting a certain fact, in particular:
■ a document recording a person's birth, marriage, or death. ■ a document attesting ownership of a certain item: *a stock certificate.*
▶v. /sər'tifə,kāt/ [trans.] (usu. **be certificated**) provide with or attest in an official document.
ORIGIN late Middle English (in the sense 'certification, attestation'): from French *certificat* or medieval Latin *certificatum,* from *certificare.*

cer•ti•o•ra•ri /ˌsersH(ē)ə'rärē; -'rerī/

▶ n. (usually as **writ of certiorari**) a writ or order from a higher court (especially the US Supreme Court) that it will review a decision of a lower court.
ORIGIN late Middle English: from Law Latin, 'to be informed,' a phrase originally occurring at the start of the writ, from *certiorare* 'inform,' from *certior,* comparative of *certus* 'certain.'

chal•lenge /'CHælinj/

▶ n. an objection or query as to the truth of something, often with an implicit demand for proof: *a challenge to the legality of the order.*
■ an objection regarding the eligibility or suitability of a jury member. See also PEREMPTORY CHALLENGE.
▶v. [trans.] object to (a jury member).
PHRASES **challenge for cause** an objection regarding the eligibility or suitability of a jury member, for which a reason is given.
DERIVATIVES **chal•lenge•a•ble** adj.; **chal•leng•er** n.
ORIGIN Middle English (in the senses 'accusation' and 'accuse'): from Old French *chalenge* (noun), *chalenger*

(verb), from Latin *calumnia* 'calumny,' *calumniari* 'calumniate.'

cham•ber /'CHāmbər/
▶n. 1 a hall used by a legislative or judicial body.
■ the body that meets in such a hall. ■ any of the houses of a legislature: *the Senate chamber.*
2 (**chambers**) a judge's office.
■ (**chambers**) Brit. rooms used by a lawyer or lawyers.
ORIGIN Middle English (in the sense 'private room'): from Old French *chambre,* from Latin *camera* 'vault, arched chamber,' from Greek *kamara* 'object with an arched cover.'

cham•per•ty /'CHæmpərtē/
▶n. an illegal agreement in which a person with no previous interest in a lawsuit finances it with a view to sharing the disputed property if the suit succeeds.
DERIVATIVES **cham•per•tous** /'CHæmpərtəs/ **adj.**
ORIGIN late Middle English: from Anglo-Norman French *champartie,* from Old French *champart* 'feudal lord's share of produce,' from Latin *campus* 'field' + *pars* 'part.'

chan•cer•y /'CHæns(ə)rē/
▶n. (pl. **chan•cer•ies**) 1 a court of equity.
■ equity. ■ (**Chancery**) Brit. the Lord Chancellor's court, a division of the High Court of Justice.
2 a public records office.

charge /CHärj/
▶v. [trans.] 1 accuse (someone) of an offense under law: *they were **charged with** assault.*
2 instruct (a jury) as to the law: *after the judge has charged the jury, you will retire to consider your verdict.*
▶n. 1 an accusation, typically one formally made against a prisoner brought to trial: *he appeared in court **on a***

charge of attempted murder | three people were arrested but released *without charge.*

2 an official instruction, esp. one given by a judge to a jury regarding points of law.

PHRASES **press** (or **prefer**) **charges** accuse someone formally of a crime so that they can be brought to trial: *police decline to press charges against protesters* | *two charges were preferred against the Air Force captain.*

ORIGIN Middle English (in the general senses 'to load' and 'a load'): from Old French *charger* (verb), *charge* (noun), from late Latin *carricare, carcare* 'to load,' from Latin *carrus* 'wheeled vehicle.'

char•ter /ˈCHärtər/
▸ n. a written grant by a country's legislative or sovereign power, by which an institution such as a company, university, or city is created and its rights and privileges defined.
▪ a written constitution or description of an organization's functions.
▸ v. [trans.] grant a charter to (a city, university, or other institution): *the company was chartered in 1553.*
ORIGIN Middle English: from Old French *chartre*, from Latin *chartula*, diminutive of *charta* 'paper.'

chat•tel /ˈCHætl/
▸ n. (in general use) a personal possession.
▪ an item of property other than real estate. See also GOODS AND CHATTELS.
ORIGIN Middle English: from Old French *chatel*, from medieval Latin *capitale*, from Latin *capitalis*, from *caput* 'head.'

chief jus•tice /ˈCHēf ˈjəstis/
▸ n. (the title of) the presiding judge in a supreme court.
▪ (**Chief Justice of the United States**) (the formal title of) the chief justice of the US Supreme Court.

child a•buse /ˈCHīld əˈbyo͞os/
▸ **n.** physical maltreatment or sexual molestation of a child.

cir•cuit /ˈsərkit/ (abbr.: **cir.** or **circ.**)
▸ **n.** a regular journey made by a judge around a particular district to hear cases in court: [as adj.] *a circuit judge.* ◼ a district of this type. ◼ a judicial region formerly administered by traveling judges.
ORIGIN late Middle English: via Old French from Latin *circuitus,* from *circuire,* variant of *circumire* 'go around,' from *circum* 'around' + *ire* 'go.'

cir•cum•stan•tial /ˌsərkəmˈstænCHəl/
▸ **adj.** (of evidence or a legal case) pointing indirectly toward someone's guilt but not conclusively proving it.
DERIVATIVES **cir•cum•stan•ti•al•i•ty** /ˌsərkəmˌstænCHē ˈælitē/ **n.; cir•cum•stan•tial•ly** adv.
ORIGIN late 16th cent.: from Latin *circumstantia.*

ci•ta•tion /sīˈtāSHən/ (abbr.: **cit.**)
▸ **n. 1** a reference to a former tried case, used as guidance in the trying of comparable cases or in support of an argument.
2 a summons: *a traffic citation.*
ORIGIN Middle English: from Old French, from Latin *citation-,* from *citare* 'cite.'

cite /sīt/
▸ **v.** [trans.] (often **be cited**) **1** induce a former tried case as a guide to deciding a comparable case or in support of an argument: *neither party is able to cite to any case that clarifies the issue* | *his lawyer cited the ancient case of the Crown vs. Madame X.*
2 summon (someone) to appear in a court of law: *the summons cited four defendants.*
DERIVATIVES **cit•a•ble** adj.

ORIGIN late Middle English (originally with reference to a court of ecclesiastical law): from Old French *citer*, from Latin *citare*, from *ciere*, *cire* 'to call.'

cit•i•zen's ar•rest /'sitəzənz ə'rest/
▸ n. an arrest by an ordinary person without a warrant, allowable in certain cases.

civ•il /'sivəl/
▸ adj. relating to private relations between members of a community; noncriminal: *a civil action* | *a civil court*.
■ of or relating to aspects of the civil (or code) law derived from European systems.
ORIGIN late Middle English: via Old French from Latin *civilis*, from *civis* 'citizen.'

civ•il court /'sivəl 'kôrt/
▸ n. a court dealing with noncriminal cases.

civ•il dis•o•be•di•ence /'sivəl ˌdisə'bēdēəns/
▸ n. the refusal to comply with certain laws or to pay taxes and fines, as a peaceful form of political protest.

civ•il law /'sivəl 'lô/
▸ n. the system of law concerned with private relations between members of a community rather than criminal, military, or religious affairs. Contrasted with CRIMINAL LAW.
■ the system of law predominant on the European continent and of which a form is in force in Louisiana, historically influenced by the codes of ancient Rome. Compare with COMMON LAW.

civ•il lib•er•ty /'sivəl 'libərtē/
▸ n. the state of being subject only to laws established for the good of the community, esp. with regard to freedom of action and speech.

◾ (**civil liberties**) a person's rights to be only so subject.
DERIVATIVES **civ•il lib•er•tar•i•an** /'sivəl ˌlibər'terēən/ n.

civ•il wrong /'sivəl 'rôNG/
▸ n. an infringement of a person's rights, such as a tort or breach of contract.

claim /klām/
▸ v. [trans.] formally request or demand; say that one owns or has earned (something): *if no one claims the items, they will become government property.*
◾ make a demand for (money) under the terms of an insurance policy: *she could have claimed the cost through her insurance.*
▸ n. a demand or request for something considered one's due: *the court had denied their **claims to** asylum.*
◾ an application for compensation under the terms of an insurance policy. ◾ a right or title to something: *they have first **claim on** the assets of the trust.* ◾ (also **mining claim**) a piece of land allotted to or taken by someone in order to be mined.
DERIVATIVES **claim•a•ble adj.**
ORIGIN Middle English: from Old French *claime* (noun), *clamer* (verb), from Latin *clamare* 'call out.'

class ac•tion /'klæs 'æksHən/
▸ n. a lawsuit filed or defended by an individual or small group acting on behalf of a large group.

clause /klôz/
▸ n. a particular and separate article, stipulation, or proviso in a treaty, bill, or contract.
DERIVATIVES **claus•al** /'klôzəl/ **adj.**
ORIGIN Middle English: via Old French *clausē*, based on Latin *claus-* 'shut, closed,' from the verb *claudere.*

clerk /klərk/
> ▸ n. an official in charge of the records of a local council or court: *a clerk to the court.*
> ▪ a person employed by a judge, or being trained by a lawyer, who does legal research, etc.
> ▸ v. [intrans.] work as a clerk: *they clerked for several judges at one time.*

ORIGIN Old English *cleric, clerc* (in the sense 'ordained minister, literate person'), from ecclesiastical Latin *clericus* 'clergyman'; reinforced by Old French *clerc*, from the same source.

clerk•ship /'klərk,SHip/
> ▸ n. the position or status of a clerk, esp. in the legal profession.

code /kōd/
> ▸ n. a systematic collection of laws or regulations: *the criminal code.*

PHRASES **bring something up to code** renovate an old building or update its features in line with the latest building regulations.

ORIGIN Middle English: via Old French from Latin *codex, codic-.* The term originally denoted a systematic collection of statutes made by one of the later Roman emperors, particularly that of Justinian; (mid 18th cent.), the earliest modern sense.

co•de•fend•ant /,kōdi'fendənt/
> ▸ n. a joint defendant.

cod•i•cil /'kädəsil/
> ▸ n. an addition or supplement that explains, modifies, or revokes a will or part of one.

DERIVATIVES **cod•i•cil•la•ry** /,kädə'silərē/ **adj.**

ORIGIN late Middle English: from Latin *codicillus*, diminutive of *codex, codic-.*

cod•i•fy /'kädə‚fī; 'kōd-/
> ▶ v. (**cod•i•fies, cod•i•fied**) [trans.] arrange (laws or rules) into a systematic code.
DERIVATIVES **cod•i•fi•ca•tion** /‚kädəfi'kāsнən; ‚kōd-/ n.; **cod•i•fi•er** /'kädə‚fīər; 'kōd-/ n.

cog•ni•za•ble /'kägnəzəbəl; käg'nīz-/
> ▶ adj. within the jurisdiction of a court: *a cognizable offense.*
ORIGIN late 17th cent.: from COGNIZANCE + -*able.*

cog•ni•zance /'kägnəzəns/
> ▶ n. formal knowledge, awareness, or notice: *he was deputed to bring the affair to the cognizance of the court.*
■ the action of taking jurisdiction. ■ the action of taking judicial notice (of a fact beyond dispute).
ORIGIN Middle English *conisance,* from Old French *conoisance,* based on Latin *cognoscere* 'get to know.' The spelling with *g,* influenced by Latin, arose in the 15th cent. and gradually affected the pronunciation.

col•lu•sion /kə'lōōzнən/
> ▶ n. secret or illegal cooperation or conspiracy, esp. between ostensible opponents in a lawsuit.
DERIVATIVES **col•lu•sive** /kə'lōōsiv; -ziv/ adj.; **col•lu•sive•ly** adv.
ORIGIN late Middle English: from Latin *collusion-,* from *colludere* 'have a secret agreement.'

col•or /'kələr/ (Brit. **col•our**)
> ▶ n. an apparent right or ground.
PHRASES **under color of law** with the apparent authority of the law.
ORIGIN Middle English (as *colo(u)r*): from Old French *colour* (noun), *colourer* (verb), from Latin *color* (noun), *colorare* (verb).

com•mit /kəˈmit/

▸ v. (**com•mit•ted, com•mit•ting**) [trans.] **1** carry out or perpetrate (a mistake, crime, or immoral act): *he committed an uncharacteristic error.*
2 pledge or bind (a person or an organization) to a certain course or policy: *the treaty commits each party to defend the other.*
3 send, entrust, or consign, in particular:
■ consign (someone) officially to prison, esp. on remand: *he was committed to prison for contempt of court.*
■ send (a person or case) for trial. ■ refer (a legislative bill) to a committee.
DERIVATIVES **com•mit•ta•ble adj.**; **com•mit•ter n.**
ORIGIN late Middle English: from Latin *committere* 'join, entrust' (in medieval Latin 'put into custody'), from *com-* 'with' + *mittere* 'put or send.'

com•mon /ˈkämən/

▸ adj. (of a crime) of relatively minor importance: *common assault.*
PHRASES **the common good** the benefit or interests of all: *it is time our elected officials stood up for the common good.* **common property** a thing or things held jointly. **in common** See TENANCY IN COMMON.
ORIGIN Middle English: from Old French *comun* (adjective), from Latin *communis.*

com•mon law /ˈkämən ˈlô/

▸ n. the part of law that is derived from judicial precedent rather than statutes: [as adj.] *this suggests the Supreme Court was invoking the common law notion that the reasonable person standard should not apply to deliberate deception.* Often contrasted with STATUTORY LAW.
■ the body of law originally developed in the English royal courts. Compare with EQUITY, PUBLIC LAW. ■ The body of law in countries that derive their law from England, including the United States, Australia, and New

Zealand. ■ [as adj.] denoting a partner in a marriage by common law (which recognized unions created by mutual agreement and public behavior), not by a civil or ecclesiastical ceremony: *a common-law husband.* ■ [as adj.] denoting a partner in a long-term relationship of cohabitation.

Com•mon Pleas /ˈkämən ˈplēz/ (in full **Court of Common Pleas**) (in some jurisdictions) a court for hearing civil cases between citizens.

ORIGIN apart from current limited usage, the term is chiefly historical.

com•mu•ni•ty pro•per•ty /kəˈmyo͞onitē ˈpräpərtē/
▶n. (in certain US states) property that is owned jointly by a husband and wife, and which is distributed equally on termination of the marriage: *property accumulated by an unmarried couple in a stable relationship is treated like community property.*

com•mu•ni•ty serv•ice /kəˈmyo͞onitē ˈsərvis/
▶n. unpaid work, intended to be of social use, that an offender is required to do instead of going to prison: *the vandals were sentenced to 600 hours of community service.*

com•mu•ta•tion /ˌkämyəˈtāsHən/
▶n. action or the process of commuting a judicial sentence: *there are circumstances concerning the handling of his trial which warrant a commutation of his sentence.*
■ the conversion of a legal obligation or entitlement into another form: *these retirees elected to receive a lump-sum payment in commutation of a monthly annuity.*
ORIGIN late Middle English (in the sense 'exchange, barter,' later 'alteration'): from Latin *commutatio(n-)*, from *commutare* 'exchange, interchange' (see COMMUTE). Usage regarding judicial sentences dates from the late 16th cent.

com•mute /kə'myoot/

▸ v. [trans.] reduce (a judicial sentence, esp. a sentence of death) to one less severe: *the governor recently commuted the sentences of dozens of women convicted of killing their husbands.*

■ (**commute something for/into**) change one kind of payment or obligation for (another): *monthly income for the remainder of the guaranteed period will be commuted into a lump-sum payment.* ■ replace (an annuity or other series of payments) with a single payment: *if he had commuted some of his pension, he would have received $330,000.*

ORIGIN late Middle English (in the sense 'interchange (two things)'): from Latin *commutare*, from *com-* 'altogether' + *mutare* 'to change.'

com•par•a•tive neg•li•gence /kəm'pæritiv 'neglijəns/

▸ n. failure of an injured plaintiff to act with reasonable care, thereby reducing the amount recovered from the defendant or preventing the plaintiff from receiving any compensation: *West Dakota has adopted comparative negligence under which the plaintiff's fault reduces recoverable damages but does not bar a cause of action.*

com•pen•sa•ble /kəm'pensəbəl/

▸ adj. (of a loss or hardship) for which compensation can be obtained: *an on-the-job injury or illness that the Department of Labor determines to be compensable.*

ORIGIN mid 17th cent.: French, from *compenser*, from Latin *compensare* 'weigh (something) against (another).'

com•pe•tence /'kämpitəns/ (also **com•pe•ten•cy** /'kämpitənsē/)

▸ n. the legal authority of a court or other body to deal with a particular matter: *the court's competence has been accepted to cover these matters.*

■ the ability of a participant in a trial, as gauged by their capacity to understand the proceedings: *it is a mental disability that does not affect the competence of the witness to testify.*

com•pe•tent /ˈkämpətənt/
▸**adj.** (chiefly of a court or other body) accepted as having legal authority to deal with a particular matter: *the governor was not the **competent authority** to deal with the matter.*
■ (of a criminal defendant) able to understand the charges and to aid in defending themselves: *the carjacking suspect was ruled not competent for trial.* ■ (of a witness) capable of testifying.
DERIVATIVES **com•pe•tent•ly** adv.
ORIGIN late Middle English (in the sense 'suitable, adequate'): from Latin *competent-*, from the verb *competere* in its earlier sense 'be fit or proper.'

com•plain•ant /kəmˈplānənt/
▸**n.** a plaintiff in certain lawsuits: *the complainant did not have proof of proper service of the notice of hearing.*
ORIGIN late Middle English: from French *compliagnant*, present participle of *complaindre* 'to lament.'

com•plaint /kəmˈplānt/
▸**n.** the pleading that states the plaintiff's reasons for proceeding in a civil action: *at the time of the collision stated in the complaint, the plaintiff was driving home from work.*
ORIGIN late Middle English: from Old French *complainte*, feminine past participle of *complaindre* 'to lament.'

com•po•si•tion /ˌkämpəˈziSHən/
▸**n.** a legal agreement to pay an amount of money in lieu of a larger debt or other obligation: *he never made a composition with his creditors in satisfaction of his debts.*
■ an amount of money paid in this way.

ORIGIN late Middle English: via Old French from Latin *composition-*, from *componere* 'put together.'

com•pound

▶ v. /kəm'pownd; käm'pownd; 'käm,pownd/ [trans.] forbear from prosecuting (a felony) in exchange for money or other consideration.

■ settle (a debt or other matter) in this way: *he compounded the case with the defendant for a cash payment.*
DERIVATIVES **com•pound•a•ble** /kəm'powndəbəl; käm-/ **adj.**
ORIGIN late Middle English *compoune* (verb), from Old French *compoun-*, present tense stem of *compondre*, from Latin *componere* 'put together.' The final -*d* was added in the 16th cent. on the pattern of *expound* and *propound*.

com•pur•ga•tion /,kämpər'gāSHən/

▶ n. historical acquittal from a charge or accusation, obtained by statements of innocence given by witnesses under oath.
ORIGIN mid 17th cent.: from medieval Latin *compurgation-*, from Latin *compurgare*, from *com-* (expressing intensive force) + *purgare* 'purify' (from *purus* 'pure').

com•pur•ga•tor /'kämpər,gātər/

▶ n. historical a sworn witness to the innocence or good character of an accused person: *the reservation would enable the compurgator to escape the charge of false swearing.*
ORIGIN mid 16th cent.: medieval Latin, from Latin *com-* 'together with' + *purgator*, from *purgare* 'purify' (see COMPURGATION).

con•cert

▶ n. /'kän,sərt; 'känsərt/ formal agreement, accordance, or harmony.
▶ v. /kən'sərt/ [trans.] formal arrange (something) by mutual agreement or coordination: *they could be liable for con-*

certing their behavior in order to deter entry into the market.

PHRASES **in concert** acting jointly: *he made his decision in concert with his son and son-in-law.*

ORIGIN late 16th cent. (in the sense 'unite, cause to agree'): from French *concerter*, from Italian *concertare* 'harmonize.'

con•demn /kənˈdem/
▶ v. [trans.] sentence (someone) to a particular punishment, esp. death: *the rebels had been* **condemned to death** | [as adj.] (**condemned**) *the condemned men.*
■ (usu. **be condemned**) officially declare (something, esp. a building) to be unfit for use: *the pool has been condemned as a health hazard.*
DERIVATIVES **con•dem•na•ble** /kənˈdem(n)əbəl/ adj.; **con•dem•na•tion** /ˌkändəmˈnāsHən; -dem-/ n.; **con•dem•na•to•ry** /kənˈdemnəˌtôrē/ adj.
ORIGIN Middle English: from Old French *condemner*, from Latin *condemnare*, from *con-* (expressing intensive force) + *damnare* 'inflict loss on.'

con•di•tion•al sale /kənˈdisHənl ˈsāl/
▶ n. the sale of goods according to a contract containing conditions, typically that ownership does not pass to the buyer until after a set time, usually after payment of the last installment of the purchase price, although the buyer has possession and is committed to acquiring ownership.

con•do•min•i•um /ˌkändəˈminēəm/
▶ n. (pl. **con•do•min•i•ums**) **1** a building or complex of buildings containing a number of individually owned apartments or houses: *a lakeshore condominium*
■ each of the individual apartments or houses in such a building or complex: *they're thinking of selling their Florida condominium.* ■ the system of ownership by which

these operate, in which owners have full title to the individual apartment or house and an undivided interest in the shared parts of the property: *all the other buildings on the block have* **gone condominium**.
2 the joint control of a country's or territory's affairs by other countries: *the Western part of the district was ruled in condominium between Trier and Luxembourg.*
■ a state so governed.
ORIGIN early 18th cent.: modern Latin, from *con-* 'together with' + *dominium* 'right of ownership' (see DOMINION). Sense 1 dates from the 1960s.

con•ju•gal rights /ˈkänjəgəl ˈrīts; kənˈjoōgəl/
▸ plural n. the rights, especially to sexual relations, regarded as exercisable in law by each partner in a marriage: *in certain cases, spouses have withdrawn conjugal rights from each other and continue to live under the same roof.*

con•ju•gal vis•it /ˈkänjəgəl ˈvizit/
▸ n. a visit by the spouse of a prisoner, especially for sexual relations.

con•science clause /ˈkänsHəns ˌklôz/
▸ n. a clause that makes concessions to the consciences of those affected by a law: *Congress passed a "conscience clause" bill, which permitted any individual opposed to abortion to refuse to perform the procedure.*

con•sent /kənˈsent/
▸ n. permission for something to happen or agreement to do something: *no change may be made without the consent of all the partners.*
▸ v. [intrans.] give permission for something to happen: *he consented to a search by a detective.*
■ [with infinitive] agree to do something: *he had consented to serve on the panel.*

PHRASES **by common consent** with the agreement of all: *the parties may by common consent agree to replace any conciliator.* **informed consent** permission granted in the knowledge of the possible consequences, typically that which is given by a patient to a doctor for treatment with full knowledge of the possible risks and benefits.
ORIGIN Middle English: from Old French *consente* (noun), *consentir* (verb), from Latin *consentire,* from *con-* 'together' + *sentire* 'feel.'

con•sent•ing a•dult /kən'sentiNG ə'dəlt; 'æd,əlt/
▶ n. an adult who willingly agrees to engage in an act, esp. a sexual act: *socially acceptable and lawful activities between consenting adults.*

con•se•quen•tial /ˌkänsə'kwenCHəl/
▶ adj. resulting from an act, but not immediately and directly: *consequential damages.*
DERIVATIVES **con•se•quen•ti•al•i•ty** /ˌkänsə,kwenCHē'ælitē/ n.; **con•se•quen•tial•ly** adv.
ORIGIN early 17th cent.: from Latin *consequentia.*

con•sid•er•a•tion /kən,sidə'rāSHən/
▶ n. 1 (in a contractual agreement) anything given or promised or forborne by one party in exchange for the promise or undertaking of another: *in consideration of the services provided under this Agreement, the company will pay the agent a commission on all sales.*
2 archaic importance; consequence.
ORIGIN late Middle English: via Old French from Latin *consideration-,* from *considerare* 'examine.'

con•sol•i•date /kən'säli,dāt/
▶ v. [trans.] combine (two or more legal actions involving similar or related questions) into one for action by a court: *the husband moved the trial court to dismiss the action on the note or, in the alternative, to consolidate the action with the pending divorce proceedings.*

DERIVATIVES **con•sol•i•da•tion** /kən₁säli'dāsHən/ n.
ORIGIN early 16th cent. (in the sense 'combine into a single whole'): from Latin *consolidare*, from *con-* 'together' + *solidare* 'make firm' (from *solidus* 'solid').

con•sor•ti•um /kən'sôrsH(ē)əm; -'sôr̲t̲ēəm/
▶ n. (pl. **con•sor•ti•a** /kən'sôrsH(ē)ə; -'sôr̲t̲ēə/ or **con•sor•ti•ums**) the right of association and companionship with one's husband or wife.
PHRASES **loss of consortium** damage to a spouse for loss of companionship (often including sexual relations) due to injury to their spouse: *the extent to which a spouse may apply for loss of consortium damages in a wrongful death claim.*
ORIGIN early 19th cent. (in the sense 'partnership'): from Latin, from *consors* 'sharing, partner.'

con•sta•ble /'känstəbəl; 'kən-/
▶ n. a peace officer with limited policing authority, typically in a small town.
■ Brit. a police officer.
ORIGIN Middle English: from Old French *conestable*, from late Latin *comes stabuli* 'count (head officer) of the stable.'

con•stab•u•lar•y /kən'stæbyə₁lerē/
▶ n. (pl. **con•stab•u•lar•ies**) the constables of a district, collectively.
■ an armed police force organized as a military unit.
■ Brit. a police force covering a particular area or city: *the Durham Constabulary.*
▶ adj. [attrib.] of or relating to a constabulary.
ORIGIN late 15th cent. (denoting the district under the charge of a constable): from medieval Latin *constabularia (dignitas)* '(rank) of constable,' from *constabulus*, based on Latin *comes stabuli* (see CONSTABLE).

con•stit•u•ent /kənˈstiCHo͞oənt/
▶ **adj.** [attrib.] being a voting member of a community or organization and having the power to appoint or elect: *the constituent body has a right of veto.*
■ able to make or change a political constitution: *a constituent assembly.*
▶**n.** a member of a constituency: *Senator Kyle offers many services to his constituents.*
ORIGIN late 15th cent. (in the legal sense of the noun): from Latin *constituent-* (partly via French *constituant*) 'establishing, appointing,' from the verb *constituere* (see CONSTITUTE).

con•sti•tute /ˈkänstiˌt(y)o͞ot/
▶ **v.** [trans.] (usu. **be constituted**) give legal or constitutional form to (an institution); establish by law: *the committee delegation was constituted by written procedure on November 28th, 2000.*
ORIGIN late Middle English: from Latin *constitut-* 'established, appointed,' from the verb *constituere*, from *con-* 'together' + *statuere* 'set up.'

con•sti•tu•tion•al•ize /ˌkänstiˈt(y)o͞oSHənl-ˌīz/
▶ **v.** [trans.] make subject to explicit provisions of a country's constitution: *divorce is not constitutionalized.*

con•struc•tion•ist /kənˈstrəkSHənist/
▶ **n.** a person who puts a particular construction upon a legal document, esp. the US Constitution.
DERIVATIVES **con•struc•tion•ism** n.

con•struc•tive /kənˈstrəktiv/
▶ **adj.** derived by inference; implied by operation of law; not obvious or explicit: *constructive notice.*
ORIGIN mid 17th cent.: from late Latin *constructivus*, from Latin *construct-* 'heaped together,' from the verb *construere*, from *con* 'together' + *struere* ' pile, build.'

con•sul /ˈkänsəl/

▸**n. 1** an official appointed by a government to live in a foreign city and protect and promote the government's citizens and interests there: *the Colombian consul in San Francisco.*
2 (in ancient Rome) one of the two annually elected chief magistrates who jointly ruled the republic.
▪ any of the three chief magistrates of the first French republic (1799–1804).
DERIVATIVES **con•su•lar** /ˈkäns(y)ələr/ **adj.**; **con•sul•ship** /ˈkänsəl͵sHip/ **n.**
ORIGIN late Middle English (denoting an ancient Roman magistrate): from Latin, related to *consulere* 'take counsel.'

con•su•late /ˈkänsəlit/

▸**n. 1** the place or building in which a consul's duties are carried out: *the American Consulate in Strasbourg.*
▪ the office, position, or period of office of a consul.
2 historical the period of office of a Roman consul.
▪ (**the consulate**) the system of government by consuls in ancient Rome.
3 (**the Consulate**) the government of the first French republic (1799–1804) by three consuls.
ORIGIN late Middle English (denoting the government of Rome by consuls, or their office or dignity): from Latin *consulatus*, from *consul* (see CONSUL).

con•tem•pla•tion /͵käntəmˈpläsHən/

▸**n.** the state of being thought about or planned; anticipation: *Mr. Truman's gift was made in contemplation of death.*
ORIGIN Middle English: from Old French, from Latin *contemplatio(n-)*, from the verb *contemplari*, based on *templum* 'place for observation.'

con•tempt /kənˈtem(p)t/

▸**n.** (also **contempt of court**) the offense of being disobedient to or disrespectful of a court of law and its officers: *several unions were* **held** *to be* **in contempt** *and were fined.*

■ the offense of being similarly disobedient to or disrespectful of the lawful operation of a legislative body (e.g., its investigations): *what are the consequences of being cited in contempt of Congress?*

ORIGIN late Middle English: from Latin *contemptus*, from *contemnere*, from *con-* (expressing intensive force) + *temnere* 'despise.'

con•test

▶ n. /'kän,test/ the act of disputing or challenging the validity of a will: *if a contest is successful, a portion of the estate may descend by intestate succession.*

▶ v. /kən'test; 'kän,test/ [trans.] dispute or challenge the validity of (a will): *what are legitimate grounds for contesting the will?*

PHRASES **no contest** another term for NOLO CONTENDERE: *he pleaded no contest to two misdemeanor counts.*

DERIVATIVES **con•test•a•ble** /kən'testəbəl/ **adj.**; **con• test•er** /kən'testər; 'kän,tes-/ **n.**

ORIGIN late 16th cent.: from Latin *contestari* 'call upon to witness, initiate an action (by calling witnesses),' from *con-* 'together' + *testare* 'to witness.'

con•test•ant /kən'testənt/

▶ n. a person who takes part in a legal contest: *a contestant is trying to establish that the testator was inebriated at the time when the testamentary instruments were signed.*

ORIGIN mid 17th cent.: from French, present participle of *contester*, from Latin *contestari* 'call upon to witness' (see CONTEST).

con•tin•u•ance /kən'tinyo͞oəns/

▶ n. a postponement or adjournment: *if this man's testimony is important, I will grant a continuance.*

ORIGIN late Middle English: from Old French, from

continuer 'continue,' from Latin *continuare*, from *continuus* 'uninterrupted,' from *continere* 'hang together' (from *con-* 'together with' + *tenere* hold) + *-ous*.

con•tin•ue /kənˈtinyo͞o/
▶ v. [trans.] (**con•tin•ues, con•tin•ued, con•tin•u•ing**) postpone or adjourn (a legal proceeding): *the case was continued without a finding until August 2.*
ORIGIN Middle English: from Old French *continuer*, from Latin *continuare*, from *continuus* (see CONTINUANCE).

con•tract
▶ n. /ˈkänˌtrækt/ a written or spoken agreement that is intended to be enforceable by law: *both parties must sign employment contracts* | *a network of doctors and hospitals are* **under contract** *to provide services.*
■ the branch of law concerned with the making and observation of such agreements. ■ dated a formal agreement to marry.
▶ v. [intrans.] **1** /ˈkänˌtrækt; kənˈtrækt/ enter into a formal and legally binding agreement: *the local authority will* **contract with** *a wide range of agencies to provide services.*
■ secure specified rights or undertake specified obligations in a formal and legally binding agreement: *a buyer may* **contract for** *the right to withhold payment* | *the paper had* **contracted to** *publish extracts from the diaries.*
■ [trans.] impose an obligation on (someone) to do something by means of a formal agreement: *health authorities contract a hospital to treat a specific number of patients.*
■ [trans.] (**contract something out**) arrange for work to be done by another organization: *local authorities will have to contract out waste management.* ■ [trans.] dated formally enter into (a marriage): *before Fanny met him, he had contracted a disastrous liaison and marriage.*
2 /kənˈtrækt/ [trans.] become liable to pay (a debt): *he contracted a debt of $3,300.*

DERIVATIVES **con•tract•ee** /ˌkäntræk'tē/ **n.**; **con•trac•tive** /kən'træktiv; 'kän,træktiv/ **adj.**

ORIGIN Middle English: via Old French from Latin *contractus*, from *contract-* 'drawn together, tightened,' from the verb *contrahere*, from *con-* 'together' + *trahere* 'draw.'

con•tra pro•fer•en•tem /'käntrə ˌpräfə'rentem/
▸ **adv.** (of the interpretation of a contract) against the party that proposed (or, more usually, drafted) the contract or a provision in the contract: *Intel argued that a decision in the district court made a mistake because it applied contra proferentum.*
▸ **n.** The rule that a contract must be construed most strictly against the drafter: *the drafting history will establish through extrinsic evidence that Nestle's interpretation is correct and that contra proferentum applies.*

ORIGIN Latin, 'against (the person) mentioning.'

con•trib•u•to•ry /kən'tribyə,tôrē/
▸ **adj.** (of or relating to a pension or insurance plan) operated by means of a fund into which people pay: *contributory benefits.*

ORIGIN late Middle English: from medieval Latin *contributorius*, from Latin *contribut-* 'added.'

con•trib•u•to•ry neg•li•gence /kən'tribyə,tôrē 'neglijəns/
▸ **n.** failure of an injured plaintiff to act with reasonable care, considered to be a contributory factor in the injury suffered, thereby barring the plaintiff from compensation by the defendant.

con•tu•ma•cious /ˌkänt(y)ə'māsнəs/
▸ **adj.** (esp. of a defendant's behavior) stubbornly or willfully disobedient to authority; in contempt: *a clear record of delay or contumacious conduct.*

DERIVATIVES **con•tu•ma•cious•ly adv.**

ORIGIN late 16th cent.: from Latin *contumax, contumac-* (perhaps from *con-* 'with' + *tumere* 'to swell') + *-ious.*

con•tu•ma•cy /kən't(y)ōōməsē; 'känt(y)əməsē/
▶ n. stubborn refusal to obey or comply with authority, esp. a court order or summons: *his refusal to comply with the Court Order is based upon contumacy rather than inability.*
ORIGIN Middle English: from Latin *contumacia* 'inflexibility,' from *contumax* (see CONTUMACIOUS).

con•ver•sion /kən'vərzHən/
▶ n. the action of wrongfully dealing with goods or money in a manner inconsistent with the owner's rights: *he was found guilty of the fraudulent conversion of clients' monies.*
ORIGIN Middle English: via Old French from Latin *conversio(n-)*, from *convers-* 'turned around,' from the verb *convertere* (see CONVERT).

con•vert
▶ v. [trans.] /kən'vərt/ wrongfully deal with (goods or money) in a manner inconsistent with the owner's rights: *the defendant converted the plaintiff's construction materials to his own use.*
ORIGIN Middle English (in the sense 'turn around, send in a different direction'): from Old French *convertir*, based on Latin *convertere* 'turn around,' from *con-* 'altogether' + *vertere* 'turn.'

con•vey /kən'vā/
▶ v. [trans.] transfer the title to (property): *the cabin was conveyed to her by inheritance.*
DERIVATIVES **con•vey•a•ble** adj.
ORIGIN Middle English: from Old French *conveier*, from medieval Latin *conviare*, from *con-* 'together' + Latin *via* 'way.'

con•vey•ance /kən'vāəns/
▶ n. the legal process of transferring property from one

owner to another: *protective measures that might be taken before the conveyance is concluded.*

■ a legal document effecting such a process.

con•vey•anc•ing /kən'vāənsiNG/

▶ n. the branch of law concerned with the preparation of documents for the transferring of property.

■ the action of preparing documents for the transfer of property: *settlement costs include transfer tax, recording fees, documentary stamps, and conveyancing.*

DERIVATIVES **con•vey•anc•er** n.

con•vict

▶ v. /kən'vikt/ [trans.] (often **be convicted**) declare (someone) to be guilty of a criminal offense by the verdict of a jury or the decision of a judge in a court of law: *her former boyfriend was **convicted of** assaulting her* | [as adj.] (**convicted**) *a convicted murderer.*

▶ n. /'kän,vikt/ a person found guilty of a criminal offense and serving a sentence of imprisonment.

ORIGIN Middle English: from Latin *convict-* 'demonstrated, refuted, convicted,' from the verb *convincere*, from *con-* 'with' + *vincere* 'conquer.' The noun is from obsolete *convict* 'convicted.'

con•vic•tion /kən'vikSHən/

▶ n. a formal declaration that someone is guilty of a criminal offense, made by the verdict of a jury or the decision of a judge in a court of law: *she had a previous conviction for a similar offense.*

ORIGIN late Middle English: from Latin *convictio(n-)*, from the verb *convincere* (see CONVICT).

cop•y•right /'käpē,rīt/

▶ n. the exclusive legal right, given to a creator or an assignee for a fixed number of years, to reproduce,

distribute, or perform literary, artistic, or musical material, and to authorize others to do the same: *they bought the copyright to the whole film archive.*
▸v. [trans.] secure copyright for (such material): *is the book copyrighted in the name of the author or the publisher?*

co•re•spond•ent /ˌkō risˈpändənt/ (also **co•re•spond•ent**)
▸ n. **1** a joint defendant in a lawsuit, esp. one on appeal: *the bank is a co-respondent in the case, but is not being represented legally.*
2 a person cited in a divorce case as having committed adultery with the respondent.

cor•po•rate /ˈkôrp(ə)rət/
▸ adj. (of a company or group of people) authorized to act as a single entity and recognized as such in law: *the historical development of corporate rights in America.*
▸n. a corporate company or group.
DERIVATIVES **cor•po•rate•ly** adv.
ORIGIN late 15th cent.: from Latin *corporatus*, past participle of *corporare* 'form into a body,' from *corpus, corpor-* 'body.'

cor•po•ra•tion /ˌkôrpəˈrāsHən/
▸ n. a company or group of people authorized to act as a single entity (legally a person) in which the individuals who make up the corporation have limited liability.
■ (also **municipal corporation**) a group of people elected to govern a city, town, or borough.
ORIGIN late Middle English: from late Latin *corporatio(n-)*, from Latin *corporare* 'combine in one body' (see CORPORATE).

cor•po•re•al /kôrˈpôrēəl/
▸ adj. consisting of material objects; tangible: *corporeal property.*
DERIVATIVES **cor•po•re•al•i•ty** /kôrˌpôrēˈælitē/ n.; **cor•po•re•al•ly** adv.

ORIGIN late Middle English (in the sense 'material'): from late Latin *corporealis*, from Latin *corporeus* 'bodily, physical,' from *corpus*, *corpor-* 'body.'

cor•pus de•lic•ti /ˈkôrpəs dəˈliktī; dəˈliktē/
▸ n. the facts and circumstances constituting a breach of a law.
■ concrete evidence of a crime, such as a corpse: *it isn't necessary to rely upon a corpus delicti to gain a murder conviction.*
ORIGIN Latin, literally 'body of offense.'

cor•rupt prac•tice /kəˈrəpt ˈpræktis/
▸ n. (often **corrupt practices**) a fraudulent activity, especially an attempt to rig an election or bribe an official.

Co•sa Nos•tra /ˌkōsə ˈnōstrə; ˌkōzə/ a US criminal organization resembling and related to the Mafia.
ORIGIN Italian, literally 'our affair.'

costs /kôsts/
▸ plural noun legal expenses, esp. those allowed in favor of the winning party or against the losing party in a suit: *the plaintiff was awarded $7,500 general damages, plus costs.*
ORIGIN Middle English: from Old French *coust* (noun), *couster* (verb), based on Latin *constare* 'stand firm, stand at a price.'

coun•sel /ˈkownsəl/
▸ n. (pl. same) the lawyer or lawyers conducting a case: *the counsel for the defense.*
ORIGIN Middle English: via Old French *counseil* (noun), *conseiller* (verb), from Latin *consilium* 'consultation, advice,' related to *consulere* 'take counsel.'

count /kownt/

▶ **n.** a separate charge in an indictment: *he pleaded guilty to five counts of murder.*

ORIGIN Middle English (as a noun): from Old French *counte* (noun), *counter* (verb), from the verb *computare* 'calculate.'

coun•ter•claim /'kowntər‚klām/

▶ **n.** a claim made to rebut a previous claim: *the employer made a counterclaim, affirming that there would be no hearing in the case.*

■ a claim made by a defendant against the plaintiff: *the defendant's counterclaim may demand money from the plaintiff.*

▶ **v.** [intrans.] make a counterclaim for something: *Century counterclaimed for the difference between the amount the Association had paid and its statutory coverage limit.*

coun•ter•mand /‚kowntər'mænd; 'kowntər‚mænd/

▶ **v.** [trans.] revoke (an order): *an order to arrest the strike leaders had been countermanded.*

■ declare (voting) invalid: *the election commission has countermanded voting on the grounds of intimidation.*

ORIGIN late Middle English: from Old French *contremander* (verb), *contremand* (noun), from medieval Latin *contramandare*, from *contra-* 'against' + *mandare* 'to order.'

coun•ter•part /'kowntər‚pärt/

▶ **n.** one of two or more copies of a legal document: *everyone ensures that the unsigned headers are identical to their signed counterparts.*

coun•ty court /'kowntē 'kôrt/

▶ **n.** a court in some states with civil and criminal jurisdiction for a given county.

court /kôrt/

▸ n. (also **court of law**) a tribunal presided over by a judge, judges, or a magistrate: *a settlement was reached during the first sitting of the court* | *she will **take** the matter **to court*** | [as adj.] *a court case.*

■ any of various other tribunals, such as military courts.

■ the place where such a tribunal meets: *reporters and photographers were waiting in front of the court.* ■ (**the court**) the judge or judges presiding at such a tribunal: PHRASES **go to court** take legal action. **in court** appearing as a party or an attorney in a court of law: *Ms. Webber is in court every day this week.* **out of court** before a legal hearing can take place: *they are trying to settle the squabble out of court* | [as adj.] *an out-of-court settlement.*

ORIGIN Middle English: from Old French *cort*, from Latin *cohors*, *cohort-* 'yard or retinue.' The verb is influenced by Old Italian *corteare*, Old French *courtoyer*.

court•house /'kôrt,hows/

▸ n. **1** a building in which a judicial court is held.
2 a building containing the administrative offices of a county.

court-mar•tial /'kôrt ,märsHəl/

▸ n. (pl. **courts-mar•tial** or **court-mar•tials**) a judicial court for trying members of the armed services accused of offenses against military law: *they appeared before a court-martial* | *he was found guilty by court-martial.*
▸ v. (**court-mar•tialed, court-mar•tial•ing**; Brit **court-mar•tialled, court-mar•tial•ling**) [trans.] try (someone) by such a court: *two Army officers were court-martialed for the security breach.*

court of ap•peals /'kôrt əv ə'pēlz/

▸ n. a court to which appeals are taken in a federal circuit or a state.

court of claims /'kôrt əv 'klāmz/
▸ n. a court in which claims against the government are adjudicated.

court of in•quir•y /'kôrt əv in'kwīrē; 'inkwīrē; 'iNGkwərē/
▸ n. a tribunal appointed in the armed forces to investigate a matter and decide whether a court-martial is called for: *the Navy will convene a court of inquiry to determine whether disciplinary action should be taken against senior officers.*

court of rec•ord /'kôrt əv 'rekərd/
▸ n. a court whose proceedings are recorded and available as evidence of fact.

court or•der /'kôrt 'ôrdər/
▸ n. a direction issued by a court or a judge requiring a person to do or not do something: *a court order banning her from being within three blocks of the White House.*

court rec•ord /'kôrt 'rekərd/
▸ n. see RECORD (sense 1).

court•room /'kôrt‚ro͞om; -‚ro͝om/
▸ n. the place or room in which a court of law meets.

cov•e•nant /'kəvənənt/
▸ n. a contract drawn up by deed: *it is agreed in the covenant that the municipalities will make these requirements known to the operators.*
▪ a clause in a contract.
▸ v. [intrans.] agree, esp. by lease, deed, or other legal contract: *the landlord **covenants to** repair the property | the county shall covenant that the real property tax assessment will reflect the fair market value.*
DERIVATIVES **cov•e•nan•tal** /‚kəvə'næntl/ adj.; **cov•e•nan•tor** /'kəvənəntər/ (also **cov•e•nan•ter**) n.
ORIGIN Middle English: from Old French, present

participle of *covenir* 'agree,' from Latin *convenire* 'assemble, agree, fit,' from *con-* 'together' + *venire* 'come.'

cov•e•nan•tee /ˌkəvənənˈtē; -næn-/
▸ n. the person to whom a promise by covenant is made.

co•vert
▸ adj. /ˈkōvərt; kōˈvərt; ˈkəvərt/ (of a woman) married and under the authority and protection of her husband. See also FEME COVERT.
ORIGIN Middle English (in the general senses 'covered' and 'a cover'): from Old French, 'covered,' past participle of *covrir*, from Latin *cooperire*, from *co-* (expressing intensive force) + *operire* 'to cover.'

cov•er•ture /ˈkəvərˌCHo͞or; -CHər/
▸ n. historical the legal status of a married woman, considered to be under her husband's protection and authority.
ORIGIN Middle English: from Old French, from *covrir* 'to cover.' It originally denoted a coverlet or a garment, later various kinds of covering or shelter.

cri•er /ˈkrīər/
▸ n. an officer who makes public announcements in a court of justice.
ORIGIN late Middle English: from Old French *criere*, from *crier* 'to shout.'

crime /krīm/
▸ n. an action or omission that constitutes an offense that may be prosecuted by the state and is punishable by law: *shoplifting was a serious crime.*
■ illegal activities: *the victims of crime.*
ORIGIN Middle English (in the sense 'wickedness, sin'): via Old French from Latin *crimen* 'judgment, offense,' based on *cernere* 'to judge.'

crim·i·nal /'krimənl/

▸ **n.** a person who has committed a crime: *these men are dangerous criminals.*

▸ **adj.** of or relating to a crime: *he is charged with conspiracy to commit criminal damage.*

■ of or relating to crime as opposed to civil matters: *a criminal court.*

DERIVATIVES **crim·i·nal·i·ty** /ˌkrimə'nælitē/ **n.**; **crim·i·nal·ly adv.** *criminally negligent*

ORIGIN late Middle English (as an adjective): from late Latin *criminalis*, from Latin *crimen, crimin-* (see CRIME).

crim·i·nal con·ver·sa·tion /'krimənl ˌkänvər'sāSHən/

▸ **n.** historical adultery, esp. as formerly constituting grounds for the recovery of legal damages by a husband from his adulterous wife's partner: *causes of action for breach of promise, alienation of affections, and criminal conversation.*

crim·i·nal·is·tics /ˌkrimənl'istiks/

▸ **plural n.** [treated as sing.] another term for **forensics** (see **forensic**).

DERIVATIVES **crim·i·nal·ist n.**

crim·i·nal law /'krimənl 'lô/

▸ **n.** a system of law concerned with the punishment of those who commit crimes. Contrasted with CIVIL LAW.

■ a law belonging to this system.

crim·i·nal li·bel /'krimənl 'lībəl/

▸ **n.** historical a malicious, defamatory statement in a permanent form, rendering the maker liable to criminal prosecution: *it is the question of whether the publication of anything with a malicious intention to cause a breach of the peace constitutes criminal libel.*

crim·i·nal re·cord /'krimənl 'rekərd/

▸ **n.** a history of being convicted for crime: *he admits he has a criminal record.*

■ a list of a person's previous criminal convictions: *the court said his criminal record would be expunged at the end of the year.*

crim·i·nol·o·gy /ˌkrimə'näləjē/
▸ n. the scientific study of crime and criminals.
DERIVATIVES **crim·i·no·log·i·cal** /ˌkrimənl'äjikəl/ **adj.**; **crim·i·nol·o·gist** /ˌkrimə'näləjist/ n.
ORIGIN late 19th cent.: from Latin *crimen, crimin-* 'crime' + *-logy.*

cross-claim /'krôs 'klām/
▸ a claim brought by one defendant against another in the same proceeding.

cross-ex·am·ine /'krôs ig'zæmin/
▸ v. [trans.] question (a witness called by the other party) in a court of law to discredit or undercut testimony already given. *the approach to cross-examining the defense medical expert varies on a case-to-case basis.* Compare with DIRECT EXAMINATION.
DERIVATIVES **cross-ex·am·i·na·tion** /'krôs ig,zæmə'nāsHən/ n.; **cross-ex·am·in·er** n.

cru·el·ty /'krōōəltē/
▸ n. (pl. **cru·el·ties**) behavior that causes physical or mental harm to another, esp. a spouse, whether intentionally or not: *the mother, 18, was charged with cruelty and attempted murder.*
ORIGIN Middle English: from Old French *crualte,* based on Latin *crudelitas,* from *crudelis.*

cui bo·no? /kwē 'bōnō/
▸ exclam. who stands, or stood, to gain (from a crime, and so might have been responsible for it)?
ORIGIN early 17th cent.: Latin, literally 'to whom (is it) a benefit?'

cur•te•sy /'kərtəsē/
▸ n. (pl. **cur•te•sies**) historical a tenure by which a husband, after his wife's death, held certain kinds of property that she had inherited.

cur•ti•lage /'kərtl-ij/
▸ n. an area of land attached to a house and forming one enclosure with it: *the roads **within the curtilage** of the development site.*
ORIGIN Middle English: from Anglo-Norman French, variant of Old French *courtillage*, from *courtil* 'small court,' from *cort* 'court.'

cus•to•dy /'kəstədē/
▸ n. the protective care or guardianship of someone or something: *the property was placed in the custody of a trustee.*
■ imprisonment: *my father was being **taken into custody**.* ■ parental responsibility, esp. as allocated to one of two divorcing parents: *he was trying to get **custody of** their child.*
DERIVATIVES **cus•to•di•al** /kə'stōdēəl/ **adj.** *the custodial parent* | *custodial sentences.*
ORIGIN late Middle English: from Latin *custodia*, from *custos* 'guardian.'

cy-pres /sē'prā/
▸ adv. & adj. as near as possible to the testator's or donor's intentions when these cannot be precisely followed: [as adj.] *these are the cy-pres options for distributions of pecuniary penalties.*
ORIGIN early 19th cent.: from a late Anglo-Norman French variant of French *si près* 'so near.'

D

DA
▶ **abbr.** district attorney: *the DA for the Third Judicial Circuit.*

dam•ages /'dæmijiz/
▶ **plural noun** a sum of money claimed or awarded in compensation for a loss or an injury: *she was awarded $284,000 in damages.*
ORIGIN Middle English: from Old French, from *dam, damne* 'loss or damage,' from Latin *damnum* 'loss or hurt.'

date rape /'dāt ˌrāp/
▶ **n.** rape committed by the victim's escort: *a former UM student was accused of a 1994 date rape.*

dead hand /'ded 'hænd/
▶ **n.** an undesirable persisting influence, especially concerning property after the death of a prior owner: *the purposes behind the rule against remoteness are to curtail dead hand domination and to facilitate marketability.*
■ see MORTMAIN.

death cer•tif•i•cate /'deTH sərˌtifikit/
▶ **n.** an official statement, signed by a physician, of the cause, date, and place of a person's death.

death pen•al•ty /'deTH ˌpenltē/
▶ **n.** the punishment of execution, administered to someone convicted of a capital crime.

death tax /'deTH ˌtæks/
▶ **n. 1** another term for ESTATE TAX.
2 another term for INHERITANCE TAX.

death war•rant /ˈdeTH ˌwôrənt; ˌwärənt/
▸ n. an official order for the execution of a condemned person: *the motion to stay execution was denied as premature as the governor has not yet signed a death warrant.*

de•cease /diˈsēs/
▸ n. [in sing.] death: *he left no property at the time of his decease.*
ORIGIN Middle English: from Old French *deces,* from Latin *decessus* 'death,' past participle (used as a noun) of *decedere* 'to die.'

de•ceased /diˈsēst/ formal
▸ n. (**the deceased**) a person who has died: *you should present any evidence you have that shows your relationship to the deceased.*
▸ adj. dead; no longer living: *the vehicle title of the deceased owner was transferred to the spouse's name.*

de•ce•dent /diˈsēdnt/
▸ n. a person who has died: *measures to make sure the decedent's property passes to his children.*
ORIGIN late 16th cent.: from Latin *decedent-* 'dying,' from the verb *decedere* (see DECEASE).

de•ci•sion /diˈsiZHən/
▸ n. a formal judgment: *last year's Supreme Court decision.*
ORIGIN late Middle English: from Latin *decisio(n-),* from *decidere* 'determine.'

de•clar•ant /diˈklerənt/
▸ n. a person or party who makes a formal declaration: *the statement was made while the declarant was under the stress of excitement.*
▪ an alien who has signed a declaration of intent to become a US citizen: *the form contains little more than the declarant's name and native country.*
▸ adj. making or having made a formal declaration.

ORIGIN late 17th cent.: from French *déclarant*, present participle of *déclarer*, from Latin *declarare* 'make quite clear.'

dec•la•ra•tion /ˌdeklə'rāsHən/
▶ n. a statement asserting or protecting a legal right: *the Universal Declaration of Human Rights.*
■ a written public announcement of intentions or of the terms of an agreement: *authors are required to submit this declaration of competing financial interests form.* ■ a plaintiff's statement of claims in proceedings: *in a declaration, the plaintiff speaks of much more than an affiliation with the Association.* ■ an affirmation made instead of taking an oath.
ORIGIN late Middle English: from Latin *declaratio(n-)*, from *declarare* 'make quite clear.'

de•cree /di'krē/
▶ n. an official order issued by a legal authority: *an interlocutory decree of divorce.*
■ the issuing of such an order: *the king **ruled by decree**.* ■ a judgment or decision of certain courts of law: *a consent decree.*
▶ v. (**de•crees, de•creed, de•cree•ing**) [trans.] order (something) by decree: *the government decreed a ban on any contact with the guerrillas* | [with clause] *the president decreed that the military was to be streamlined.*
ORIGIN Middle English (denoting an edict issued by an ecclesiastical council to settle a point of doctrine or discipline): from Old French *decre, decret*, from Latin *decretum* 'something decided,' from *decernere* 'decide.'

de•crim•i•nal•ize /dē'krimənl‚īz/
▶ v. [trans.] cease to treat (something) as illegal, typically by legislation: *a battle to decriminalize drugs.*
DERIVATIVES **de•crim•i•nal•i•za•tion** /dē‚krimənli'zāsHən/ n.

deed /dēd/

▸ **n.** a legal document that is signed and delivered, esp. one regarding the ownership of property or legal rights. See also TITLE DEED.

▸ **v.** [trans.] convey or transfer (property or rights) by legal deed: *they **deeded** their property to their children.*

ORIGIN Old English *dēd*, *dǣd*, of Germanic origin; related to Dutch *daad* and German *Tat*, from an Indo-European root shared by *do*.

deed of trust /'dēd əv 'trəst/

▸ **n.** another term for TRUST DEED.

de fac•to /di 'fæktō; dā/

▸ **adv.** in fact, whether by right or not: *assume he is de facto stateless if he says he is stateless but cannot establish he is de jure stateless.* Often contrasted with DE JURE.

▸ **adj.** [attrib.] denoting someone or something that is such in fact: *evidence that the child has been cared for by a de facto custodian.*

ORIGIN early 17th cent.: Latin, literally 'of fact.'

de fac•to seg•re•ga•tion /di 'fæktō segri'gāsHən/

▸ **n.** segregation that exists as a consequence of social, economic, and political circumstances, and not as the result of legislation: *busing was ordered as a way to deal with de facto segregation brought about by housing patterns.*

de•fal•cate /di'fælkāt; -'fôl-/

▸ **v.** [trans.] misappropriate or fail to turn over (funds with which one has been entrusted): *the officials were charged with defalcating government money.* Compare with EMBEZZLE.

DERIVATIVES **de•fal•ca•tion** /ˌdēfæl'kāsHən; -fôl-/ n.; **de•fal•ca•tor** n.

ORIGIN mid 16th cent. (in the sense 'deduct, subtract'):

from medieval Latin *defalcat-* 'lopped,' from the verb *defalcare*, from *de-* 'away from, off' + Latin *falx, falc-* 'sickle.'

def•a•ma•tion /ˌdefəˈmāsHən/

▶ n. the modern form of the action for slander or libel: *defamation of character* | *the group was initially organized to speak out against defamation and hate crimes.*

ORIGIN see **DEFAME.**

de•fame /diˈfām/

▶ v. [trans.] damage the good reputation of (someone); slander or libel: *he claimed that the article defamed his family.*

DERIVATIVES **de•fam•a•to•ry** /diˈfæməˌtôrē/ adj.; **de•fam•er** n.

ORIGIN Middle English: from Old French *diffamer*, from Latin *diffamare* 'spread evil report,' from *dis-* (expressing removal) + *fama* 'report.'

de•fault /diˈfôlt/

▶ n. failure to fulfill an obligation, esp. to repay a loan or appear in a court of law: *it will have to restructure its debts to avoid default.*

▶v. [intrans.] fail to fulfill an obligation, esp. to repay a loan or to appear in a court of law: *some had **defaulted on** student loans.*

◼ [trans.] declare (a party) in default and give judgment against that party: *the possibility that cases would be defaulted and defendants released.*

PHRASES **by default** through lack of positive action rather than conscious choice: *legislation dies by default if the governor fails to act on it.* **in default** guilty of failing to repay a loan or appear in a court of law: *the company is already **in default on** its loans.* **in default of** in the absence of: *in default of agreement, the rent was to be determined by a surveyor.*

ORIGIN Middle English: from Old French *defaut*, from *defaillir* 'to fail,' based on Latin *fallere* 'disappoint, deceive.'

de•fault judg•ment /di'fôlt ˌjəjmənt/
▸ n. judgment awarded to the plaintiff on the defendant's failure to plead.

de•fea•sance /di'fēzəns/
▸ n. the action or process of rendering something null and void: *riparian rights held by the United States under California law are subject to defeasance by subsequent appropriators.*
■ a clause or condition which, if fulfilled, renders a deed or contract null and void.
ORIGIN late Middle English (as a legal term): from Old French *defesance*, from *defaire*, *desfaire* 'undo.'

de•fea•si•ble /di'fēzəbəl/
▸ adj. (especially of an interest in land) subject to being defeated or extinguished: *in the typical mortgage relationship a mortgagee holds defeasible legal title to the mortgaged property interest.*
DERIVATIVES **de•fea•si•bil•i•ty** /diˌfēzə'bilitē/ n.; **de•fea•si•bly** /di'fēzəblē/ adv.
ORIGIN Middle English: via Anglo-Norman French from the stem of Old French *desfesant* 'undoing' (see also DEFEASANCE).

de•feat /di'fēt/
▸ v. [trans.] reject or block (a motion or proposal): *the amendment was defeated.*
■ render null and void; annul: *title to goods may be defeated under certain conditions involving irregularities in warehousing and freight forwarding.*
▸ n. an instance of defeating or being defeated.

ORIGIN late Middle English (in the sense 'undo, destroy, annul'): from Old French *desfait* 'undone,' past participle of *desfaire*, from medieval Latin *disfacere* 'undo.'

de•fend /di'fend/
▶ v. [trans.] conduct the case for (the party being accused or sued) in a lawsuit: *their lawyer had defended dozens of indigent clients.*
DERIVATIVES **de•fend•a•ble adj.**
ORIGIN Middle English: from Old French *defendre*, from Latin *defendere*, from *de-* 'off' + *-fendere* 'to strike.'

de•fend•ant /di'fendənt/
▶ n. an individual or entity sued or accused in a court of law. *this defendant identifies himself in his deposition as Timothy E. Nickel.* Compare with PLAINTIFF.
ORIGIN Middle English (as an adjective in the sense 'defending'): from Old French, 'warding off,' present participle of *defendre* (see DEFEND).

de•fense /di'fens; 'dēfens/ (Brit. de•fence)
▶ n. 1 the case presented by or on behalf of the party being accused or sued in a lawsuit.
2 one or more defendants in a trial.
▣ (usu. **the defense**) [treated as sing. or pl.] the counsel for the defendant in a lawsuit: *the defense requested more time to prepare their case.*
ORIGIN Middle English: from Old French *defens*, from late Latin *defensum* (neuter), *defensa* (feminine), past participles of *defendere* 'defend.'

de•gree /di'grē/
▶ n. [in combination] a legal grade of crime or offense, esp. murder: *second-degree murder.*
ORIGIN Middle English (in the senses 'step,' 'tier,' 'rank,'

or 'relative state'): from Old French, based on Latin *de-* 'down' + *gradus* 'step or grade.'

de ju•re /di 'jŏŏrē; dā 'jŏŏrä/
▸ **adv.** according to rightful entitlement or law; by right: *if the product configuration is not de jure functional, the mark may be registered on the Supplemental Register*. Often contrasted with DE FACTO.
▸ **adj.** denoting something or someone that is such by law: *he has been the de jure president of the company since his father's death.*
ORIGIN mid 16th cent.: Latin, literally 'of law.'

de•lict /di'likt/
▸ **n.** a violation of the law; a tort or crime: *an international delict.*
DERIVATIVES **de•lict•u•al** /di'liksHŏŏəl/ **adj.**
ORIGIN late Middle English: from Latin *delictum* 'something showing fault,' neuter past participle of *delinquere*, from *de-* 'away' + *linquere* 'to leave.'

de•liv•er /di'livər/
▸ **v.** [trans.] **1** transfer (property), acknowledging that one intends to be bound by a deed, either explicitly by declaration or implicitly by formal handover.
2 (of a judge or court) give (a judgment or verdict): *the judge delivered his verdict.*
ORIGIN Middle English: from Old French *delivrer*, based on Latin *de-* 'away' + *liberare* 'set free.'

de•liv•er•y /di'livərē/
▸ **n.** (pl. **de•liv•er•ies**) the formal or symbolic handing over of property, esp. by deed, to a grantee or third party.
ORIGIN late Middle English: from Anglo-Norman French *delivree*, feminine past participle of *delivrer* (see DELIVER).

de•mand /di'mænd/
> ▸ n. a formal request, as a right: *there is no fee in federal court for filing a jury demand.*
> ▸ v. [trans.] **1** call into court; summon.
> **2** make a formal request: *the court demanded that the FDA support its claims with evidence.*

DERIVATIVES **de•mand•er** n.

ORIGIN Middle English (as a noun): from Old French *demande* (noun), *demander* (verb), from Latin *demandare* 'hand over, entrust' (in medieval Latin 'demand'), from *de-* 'formally' + *mandare* 'to order.'

de•mise /di'mīz/
> ▸ v. [trans.] convey or grant (an estate) by will or lease: *the premises hereby demised may be used for any lawful retail purpose.*
> ▸ n. [in sing.] conveyance or transfer of property or a title by demising: *documents that confirm any demise of title to real estate are fully taxable.*

ORIGIN late Middle English (as a legal term): from Anglo-Norman French, past participle (used as a noun) of Old French *desmettre* 'dismiss,' (in reflexive) 'abdicate,' based on Latin *dimittere* (see DISMISS).

de•mon•stra•tive ev•i•dence /di'mänstrətiv 'evidns/
> ▸ n. evidence that makes use of a demonstration or display or an addition to testimony: *computer-generated demonstrative evidence.*

de•mur /di'mər/
> ▸ v. (**de•murred, de•mur•ring**) [intrans.] dated put forward a demurrer.
> ▸ n. [usu. with negative] the action or process of objecting to or hesitating over something: *they accepted this ruling without demur.*

ORIGIN Middle English (in the sense 'linger, delay'):

from Old French *demourer* (verb), *demeure* (noun), based on Latin *de-* 'away, completely' + *morari* 'delay.'

de•mur•rage /di'mərij/

▸ n. a charge payable to the owner of a chartered ship in the event of failure to load or discharge the ship within the time agreed.

ORIGIN mid 17th cent. (also in the general sense 'procrastination, delay'): from Old French *demourage*, from the verb *demourer* (see DEMUR).

de•mur•rer /di'mərər/

▸ n. an objection that a plaintiff's claim is irrelevant or invalid, while granting the factual basis of the point: *on demurrer it was held that the plaintiff's claim succeeded.*

ORIGIN early 16th cent.: from Anglo-Norman French (infinitive used as a noun), from Old French *demourer* 'remain, stay' (see DEMUR).

de•po•nent /di'pōnənt/

▸ n. a person who makes a deposition or affidavit under oath: *the attorney may instruct the deponent not to answer a question.*

ORIGIN late Middle English: from Latin *deponent-* 'laying aside, putting down' (in medieval Latin 'testifying'), from the verb *deponere*, from *de-* 'down' + *ponere* 'place.'

de•port /di'pôrt/

▸ v. [trans.] expel (a foreigner) from a country, typically on the grounds of illegal status or for having committed a crime: *he was deported for violation of immigration laws.*

■ exile (a native) to another country or territory.

DERIVATIVES **de•port•a•ble** adj.; **de•por•ta•tion** /ˌdēpôr'tāSHən/ n. *deportation proceedings.*

ORIGIN late 16th cent.: from French *déporter*, from Latin *deportare*, from *de-* 'away' + *portare* 'carry.'

de•pose /di'pōz/

▶ v. [trans.] **1** remove from office suddenly and forcefully: *he had been deposed by a military coup.*
2 testify to or give (evidence) on oath, typically in a written statement: *every affidavit shall state which of the facts* **deposed to** *are within the deponent's knowledge.*
3 question (a witness) in deposition: *we conclude that deposing the accused's mother-in-law would provide no conceivable benefit.*
ORIGIN Middle English: from Old French *deposer,* from Latin *deponere* (see DEPONENT), but influenced by Latin *depositus* and Old French *poser* 'to place.'

dep•o•si•tion /ˌdepə'zishən/

▶ n. the process of giving sworn testimony out of court, typically as part of discovery: *claimants and representatives have the same rights during deposition that they have during hearings.*
■ the record of such a process: *his deposition stated he intended to use the product for business purposes.*
ORIGIN late Middle English: from Latin *depositio(-n),* from the verb *deponere* 'lay aside.'

der•e•lict /'derə,likt/

▶ adj. in a very poor condition as a result of disuse and neglect: *derelict buildings.*
■ (of a person) shamefully negligent in not having done what one should have done: *he was* **derelict in** *his duty to conduct the review process.*
▶ n. a person without a home, job, or property: *streets lined with derelicts.*
■ a piece of property, esp. a ship, abandoned by the owner or crew: *the government determined her a derelict and a menace* | [as adj.] *a derelict orchard.*
ORIGIN mid 17th cent.: from Latin *derelictus* 'abandoned,' past participle of *derelinquere,* from *de-* 'completely' + *relinquere* 'forsake.'

der•e•lic•tion /ˌderə'likSHən/
> ▸ n. the state of having been abandoned and become di-lapidated: *the neighborhood already shows signs of dereliction.*

■ (usu. **dereliction of duty**) the willful failure to fulfill one's obligations: *their dereliction of duty in refusing to cooperate with him in lifting the easement.*

ORIGIN late 16th cent.: from Latin *derelictio(n-)*, from the verb *derelinquere* (see DERELICT).

de•re•strict /ˌdēri'strikt/
> ▸ v. [trans.] remove restrictions from: *the reports were put in final form and derestricted for public distribution later in the year.*

DERIVATIVES **de•re•stric•tion** /ˌdēri'strikSHən/ n.

der•mat•o•glyph•ics /ˌdərmətə'glifiks; dərˌmætə-/
> ▸ plural n. [treated as sing.] the study of skin markings or patterns on fingers, hands, and feet, and its application, esp. in criminology.

DERIVATIVES **der•mat•o•glyph** /dər'mætəˌglif/ n.; **der•mat•o•glyph•ic** adj.; **der•mat•o•glyph•i•cal•ly** adv.

ORIGIN 1920s: from DERMATO-'skin' + Greek *gluphikos* 'carved' (from *gluphē* 'carving').

de•scend•i•ble /di'sendəbəl/
> ▸ adj. (of property) able to be inherited by a descendant: *the property rights are freely transferable and descendible.*

de•scent /di'sent/
> ▸ n. the transmission of qualities, property (in the case of intestacy), or privileges by inheritance: *the legislature regulates the descent and distribution of property.*

ORIGIN Middle English: from Old French *descente*, from *descendre* 'to descend.'

de•tain /di'tān/
▶ v. [trans.] keep (someone) in official custody, typically for questioning about a crime or in politically sensitive situations: *she was detained without trial for two years.*
DERIVATIVES **de•tain•ment** n.
ORIGIN late Middle English (in the sense 'be afflicted with sickness or infirmity'): from Old French *detenir,* from a variant of Latin *detinere,* from *de-* 'away, aside' + *tenere* 'to hold.'

de•tain•er /di'tānər; dē-/
▶ n. **1** the action of detaining or withholding property: *detainer of the premises was part of the drug investigation.*
■ the detention of a person in custody: *a charge of unlawful detainer.* ■ an order authorizing the continued detention of a person in custody: *the federal prosecutor handling this case has lodged a detainer against Thorpe with the Florida authorities.*
2 a person who detains someone or something.
ORIGIN early 17th cent.: from Anglo-Norman French *detener* 'detain' (used as a noun), variant of Old French *detenir* (see DETAIN).

de•ten•tion /di'tensHən/
▶ n. the action of detaining someone or the state of being detained in official custody: *he committed suicide while in police detention.*
ORIGIN late Middle English (in the sense 'withholding of what is claimed or due'): from late Latin *detentio(n-),* from Latin *detinere* 'hold back' (see DETAIN).

de•ten•tion cen•ter /di'tensHən ˌsentər/
▶ n. an institution where people are held in detention, usually for short periods, in particular illegal immigrants, refugees, people awaiting trial or sentence, or young offenders.

de•ter•mi•na•ble /di'tərmənəbəl/

▸ **adj.** capable of being brought to an end under given conditions; terminable.

ORIGIN late Middle English: via Old French from late Latin *determinabilis* 'finite,' from the verb *determinare* (see DETERMINE).

de•ter•mi•na•tion /di,tərmə'nāsHən/

▸ **n. 1** the settlement of a dispute by the authoritative decision of a judge or arbitrator.

■ a judicial decision or sentence: *the secretary shall file in the court the record of the proceedings on which he based his determination as provided in this section.*

2 the cessation of an estate or interest.

ORIGIN late Middle English: via Old French from Latin *determinatio(n-)*, from the verb *determinare* (see DETER-MINE).

de•ter•mine /di'tərmin/

▸ **v.** [trans.] archaic bring or come to an end.

ORIGIN late Middle English: from Old French *determiner*, from Latin *determinare* 'limit, fix,' from *de-* 'completely' + *terminare* 'terminate.'

det•i•nue /'detn,(y)o͞o/

▸ **n.** a common-law claim or action to recover wrongfully detained goods or possessions.

ORIGIN late Middle English: from Old French *detenue*, past participle (used as a noun) of *detenir* 'detain.'

de•vise /di'vīz/

▸ **v.** [trans.] leave (property, especially real estate) to someone by the terms of a will: *the court determined that the decedent had not devised the property to the petitioner.*

▸ **n.** a clause in a will leaving property, especially real estate, to someone: *they are authorized to receive donations of money, lands, goods, chattels and the like, either by gift or devise.*

DERIVATIVES **de•vi•see** /di͵vīˈzē/ n.; **de•vi•sor** n.; **de• vis•er** n.

ORIGIN Middle English: the verb from Old French *deviser*, from Latin *divis-* 'divided,' from the verb *dividere* (this sense being reflected in the original English sense of the verb); the noun is a variant of *device* (in the early sense 'will, desire').

dev•o•lu•tion /͵devəˈloͻoSHən/

▶ n. the transfer or delegation of power to a lower level, esp. by central government to local or regional administration: *the devolution of housing programs from federal housing resources closer to communities.*

■ the transfer of property from one owner to another.
DERIVATIVES **dev•o•lu•tion•ar•y** /͵devəˈloͻoSHə͵nerē/ adj.; **dev•o•lu•tion•ist** /͵devəˈloͻoSHənist/ n.

ORIGIN late 15th cent. (in the sense 'transference by default'): from late Latin *devolutio(n-)*, from Latin *devolvere* 'roll down' (see DEVOLVE).

de•volve /diˈvälv/

▶ v. [trans.] transfer or delegate (power) to a lower level, esp. from central government to local or regional administration: *measures to **devolve** power to the provinces* | [as adj.] (**devolved**) *devolved and decentralized government.*

■ [intrans.] (**devolve on/upon/to**) (of duties or responsibility) pass to (a body or person at a lower level): *his duties devolved on a comrade.*
DERIVATIVES **de•volve•ment** n.

ORIGIN late Middle English (in the sense 'roll down'): from Latin *devolvere*, from *de-* 'down' + *volvere* 'to roll.'

dic•tum /ˈdiktəm/

▶ n. (pl. **dic•ta** /ˈdiktə/ or **dic•tums**) a formal pronouncement from an authoritative source: *the Politburo's dictum that the party will become a "left-wing parliamentary party."*

◼ short for OBITER DICTUM.
ORIGIN late 16th cent.: from Latin, literally 'something said,' neuter past participle of *dicere*.

di•es non /ˌdēäz 'nän/
▶ n. (pl. same) a day on which no court is in session or which does not count for legal or other purposes.
ORIGIN Latin, short for *dies non juridicus* 'nonjudicial day.'

di•gest
▶ n. /'dīˌjest/ a methodical summary of a body of laws, decided cases, legal rules, etc.
ORIGIN late Middle English: from Latin *digest-* 'distributed, dissolved, digested,' from the verb *digerere*, from *di-* 'apart' + *gerere* 'carry'; the noun from Latin *digesta* 'matters methodically arranged,' from *digestus* 'divided,' from *digerere*.

di•min•ished ca•pac•i•ty /di'minisHt kə'pæsitē/
▶ n. an unbalanced mental state that is considered to make a person unable to act with the intent necessary for a particular crime and is recognized as grounds to reduce the charge: *she had wished to convince the court that she suffered from diminished capacity at the time of the murder.*

di•rect ex•am•i•na•tion /də'rekt igˌzæmə'nāsHən/
▶ n. the questioning of a witness by the party that has called that witness to give evidence, in order to support the case that is being made: *on direct examination of Airman TJ, trial counsel sought to explain these circumstances.* Compare with CROSS-EXAMINE.

dis•a•bil•i•ty /ˌdisə'bilitē/
▶ n. (pl. **dis•a•bil•i•ties**) a disadvantage or handicap, esp. one imposed or recognized by the law.

■ welfare income provided because of this: *he had to quit his job and go* **on disability**.
■ an incapacity to perform all one's legal rights.

dis•af•firm /ˌdisə'fərm/
▸v. [trans.] repudiate; declare void: *to disaffirm a contract is to say it never existed.*
DERIVATIVES **dis•af•fir•ma•tion** /disˌæfər'māsʜən/ n.

dis•bar /dis'bär/
▸v. (**dis•barred, dis•bar•ring**) [trans.] (usu. **be disbarred**) expel (a lawyer) from the Bar, so that they no longer have the right to practice law: *he was unable to show cause why he should not be disbarred.*
DERIVATIVES **dis•bar•ment** n.

dis•charge
▸v. /dis'cʜärj/ [trans.] **1** (often **be discharged**) tell (someone) officially that they can or must leave, in particular:
■ release (someone) from the custody or restraint of the law: *he ordered that 1,671 prisoners of war be **discharged from** prison.* ■ relieve (a juror or jury) from serving in a case: *the district court discharged the jury over the objections of defense counsel.* ■ relieve (a bankrupt) of liability.
■ release (a party) from a contract or obligation: *the insurer is discharged from liability from the day of breach.*
2 pay off (a debt or other financial claim): *her membership was suspended until such time as she could discharge her debts.*
3 dated (of a judge or court) cancel (an order of a court). ■ cancel (a contract) because of completion or breach: *the existing mortgage will be discharged on completion.*
▸n. /'dis,cʜärj/ **1** an act of releasing someone from the custody or restraint of the law: *four days in jail and one year conditional discharge.*
■ the action of relieving a bankrupt from residual liability: *the debtor may be entitled to a discharge.*

2 the payment of a debt or other financial claim: *money paid in discharge of a claim.*

3 dated the action of canceling an order of a court.

DERIVATIVES **dis•charge•a•ble** /dis'CHärjəbəl/ **adj.; dis• charg•er** /dis'CHärjər/ **n.**

ORIGIN Middle English (in the sense 'relieve of (an obligation)'): from Old French *descharger*, from late Latin *discarricare* 'unload,' from *dis-* (expressing reversal) + *carricare* 'to load' (see CHARGE).

dis•claim /dis'klām/

▶**v.** [trans.] renounce a legal claim to (a property or title): *a statement disclaiming any interest in a specifically described aircraft may be recorded upon payment of a $5 recording fee.*

ORIGIN late Middle English (in legal contexts): from Anglo-Norman French *desclamer*, from *des-* (expressing reversal) + *clamer* 'to claim' (see CLAIM).

dis•claim•er /dis'klāmər/

▶**n.** a statement that denies something, esp. responsibility: *Amtrak's disclaimer of liability is printed on the ticket.* ◾ an act of repudiating another's claim or renouncing one's own: *the court concluded that her disclaimer constituted a taxable gift.*

ORIGIN late Middle English (as a legal term): from Anglo-Norman French *desclamer* (infinitive used as noun: see DISCLAIM).

dis•clo•sure /dis'klōzHər/

▶**n.** the action of making new or secret information known: *a judge ordered the disclosure of the government documents.*

ORIGIN late 16th cent.: from *disclose*, on the pattern of *closure*.

dis•cov•er•y /dis'kəvərē/

▶**n.** (pl. **dis•cov•er•ies**) the compulsory disclosure, by a party to a civil or criminal action, of relevant documents referred to by the other party: *material obtained by discovery or otherwise.*

■ the process by which parties to an action investigate facts prior to trial, including depositions, interrogatories, and examinations: *counsel should take advantage of the potential for discovery offered by a hearing.*

ORIGIN mid 16th cent.: from *discover*, on the pattern of the pair *recover, recovery.*

dis•en•fran•chise /ˌdisen'frænCHīz/ (also **dis•fran•chise** /dis'frænCHīz/)

▸v. [trans.] deprive (someone) of the right to vote: *the law disenfranchised some 3,000 voters on the basis of a residence qualification.*

■ deprive (someone) of a right or privilege: *the move would disenfranchise the disabled from using the transit system.* ■ archaic deprive (someone) of the rights and privileges of a free inhabitant of a borough, city, or country.

DERIVATIVES **dis•en•fran•chise•ment** n.

dis•miss /dis'mis/

▸v. [trans.] refuse further hearing to (a case): *the judge dismissed the case for lack of evidence.*

■ revoke an order of a court: *the writ of certiorari is dismissed as improvidently granted.*

DERIVATIVES **dis•miss•al** /dis'misəl/ n.; **dis•miss•i•ble** /dis'misəbəl/ adj.

ORIGIN late Middle English: from medieval Latin *dismiss-*, variant of Latin *dimiss-* 'sent away,' from the verb *dimittere.*

dis•or•der•ly /dis'ôrdərlē/

▸adj. involving or contributing to a breakdown of peaceful and law-abiding behavior: *they had no intention of staging a disorderly protest.*

DERIVATIVES **dis•or•der•li•ness** n.

dis•or•der•ly con•duct /dis'ôrdərlē 'kändəkt/
▸ **n.** unruly behavior constituting a minor offense: *McDonald was arrested and charged with assault in the fourth degree and convicted of disorderly conduct.*

dis•or•der•ly house /dis'ôrdərlē ˌhows/
▸ **n.** archaic a brothel.

dis•pose /dis'pōz/
▸ **v.** [intrans.] (**dispose of**) make a final resolution of: *there was no heritable property to be disposed of | most cases are disposed of by motion or settlement.*
ORIGIN late Middle English: from Old French *disposer*, from Latin *disponere* 'arrange,' influenced by *dispositus* 'arranged' and Old French *poser* 'to place.'

dis•po•si•tion /ˌdispə'zisHən/
▸ **n. 1** conclusive action on a matter by a court or other tribunal: *they'll stay the schedule for record preparation and briefing pending the court's disposition of the motion.*
2 the action of distributing or transferring property or money to someone, in particular by bequest: *this is a tax that affects the disposition of assets on death.*
ORIGIN late Middle English: via Old French from Latin *dispositio(n-)*, from *disponere* 'arrange' (see DISPOSE).

dis•pos•i•tive /dis'päziṯiv/
▸ **adj.** relating to or bringing about the settlement of an issue or the disposition especially of property: *such litigation will rarely be dispositive of any question.*
■ dealing with the disposition of property by deed or will: *the testator had to make his signature after making the dispositive provisions.* ■ dealing with the settling of international conflicts by an agreed disposition of disputed territories: *a peace settlement in the nature of a dispositive treaty.*
ORIGIN late Middle English (in the sense 'contributory,

conducive'): from Old French, or from medieval Latin *dispositivus*, from Latin *disposit-* 'arranged, disposed,' from the verb *disponere* (see DISPOSE).

dis•qual•i•fy /disˈkwäləˌfī/

▶v. (**dis•qual•i•fies, dis•qual•i•fied**) [trans.] (often **be disqualified**) pronounce (someone) ineligible for an office or activity because of an offense, infringement, or conflict of interest: *he was **disqualified from** driving for six months.*

dis•train /disˈtrān/

▶v. [trans.] seize (someone's property) to obtain payment of rent or other money owed: *legislation has restricted the right to distrain goods found on the premises.*
■ seize the property of (someone) for this purpose: *the government applied political pressure by distraining debtors.*
DERIVATIVES **dis•train•er** n.; **dis•train•ment** n.
ORIGIN Middle English: from Old French *destreindre*, from Latin *distringere* 'stretch apart,' from *dis-* 'apart' + *stringere* 'tighten.'

dis•traint /disˈtrānt/

▶n. the seizure of someone's property in order to obtain payment of money owed, esp. rent: *many faced heavy fines and the distraint of goods.*
ORIGIN mid 18th cent.: from DISTRAIN, on the pattern of *constraint.*

dis•tress /disˈtres/

▶n. 1 (esp. as **emotional distress**) extreme anxiety, sorrow, or pain: *damages for emotional distress have been permitted.*
2 another term for DISTRAINT.
ORIGIN Middle English: from Old French *destresce* (noun), *destrecier* (verb), based on Latin *distringere* 'stretch apart.'

dis•trict at•tor•ney /'distrikt ə'tərnē/ (abbr.: **DA**)
 ▸ n. a public official who acts as prosecutor for the state or the federal government in court in a particular district.

dis•trict court /'distrikt 'kôrt/
 ▸ n. a state or federal trial court.

dis•tur•bance /dis'tərbəns/
 ▸ n. the interruption of a settled and peaceful condition, specifically:
 ■ a breakdown of peaceful and law-abiding behavior; a riot: *the disturbances were precipitated when four men were refused bail.* ■ interference with rights or property: *the field party shall assure the landowner that every effort will be made to minimize disturbance or disruption to the property.*
 ORIGIN Middle English: from Old French *destourbance,* from *destourber,* from *dis-* 'utterly' + *turbare* 'disturb' (from *turba* 'tumult').

di•vorce /di'vôrs/
 ▸ n. the legal dissolution of a marriage by a court or other competent body: *her **divorce from** her first husband | one in three marriages ends in divorce | [as adj.] divorce proceedings.*
 ■ a legal decree dissolving a marriage: *the wife obtained a divorce in a Mexican court.*
 ▸ v. [trans.] legally dissolve one's marriage with (someone): *he divorced his first wife after 10 months | [as adj.]* (**divorced**) *a divorced couple | [intrans.] they divorced eight years later.*
 DERIVATIVES **di•vorce•ment** n.
 ORIGIN late Middle English: the noun from Old French *divorce,* from Latin *divortium,* based on *divertere,* from *di-* 'aside' + *vertere* 'to turn'; the verb from Old French *divorcer,* from late Latin *divortiare,* from *divortium.*

dock /däk/

▶ n. (usu. **the dock**) the enclosure in a criminal court where a defendant is placed.

PHRASES **in the dock** (of a defendant) on trial in court.

ORIGIN late 16th cent.: probably originally slang and related to Flemish *dok* 'chicken coop, rabbit hutch,' of unknown origin.

dock•et /'däkit/

▶ n. a calendar or list of cases for trial or people having cases pending: *orders and opinions appear here for only sixty days after the date of entry on the court's docket.*
◾ an abridged account of legal proceedings.

▶ v. (**dock•et•ed, dock•et•ing**) [trans.] (usu. **be docketed**) enter (a case or suit) onto a list of those due to be heard: *the case will go to the Supreme Court, and may be docketed for the fall term.*

ORIGIN late 15th cent. The word originally denoted a short summary or abstract; hence, in the early 18th cent., 'a document giving particulars of a consignment.'

doc•trine /'däktrin/

▶ n. a rule or standard of law; the body of such rule: *the doctrine of the separation of powers.*

DERIVATIVES **doc•tri•nal** /'däktrənl/ adj.; **doc•tri•nal•ly** adv.

ORIGIN late Middle English: from Old French, from Latin *doctrina* 'teaching, learning,' from *doctor* 'teacher,' from *docere* 'teach.'

dom•i•cile /'dämə͵sīl; 'dō-; 'däməsəl/ (also **dom•i•cil** /'däməsəl/)

▶ n. the state or country that a person treats as their permanent home, or lives in and has a substantial connection with: *his wife has a **domicile of origin** in Germany.*
◾ a person's residence or home: *he is a financially independent student who has had a domicile in the state of Wash-*

ington for the period of one year. ■ the place at which a corporation or other body is registered, esp. for tax purposes.

▸v. [with adverbial of place] (**be domiciled**) formal or treat a specified country as a permanent home: *the tenant is domiciled in the United States.*

■ reside; be based: *he was domiciled in a frame house on the outskirts of town.*

ORIGIN late Middle English: via Old French from Latin *domicilium* 'dwelling,' from *domus* 'home.'

do•nee /dōˈnē/
▸n. a person who receives a gift: *the third party was a donee of the 20 shares.*
■ a person who is given a power of appointment.
ORIGIN early 16th cent.: from *donor* + *-ee.*

dou•ble jeop•ard•y /ˈdəbəl ˈjepərdē/
▸n. the prosecution of a person twice for the same offense.

dow•er /ˈdow(-ə)r/
▸n. historical a widow's share for life of her husband's estate: *W expressly waived all right to alimony, dower, and future interest in R's property.*
■ archaic a dowry.
▸v. [trans.] archaic give a dowry to.
ORIGIN late Middle English: from Old French *douaire,* from medieval Latin *dotarium,* from Latin *dotare* 'endow,' from *dos, dot-* 'dowry'; related to *dare* 'give.'

drunk driv•ing /ˈdrəngk ˈdrīviNG/ (also **drunk•en driv•ing** /ˈdrəngkən ˈdrīviNG/)
▸n. the crime of driving a vehicle with an excess of alcohol in the blood.
DERIVATIVES **drunk driv•er** n.

due dil•i•gence /'d(y)oo 'diləjəns/
▶ **n.** reasonable steps taken by a person in order to satisfy a legal requirement, esp. in performing a professional duty: *any person can file a petition challenging the due diligence of an applicant for patent.*

due proc•ess /'d(y)oo 'präses/ (also **due proc•ess of law**)
▶ **n.** fair treatment through the normal judicial system, esp. as a citizen's entitlement. Due process is guaranteed by the Fifth and Fourteenth Amendments to the US Constitution: *plaintiff claims that defendants violated his due process rights when he was discharged from his employment.*

DUI
▶ **abbr.** driving under the influence (of drugs or alcohol): *the charge was originally filed as a DUI* | [as adj.] *a DUI program.*

du•plic•i•tous /d(y)oo'plisitəs/
▶ **adj.** (of a charge or plea) containing more than one allegation: *the risk behind a duplicitous charge is that a jury may convict the defendant without unanimous agreement on a particular offense.*

du•ress /d(y)oo'res/
▶ **n.** constraint illegally exercised to force someone to perform an act: *the question is whether the defendant acted in self-defense or was **under duress**.*
▪ archaic forcible restraint or imprisonment.
ORIGIN Middle English (in the sense 'harshness, severity, cruel treatment'): via Old French from Latin *duritia,* from *durus* 'hard.'

dwell•ing house /'dweliNG ,hows/
▶ **n.** a house used as a residence and not for business pur-

poses: *distilled spirits plants shall not be located in any dwelling house.*

DWI

▸ **abbr.** driving while intoxicated: *Holden has vowed that drivers charged with DWI will face stiffer penalties.*

E

ear•nest /'ərnist/
▸ n. [in sing.] earnest money
ORIGIN Middle English *ernes*, literally 'installment paid to confirm a contract,' based on Old French *erres*, from Latin *arra*, shortened form of *arrabo* 'a pledge.' The spelling was influenced by words ending in -*ness*; the final -*t* is probably by association with the adjective *earnest*.

ear•nest mon•ey /'ərnist 'mənē/
▸ n. money paid to confirm a contract: *there are discrepancies in the amount of earnest money on deposit.*

ease•ment /'ēzmənt/
▸ n. a right to cross or otherwise use someone else's land for a specified purpose: *an agricultural conservation easement.*
ORIGIN late Middle English: from Old French *aisement*, from *aisier*, from the phrase *a aise* 'at ease.'

e•ject /i'jekt/
▸ v. [trans.] (often **be ejected**) dispossess (a tenant or occupant) by legal process: *after interrogating the organizers, casino security guards again ejected them from the property.*
DERIVATIVES **e•jec•tion** /i'jekSHən/ n.
ORIGIN late Middle English: from Latin *eject-* 'thrown out,' from the verb *eicere*, from *e-* (variant of *ex-*) 'out' + *jacere* 'to throw.'

e•ject•ment /i'jektmənt/
▸ n. the action or process of evicting a tenant from property: *the landlord shall serve a **writ in ejectment**.*

■ the action or process in which a person evicted from property seeks to recover possession and damages.

e•man•ci•pate /i'mænsə,pāt/
▶ v. [trans.] set free, esp. from legal, social, or political restrictions: *it was the first effort of an infant community to assert its individuality and emancipate itself from the tutelage of Oregon.*
■ set (a child) free from the authority of its parents: *attaining the age of majority does not automatically emancipate the child.* ■ free from slavery: *it is estimated that he emancipated 8,000 slaves.*
DERIVATIVES **e•man•ci•pa•tion** /i,mænsə'pāsHən/ n.; **e•man•ci•pa•tor** /i'mæmsə,pāt̲ər/ n.; **e•man•ci•pa•to•ry** /i'mænsəpə,tôrē/ **adj.**
ORIGIN early 17th cent.: from Latin *emancipat-* 'transferred as property,' from the verb *emancipare*, from *e-* (variant of *ex-*) 'out' + *mancipium* 'slave.'

em•bez•zle /em'bezəl/
▶ v. [trans.] steal or misappropriate (money or property placed in one's trust or belonging to the organization for which one works): *she had embezzled $5,600,000 in company funds.* Compare with DEFALCATE.
DERIVATIVES **em•bez•zle•ment** n.; **em•bez•zler** /em'bezlər/ n.
ORIGIN late Middle English (in the sense 'steal'): from Anglo-Norman French *embesiler*, from *besiler* in the same sense (compare with Old French *besillier* 'maltreat, ravage'), of unknown ultimate origin. The current sense dates from the late 16th cent.

em•i•nent do•main /'emənənt dō'mān/
▶ n. the right of a government or its agent to expropriate private property for public use, with payment of compensation.

em•pan•el /im'pænl/
▸v. variant spelling of IMPANEL.

en•a•bling act /en'ābliNG 'ækt/
▸n. a statute empowering a person or body to take certain action, esp. to make regulations, rules, or orders: *a statehood enabling act.*

en•act•ment /en'æktmənt/
▸n. the process of passing legislation: *within 90 days after the enactment of the bill, the FCC is directed to adopt waiver procedures.*
■ a law that is passed.
DERIVATIVES **en•ac•tive** /en'æktiv/ **adj.**

en•cum•brance /en'kəmbrəns/
▸n. a burden or impediment: *plaintiff's easement by way of necessity does not constitute an encumbrance.*
■ a mortgage or other charge on property or assets: *a motor vehicle or trailer may be subject to a lien or encumbrance.* ■ archaic a person, esp. a child, who is dependent on someone else for support.
ORIGIN Middle English (denoting an encumbered state; formerly also as *incumbrance*): from Old French *encombrance*, from *encombrer* 'block up.'

en•dorse /en'dôrs/ (also dated **in•dorse** /in'dôrs/)
▸v. [trans.] sign (a check or bill of exchange) on the back to make it payable to someone other than the stated payee or to accept responsibility for paying it: *the claimant endorsed this check over to the City.*
■ (usu. **be endorsed on**) write (a comment) on the front or back of a document: *the court shall endorse on the reverse side of the license that the person was ordered not to drive.*
DERIVATIVES **en•dors•a•ble adj.; en•dors•er n.**

ORIGIN late 15th cent. (in the sense 'write on the back of'; formerly also as *indorse*): from medieval Latin *indorsare*, from Latin *in-* 'in, on' + *dorsum* 'back.'

en•dorse•ment /en'dôrsmənt/ (also dated **in•dorse•ment** /in'dôrsmənt/)

▸ n. 1 a clause in an insurance policy detailing an exemption from or change in coverage: *carriers often include endorsements that waive exclusions and offer coverages additional to those included in a standard policy.*
2 the action of endorsing a check or bill of exchange.

en•force /en'fôrs/

▸ v. [trans.] compel observance of or compliance with (a law, rule, or obligation): *evidence indicates that the ordinance is rarely enforced.*
DERIVATIVES **en•force•a•bil•i•ty** /en,fôrsə'bilitē/ n.; **en•force•a•ble** /en'fôrsəbəl/ adj.; **en•forc•ed•ly** /en'fôrsidlē/ adv.; **en•force•ment** n.; **en•forc•er** n.
ORIGIN Middle English (in the senses 'strive' and 'impel by force'; formerly also as *inforce*): from Old French *enforcir, enforcier,* based on Latin *in-* 'in' + *fortis* 'strong.'

en•gross /en'grōs/

▸ v. [trans.] produce (a legal document) in its final or definitive form: *the judge may direct the appellant to engross the statement or transcript, or both, as settled.*
DERIVATIVES **en•gross•ment** n.
ORIGIN late Middle English (formerly also as *ingross*): based on *en-, in-* 'in' + late Latin *grossus* 'large.'

en•join /en'join/

▸ v. [trans.] (**enjoin someone from**) prohibit someone from performing (a particular action) by issuing an injunction: *Judge Sessions has enjoined USDA from implementing milk market order reform.*
DERIVATIVES **en•join•er** n.; **en•join•ment** n.

ORIGIN Middle English (formerly also as *injoin*): from Old French *enjoindre*, from Latin *injungere* 'join, attach, impose,' from *in-* 'in, toward' + *jungere* 'to join.'

en•ter /'entər/
▸ v. submit (a statement) in an official capacity, usually in a court of law: *an attorney entered a plea of guilty on her behalf.*
▸**enter into** undertake to bind oneself by (an agreement or other commitment): *the council entered into an agreement with a private firm.*
enter on/upon (as a legal entitlement) go freely into property as or as if the owner: *you are not allowed to enter upon railroad property.*
ORIGIN Middle English: from Old French *entrer*, from Latin *intrare*, from *intra* 'within.'

en•try /'entrē/
▸ n. (pl. **-ies**) the action of taking up the legal right to property.
ORIGIN Middle English: from Old French *entree*, based on Latin *intrata*, feminine past participle of *intrare* (see ENTER).

e•qual /'ēkwəl/
▸ adj. (of people) having the same status, rights, or opportunities.
■ uniform in application or effect; without discrimination on any grounds: *a dedicated campaigner for equal rights.*
ORIGIN late Middle English: from Latin *aequalis*, from *aequus* 'even, level, equal.'

eq•ui•ta•ble /'ekwitəbəl/
▸ adj. valid in equity as distinct from law: *the beneficiaries have an equitable interest in the property.*
DERIVATIVES **eq•ui•ta•bil•i•ty** /ˌekwitəˈbilitē/ n.; **eq•ui•ta•ble•ness** n.; **eq•ui•ta•bly** /'ekwitəblē/ adv.

ORIGIN mid 16th cent.: from French *équitable*, from *équité* (see EQUITY).

eq•ui•ty /'ekwitē/
▸ n. (pl. **eq•ui•ties**) 1 a branch of law that developed alongside common law in order to remedy some of its defects in fairness and justice, formerly, and still in some jurisdictions, administered in special courts.
2 the value of a mortgaged property after deduction of charges against it: *negative equity arises from plummeting house prices.*
ORIGIN Middle English: from Old French *equité*, from Latin *aequitas*, from *aequus* 'equal.'

eq•ui•ty of re•demp•tion /'ekwitē əv ri'dempSHən/
▸ n. the right of a mortgagor over the mortgaged property, esp. the right to redeem the property on payment of the principal, interest, and costs.

er•ror /'erər/
▸ n. a mistake of fact or of law in a court's opinion, judgment or order: *the District Court's procedural errors.*
ORIGIN Middle English: via Old French from Latin *error*, from *errare* 'to stray, err.'

es•cape clause /i'skāp ˌklôz/
▸ n. a clause in a contract that specifies the conditions under which one party can be freed from an obligation: *OMSF left itself many escape clauses that could have important effects on the scientific program.*

es•cheat /es'CHēt/
▸ n. the reversion of property to the state, or (in feudal law) to a lord, on the owner's dying without legal heirs: *if it appears that there may be an escheat, notice of hearing and a copy of the petition must be sent to the Attorney General.*

■ an item of property affected by this.

▸v. [intrans.] (of land) revert to a lord or the state by escheat: *probate of estates in which property escheated to Indian tribes.*

■ [trans.] [usu. as adj.] (**escheated**) hand over (land) as an escheat.

ORIGIN Middle English: from Old French *eschete*, based on Latin *excidere* 'fall away,' from *ex-* 'out of, from' + *cadere* 'to fall.'

es•crow /ˈeskrō/

▸n. a bond, other document, or payment kept in the custody of a third party, taking effect only when a specified condition has been fulfilled: *a mechanism for the escrow of digital signature keys is desirable.*

■ [usu. as adj.] a deposit or fund held in trust or as a security: *an escrow account.* ■ the state of being kept in custody or trust in this way: *the board holds funds in escrow.*

▸v. [trans.] place in custody or trust in this way: *the cooperative has received and escrowed the amount of $75,016.22.*

ORIGIN late 16th cent.: from Old French *escroe* 'scrap, scroll,' from medieval Latin *scroda*, of Germanic origin; related to *shred*.

es•quire /ˈeskwīr; iˈskwīr/

▸n. (**Es•quire**) (abbr.: **Esq.**) a title appended to a lawyer's surname.

ORIGIN late Middle English: from Old French *esquier*, from Latin *scutarius* 'shield-bearer,' from *scutum* 'shield.'

es•tate /iˈstāt/

▸n. the interest that a person possesses in land or other property.

◼ all the money and property owned by a particular person, esp. at death: *in his will, he divided his estate between his wife and daughter.*
ORIGIN Middle English (in the sense 'state or condition'): from Old French *estat*, from Latin *status* 'state, condition,' from *stare* 'to stand.'

es•tate tax /i'stāt ˌtæks/
▸ n. a tax levied on the net value of the estate of a deceased person before distribution to the heirs. Also called DEATH TAX.

es•top /e'stäp/
▸ v. (**es•topped, es•top•ping**) [trans.] (usu. **be estopped from**) bar or preclude by estoppel: *estopping the government from enforcing the laws disserves the public interest.*
ORIGIN late Middle English (in the sense 'stop up, dam, plug'): from Old French *estopper* 'stop up, impede,' from late Latin *stuppare*, from Latin *stuppa* 'tow, oakum.'

es•top•pel /e'stäpəl/
▸ n. the principle that precludes a person from asserting something contrary to what is implied by a previous action or statement of that person or by a previous pertinent judicial determination: *estoppel could not be invoked to prevent recoupment of an overpayment to a medical provider under Part A of Medicare.*
ORIGIN mid 16th cent.: from Old French *estouppail* 'bung,' from *estopper* (see ESTOP).

Eu•ro•pe•an Com•mis•sion for Hu•man Rights /ˌyŏŏrə'pēən kə'misHən fər '(h)yŏŏmən 'rīts/ an institution of the Council of Europe, set up to examine complaints of alleged breaches of the European Convention on Human Rights (an international agreement set up by the Council of Europe in 1950 to protect human rights). It is based in Strasbourg, France.

Eu•ro•pe•an Court of Jus•tice /ˌyo͝orə'pēən 'kôrt əv 'jəstis/ an institution of the European Union, with thirteen judges appointed by its member governments, meeting in Luxembourg. Established in 1958, it exists to safeguard the law in the interpretation and application of Community treaties.

eu•tha•na•sia /ˌyo͞oTHə'nāZHə/
▸ n. the painless killing of a patient suffering from an incurable and painful disease or in an irreversible coma. The practice is illegal in most countries.
ORIGIN early 17th cent. (in the sense 'easy death'): from Greek, from *eu* 'well' + *thanatos* 'death.'

e•vade /i'vād/
▸ v. escape or avoid, in particular:
◼ avoid giving a direct answer to (a question): *he denied evading the question.* ◼ avoid dealing with or accepting; contrive not to do (something morally or legally required): *these are difficulties to be faced and not evaded.* ◼ escape paying (tax or duty), esp. by illegitimate presentation of one's finances: *he allegedly evaded payment of property taxes.* ◼ defeat the intention of (a law or rule), esp. while complying with its letter.
DERIVATIVES **e•vad•a•ble** adj.; **e•vad•er** n.
ORIGIN late 15th cent.: from French *évader*, from Latin *evadere*, from *e-* (variant of *ex-*) 'out of' + *vadere* 'go.'

e•ven date /'ēvən 'dāt/
▸ phrase (**of even date**) of the same date: *please refer to our attached report of even date.*

e•vict /i'vikt/
▸ v. [trans.] expel (someone, usually a tenant) from a property, esp. with the support of the law: *he had court orders to **evict** the trespassers **from** three camps.*

DERIVATIVES **e•vic•tion** /i'vikSHən/ n.; **e•vic•tor** /i'vik-tər/ n.
ORIGIN late Middle English (in the sense 'recover property, or the title to property, by legal process'): from Latin *evict-* 'overcome, defeated,' from the verb *evincere*, from *e-* (variant of *ex-*) 'out' + *vincere* 'conquer.'

ev•i•dence /'evədəns/
▸ n. information given personally, drawn from a document, or in the form of material objects, tending or used to establish facts in a legal investigation or as testimony in a court of law: *without evidence, they can't bring a charge.*
PHRASES **give evidence** give information formally and in person in a law court or at an inquiry. **turn state's** (or Brit. **King's** or **Queen's**) **evidence** (of a criminal) give information in court against one's partners in order to receive a less severe punishment oneself.
ORIGIN Middle English: via Old French from Latin *evidentia*, from *evident-* 'obvious to the eye or mind.'

ev•i•den•tial /ˌevi'denCHəl/
▸ adj. another term for EVIDENTIARY.
DERIVATIVES **ev•i•den•ti•al•i•ty** /ˌevi,denCHē'ælitē/ n.; **ev•i•den•tial•ly** adv.
ORIGIN early 17th cent.: from medieval Latin *evidentialis*, from Latin *evidentia* (see EVIDENCE).

ev•i•den•tia•ry /ˌevi'denCHərē/
▸ adj. of or providing evidence: *the evidentiary value of the record.*

ex•am•i•na•tion /ig,zæmə'nāSHən/
▸ n. the formal questioning of a witness in court: *attorneys may move about the courtroom as they like during examination of witnesses.*

ORIGIN late Middle English (also in the sense 'testing (one's conscience) by a standard'): via Old French from Latin *examinatio(n-)*, from *examinare* 'weigh, test' (see EXAMINE).

ex•am•ine /igˈzæmin/
▸ v. [trans.] formally question (a defendant or witness) in court. Compare with CROSS-EXAMINE.
DERIVATIVES **ex•am•in•a•ble** adj.; **ex•am•i•nee** /igˌzæməˈnē/ n.; **ex•am•in•er** n.
ORIGIN Middle English: from Old French *examiner*, from Latin *examinare* 'weigh, test,' from *examen*.

ex•clude /ikˈsklo͞od/
▸ v. [trans.] prevent the occurrence of; preclude: *clauses seeking to exclude liability for loss or damage.*
ORIGIN late Middle English: from Latin *excludere*, from *ex-* 'out' + *claudere* 'to shut.'

ex•clu•sion /ikˈsklo͞ozHən/
▸ n. the process or state of excluding or being excluded: *drug users are subject to exclusion from the military.*
◾ an item or risk specifically not covered by an insurance policy or other contract: *exclusions can be added to your policy.*
DERIVATIVES **ex•clu•sion•ar•y** /ikˈsklo͞ozHəˌnerē/ adj.
ORIGIN late Middle English: from Latin *exclusio(n-)*, from *excludere* 'shut out.'

ex•cul•pate /ˈekskəlˌpāt/
▸ v. [trans.] show or declare that (someone) is not guilty of wrongdoing: *he used this evidence to exculpate him-self.*
DERIVATIVES **ex•cul•pa•tion** /ˌekskəlˈpāsHən/ n.; **ex•cul•pa•to•ry** /iksˈkəlpəˌtôrē/ adj.
ORIGIN mid 17th cent.: from medieval Latin *exculpat-* 'freed from blame,' from the verb *exculpare*, from *ex-* 'out, from' + Latin *culpa* 'blame.'

ex•e•cute /ˈeksiˌkyo͞ot/
▸ v. [trans.] **1** carry out or put into effect (a plan, order, or course of action), in particular:
■ make (a legal instrument) valid by signing or sealing it: *the documents were executed before a notary public.*
■ carry out (a judicial sentence, the terms of a will, or other order): *police executed a search warrant.*
2 (often **be executed**) carry out a sentence of death on (a legally condemned person): *he was convicted of treason and executed.*
ORIGIN late Middle English: from Old French *executer*, from medieval Latin *executare*, from Latin *exsequi* 'follow up, carry out, punish,' from *ex-* 'out' + *sequi* 'follow.'

ex•e•cu•tion /ˌeksiˈkyo͞oSHən/
▸ n. **1** the carrying out or putting into effect of a plan, order, or course of action, in particular:
■ the putting into effect of a legal instrument or order.
■ seizure of the property or person of a debtor in default of payment.
2 short for WRIT OF EXECUTION.
3 the carrying out of a sentence of death on a condemned person: *the place of execution* | *executions of convicted murderers.*

ex•e•cu•tion•er /ˌeksiˈkyo͞oSH(ə)nər/
▸ n. an official who carries out a sentence of death on a legally condemned person.

ex•ec•u•tive ses•sion /igˈzekyətiv ˈseSHən/
▸ n. a private meeting of a legislative body: *the Committee met today in executive session.*

ex•ec•u•tor
▸ n. /igˈzekyətər/ a person or institution appointed by a testator to carry out the terms of their will: *the brother she appointed as executor predeceased her.*

DERIVATIVES **ex•ec•u•to•ri•al** /ig,zekyə'tôrēəl/ adj. (rare); **ex•ec•u•tor•ship** /ig'zikyətər,SHip/ n.; **ex•ec•u•to•ry** /ig'zekyə,tôrē/ adj.
ORIGIN Middle English: via Anglo-Norman French from Latin *execut-* 'carried out,' from *exsequi* (see EXECUTE).

ex•em•pla•ry /ig'zemplərē/

▸ **adj.** (of a punishment) serving as a warning or deterrent: *exemplary sentencing may discourage the ultraviolent minority.*
▪ (of damages) exceeding the amount needed for simple compensation, and intending to mark disapproval of the defendant's conduct; punitive. See also PUNITIVE DAMAGES.
DERIVATIVES **ex•em•pla•ri•ly** /ig'zemplərəlē/ adv.; **ex•em•pla•ri•ness** n.; **ex•em•plar•i•ty** /,egzem'plærit̯ē; -'pler-/ n.
ORIGIN late 16th cent.: from late Latin *exemplaris,* from Latin *exemplum* 'sample, imitation.'

ex•hib•it /ig'zibit/

▸ **n.** a document or other object produced in a court as evidence.
ORIGIN late Middle English (in the sense 'submit for consideration,' also specifically 'present a document as evidence in court'): from Latin *exhibit-* 'held out,' from the verb *exhibere,* from *ex-* 'out' + *habere* 'hold.'

ex par•te /eks 'pärtē/

▸ **adj. & adv.** with respect to or in the interests of one side only, without notice to the other party: *the petitions included are for the ex parte order as well as the 150-day order.*
▪ one-sided; partial.
PHRASES **ex parte contact** contact with a judge made

by only one party to a proceeding: *a telephone call to the judge would be a prohibited ex-parte contact.*
ORIGIN late 17th cent.: Latin, literally 'from a side.'

ex•pert wit•ness /'ekspərt 'witnis/
▸ n. a person who is permitted to testify at a trial because of their special knowledge or proficiency in a particular field that is relevant to the case: *Bachman was hired as an expert witness because she had assisted in more than 100 similar surgical procedures.*

ex post fac•to /ˌeks ˌpōst 'fæktō/
▸ adj. & adv. with retroactive effect or force: [as adj.] *ex post facto laws.*
ORIGIN erroneous division of Latin *ex postfacto* 'in the light of subsequent events.'

ex•pro•pri•ate /eks'prōprēˌāt/
▸ v. [trans.] (esp. of the state) take away (property) from its owner: *they were protesting government plans to expropriate farmland.*
■ dispossess (someone) of property: *the land reform expropriated the Irish landlords.*
DERIVATIVES **ex•pro•pri•a•tion** /eksˌprōprē'āsHən/ n.; **ex•pro•pri•a•tor** /eks'prōprēˌātər/ n.
ORIGIN late 16th cent.: from medieval Latin *expropriat-* 'taken from the owner,' from the verb *expropriare*, from *ex-* 'out, from' + *proprium* 'property,' neuter singular of *proprius* 'own.'

ex•tin•guish /ik'stiNGgwisH/
▸ v. [trans.] render (a right or obligation) void: *rights of common pasture were extinguished.*
■ (often **be extinguished**) cancel (a debt) by full payment: *the debt was absolutely extinguished.*
DERIVATIVES **ex•tin•guish•a•ble** adj.; **ex•tin•guish•ment** n.

ORIGIN mid 16th cent.: from Latin *exstinguere*, from *ex-* 'out' + *stinguere* 'quench.'

ex·tra·dit·a·ble /'ekstrə,dīṯəbəl/
▸ adj. (of a crime) making a criminal liable to extradition: *possession of explosives will be an extraditable offense.*
■ (of a criminal) liable to extradition.

ex·tra·dite /'ekstrə,dīt/
▸ v. [trans.] hand over (a person accused or convicted of a crime) to the jurisdiction of another state or country: *Greece refused to **extradite** him to Italy.*
ORIGIN mid 19th cent.: back-formation from EXTRADITION.

ex·tra·di·tion /,ekstrə'disHən/
▸ n. the action of extraditing a person accused or convicted of a crime: *they fought to prevent his extradition to the US | extraditions of drug suspects.*
ORIGIN mid 19th cent.: from French, from *ex-* 'out, from' + *tradition* 'delivery.'

ex·tra·ju·di·cial /,ekstrəjoo'dishəl/
▸ adj. (of a sentence) not legally authorized: *there have been reports of extrajudicial executions.*
■ (of a settlement, statement, or confession) not made in court; out-of-court: *lawyers involved must abstain from making any extrajudicial statement about the case.*
DERIVATIVES **ex·tra·ju·di·cial·ly** adv.

ex·tra·le·gal /,ekstrə'lēgəl/
▸ adj. (of an action or situation) beyond the authority of the law; not regulated by the law: *the president has extensive legal and estralegal powers.*

ex·tra·ter·ri·to·ri·al /,ekstrə,terə'tôrēəl/
▸ adj. (of a law or decree) valid outside a country's territory.

■ denoting the freedom of an ambassador or other embassy staff from the jurisdiction of the territory of residence: *foreign embassies have extraterritorial rights.* ■ situated outside a country's territory: *extraterritorial industrial zones.*

DERIVATIVES **ex•tra•ter•ri•to•ri•al•i•ty** /ˌekstrəˌterə ˌtôrēˈælit̪ē/ **n.**

ORIGIN mid 19th cent.: from Latin *extra territorium* 'outside the territory' + *-al*.

eye•wit•ness /ˈīˈwitnəs/
▸n. [often as adj.] a person who has personally seen something happen and so can give a firsthand description of it: *eyewitness accounts* of the robbery.

F

fact /fækt/

▶ n. the truth about events as opposed to interpretation: *there was a question of fact as to whether they had received the letter.*

PHRASES **before** (or **after**) **the fact** before (or after) the committing of a crime: *an accessory before the fact.*

ORIGIN late 15th cent.: from Latin *factum*, neuter past participle of *facere* 'do.' The original sense was 'an act or feat,' later 'bad deed, a crime,' surviving in the phrase *before (or after) the fact.* The earliest of the current senses ('truth, reality') dates from the late 16th cent.

fair use /'fer 'yo͞os/

▶ n. the doctrine that, under certain conditions, copyright material may be quoted verbatim without need for permission from or payment to the copyright holder: *the court is trying to address whether parody can constitute fair use.*

fault /fôlt/

▶ n. responsibility for an accident or misfortune: *it was his fault she had died.*

■ responsibility for an act or omission, usually intentional and leading to liability. Compare with NEGLIGENCE.

PHRASES **at fault** responsible for an undesirable situation or event; in the wrong, sometimes legally liable: *we recover compensation from the person at fault.*

ORIGIN Middle English *faut(e)* 'lack, failing,' from Old French, based on Latin *fallere* 'deceive.' The *-l-* was added (in French and English) in the 15th cent. to conform with the Latin word, but did not become standard in English until the 17th cent., remaining silent in pronunciation until well into the 18th.

fee /fē/

▸ **n. 1** a payment made to a professional person or to a professional or public body in exchange for advice or services: *all land transfers require the payment of a recording fee.*

2 an inheritable estate of land, either absolute (see FEE SIMPLE) or conditional.

■ historical an estate held on condition of feudal service.

▸**v.** (**fees, fee'd** or **feed, fee•ing**) [trans.] rare make a payment to (someone) in return for services.

PHRASES **hold something in fee** hold an estate in land, especially absolutely.■ historical hold an estate in return for feudal service to a superior.

ORIGIN Middle English: from an Anglo-Norman French variant of Old French *feu, fief,* from medieval Latin *feodum, feudum,* ultimately of Germanic origin.

fee sim•ple /'fē 'simpəl/

▸ **n.** (pl. **fees sim•ple**) a permanent and absolute tenure of an estate in land with freedom to dispose of it at will, esp. (in full **fee simple absolute**) a freehold tenure, which is the main type of land ownership.

fee tail /'fē 'tāl/

▸ **n.** (pl. **fees tail**) historical a former type of tenure of an estate in land with restrictions or entailment regarding the line of heirs to whom it may be willed.

ORIGIN late Middle English: from Anglo-Norman French *fee tailé.*

fel•on /'felən/

▸ **n.** a person who has been convicted of a felony: *fugitive felons.*

▸**adj.** [attrib.] archaic cruel; wicked: *the felon undermining hand of dark corruption.*

ORIGIN Middle English: from Old French, literally

'wicked, a wicked person' (oblique case of *fel* 'evil'), from medieval Latin *fello*, *fellon-*, of unknown origin.

fe•lo•ni•ous /fəˈlōnēəs/
▸ **adj.** of, relating to, or involved in a felony or felonies: *they turned their felonious talents to the smuggling trade.*
■ relating to or of the nature of felony: *his conduct was felonious.*
DERIVATIVES **fe•lo•ni•ous•ly adv.**

fel•o•ny /ˈfelənē/
▸ **n.** (pl. **fel•o•nies**) a crime, often one involving violence, regarded as more serious than a misdemeanor, and usually punishable by imprisonment for more than one year or by death: *he pleaded guilty to six felonies | an accusation of felony.*

The distinction between felonies and misdemeanors usually depends on the penalties or consequences attaching to the crime, felonies typically involving prison sentences of at least one year. In English common law, felony originally comprised those offenses (murder, wounding, arson, rape, and robbery) for which the penalty included forfeiture of land and goods.

ORIGIN Middle English: from Old French *felonie*, from *felon* (see FELON).

feme cov•ert /ˈfem ˈkəvərt; ˈfēm/
▸ **n.** historical a married woman.
ORIGIN early 16th cent.: from Anglo-Norman French, literally 'a woman covered (i.e., protected by marriage).'

feme sole /ˈfem ˈsōl; ˈfēm/
▸ **n.** historical a woman without a husband, esp. one who is divorced.
ORIGIN early 16th cent.: from Anglo-Norman French *feme soule* 'a woman alone.'

fi•du•ci•ar•y /fəˈdo͞oSHē,erē; -SHərē/
▸ **adj.** involving trust, esp. with regard to the relationship between a trustee and a beneficiary: *the company has a fiduciary duty to shareholders.*
▪ archaic held or given in trust: *fiduciary estates.*
▸**n.** (pl. **fi•du•ci•ar•ies**) a trustee.
ORIGIN late 16th cent. (in the sense 'something inspiring trust; credentials'): from Latin *fiduciarius*, from *fiducia* 'trust,' from *fidere* 'to trust.'

fi•e•ri fa•ci•as /ˌfīərē ˈfāsH(ē)əs/
▸ **n.** a writ commanding a sheriff to seize and sell a debtor's goods in executing a judgment.
ORIGIN late Middle English: Latin, 'you shall make happen.'

Fifth /fi(f)TH/
▸**n.** (**the Fifth**) the Fifth Amendment to the US Constitution, used in particular reference to the amendment's provision that no person "shall be compelled in any criminal case to be a witness against himself."
PHRASES **take** (or **plead**) **the Fifth** exercise the right guaranteed by the Fifth Amendment of refusing to answer questions in order to avoid incriminating oneself.

fight•ing words /ˈfītiNG ˈwərdz/
▸ **plural n.** informal words, such as those expressing an insult, esp. of an ethnic, racial, or sexist nature, which are considered likely to provoke a violent response: *Mr. Posson allegedly shouted fighting words at the others in the group.*

file /fīl/
▸ **v.** [trans.] submit (a legal document, application, or charge) to be placed on record by the appropriate authority: *criminal charges were **filed against** the firm* | [intrans.] *the company had **filed for** bankruptcy.*

ORIGIN late Middle English (as a verb meaning 'string documents on a thread or wire to keep them in order'): from French *filer* 'to string,' *fil* 'a thread,' both from Latin *filum* 'a thread.'

find /fīnd/

▶ v. (past and past part. **found** /fownd/) [trans.] (often **be found**) (of a court) officially declare to be the case: *he was found guilty of speeding* | [with clause] *the court found that a police lab expert had fabricated evidence.*
PHRASES **find in favor of** see **find for** below.
▶**find against** (of a court) make a decision against or judge to be guilty: *the panel found against the United States on three of the five principal claims.*
find for (or **find in favor of**) (of a court) make a decision in favor of or judge to be innocent: *a jury found for the plaintiff.*
ORIGIN Old English *findan*, of Germanic origin; related to Dutch *vinden* and German *finden*.

fine /fīn/

▶ n. a sum of money exacted as a penalty by a court of law or other authority: *a parking fine.*
▶ v. [trans.] (often **be fined**) punish (someone) by making them pay a sum of money, typically as a penalty for breaking the law: *he was fined $600 and sentenced to one day in jail.*
DERIVATIVES **fine•a•ble** /'fīnəbəl/ **adj.**
ORIGIN Middle English: from Old French *fin* 'end, payment,' from Latin *finis* 'end' (in medieval Latin denoting a sum paid on settling a lawsuit). The original sense was 'conclusion'; also used in the medieval Latin sense, the word came to denote a penalty of any kind, later specifically a monetary penalty.

fine print /'fīn 'print/

▶ n. inconspicuous details or conditions printed in an

agreement or contract, esp. ones that may prove unfavorable: *read the fine print of whatever loan document is shoved under your nose.*

first-de•gree /'fərst də'grē/
▸ **adj.** [attrib.] denoting the most serious category of a crime, esp. murder.

first of•fend•er /'fərst ə'fendər/
▸ **n.** a person who is convicted of a criminal offense for the first time: *a first offender prostitution program.*

fix•tures /'fiksCHərz/
▸ **plural n.** articles attached to a house or land and considered legally part of it so that they normally remain in place when an owner moves: *the hotel retains many original fixtures.*
ORIGIN late 16th cent. (in the sense 'fixing, becoming fixed'): alteration (first found in Shakespeare) of obsolete *fixure* (from late Latin *fixura*, from Latin *figere* 'to fix'), with *t* inserted on the pattern of *mixture*.

force ma•jeure /ˌfôrs mä'ZHər/
▸ **n.** unforeseeable circumstances that prevent someone from fulfilling a contract: *the company may suspend bargaining agreements if required by force majeure or economic conditions.*
PHRASES **force majeure clause** a contract provision excusing performance in the event of unforeseeable circumstances.
ORIGIN late 19th cent.: French, literally 'superior strength.'

fore•close /fôr'klōz/
▸ **v.** [intrans.] take possession of a mortgaged property as a result of someone's failure to keep up their mortgage payments: *the bank was threatening to **foreclose** on his mortgage.*

■ [trans.] take away someone's power of redeeming (a mortgage) and take possession of the mortgaged property.

ORIGIN Middle English: from Old French *forclos*, past participle of *forclore*, from *for-* 'out' (from Latin *foras* 'outside') + *clore* 'to close.' The original sense was 'bar from escaping,' in late Middle English 'shut out,' and 'bar from doing something', hence specifically 'bar someone from redeeming a mortgage' (early 18th cent.).

fore•clo•sure /fôr'klōzHər/
▶ n. the process of taking possession of a mortgaged property as a result of someone's failure to keep up mortgage payments.

fore•man /'fôrmən/
▶ n. (pl. **fore•men**) (in a court of law) a person, esp. a man, who presides over a jury and speaks on its behalf.

fo•ren•sic /fə'renzik; -sik/
▶ adj. of, relating to, or denoting the application of scientific methods and techniques to the investigation of crime: *forensic evidence*.
■ of or relating to courts of law.
▶ n. (**forensics**) scientific tests or techniques used in connection with the detection of crime.
■ (also **forensic**) [treated as sing. or pl.] informal a laboratory or department responsible for such tests.
DERIVATIVES **fo•ren•si•cal•ly** /fə'renziklē; -sik-/ **adv.**
ORIGIN mid 17th cent.: from Latin *forensis* 'in open court, public,' from *forum* (see FORUM).

fo•ren•sic med•i•cine /fə'renzik 'medisən; fə'rensik/
▶ n. the application of medical knowledge to the investigation of crime, particularly in establishing the causes of injury or death.

fore•per•son /'fôr‚pərsən/
▸ n. (in a court of law) a person who presides over a jury and speaks on its behalf (used as a neutral alternative to FOREMAN).

fore•feit /'fôrfit/
▸ v. (**for•feit•ed, for•feit•ing**) [trans.] lose or be deprived of (property or a right or privilege) as a penalty for wrongdoing: *those unable to meet their taxes were liable to forfeit their property.*
◼ (of a court or other authority) cause or order (property, a right, etc,) to be lost or surrendered.
▸n. a fine or penalty for wrongdoing or for a breach of the rules in a club or game.
◼ an item of property or a right or privilege lost as a legal penalty.
▸adj. [predic.] lost or surrendered as a penalty for wrongdoing or neglect: *the lands which he had acquired were automatically forfeit.*
DERIVATIVES **for•feit•a•ble adj.; for•feit•er** /'fôrfitər/ n.; **for•fei•ture** /'fôrfəCHər/ n.
ORIGIN Middle English (originally denoting a crime or transgression, hence a fine or penalty for this): from Old French *forfet, forfait,* past participle of *forfaire* 'transgress,' from *for-* 'out' (from Latin *foris* 'outside') + *faire* 'do' (from Latin *facere*).

forge /fôrj/
▸ v. [trans.] produce a copy or imitation of (a document, signature, banknote, or work or art) for the purpose of deception: *Walton admitted that he had forged the initials on the painting.*
DERIVATIVES **forge•a•ble adj.; forg•er** n.
ORIGIN Middle English (also in the general sense 'make, construct'): from Old French *forger,* from Latin *fabricare* 'fabricate,' from *fabrica* 'manufactured object,

workshop.' The noun is via Old French from Latin *fabrica*.

for•ger•y /'fôrjərē/
▸ n. (pl. **for•ger•ies**) the action of forging or producing a copy of a document, signature, banknote, or work of art.
■ a forged or copied document, signature, banknote, or work of art.

fo•rum /'fôrəm/
▸ n. (pl. **fo•rums**) a court or tribunal.
ORIGIN from Latin, literally 'what is out of doors,' originally denoting an enclosure surrounding a house; related to *fores* '(outside) door.'

fran•chise /'fræn‚CHīz/
▸ n. **1** an authorization granted by a government or company to an individual or group enabling them to carry out specified commercial activities, e.g., providing a broadcasting service or acting as an agent for a company's products: *the use of franchises to sell foreign goods and supplies has been growing rapidly.*
■ a business or service given such authorization to operate.
2 (usu. **the franchise**) the right to vote.
■ the rights of citizenship.
▸ v. [trans.] grant a franchise to (an individual or group): *the state franchises the various power companies to operate in different areas.*
■ grant a franchise for the sale of (goods) or the operation of (a service): *all the catering was **franchised out**.*
DERIVATIVES **fran•chi•see** /‚frænCHī'zē/ n.; **fran•chis•er** (also **fran•chi•sor** /‚frænCHə'zôr/) **n.**
ORIGIN Middle English (denoting a grant of legal immunity): from Old French, based on *franc, franche* 'free.' Sense 2 dates from the late 18th cent. and sense 1 from the 20th cent.

fraud /frôd/

▸ **n.** wrongful or criminal deception intended to result in unjust advantage, especially financial or personal gain: *he was convicted of fraud | prosecutions for social security frauds.*

■ a person or thing intended to deceive others, typically by unjustifiably claiming or being credited with accomplishments or qualities: *mediums exposed as tricksters and frauds.*

ORIGIN Middle English: from Old French *fraude*, from Latin *fraus, fraud-* 'deceit, injury.'

fraud•u•lent /ˈfrôjələnt/

▸ **adj.** obtained, done by, or involving deception, esp. criminal deception: *the fraudulent copying of American software.*

■ unjustifiably claiming or being credited with particular accomplishments or qualities: *he unmasked fraudulent psychics.*

DERIVATIVES **fraud•u•lence** n.; **fraud•u•lent•ly** adv.

ORIGIN late Middle English: from Old French, or from Latin *fraudulentus*, from *fraus, fraud-* 'deceit, injury.'

free•hold /ˈfrēˌhōld/

▸ **n.** permanent and absolute tenure of land or property with freedom to dispose of it at will. Often contrasted with LEASEHOLD.

■ **(the freehold)** the ownership of a piece of land or property by such tenure. ■ a piece of land or property held by such tenure.

▸**adj.** held by or having the status of freehold: *a freehold interest in a property.*

DERIVATIVES **free•hold•er** n.

friend of the court /ˈfrend əv T͟Hə ˈkôrt/

▸ **n.** See AMICUS.

fun•gi•ble /ˈfənjəbəl/
> ▸ **adj.** (of goods contracted for without an individual specimen being specified) able to replace or be replaced by another identical item; mutually interchangeable: *money is fungible—money that is raised for one purpose can easily be used for another.*
> DERIVATIVES **fun•gi•bil•i•ty** /ˌfənjəˈbilətē/ n.
> ORIGIN late 17th cent.: from medieval Latin *fungibilis*, from *fungi* 'perform, enjoy,' with the same sense as *fungi vice* 'serve in place of.'

G

gar•nish /'gärnisн/
> ▸ v. [trans.] serve notice of garnishment.
> ■ seize (money, esp. part of a person's salary) to settle a debt or claim: *the IRS garnished his earnings.*
> ORIGIN Middle English (in the sense 'equip, arm'): from Old French *garnir*, probably of Germanic origin and related to *warn.*

gar•nish•ee /ˌgärni'sнē/
> ▸ n. a third party who is served notice by a court to surrender money in settlement of a debt or claim: [as adj.] *a garnishee order.*
> ▸ v. (**gar•nish•ees, gar•nish•eed**) another term for GAR-NISH.

gar•nish•ment /'gärnisнmənt/
> ▸ n. a court order directing that money or property of a third party (usually wages paid by an employer), be seized to satisfy a debt owed by a debtor to a plaintiff creditor.

GBH
> ▸ abbr. grievous bodily harm.

gen•er•al jur•is•dic•tion /'jen(ə)rəl ˌjo͞oris'diksнən/
> ▸ n. the authority of a court to hear civil or criminal cases within its geographic area: *Alabama's trial courts of general jurisdiction are the circuit courts.*
> ■ the authority of a court to hear a defendant's claims within the geographic area in which the defendant resides, when there is no connection between this area and the claims.

goods and chat•tels /'go͞odz ən(d) 'cнætlz/
> ▸ plural n. all kinds of personal possessions.

grace /grās/

▶ n. (also **grace period**) a period officially allowed for payment of a sum due or for compliance with a law or condition, esp. an extended period granted as a special favor: *another three days' grace.*

ORIGIN Middle English: via Old French from Latin *gratia*, from *gratus* 'pleasing, thankful'; related to *grateful*.

grand /grænd/

▶ adj. (of a crime) involving money or items with a value over a statutorily defined amount; serious: *grand theft.* Compare with PETTY.

ORIGIN Middle English: from Old French *grant, grand*, from Latin *grandis* 'full-grown, big, great.' The original uses were to denote family relationships and as a title (*the Grand*, translating Old French *le Grand*); hence the senses 'of the highest rank,' 'of great importance.'

grand·fa·ther clause /ˈgræn(d),fäTHər ,klôz/

▶ n. informal a clause exempting certain classes of people or things from the requirements of a piece of legislation affecting their previous rights, privileges, or practices.

ORIGIN early 20th cent.: so called because under constitutional clauses in some southern states, permitting whites to vote and disenfranchising blacks, the descendants of those voting before 1867 were permitted to vote without having to meet certain stringent conditions.

grand ju·ry /ˈgrænd ˈjo͝orē/

▶ n. a jury, typically of twenty-three jurors, selected to examine whether the evidence supporting a criminal accusation is sufficient for an indictment and trial by (petty) jury: *the grand jury returned a 21-count indictment.*

grand lar·ce·ny /ˈgrænd ˈlärsənē/

▶ n. (in many US states and formerly in Britain) theft of

personal property having a value above a legally specified amount.

grant /grænt/

▸ v. [trans., with two objs.] give (a right, power, property,
etc.) formally or legally to: *the amendment that granted
women the right to vote.*

▸ n. a legal conveyance or formal conferment: *a grant of
land* | *a grant of probate.*

DERIVATIVES **grant•a•ble** adj.; **grant•er** n.

ORIGIN Middle English: from Old French *granter* 'consent to support,' variant of *creanter* 'to guarantee,' based
on Latin *credere* 'entrust.'

gran•tee /græn'tē/

▸ n. a person or institution to whom a grant or conveyance is made.

gran•tor /græn'tôr; 'græntər/

▸ n. a person or institution that makes a grant or conveyance.

gra•va•men /grə'vāmən/

▸ n. (pl. **gra•va•mi•na** /grə'væmənə/) the essence or most
serious part of a complaint or accusation: *the gravamen
of a conspiracy charge is the agreement to commit an illegal
act.*

■ a grievance.

ORIGIN early 17th cent. (as an ecclesiastical term denoting formal presentation of a grievance): from late
Latin, literally 'physical inconvenience,' from Latin
gravare 'to load,' from *gravis* 'heavy.'

griev•ous bod•i•ly harm /'grēvəs 'bädəlē 'härm/ (abbr.:
GBH)

▸ n. serious physical injury inflicted on a person by the
deliberate action of another.

guar•an•tee /ˌgerənˈtē/
▶ n. a formal promise or assurance (typically in writing) that certain conditions will be fulfilled, esp. that a product will be repaired or replaced if not of a specified quality and durability: *we offer a 10-year **guarantee against** rusting.*
■ variant spelling of GUARANTY. ■ less common term for GUARANTOR.
▶ v. (**guar•an•tees, guar•an•teed, guar•an•tee•ing**) [intrans.] provide a formal assurance or promise, esp. that certain conditions shall be fulfilled relating to a product, service, or transaction.
■ [trans.] provide such an assurance regarding (something, esp. a product): *the repairs will be guaranteed for three years* | [as adj.] (**guaranteed**) *the guaranteed bonus is not very high.* ■ [trans.] provide financial security for; underwrite: *a demand that $100,000 be deposited to guarantee their costs.*
ORIGIN late 17th cent. (in the sense 'guarantor'): perhaps from Spanish *garante*, corresponding to French *garant* (see WARRANT), later influenced by French *garantie* 'guaranty.'
USAGE: **Guarantee** and **guaranty** are interchangeable for both noun and verb, although the latter is now rare as a verb. **Warranty** is widely used in their place.

guar•an•tor /ˌgerənˈtôr; ˈgerəntər/
▶ n. a person or organization that provides a guaranty.

guar•an•ty /ˈgerənˌtē/ (also **guar•an•tee**)
▶ n. (pl. **guar•an•ties**) a formal pledge to pay another person's debt or to perform another person's obligation in the case of default.
■ a thing serving as security for a such a pledge.
ORIGIN early 16th cent.: from Old French *garantie*, from *garantir*; related to WARRANT.

guard•i•an /'gärdēən/
▸ n. a person who looks after and is legally responsible for someone who is unable to manage their own affairs, esp. an incompetent or disabled person or a child whose parents have died.
DERIVATIVES **guard•i•an•ship** /'gärdē,ən,sHip/ n.
ORIGIN late Middle English: from Old French *garden*, of Germanic origin; compare with WARD. The ending was altered by association with *-ian*.

guilt•y /'giltē/
▸ adj. (**guilt•i•er, guilt•i•est**) culpable of or responsible for a specified wrongdoing: *the police will soon discover who the guilty party is* | *he was found **guilty of** manslaughter* | *he found them **guilty on** a lesser charge.* See also FIND, PLEAD.
DERIVATIVES **guilt•i•ness** n.

H

ha•be•as cor•pus /ˈhābēəs ˈkôrpəs/
▸ **n.** a writ requiring a person under custody to be brought before a judge or into court, esp. to secure the person's release unless lawful grounds are shown for their detention.
■ the legal right to apply for such a writ.
ORIGIN late Middle English: Latin, literally 'you shall have the body (in court).'

ha•ben•dum /həˈbendəm/
▸ **n.** the part of a deed or conveyance that states the estate or quantity of interest to be granted: [as adj.] *a habendum clause.*
ORIGIN early 17th cent.: Latin, literally '(that is) to be had'.

half•way house /ˈhæf,wā ˌhows/
▸ **n.** a center for helping former drug addicts, prisoners, psychiatric patients, or others to adjust to life in general society.

head•note /ˈhed,nōt/
▸ **n.** a summary of a decided case prefixed to the case report, setting out the principles behind the decision and an outline of the facts.

hear /hir/
▸ **v.** (past and past part. **heard** /hərd/) [trans.] listen to and judge (a case, appeal, etc.): *an all-woman jury heard the case.*
ORIGIN Old English *hīeran, hēran,* of Germanic origin; related to Dutch *hooren* and German *hören.*

hear•ing /'hiriNG/
> ▸ n. an act of listening to evidence or arguments in a court of law or before an official, esp. a trial before a judge without a jury.

hear•say /'hir,sā/
> ▸ n. the report of another person's words by a witness, usually disallowed as evidence in a court of law: *everything they had told him would have been ruled out as hearsay* | [as adj.] *hearsay evidence.*

heir /er/
> ▸ n. a person legally entitled to the property or rank of another on that person's death: *his eldest son and heir* | *she aspired to marry the heir to the throne.*
> DERIVATIVES **heir•dom** /'erdəm/ n.; **heir•less** adj.; **heir•ship** /'er,SHip/ n.
> ORIGIN Middle English: via Old French from Latin *heres.*

heir•ess /'eris/
> ▸ n. a female heir, esp. to vast wealth: *the heiress to the Postum Cereal Company.*

her•e•dit•a•ment /,herə'ditəmənt/
> ▸ n. dated any item of inheritable property, either a **corporeal hereditament** (such as land or a building) or an **incorporeal hereditament** (such as a rent or a right of way).
> ■ an item of inheritance.
> ORIGIN late Middle English: from medieval Latin *hereditamentum,* from ecclesiastical Latin *hereditare* 'inherit,' from Latin *heres, hered-* 'heir.'

here•in•af•ter /,hirin'æftər/
> ▸ adv. formal further on in this document: *the Cincinnati Gas & Electric Company (hereinafter CG&E).*

here•in•be•fore /ˌhirinbəˈfôr/
▸ adv. formal before this point in this document: *defendant denies each and every allegation of the petition not hereinbefore specifically admitted.*

her•it•a•ble /ˈheritəbəl/
▸ adj. (of property) capable of being inherited.
DERIVATIVES **her•it•a•bil•i•ty** /ˌheritəˈbilitē/ n.; **her•it•a•bly** /ˈheritəblē/ adv.
ORIGIN late Middle English: from Old French *heriter* 'inherit,' from ecclesiastical Latin *hereditare*, from Latin *heres*, *hered*- 'heir.'

high court /ˈhī ˈkôrt/
▸ n. the court of final appeal in a state or national judicial system.
■ the US Supreme Court. ■ (in the US) the supreme court in a state. ■ a higher court, such as an appeals court in relation to a trial court. ■ (in full **High Court of Justice**) (in England and Wales) the court of unlimited civil jurisdiction forming part of the Supreme Court and comprising three divisions: Queen's Bench, Chancery, and the Family Division.

high•er court /ˈhīər ˈkôrt/
▸ n. a court that can overrule the decision of another.

high seas /ˈhī ˈsēz/
▸ plural n. (**the high seas**) the open ocean, esp. that not within any country's territorial jurisdiction but governed by maritime law: *they commited the crime of piracy on the high seas*.

hold /hōld/
▸ v. (past and past part. **held** /held/) 1 [trans.] keep or detain (someone): *the police were holding him on a murder charge | she was held prisoner for two days.*

2 [trans.] have in one's possession: *the managing director still holds fifty shares in the company.*

■ [intrans.] informal be in possession of illegal drugs: *he was holding, and the police hauled him off to jail.* ■ [with clause] (of a judge or court) rule; decide: *the Court of Appeals held that there was no evidence to support the judge's assessment.*

PHRASES **hold someone/something harmless** indemnify.

ORIGIN Old English *haldan, healdan,* of Germanic origin; related to Dutch *houden* and German *halten*; the noun is partly from Old Norse *hald* 'hold, support, custody.'

home•stead /'hōm,sted/
▸ n. **1** a person's or family's residence, which comprises the land, house, and outbuildings, and in most states is exempt from forced sale for collection of debt.
2 historical (as provided by the federal Homestead Act of 1862) an area of public land in the West (usually 160 acres) granted to any US citizen willing to settle on and farm the land for at least five years.
DERIVATIVES **home•stead•er** n.
ORIGIN Old English *hāmstede* 'a settlement.'

hom•i•cide /'hämə,sīd; 'hōmə-/
▸ n. the killing of one person by another: *he was charged with homicide* | *two thirds of homicides in the county were drug-related.* Compare with MANSLAUGHTER, MURDER.
■ (**Hom•i•cide**) the police department that deals with such crimes: *a detective from Homicide.* ■ dated a murderer.
ORIGIN Middle English: from Old French, from Latin *homicidium,* from *homo, homin-* 'man.'

hon•or /'änər/ (Brit. **honour**)
▸ n. (**His, Your,** etc., **Honor**) a title of respect given to or used in addressing a judge or a mayor.

ORIGIN Middle English: from Old French *onor* (noun), *onorer* (verb), from Latin *honor*.

horn•book /ˈhôrnˌbo͝ok/
▸ n. historical a one-volume treatise summarizing the law in a specific field: [as adj.] *the hornbook explanation of the rule of reason is that it calls for balancing of pro- and anticompetitive effects.*

hos•tile wit•ness /ˈhästl ˌwitnis; ˈhästīl/
▸ n. a witness who is antagonistic to the party calling them, and who may, if the judge permits, be cross-examined by that party.

house•break•ing /ˈhowsˌbrākiNG/
▸ n. the action of breaking into a building, esp. in daytime, to commit a felony.
DERIVATIVES **house•break•er** /ˈhowsˌbrākər/ n.

hy•poth•e•cate /həˈpäTHiˌkāt; hī-/
▸ v. [trans.] pledge (money) by law to a specific purpose: *No beneficiary shall have any right to alienate, encumber, or hypothecate his or her interest in the principal.*
■ pledge (property) as security without handing over possession; mortgage: *you need the landlord's permission to hypothecate the property to guarantee a loan.*
DERIVATIVES **hy•poth•e•ca•tion** /həˌpäTHiˈkāSHən; hī-/ n.
ORIGIN early 17th cent.: from medieval Latin *hypothecat-* 'given as a pledge,' from the verb *hypothecare*, based on Greek *hypothēkē*.

I

il•le•gal /i(l)'lēgəl/
▸**adj.** contrary to or forbidden by law, esp. criminal law: *illegal drugs.*
▸**n.** an illegal immigrant: *five of the illegals carried base clearance cards.*
DERIVATIVES **il•le•gal•i•ty** /ˌi(l)li'gælitē/ n. (pl. **il•le•gal•i•ties**); **il•le•gal•ly** adv.
ORIGIN early 17th cent.: from French *illégal* or medieval Latin *illegalis*, from Latin *in-* 'not' + *legalis* 'according to the law.'

il•le•git•i•mate
▸**adj.** /ˌi(l)lə'jitəmit/ not authorized by the law; not in accordance with accepted standards or rules: *an illegitimate exercise of power by the military.*
■ (of a child) born of parents not lawfully married to each other.
▸**n.** a person who is illegitimate by birth.
DERIVATIVES **il•le•git•i•ma•cy** /ˌi(l)lə'jitəməsē/ n.; **il•le•git•i•mate•ly** adv.
ORIGIN mid 16th cent.: from late Latin *illegitimus* (from *in-* 'not' + *legitimus* 'lawful'), suggested by LEGITIMATE.

im•mi•gra•tion /ˌimə'grāsHən/
▸**n.** the action of coming to live permanently in a country of which one is not a native or citizen: *a barrier to control illegal immigration from Mexico.*
■ the place at an airport or country's border where government officials check the documents of people entering that country.

im•mov•a•ble /i(m)'mo͞ovəbəl/
▸**adj.** (of property) consisting of land, buildings, or other permanent items.

▸n. (**immovables**) immovable property: *most of the local notary's business dealt with sales of immovables in the surrounding parishes.*

im•pan•el /im'pænl/ (also **em•pan•el**)

▸ v. (**im•pan•eled, im•pan•el•ing**; Brit. **im•pan•elled, im•pan•el•ling**) [trans.] enlist or enroll (a jury): *the General Duty Judge is empowered to impanel one or more grand juries as the public interest requires.*

■ enroll (someone) on to a jury: *several of her friends have been impaneled.*

DERIVATIVES **im•pan•el•ment** n.

ORIGIN late Middle English (originally as *empanel*): from Anglo-Norman French *empaneller*, from *em-* 'in' + Old French *panel* 'panel.'

im•peach /im'pēCH/

▸ v. [trans.] call into question the integrity or validity of (a judgment, etc.): *any deposition may be used for the purpose of impeaching the testimony of the deponent as a witness.*

■ charge (the holder of a public office) with misconduct: *the governor served only one year before being impeached and convicted for fiscal fraud.* ■ cast doubt on the credibility of (a witness).

DERIVATIVES **im•peach•a•ble** adj.; **im•peach•ment** n.

ORIGIN late Middle English (also in the sense 'hinder, prevent'; earlier as *empeche*): from Old French *empecher* 'impede,' from late Latin *impedicare* 'catch, entangle' (based on *pedica* 'a fetter,' from *pes, ped-* 'foot').

im•ped•i•ment /im'pedəmənt/

▸ n. an obstruction to a legal right or power: *our current Building Code's complexity is often an impediment to new construction and drives up the cost of building.*

DERIVATIVES **im•ped•i•men•tal** /im,pedə'mentl/ adj.

ORIGIN late Middle English: from Latin *impedimentum*, from *impedire*.

im•pound /im'pownd/
▸ v. [trans.] seize and take legal custody of (something, esp. a vehicle, goods, or documents) because of an infringement of a law or regulation: *vehicles parked where they cause an obstruction will be impounded.*
DERIVATIVES **im•pound•a•ble** adj.; **im•pound•er** n.; **im•pound•ment** n.

in•ad•mis•si•ble /ˌinəd'misəbəl/
▸ adj. not able to be introduced in evidence (because prejudicial, irrelevant, etc.): *her written expression of sympathy for the victim was ruled inadmissible as evidence of liability.*
DERIVATIVES **in•ad•mis•si•bil•i•ty** /ˌinəd,misə'bilitē/ n.; **in•ad•mis•si•bly** /ˌinəd'misəblē/ adv.

in•al•ien•a•ble /in'ālēənəbəl/
▸ adj. unable to be given away or transferred by the possessor: *the giant sequoias were granted to the State of California as an inalienable public trust.*
DERIVATIVES **in•al•ien•a•bil•i•ty** /in,ālēənə'bilitē/ n.; **in•al•ien•a•bly** /in'ālēənəblē/ adv.

in cam•er•a /in 'kæm(ə)rə/
▸ phrase in private, in particular taking place in the private chambers of a judge, with the press and public excluded: *judges assess the merits of such claims in camera.*
ORIGIN late Latin, 'in the chamber.'

in•ca•pac•i•tate /ˌinkə'pæsi,tāt/
▸ v. [trans.] deprive (someone) of their legal capacity.
DERIVATIVES **in•ca•pac•i•tant** /ˌinkə'pæsitnt/ n.; **in•ca•pac•i•ta•tion** /ˌinkə,pæsi'tāsHən/ n.

in•ca•pac•i•ty /ˌinkəˈpæsitē/

> ▸ n. (pl. **in•ca•pac•i•ties**) legal disqualification: *they are not subject to any legal incapacity.*

ORIGIN early 17th cent.: from French *incapacité* or late Latin *incapacitas*, from *in-* (expressing negation) + *capacitas* (see CAPACITY).

in•cest /ˈinˌsest/

> ▸ n. sexual relations between people classed as being too closely related to marry each other.

> ■ the crime of having sexual intercourse with a parent, child, sibling, or grandchild.

ORIGIN Middle English: from Latin *incestus, incestum* 'unchastity, incest,' from *in-* 'not' + *castus* 'chaste.'

in•ces•tu•ous /inˈsesCHo͞oəs/

> ▸ adj. involving or guilty of incest: *the child of an incestuous relationship.*

DERIVATIVES **in•ces•tu•ous•ly** adv.; **in•ces•tu•ous•ness** n.

ORIGIN early 16th cent.: from late Latin *incestuosus*, from Latin *incestus* (see INCEST).

in•cho•ate

> ▸ /inˈkō-it; -āt/ adj. (of an offense, such as incitement or conspiracy) anticipating a further criminal act: *the danger of inchoate crimes lies in the possibility that they will be carried to fruition.*

DERIVATIVES **in•cho•ate•ly** adv.; **in•cho•ate•ness** n.

ORIGIN mid 16th cent.: from Latin *inchoatus*, past participle of *inchoare*, variant of *incohare* 'begin.'

in•ci•dent /ˈinsidənt/

> ▸ adj. attaching to: *the costs properly incident to a suit for foreclosure or redemption.*

ORIGIN late Middle English: via Old French from Latin

incident- 'falling upon, happening to,' from the verb *incidere,* from *in-* 'upon' + *cadere* 'to fall.'

in•com•pe•tent /in'kämpətənt; iNG-/
▶**adj.** not qualified to act in a particular capacity: *the patient is deemed legally incompetent.*
▶**n.** an incompetent person.
DERIVATIVES **in•com•pe•tence** n.; **in•com•pe•ten•cy** n.; **in•com•pe•tent•ly** adv.
ORIGIN late 16th cent. (in the sense 'not legally competent'): from French, or from late Latin *incompetent-,* from *in-* 'not' + Latin *competent-* 'being fit or proper' (see COMPETENT).

in•cor•po•rate
▶**v.** /in'kôrpə,rāt/ [trans.] (often **be incorporated**) constitute (a company, city, or other organization) as a legal corporation: *the Trust is incorporated as a national banking association.*
▶**adj.** /in'kôrp(ə)rit/ archaic another term for INCORPORATED.
DERIVATIVES **in•cor•po•ra•tion** /in,kôrpə'rāSHən/ n.; **in•cor•po•ra•tor** /in'kôrpə,rātər/ n.
ORIGIN late Middle English: from late Latin *incorporat-* 'embodied,' from the verb *incorporare,* from *in-* 'into' + Latin *corporare* 'form into a body' (from *corpus, corpor-* 'body').

in•cor•po•re•al /,inkôr'pôrēəl/
▶**adj.** (often of a property interest) having no material existence: *there is no reason for the government to favor an incorporeal entity over a human developer.*
DERIVATIVES **in•cor•po•re•al•i•ty** /,inkôr,pôrē'ælitē/ n.; **in•cor•po•re•al•ly** adv.; **in•cor•po•re•i•ty** /in,kôrpə'rēitē/ n.
ORIGIN late Middle English: from Latin *incorporeus,* from *in-* 'not' + *corporeus* (from *corpus, corpor-* 'body') + *-al.*

in•crim•i•nate /inˈkriməˌnāt/
▸ v. [trans.] make (someone) appear guilty of a crime or wrongdoing; strongly imply the guilt of (someone): *he refused to answer questions in order not to incriminate himself* | [as adj.] (**incriminating**) *incriminating evidence.*
DERIVATIVES **in•crim•i•na•tion** /inˌkriməˈnāsHən/ n.; **in•crim•i•na•to•ry** /inˈkrimənəˌtôrē/ adj.
ORIGIN mid 18th cent.: from late Latin *incriminat-* 'accused,' from the verb *incriminare,* from *in-* 'into, toward' + Latin *crimen* 'crime.'

in•de•cen•cy /inˈdēsənsē/
▸ n. (pl. **in•de•cen•cies**) indecent behavior: *a law governing indecency on cable television.*
■ an indecent act, gesture, or expression.

in•de•cent as•sault /inˈdēsənt əˈsôlt/
▸ n. see SEXUAL ASSAULT.

in•de•cent ex•po•sure /inˈdēsənt ikˈspōzHər/
▸ n. the crime of intentionally showing one's sexual organs in public.
■ the act of outraging public decency by being naked in a public place.

in•de•fea•si•ble /ˌindəˈfēzəbəl/
▸ adj. Philosophy not able to be lost, annulled, or overturned: *an indefeasible right.*
DERIVATIVES **in•de•fea•si•bil•i•ty** /ˌindəˌfēzəˈbilitē/ n.; **in•de•fea•si•bly** /ˌindəˈfēzəblē/ adv.

in•dem•ni•fy /inˈdemnəˌfī/
▸ v. (**in•dem•ni•fies, in•dem•ni•fied**) [trans.] compensate (someone) for harm or loss: *the insurance was inadequate to indemnify the owner.*
■ secure (someone) against such harm or loss: *are you sure that these arrangements will indemnify us?* ■ secure

(someone) against legal responsibility for their actions: *the newspaper could not be forced to **indemnify** the city for personal-injury liability that might result from accidents involving newsstands.*

DERIVATIVES **in•dem•ni•fi•ca•tion** /in,demnəfiˈkā- SHən/ n.; **in•dem•ni•fi•er** n.

ORIGIN early 17th cent.: from Latin *indemnis* 'unhurt, free from loss or damage,' from *in-* (expressing negation) + *damnum* 'loss, damage.'

in•dem•ni•ty /inˈdemnitē/

▶ n. (pl. **in•dem•ni•ties**) security or protection against a loss or other financial burden: *no indemnity will be given for loss of cash.*

■ security against or exemption from legal responsibility for one's actions: *a deed of indemnity* | *even warranties and indemnities do not provide complete protection.* ■ a sum of money paid as compensation, esp. a sum exacted by a victor in war as one condition of peace.

ORIGIN late Middle English: from French *indemnite*, from late Latin *indemnitas*, from *indemnis* 'unhurt, free from loss.'

in•den•ture /inˈdenCHər/

▶ n. a formal legal agreement, contract, or document, in particular:

■ an agreement binding an apprentice to a master: *the 30 apprentices received their indentures on completion of their training.* ■ historical a deed of contract of which copies were made for the contracting parties with the edges indented for identification. ■ a formal list, certificate, or inventory. ■ historical a contract by which a person agreed to work for a set period for a landowner in a British colony in exchange for passage to the colony. ■ the fact of being bound to service by such an agreement: *men in their first year after **indenture to** the Company of Watermen and Lightermen.*

▸**v.** [trans.] (usu. **be indentured to**) chiefly historical bind (someone) by an indenture as an apprentice or laborer: [as adj.] (**indentured**) *landowners tried to get their estates cultivated by indentured laborers.*
DERIVATIVES **in•den•ture•ship** /in'denchər͵ship/ **n.**

in•de•ter•mi•nate /͵indi'tərmənit/
▸**adj. 1** (of a judicial sentence) not fixed in length, typically so that the convicted person's conduct determines the date of release.
2 (of rules) not capable of mechanical application: *the initial pleading in this case was indeterminate as to removability.*
DERIVATIVES **in•de•ter•mi•na•cy** /͵indi'tərmənəsē/ **n.;** **in•de•ter•mi•nate•ly** adv.; **in•de•ter•mi•nate•ness** n.
ORIGIN early 17th cent.: from late Latin *indeterminatus,* from *in-* 'not' + Latin *determinatus* 'limited, determined.'

in•dict /in'dīt/
▸**v.** [trans.] (usu. **be indicted**) formally, by a grand jury, accuse or charge (someone) with a crime: *his former manager was indicted for fraud.*
DERIVATIVES **in•dict•ee** /͵indī'tē/ **n.;** **in•dict•er** n.
ORIGIN Middle English *endite, indite,* from Anglo-Norman French *enditer,* based on Latin *indicere* 'proclaim, appoint,' from *in-* 'toward' + *dicere* 'pronounce, utter.'

in•dict•a•ble /in'dītəbəl/
▸**adj.** (of an offense) rendering the person who commits it liable to be charged with a crime that warrants a trial by jury.
■ (of a person) liable to be charged with a crime.

in•dict•ment /in'dītmənt/
▸**n.** a formal charge or accusation, by a grand jury, of a crime: *an indictment for conspiracy.* See also BILL OF IN-DICTMENT.

■ the action of indicting or being indicted: *the indictment of twelve people who had imported cocaine.*
ORIGIN Middle English *enditement, inditement,* from Anglo-Norman French *enditement,* from *enditer* (see IN-DICT).

in•dis•pen•sa•ble /ˌindiˈspensəbəl/
▶ n. a person who must be made party to a legal action: *in a suit against a subordinate officer, the head of a department or other superior officer is an indispensable.*
ORIGIN mid 16th cent.: from medieval Latin *indispensabilis,* from *in-* 'not' + *dispensabilis* 'dispensable.'

in•duce•ment /inˈd(y)ōōsmənt/
▶ n. a thing that persuades or influences someone to do something, especially enter into a contract: *companies were prepared to build only in return for massive inducements* | *there is no* **inducement to** *wait for payment.*
■ a bribe.

in•fa•mous /ˈinfəməs/
▶ adj. historical (of a person) deprived of all or some of a citizen's rights as a consequence of conviction for a serious crime.
■ (of a crime) leading to such deprivation.
DERIVATIVES **in•fa•mous•ly** adv.; **in•fa•my** /ˈinfə,mē/ n. (pl. **in•fa•mies**) .
ORIGIN late Middle English: from medieval Latin *infamosus,* from Latin *infamis* (based on *fama* 'fame').

in•fan•cy /ˈinfənsē/
▶ n. the condition of being a minor; minority: *the disabilities of insanity or infancy.*
ORIGIN late Middle English: from Latin *infantia* 'childhood, inability to speak,' from *infans, infant-* (see INFANT).

in•fant /'infənt/
▶ **n.** a person who has not attained legal majority: *the creditor was unaware that the debtor was an infant.*
ORIGIN late Middle English: from Old French *enfant*, from Latin *infant-* 'unable to speak,' from *in-* 'not' + *fant-* 'speaking' (from the verb *fari*).

in•fan•ti•cide /in'fænti,sīd/
▶ **n. 1** the crime of killing one's newborn or a very young child.
2 a person who kills an infant, esp. their own child.
DERIVATIVES **in•fan•ti•cid•al** /in,fænti'sīdl/ **adj.**
ORIGIN mid 17th cent.: via French from late Latin *infanticidium*, from Latin *infant-* (see INFANT) + *-cidium*, from *caedere* 'kill.'

in•fe•ri•or /in'firēər/
▶ **adj.** (of a court or tribunal) subordinate to, and able to have its decisions overturned by, a higher court.
ORIGIN from Latin, comparative of *inferus* 'low.'

in fla•gran•te de•lic•to /,in flə'gräntā də'liktō; flə'græntē/ (also informal **in fla•gran•te**)
▶ **adv.** in the very act of wrongdoing, esp. in an act of sexual misconduct: *he had been **caught in flagrante** with the wife of the association's treasurer.*
ORIGIN late 18th cent.: Latin, literally 'in blazing crime.'

in•flu•ence /'inflōŏəns/
▶ **n.** see UNDER THE INFLUENCE.

in•form•ant /in'fômənt/
▶ **n.** a person who informs on another person to the police or other authority: *an informant told the police that a large shipment of heroin would arrive in Rochester from New York City.*

in•for•ma•tion /ˌinfərˈmāsHən/
▸ **n.** a formal criminal charge lodged with a court or magistrate by a prosecutor without the aid of a grand jury: *the tenant may lay an information against his land-lord.*
ORIGIN late Middle English (also in the sense 'formation of the mind, teaching'), via Old French from Latin *informatio(n-)*, from the verb *informare* 'shape, fashion, describe,' from *in-* 'into' + *forma* 'a form.'

in•form•er /inˈfôrmər/
▸ **n.** another term for INFORMANT.

in•frac•tion /inˈfraksHən/
▸ **n.** a violation or infringement of a law, an agreement, the rights of others, or a set of rules. An infraction typically is a minor offense: *traffic infractions.*
DERIVATIVES **in•frac•tor** /inˈfraktər/ n.
ORIGIN late Middle English: from Latin *infractio(n-)*, from the verb *infringere* (see INFRINGE).

in•fringe /inˈfrinj/
▸ **v.** [trans.] actively break the terms of (a law, agreement, etc.): *making an unauthorized copy would infringe copyright.*
■ act so as to limit or undermine (something); encroach on: *his legal rights were being infringed* | [intrans.] *I wouldn't infringe on his privacy.*
DERIVATIVES **in•fringe•ment** n.; **in•fring•er** n.
ORIGIN mid 16th cent.: from Latin *infringere*, from *in-* 'into' + *frangere* 'to break.'

in•here /inˈhir/
▸ **v.** [intrans.] (**inhere in/within**) (of rights, powers, etc.) be vested in a person or group or attached to the ownership of a property: *the rights inhering in the property they owned.*

ORIGIN mid 16th cent. (in the sense 'stick, cling to'): from Latin *inhaerere* 'stick to.'

in•her•ent /in'hirənt; -'her-/
▶ **adj.** vested in (someone) as a right or privilege: *the president's inherent foreign affairs power.*
DERIVATIVES **in•her•ence** n.; **in•her•ent•ly** adv.
ORIGIN late 16th cent.: from Latin *inhaerent-* 'sticking to,' from the verb *inhaerere*, from *in-* 'in, toward' + *haerere* 'to stick.'

in•her•it /in'herit/
▶ **v.** (**in•her•it•ed**, **in•her•it•ing**) [trans.] receive (money, property, or a title) as an heir, by will or operation of law, at the death of the previous holder: *she inherited a fortune from her father.*
DERIVATIVES **in•her•i•tor** /in'heritər/ n.
ORIGIN Middle English *enherite* 'receive as a right,' from Old French *enheriter*, from late Latin *inhereditare* 'appoint as heir,' from Latin *in-* 'in' + *heres, hered-* 'heir.'

in•her•it•a•ble /in'heritəbəl/
▶ **adj.** capable of being inherited: *inheritable property.*
■ capable of inheriting.
DERIVATIVES **in•her•it•a•bil•i•ty** /in,heritə'bilitē/ n.
ORIGIN late Middle English (formerly also as *enheritable*): from Anglo-Norman French *enheritable* 'able to be made heir,' from Old French *enheriter* (see INHERIT).

in•her•it•ance /in'heritns/
▶ **n.** a thing that is inherited: *he came into a comfortable inheritance.*
ORIGIN late Middle English (formerly also as *enheritance*): from Anglo-Norman French *enheritaunce* 'being admitted as heir,' from Old French *enheriter* (see INHERIT).

in•her•it•ance tax /in'heritns ˌtæks/
▶ n. a tax imposed on someone who inherits property or money. Also called DEATH TAX.

in•i•ti•a•tive /i'nɪSH(ē)ətiv/
▶ n. **(the initiative)** (esp. in some US states and Switzerland) the right of citizens outside the legislature to originate legislation.
ORIGIN late 18th cent.: from French, from Latin *initiare*, from *initium* 'beginning.'

in•junc•tion /in'jəNG(k)sHən/
▶ n. a judicial order, equitable in origin and enforceable by contempt proceedings, that restrains a person from beginning or continuing an action threatening or invading the legal right of another, or that compels a person to carry out a certain act, e.g., to make restitution to an injured party: *an injunction prohibiting plutonium shipments.*
DERIVATIVES **in•junc•tive** /in'jəNG(k)tiv/ **adj.**
ORIGIN late Middle English: from late Latin *injunctio(n-)*, from Latin *injungere* 'enjoin, impose.'

in•ju•ri•ous /in'jŏŏrēəs/
▶ adj. causing or likely to cause damage or harm: *fish above the tolerance level are deemed to be injurious to people's health.*
■ (of language) maliciously insulting; libelous.
DERIVATIVES **in•ju•ri•ous•ly adv.; in•ju•ri•ous•ness n.**
ORIGIN late Middle English: from French *injurieux* or Latin *injuriosus*, from *injuria* 'a wrong' (see INJURY).

in•ju•ry /'injərē/
▶ n. (pl. **in•ju•ries**) an instance of being injured.
■ the fact of being injured; harm or damage: *awards are only available where injury is actually proved.* ■ wrong or

harm done to another: *they held that exercise of the contract provisions inflicted injury.*
ORIGIN late Middle English: from Anglo-Norman French *injurie,* from Latin *injuria* 'a wrong,' from *in-* (expressing negation) + *jus, jur-* 'right.'

in•no•cent /ˈinəsənt/
▶ adj. not guilty of a crime or offense: *the arbitrary execution of an innocent man* | *he was **innocent of** any fraud.*
ORIGIN Middle English: from Old French, or from Latin *innocent-* 'not harming,' from *in-* 'not' + *nocere* 'to hurt.'

USAGE: **Innocent** properly means 'harmless,' but it has long been extended in general language to mean 'not guilty.' The jury (or judge) in a criminal trial does not, strictly speaking, find a defendant 'innocent.' Rather, a defendant may be *guilty* or *not guilty* of the charges brought. In common use, however, owing perhaps to the concept of the *presumption of innocence,* which instructs a jury to consider a defendant free of wrongdoing until proven guilty on the basis of evidence, 'not guilty' and 'innocent' have come to be thought of as synonymous.

Inn of Court /ˈin əv ˈkôrt/
▶ n. (pl. **Inns of Court**) (in the UK) each of the four legal societies having the exclusive right of admitting people to the English bar.
■ any of the sets of buildings in London occupied by these societies.

in•nu•en•do /ˌinyo͞oˈendō/
▶ n. (pl. **in•nu•en•does** or **in•nu•en•dos**) the defamatory meaning of a libel: *we disagree with the assertion that the sexual references rely solely on innuendo.*
ORIGIN 17th cent.: Latin, 'by nodding at, by pointing to,' ablative gerund of *innuere,* from *in-* 'toward' + *nuere* 'to nod.'

in per•so•nam /ˌin pərˈsōnəm/
▸ **adj.** & **adv.** made or availing against or affecting a specific person only; imposing a personal duty or liability: [as postpositive adj.] *rights and duties in personam* | [as adv.] *the view that trusts operate in personam.* Compare with **IN REM.**
ORIGIN late 18th cent.: Latin, literally 'against a person.'

in•quest /ˈin,kwest; -ˈiNG-/
▸ **n.** a judicial inquiry to ascertain the facts relating to an incident, such as a death.
■ a body of people appoginted to make such an inquiry.
ORIGIN Middle English: from Old French *enqueste,* based on Latin *inquirere* (see **INQUIRE**).

in•qui•si•tion /ˌinkwiˈziSHən; ˌiNG-/
▸ **n.** the verdict or finding of an official inquiry.
■ historical a judicial or official inquiry.
ORIGIN late Middle English (denoting a searching examination): via Old French from Latin *inquisitio(n-)* 'examination.'

in•quis•i•to•ri•al /in,kwiziˈtôrēəl; iNG-/
▸ **adj.** (of a trial or legal procedure) in which the judge has an examining or inquiring role: *administration is accompanied by a form of inquisitorial justice.* Compare with **ACCUSATORIAL, ADVERSARIAL.**
DERIVATIVES **in•quis•i•to•ri•al•ly adv.**
ORIGIN mid 18th cent.: from medieval Latin *inquisitorius* (from Latin *inquisitor,* from *inquirere* 'inquire') + *-al.*

in re /ˌin ˈrā; ˈrē/
▸ **prep.** in the legal case of; with regard to: *in re Mancet's Estate.*
ORIGIN early 17th cent.: Latin, 'in the matter of.'

in rem /ˌin ˈrem/
▸ **adj.** [often postpositive] made or availing against or affecting a thing, and therefore other people generally; imposing a general duty or liability: *it confers a right in rem.* Compare with IN PERSONAM.
ORIGIN mid 18th cent.: Latin, 'against a thing.'

in•san•i•ty /inˈsænitē/
▸ **n.** the state of being seriously mentally ill; madness.
■ such a state when it makes one not liable or responsible for one's actions: [as complement] *he attempted to plead insanity.*
ORIGIN late 16th cent.: from Latin *insanitas*, from *insanus* (see INSANE).

in•sid•er trad•ing /ˈinˌsīdər ˈtrādiNG/ (Brit. also **in•sid•er deal•ing** /ˈinˌsīdər ˈdēliNG/)
▸ **n.** the illegal practice of trading on the stock exchange to one's own advantage through having access, because of personal or business relationship, to confidential information.

in•sti•tute /ˈinstiˌt(y)o͞ot/
▸ **v.** [trans.] **1** begin (legal proceedings) in a court: *before instituting any action under this section, the Secretary shall attempt to eliminate discriminatory practice.*
2 (often **be instituted**) appoint (someone) to a position, esp. as a cleric: *his sons were **instituted to** his benefice in 1986* | *McAndrews, the testator, has instituted his daughter heir.*
▸ **n.** [usu. in names] (usu. **institutes**) archaic a commentary, treatise, or summary of principles, esp. concerning law.
ORIGIN Middle English (sense 2 of the **verb**): from Latin *institut-* 'established,' from the verb *instituere*, from *in-* 'in, toward' + *statuere* 'set up.' The noun is from Latin *institutum* 'something designed, precept.'

in•struct /in'strəkt/

▶ v. [trans.] give a person direction, information, or authorization, in particular:

■ (of a judge) give information, esp. clarification of legal principles, to (a jury): *there were two minutes of testimony that the jury was instructed to disregard.*

ORIGIN from Latin *instruct-* 'constructed, equipped, taught,' from the verb *instruere,* from *in-* 'upon, toward' + *struere* 'pile up.'

in•struc•tions /in'strəkSHənz/

▶ plural noun directions to a jury.

ORIGIN late Middle English: via Old French from late Latin *instructio(n-),* from the verb *instruere* (see IN-STRUCT).

in•stru•ment /'instrəmənt/

▶ n. a formal document, esp. a legal one: *execution involves signature and unconditional delivery of the instrument.*

▶ v. [trans.] equip (something) with measuring instruments.

ORIGIN Middle English: from Old French, or from Latin *instrumentum* 'equipment, implement,' from the verb *instruere* 'construct, equip.'

in•sur•ance pol•i•cy /in'SHŏŏrəns ˌpäləsē/

▶ n. a document detailing the terms and conditions of a contract of insurance.

in•tel•lec•tu•al prop•er•ty /ˌintl'eksHŏŏəl 'präpərtē/

▶ n. a work or invention that is the result of creativity, such as a manuscript or a design, to which one has rights and for which one may apply for a patent, copyright or trademark.

in•tent /in'tent/

▶ n. intention or purpose.

PHRASES **with intent** with the intention of committing a specified wrongful act (tort) or crime: *he denied arson with intent to endanger life* | *charges of wounding with intent.*
ORIGIN Middle English: from Old French *entent, entente,* based on Latin *intendere* 'intend.'

in•ter•dict

▸ n. /ˈintərˌdikt/ an authoritative prohibition: *an interdict against marriage of those of close kin.*
▸ v. /ˌintərˈdikt/ [trans.] **1** prohibit or forbid (something).
■ **(interdict someone from)** prohibit someone from (doing something): *I have not been interdicted from consuming or holding alcoholic beverages.*
2 intercept and prevent the movement of (a prohibited commodity or person): *the police established roadblocks throughout the country for interdicting drugs.*
DERIVATIVES **in•ter•dic•tion** /ˌintərˈdikSHən/ n.
ORIGIN from Old French *entredit,* from Latin *interdictum,* past participle of *interdicere* 'interpose, forbid by decree,' from *inter-* 'between' + *dicere* 'say.'

in•ter•est /ˈint(ə)rist/

▸ n. a legal concern, title, or right in property: *third parties having an interest in a building.*
ORIGIN late Middle English (originally as *interess*): from Anglo-Norman French *interesse,* from Latin *interesse* 'differ, be important,' from *inter-* 'between' + *esse* 'be.' The *-t* was added partly by association with Old French *interest* 'damage, loss,' apparently from Latin *interest* 'it is important.' The original sense was 'the possession of a share in or a right to something.'

in•ter•loc•u•to•ry /ˌintərˈläkyəˌtôrē/

▸ adj. (of a decree or judgment) given provisionally during the course of a legal action; preliminary: *an interlocutory appeal.*

ORIGIN late 15th cent.: from medieval Latin *interlocutorius*, from Latin *interloqui* 'interrupt.'

in•ter•na•tion•al Court of Jus•tice /ˌintərˈnæsHənl ˈkôrt əv ˈjəstis/ a judicial court of the United Nations, formed in 1945, that meets at The Hague.

in•ter•na•tion•al law /ˌintərˈnæsHənl ˈlô/
▸ n. a body of rules established by custom or treaty and recognized by nations as binding in their relations with one another.

in•ter•plead•er /ˌintərˈplēdər/
▸ n. a suit pleaded between two parties to determine a matter of claim or right to property held by a third party: *an action **in interpleader** was filed to determine how the proceeds should be divided between the heirs.*
DERIVATIVES **in•ter•plead** /ˌintərˈplēd/ v.
ORIGIN mid 16th cent.: from Anglo-Norman French *enterpleder*, from *enter-* 'between' + *pleder* 'to plead.'

in•ter•rog•a•to•ry /ˌintəˈrägəˌtôrē/
▸ n. (pl. **in•ter•rog•a•to•ries**) a written question that is formally put to one party in a case by another party and that must be answered.
ORIGIN mid 16th cent.: the noun from medieval Latin *interrogatoria*, plural of *interrogatorium*; the adjective from late Latin *interrogatorius*, based on Latin *interrogare*, from *inter-* 'between' + *rogare* 'ask.'

in•ter•vene /ˌintərˈvēn/
▸ v. [intrans.] interpose in a lawsuit as a third party: *the university challenged NIH's action in court just days before the United States intervened in the case.*
DERIVATIVES **in•ter•ven•er** n.; **in•ter•ven•ient** /ˌintər ˈvēnyənt/ adj.; **in•ter•ve•nor** /ˌintərˈvēnər/ n.
ORIGIN late 16th cent. (in the sense 'come in as an ex-

traneous factor or thing'): from Latin *intervenire*, from *inter-* 'between' + *venire* 'come.'

in•tes•tate /in'testāt; -tit/
▸ **adj.** [predic.] not having made a will before one dies: *he died intestate* | [postpositive] *in the event of his death intestate.*
■ [attrib.] of or relating to a person who dies without having made a will: *his brother's posthumous children are admissible as intestate heirs.*
▸**n.** a person who has died without having made a will.
DERIVATIVES **in•tes•ta•cy** /in'testəsē/ **n.**
ORIGIN late Middle English: from Latin *intestatus*, from *in-* 'not' + *testatus* 'testified, witness' (see TESTATE).

in•ure /i'n(y)ŏŏr/ (also **en•ure**)
▸ **v.** [intrans.] (**inure for/to**) come into operation; take effect: *a release given to one of two joint contractors inures to the benefit of both.*
DERIVATIVES **in•ure•ment n.**
ORIGIN late Middle English *inure, enure*, from an Anglo-Norman French phrase meaning 'in use or practice,' from *en* 'in' + Old French *euvre* 'work' (from Latin *opera*).

in•val•id /in'vælid/
▸ **adj.** (esp. of an official document or procedure) not valid; void because contravening a regulation or law: *the vote was declared invalid due to a technicality.*
DERIVATIVES **in•val•id•ly adv.**
ORIGIN mid 16th cent. (earlier than *valid*): from Latin *invalidus*, from *in-* 'not' + *validus* 'strong.'

in•val•i•date /in'væli,dāt/
▸ **v.** [trans.] deprive (an official document or procedure) of legal efficacy because of contravention of a regulation or law: *a technical flaw in her papers invalidated her nomination.*

DERIVATIVES **in•val•i•da•tion** /in,væli'dāsHən/ n.; **in•val•i•da•tor** /in'væli,dātər/ n.

ORIGIN mid 17th cent.: from medieval Latin *invalidat-* 'annulled,' from the verb *invalidare* (based on Latin *validus* 'strong').

is•sue /'isHŏŏ/

▸ **n. 1** a point of fact or law that is the subject of litigation and of the court's final determination. *most of her testimony did not involve the time periods* **at issue** *in this case* | *the state court had concurrent jurisdiction to decide the issue of the debtor's liability.*

2 children of one's own: *he died without male issue.*

DERIVATIVES **is•sue•less** adj.

ORIGIN Middle English (in the sense 'outflowing'): from Old French, based on Latin *exitus*, past participle of *exire* 'go out.'

J

J
▸ **abbr.** ▪ judge. ▪ justice.

JAG
▸ **abbr.** judge advocate general.

Jane Doe /'jān 'dō/
▸ **n.** an anonymous female party, typically the plaintiff, in a legal action. See also JOHN DOE.

JD
▸ **abbr.** juris doctor, the primary degree granted at most US law schools.

jeop•ard•y /'jepərdē/
▸ **n.** danger (of conviction) arising from being on trial for a criminal offense: *pesticide retailers and end-users could also be subject to legal jeopardy*. See also DOUBLE JEOPARDY.
ORIGIN Middle English *iuparti*, from Old French *ieu parti* '(evenly) divided game.' The term was originally used in chess and other games to denote a problem, or a position in which the chances of winning or losing were evenly balanced, hence 'a dangerous situation.'

John Doe /'jän 'dō/
▸ **n.** an anonymous male party, typically the plaintiff, in a legal action. See also JANE DOE.
ORIGIN mid 18th cent.: originally in legal use as a name of a fictitious plaintiff, corresponding to *Richard Roe*, used to represent the defendant.

join•der /'joindər/
▸ **n.** the action of bringing parties (e.g., codefendants) or claims together in a legal action.

ORIGIN late Middle English: from Anglo-Norman French, from Old French *joindre* 'to join.'

joint /joint/
▸ **adj.** [attrib.] shared, held, or made by both houses of a bicameral legislature: *a joint session of Congress* | *a joint congressional hearing.*
■ applied, joined, or regarded together: *joint ownership.* Often contrasted with SEVERAL.
▸ **n.** informal (**the joint**) prison.
DERIVATIVES **joint•ly** adv.
ORIGIN Middle English: from Old French, past participle of *joindre* 'to join.'

joint and sev•er•al /'joint ən(d) 'sev(ə)rəl/
▸ **adj.** (of a legal obligation) undertaken by two or more people, each individual having liability for the whole: *she was ordered to pay restitution, joint and several with her codefendants.*

joint ten•an•cy /'joint 'tenənsē/
▸ **n.** the holding of an estate or property jointly by two or more parties, the share of each passing to the other or others on death.
DERIVATIVES **joint ten•ant** /'joint 'tenənt/ n.

JP
▸ **abbr.** justice of the peace.

judge /jəj/
▸ **n.** a public official appointed or elected to decide cases in a court of law.
▸ **v.** [trans.] decide (a case) in a court of law: *other cases were judged by tribunal.*
■ [with complement] give a verdict on (someone) in a law court: *she was judged guilty of manslaughter.*
DERIVATIVES **judge•ship** /'jəj,SHip/ n.

ORIGIN Middle English: from Old French *juge* (noun), *juger* (verb), from Latin *judex, judic-,* from *jus* 'law' + *dicere* 'to say.'

judge ad•vo•cate /'jəj 'advəkit/
▸ n. a lawyer who advises a courtmartial on points of law and sums up the case.
■ a military lawyer.

judge ad•vo•cate gen•er•al /'jəj 'advəkit 'jen(ə)rəl/ (abbr.: **JAG**)
▸ n. the officer in supreme control of the courts-martial of one of the armed forces.

judge-made /'jəj 'mād/
▸ adj. created by judicial decisions rather than legislation: *such an exemption from double patenting would contravene more than 100 years of judge-made law.*

judg•ment /'jəjmənt/ (also **judge•ment**)
▸ n. a decision of a court of law or a judge.
■ a monetary or other obligation awarded by a court: *it reversed a lower court decision upholding the $100,000 judgment.* ■ the document recording this obligation.
PHRASES **pass judgment** (of a court of law or a judge) give a decision concerning a defendant or legal matter: *he **passed judgment on** the accused.*
ORIGIN Middle English: from Old French *jugement,* from *juger* 'to judge.'

judg•ment in de•fault /'jəjmənt in di'fôlt/
▸ chiefly Brit. another term for DEFAULT JUDGMENT.

ju•di•ca•ture /'jo͞odikə,CHo͞or; -,kāCHər/
▸ n. the administration of justice.
■ (**the judicature**) judges collectively; the judiciary.
DERIVATIVES **ju•di•ca•to•ry** /'jo͞odikə,tôrē/ adj.

ORIGIN mid 16th cent.: from medieval Latin *judicatura*, from Latin *judicare* 'to judge.'

ju•di•cial /jŏŏ'disHəl/

▶ **adj.** of, by, or appropriate to a court of law or a judge: *a judicial inquiry into the allegations* | *a judicial system.*
DERIVATIVES **ju•di•cial•ly** adv.
ORIGIN late Middle English: from Latin *judicialis*, from *judicium* 'judgment,' from *judex* (see JUDGE).

USAGE: **Judicial** means 'relating to judgment and the administration of justice': *the judicial system*; | *judicial robes.* Do not confuse it with **judicious**, which means 'prudent, reasonable': *getting off the highway the minute you felt tired was a judicious choice.* **Judiciary**, usually a noun and sometimes an adjective, refers to the judicial branch of government, the court system, or judges collectively.

ju•di•cial re•view /jŏŏ'disHəl ri'vyŏŏ/

▶ **n.** (in the US) review by a court, especially the Supreme Court, of the constitutional validity of a legislative or administrative act or procedure.
■ (in the UK) a procedure by which a court can review an administrative action by a public body and (in England) secure a declaration, order, or award.

ju•di•cial sep•a•ra•tion /jŏŏ'disHəl ,sepə'rāsHən/

▶ **n.** another term for LEGAL SEPARATION (sense 1).

ju•di•ci•ar•y /jŏŏ'disHē,erē; -'disHərē/

▶ **n.** (pl. **ju•di•ci•ar•ies**) (usu. **the judiciary**) the judicial authorities of a country; judges collectively.
ORIGIN early 19th cent.: from Latin *judiciarius*, from *judicium* 'judgment.'

USAGE: See **usage** at JUDICIAL.

ju•ral /'jŏŏrəl/

▶ **adj.** formal of or relating to the law: *American jural heritage.*

ORIGIN mid 17th cent.: from Latin *jus, jur-* 'law, right' + *-al.*

ju•rat /ˈjo͝oræt/
▸ **n. 1** chiefly historical a person who has taken an oath or who performs a duty on oath, e.g., a juror.
2 a statement on an affidavit of when, where, and before whom it was sworn.
ORIGIN late Middle English: based on Latin *juratus* 'sworn,' past participle of *jurare* .

ju•rid•i•cal /jo͝oˈridikəl/
▸ **adj.** of or relating to judicial proceedings and the administration of the law: *the facts of the case did not involve any misuse of the juridicial process.*
DERIVATIVES **ju•rid•i•cal•ly adv.**
ORIGIN early 16th cent.: from Latin *juridicus* (from *jus, jur-* 'law' + *dicere* 'say') + *-al.*

ju•ris•dic•tion /ˌjo͝orisˈdiksHən/
▸ **n.** the official power to make legal decisions and judgments: *federal courts had no **jurisdiction over** the case | the District of Columbia was placed under the **jurisdiction of** Congress.*
■ the extent of this power: *the claim will be **within the jurisdiction** of the Department of Transportation.* ■ a system of law courts; a judicature: *in some jurisdictions there is a mandatory death sentence for murder.* ■ the territory or sphere of activity over which the legal authority of a court or other institution extends: *several different tax jurisdictions.*
DERIVATIVES **ju•ris•dic•tion•al** /ˌjo͝orisˈdiksHənl/ **adj.**
ORIGIN Middle English: from Old French *jurediction,* from Latin *jurisdictio(n-),* from *jus, jur-* 'law' + *dictio* 'saying' (from *dicere* 'say').

ju•ris doc•tor /ˈjo͝oris ˈdäktər/
▸ **n.** see **JD.**

ju•ris•pru•dence /ˌjŏŏrisˈprŏŏdns/
▸ n. the theory or philosophy of law.
◼ a legal system: *American jurisprudence.*
DERIVATIVES **ju•ris•pru•dent** adj. & n.; **ju•ris•pru•den•tial** /ˌjŏŏrisprŏŏˈdenCHəl/ **adj.**
ORIGIN early 17th cent.: from late Latin *jurisprudentia*, from Latin *jus, jur-* 'law' + *prudentia* 'knowledge.'

ju•rist /ˈjŏŏrist/
▸ n. an expert in or writer on law.
◼ a lawyer or a judge.
DERIVATIVES **ju•ris•tic** /jŏŏˈristik/ **adj.**
ORIGIN late 15th cent. (in the sense 'lawyer'): from French *juriste*, medieval Latin *jurista*, from *jus, jur-* 'law.'

ju•ror /ˈjŏŏrər; -ôr/
▸ n. a member of a jury.
ORIGIN late Middle English: from Old French *jureor*, from Latin *jurator*, from *jurare* 'swear,' from *jus, jur-* 'law.'

ju•ry /ˈjŏŏrē/
▸ n. (pl. **ju•ries**) a body of people (historically twelve in number) sworn to give a verdict in a legal case on the basis of evidence submitted to them in court. Also called PETIT JURY, PETTY JURY.
ORIGIN late Middle English: from Old French *juree* 'oath, inquiry,' from Latin *jurata*, feminine past participle of *jurare* 'swear' (see JUROR).

ju•ry box /ˈjŏŏrē ˌbäks/
▸ n. a segregated area in which the jury sits in a court of law.

jus co•gens /ˈjəs ˈkōjənz/
▸ n. the principles that form the norms of international law and that cannot be set aside by treaty, etc.: [as adj.] *jus cogens norms.*
ORIGIN Latin, literally 'compelling law.'

jus gen•ti•um /ˈjəs ˈjensHēəm/
▸ n. international law.
ORIGIN Latin, literally 'law of nations.'

jus•tice /ˈjəstis/
▸ n. **1** just behavior or treatment.
■ the administration of the law or authority in maintaining this: *a tragic miscarriage of justice.* ■ (**Justice**) the personification of justice, usually a blindfolded woman holding scales and a sword.
2 a judge or magistrate, in particular a judge of the supreme court of a country or state.
PHRASES **bring someone to justice** arrest someone for a crime and ensure that they are tried in court.
DERIVATIVES **jus•tice•ship** /ˈjəstis,SHip/ n. (in sense 2).
ORIGIN late Old English *iustise* 'administration of the law,' via Old French from Latin *justitia*, from *justus*, from *jus* 'law, right.'

jus•tice of the peace /ˈjəstis əv ᴛʜə ˈpēs/
▸ n. a magistrate appointed to hear minor cases, perform marriages, grant licenses, etc., in a town, county, or other local district.

jus•ti•ci•a•ble /jəˈstisH(ē)əbəl/
▸ adj. subject to trial in a court of law; capable of being tried: *defendant maintains that plaintiff's claim is not justiciable.*
ORIGIN late Middle English: from Old French, from *justicier* 'bring to trial,' from medieval Latin *justitiare*, from Latin *justitia* 'equity,' from *justus* (see JUSTICE).

jus•ti•fi•a•ble hom•i•cide /ˌjəstəˈfīəbəl ˈhämə,sīd/
▸ n. the killing of a person in circumstances (especially self-defense) that allow the act to be regarded in law as without criminal guilt.

ju•ve•nile /ˈjo͞ovə‚nīl; -vənl/
▶ n. a person below the age at which adult criminal prosecution is possible (18 in most countries).
ORIGIN early 17th cent.: from Latin *juvenilis*, from *juvenis* 'young, a young person.'

ju•ve•nile court /ˈjo͞ovə‚nīl ˈkôrt; ˈjo͞ovənl/
▶ n. a court of law responsible for the trial or legal supervision of children under a specified age (18 in most countries).

ju•ve•nile de•lin•quen•cy /ˈjo͞ovə‚nīl dəˈliNGkwənsē; ˈjo͞ovənl/
▶ n. the committing of criminal acts or offenses by a young person, esp. one below the age at which ordinary criminal prosecution is possible.
DERIVATIVES **ju•ve•nile de•lin•quent** n.

ju•ve•nile of•fend•er /ˈjo͞ovə‚nīl əˈfendər; ˈjo͞ovənl/
▶ n. a person below a specific age (18 in most countries) who has committed a crime.

K

kan•ga•roo court /ˌkæNGgəˈroo ˌkôrt/
  ▸ n. an improperly constituted court with no legal standing, which ignores procedures guaranteeing fair trials.

KC
  ▸ abbr. (in the UK) King's Counsel.

King's Bench /ˈkiNGz ˈbenCH/
  ▸ n. (in the UK) in the reign of a king, the term for QUEEN'S BENCH.

King's Coun•sel /ˈkiNGz ˈkownsəl/ (abbr.: **KC**)
  ▸ n. (in the UK) in the reign of a king, the term for QUEEN'S COUNSEL.

L

lach•es /'læCHiz/
▶ n. unreasonable delay in making an assertion or claim, such as asserting a right, claiming a privilege, or making an application for redress, which may result in refusal: *the court did not reach the issue of compliance because it found plaintiffs' claim to be barred by the doctrine of laches.*
ORIGIN late Middle English (in the sense 'slackness, negligence'): from Old French *laschesse,* from *lasche* 'loose, lax,' based on Latin *laxus* . The current sense dates from the late 16th cent.

lapse /læps/
▶ n. the termination of a right or privilege through disuse or failure to follow appropriate procedures: *statutory exceptions had prevented a lapse of the water rights in question.*
▶ v. [intrans.] (of a right, privilege, or agreement) become invalid because it is not used, claimed, or renewed; expire: *the time for an appeal has not yet lapsed.*
ORIGIN late Middle English: from Latin *lapsus,* from *labi* 'to glide, slip, or fall'; the verb reinforced by Latin *lapsare* 'to slip or stumble.'

lar•ce•ny /'lärs(ə)nē/
▶ n. (pl. **lar•ce•nies**) theft of personal property. See also GRAND LARCENY, PETTY LARCENY.
DERIVATIVES **lar•ce•ner** /'lärs(ə)nər/ n. (archaic); **lar•ce•nist** /'lärs(ə)nist/ n.; **lar•ce•nous** /'lärs(ə)nəs/ adj.
ORIGIN late 15th cent.: from Old French *larcin,* from Latin *latrocinium,* from *latro(n-)* 'robber,' earlier 'mercenary soldier,' from Greek *latreus.*

law /lô/

▸ **n.** (often **the law**) the system of rules that a particular country or community recognizes as regulating the actions of its members and may enforce by the imposition of penalties, award of damages, and injunction: *they were taken to court for* **breaking the law** | *a license is required by law* | [as adj.] *law enforcement.*

■ an individual rule as part of such a system: *an initiative to tighten up the laws on pornography.* ■ such systems as a subject of study or as the basis of the legal profession: *he was still practicing law* | [as adj.] *a law firm.* Compare with JURISPRUDENCE. ■ **(the law)** informal the police: *he'd never been in trouble with the law in his life.* ■ statutory law and the common law. Compare with EQUITY.

PHRASES **at** (or **in**) **law** according to or concerned with the laws of a country: *an agreement enforceable at law* | *an attorney-at-law.* **go to law** resort to legal action in order to settle a matter. **law and order** a situation characterized by respect for and obedience to the rules of a society. **take someone to law** initiate legal proceedings against someone.

ORIGIN Old English *lagu*, from Old Norse *lag* 'something laid down or fixed,' of Germanic origin and related to the verb *lay.*

law•break•er /'lô‚brākər/
▸ **n.** a person who violates the law.
DERIVATIVES **law•break•ing n. & adj.**

law court /'lô ‚kôrt/
▸ **n.** a court of law.

law•ful /'lôfəl/
▸ **adj.** conforming to, permitted by, or recognized by law or rules: *it is an offense to carry a weapon in public without lawful authority.*
DERIVATIVES **law•ful•ly adv.; law•ful•ness n.**

law•giv•er /'lô,givər/
▸ n. a person who draws up and enacts laws.

law•mak•er /'lô,mākər/
▸ n. a legislator.
DERIVATIVES **law•mak•ing** /'lô,mākiNG/ adj. & n.

law•man /'lômən; -,mæn/
▸ n. (pl. **-men**) a law-enforcement officer, esp. a sheriff.

law of•fice /'lô ,ôfis; ,äfis/
▸ n. a lawyer's office.

law of na•tions /'lô əv 'nāsHənz/
▸ n. international law.

law of suc•ces•sion /'lô əv sək'sesHən/
▸ n. the law regulating the inheritance of property.
■ the law regulating the appointment of a new monarch or head of state.

law•suit /'lô,soot/
▸ n. a claim or dispute brought to a court of law for adjudication: *his lawyer **filed a lawsuit against** Los Angeles County.*

law•yer /'loi-ər; 'lôyər/
▸ n. a person who practices or studies law; an attorney or a counselor.
▸ v. [intrans.] practice law; work as a lawyer: [as n.] (**lawyering**) *lawyering is a craft that takes a long time to become proficient at.*
■ [trans.] (of a lawyer) work on the legal aspects of (a contract, lawsuit, etc.): *there is always a danger that the deal will be lawyered to death.*
DERIVATIVES **law•yer•ly** adj.

lease /lēs/

▶ n. a contract by which one party conveys land, property, services, etc., to another for a specified time, usually in return for a periodic payment: *the company occupies 89 acres at Port Newark* **under a lease** *that expires in 2006.*

▶ v. [trans.] grant (property) on lease; let: *she* **leased** *the site* **to** *a local company.*

■ take (property) on lease; rent: *land was* **leased from** *the city.*

DERIVATIVES **leas•a•ble adj.**

ORIGIN late Middle English: from Old French *lais, leis,* from *lesser, laissier* 'let, leave,' from Latin *laxare* 'make loose,' from *laxus* 'loose, lax.'

lease•back /'lēs,bæk/

▶ n. [often as adj.] the leasing of a property back to its seller: *leaseback agreements.*

lease•hold /'lēs,hōld/

▶ n. the holding of property by lease: *a form of leasehold* | [as adj.] *leasehold premises.* Often contrasted with FREE-HOLD.

■ a property held by lease.

DERIVATIVES **lease•hold•er n.**

ORIGIN early 18th cent.: from LEASE, on the pattern of *freehold.*

leg•a•cy /'legəsē/

▶ n. (pl. **leg•a•cies**) an amount of money or property left to someone in a will: *the bonds were redeemed to satisfy a specific dollar amount legacy.*

■ a thing handed down by a predecessor.

ORIGIN late Middle English (also denoting the function or office of a deputy, esp. a papal legate): from Old French *legacie,* from medieval Latin *legatia* 'legateship,' from *legatus* 'person delegated.'

le•gal /ˈlēgəl/

▶ adj. 1 [attrib.] of, based on, or concerned with the law: *the American legal system.*

■ appointed or required by the law: *a legal requirement.*

■ recognized by common or statutory law, as distinct from equity.

2 permitted by law: *he claimed that it had all been legal.*

DERIVATIVES **le•gal•ly adv.** [sentence adverb] *legally, we're still very much married.*

ORIGIN late Middle English (in the sense 'to do with Mosaic law'): from French, or from Latin *legalis*, from *lex, leg-* 'law.'

le•gal aid /ˈlēgəl ˈād/

▶ n. payment from public funds allowed, in cases of need, to help pay for legal advice or proceedings.

■ (**Legal Aid**) an organization that provides free legal services to the indigent.

le•gal ca•pac•i•ty /ˈlēgəl kəˈpæsitē/

▶ n. a person's authority under law to engage in a particular undertaking or maintain a particular status.

le•gal ea•gle /ˈlēgəl ˈēgəl/ (also **le•gal bea•gle** /ˈlēgəl ˈbēgəl/)

▶ n. informal a lawyer, esp. one who is keen and astute.

le•gal•ese /ˌlēgəˈlēz; -ˈlēs/

▶ n. informal, derogatory the formal and technical language of legal documents.

le•gal fic•tion /ˈlēgəl ˈfiksHən/

▶ n. an assertion accepted as true, though probably fictitious, to achieve a useful purpose in legal matters: *an unqualified claim of "Made in USA" for products that are partly foreign is a legal fiction.*

le•gal•i•ty /li'gælitē/
▶ n. (pl. **le•gal•i•ties**) the quality or state of being in accordance with the law: *documentation testifying to the legality of the arms sale.*
■ (**legalities**) obligations imposed by law; legal procedures.
ORIGIN late Middle English: from French *légalité* or medieval Latin *legalitas* 'relating to the law,' from Latin *legalis* (see LEGAL).

le•gal•ize /'lēgə,līz/
▶ v. [trans.] make (something that was previously illegal) permissible by law: *a measure legalizing gambling in Deadwood.*
DERIVATIVES **le•gal•i•za•tion** /ˌlēgələ'zāsHən; -ˌlī'zā-/ n.

le•gal per•son /'lēgəl 'pərsən/
▶ n. an individual or incorporated entity that has legal rights and is subject to obligations.

le•gal sep•a•ra•tion /'lēgəl ˌsepə'rāsHən/
▶ n. 1 an arrangement by which a husband or wife remain married but live apart, following a court order. Also called JUDICIAL SEPARATION.
2 an arrangement by which a child lives apart from a natural parent and with the other natural parent or a foster parent, following a court order.

le•gal ten•der /'lēgəl tendər/
▶ n. coins or banknotes that must be accepted if offered in payment of a debt: *only the federal government can mint coins that are legal tender.*

leg•a•tee /ˌlegə'tē/
▶ n. a person who receives a legacy.
ORIGIN late 17th cent.: from 15th-cent. *legate* 'bequeath' (from Latin *legare* 'delegate, bequeath') + *-ee.*

le•ga•tor /liˈgātər/
▶ n. rare a testator, esp. one who leaves a legacy.
ORIGIN mid 17th cent.: from Latin, from *legat-* 'deputed, delegated, bequeathed,' from the verb *legare*.

leg•is•late /ˈlejiˌslāt/
▶ v. [intrans.] make or enact laws: *he didn't want to name anyone to the Court who would legislate from the bench.*
■ [trans.] cover, affect, or create by making or enacting laws: *Congress must legislate strong new laws.*
ORIGIN early 18th cent.: back-formation from LEGISLATION.

leg•is•la•tion /ˌlejiˈslāsʜən/
▶ n. the action of making or enacting laws: *the framework for the market should be developed through legislation, not dictation.*
■ laws enacted by a legislature, considered collectively: *tax legislation.*
ORIGIN mid 17th cent. (denoting the enactment of laws): from late Latin *legis latio(n-)*, literally 'proposing of a law,' from *lex* 'law' and *latus* 'raised' (past participle of *tollere*).

leg•is•la•tive /ˈlejiˌslātiv/
▶ adj. having the power to make laws: *the country's supreme legislative body.*
■ of or relating to laws or the making of them: *legislative proposals.* Often contrasted with EXECUTIVE. ■ of or relating to a legislature: *legislative elections.*
DERIVATIVES **leg•is•la•tive•ly** adv.

leg•is•la•tor /ˈlejiˌslātər/
▶ n. a person who makes laws; a member of a legislative body.
ORIGIN late 15th cent.: from Latin *legis lator*, literally 'proposer of a law,' from *lex* 'law' and *lator* 'proposer, mover' (see also LEGISLATION).

leg•is•la•ture /'leji,slācHər/
▶ n. the legislative body of a country or state.
ORIGIN late 17th cent.: from LEGISLATION, on the pattern of *judicature*.

le•git•i•mate
▶ adj. /li'jiṯəmit/ conforming to the law or to rules: *his claims to legitimate authority*.
◼ (of a child) born of parents lawfully married to each other.
▶v. /li'jiṯə,māt/ [trans.] make legitimate; justify or make lawful: *the regime was not legitimated by popular support*.
DERIVATIVES **le•git•i•ma•cy** /li'jiṯəməsē/ n.; **le•git•i•mate•ly** /li'jiṯəmitlē/ adv.; **le•git•i•ma•tion** /li,jiṯə'māsHən/ n.; **le•git•i•ma•tize** /li'jiṯəmə,tīz/ v.
ORIGIN late Middle English (in the sense 'born of parents lawfully married to each other'): from medieval Latin *legitimatus* 'made legal,' from the verb *legitimare*, from Latin *legitimus* 'lawful,' from *lex, leg-* 'law.'

le•git•i•mize /li'jiṯə,mīz/
▶ v. [trans.] make legitimate: *voters legitimize the government through the election of public officials*.
DERIVATIVES **le•git•i•mi•za•tion** /li,jiṯəmə'zāsHən/ n.

les•see /le'sē/
▶ n. a person who holds the lease of a property; a tenant.
DERIVATIVES **les•see•ship** /le'sē,sHip/ n.
ORIGIN late 15th cent.: from Old French *lesse*, past participle of *lesser* 'to let, leave,' + *-ee*.

les•sor /'lesôr; le'sôr/
▶ n. a person who leases or lets a property to another; a landlord.
ORIGIN late Middle English: from Anglo-Norman French, from Old French *lesser* 'let, leave.'

let•ters of ad•min•is•tra•tion /ˈleṭərz əv əd‚minəˈstrāsʜən/
▸ **plural n.** authority to administer the estate of someone
who has died without making a will.

let•ters pat•ent /ˈleṭərz ˈpætnt/
▸ **plural n.** a public document issued by a government or
monarch conferring a patent or other right.
ORIGIN late Middle English: from medieval Latin *lit-
terae patentes*, literally 'letters lying open.'

let•ters rog•a•to•ry /ˈleṭərz ˈrōgə‚tôrē; ˈrägə‚tôrē/
▸ **plural n.** documents making a request through a foreign
court for the obtaining of information or evidence from
a specified person within the jurisdiction of that court.
ORIGIN mid 19th cent.: *rogatory* from medieval Latin
rogatorius 'interrogatory.'

le•vy /ˈlevē/
▸ **v.** (**lev•ies, lev•ied**) [intrans.] (**levy on/upon**) seize (property) to satisfy a legal judgment: *there were no goods to
levy upon.*
▸ **n.** (pl. **lev•ies**) an item or set of items of property seized
to satisfy a legal judgment.
ORIGIN Middle English (as a noun): from Old French
levee, feminine past participle of *lever* 'raise,' from Latin
levare, from *levis* 'light.'

lex fo•ri /ˈleks ˈfôr‚ī; ˈfôr‚ē/
▸ **n.** the law of the state or country in which an action is
brought.
ORIGIN Latin, 'law of the court.'

lex lo•ci /ˈleks ˈlōsī; ˈlōsē; ˈlōkē; ˈlōkī/
▸ **n.** the law of the state or country in which a contract
is made, a transaction is performed, a tort is committed, or a property is situated.
ORIGIN Latin, 'law of the place.'

lex ta•li•o•nis /ˈleks ˌtälēˈōnis; ˌtælēˈōnis/
▸ n. the (supposed) law of retaliation, whereby a punishment resembles the offense committed in kind and degree.
ORIGIN Latin, from *lex* 'law' and *talio(n-)* 'retaliation' (from *talis* 'such').

li•a•ble /ˈlī(ə)bəl/
▸ adj. responsible by law; legally answerable, especially when required to pay damages: *the supplier of goods or services can become **liable for** breach of contract in a variety of ways.*
ORIGIN late Middle English: perhaps from Anglo-Norman French, from French *lier* 'to bind,' from Latin *ligare*.

li•bel /ˈlībəl/
▸ n. **1** a published false statement that is damaging to a person's reputation; a written defamation. Compare with SLANDER.
■ the action or crime of publishing such a statement: *a teacher who sued two newspapers for libel* | [as adj.] *a libel action.* ■ a false and malicious statement about a person. ■ a thing or circumstance that brings undeserved discredit on a person by misrepresentation.
2 (in admiralty, civil, and ecclesiastical law) a plaintiff's written declaration.
▸ v. (**li•beled, li•bel•ing**; Brit. **li•belled, li•bel•ling**) [trans.]
1 defame (someone) by publishing a libel: *she alleged the magazine had libeled her.*
■ make a false and malicious statement about.
2 (in admiralty, civil, and ecclesiastical law) bring a suit against (someone).
DERIVATIVES **li•bel•er** n.
ORIGIN Middle English (in the general sense 'a document, a written statement'): via Old French from Latin *libellus*, diminutive of *liber* 'book.'

li•bel•ous /'lībələs/ (Brit. **li•bel•lous**)

▶ adj. containing or constituting a libel: *a libelous newspaper story.*

DERIVATIVES **li•bel•ous•ly** adv.

lib•er•ty /'libərtē/

▶ n. (pl. **-ies**) the state of being free within society from oppressive restrictions imposed by authority on one's way of life, behavior, or political views: *compulsory retirement would interfere with individual liberty.*

■ (usu. **liberties**) an instance of this; a right or privilege, esp. a statutory one: *the Bill of Rights was intended to secure basic civil liberties.* ■ the state of not being imprisoned or enslaved: *people who have lost property or liberty without due process.*

PHRASES **at liberty** not imprisoned: *he was at liberty for three months before he was recaptured.*

ORIGIN late Middle English: from Old French *liberte*, from Latin *libertas*, from *liber* 'free.'

li•cense /'līsəns/

▶ n. (Brit. **li•cence**) a permit from an authority to own or use something, do a particular thing, or carry on a trade (esp. in alcoholic beverages): *a gun license* | [as adj.] *vehicle license fees.*

■ formal or official permission to do something: *logging is permitted **under license** from the Forest Service.*

▶ v. (Brit. also **li•cence**) [trans.] (often **be licensed**) grant a license to (someone or something) to permit the use of something or to allow an activity to take place: *brokers must be licensed to sell health-related insurance* | [with obj. and infinitive] *he ought not to have been licensed to fly a plane* | [as adj.] (**licensing**) *a licensing authority.*

■ authorize the use, performance, or release of (something): *the drug is already licensed for human use* | *firearms importers must be federally licensed.*

DERIVATIVES **li•cens•a•ble** adj.; **li•cens•er** n.; **li•cen• sor** /'līsənsər; ˌlīsən'sôr/ n.
ORIGIN late Middle English: via Old French from Latin *licentia* 'freedom, licentiousness' (in medieval Latin 'authority, permission'), from *licere* 'be lawful or permitted.'

li•censed /'līsənst/
▸ adj. having an official license: *a licensed taxi operator.*

li•cen•see /ˌlīsən'sē/
▸ n. the holder of a license.

lie /lī/
▸ v. (**lied** /līd/, **ly•ing** /'lī-iNG/; past **lay** /lā/; past part. **lain** /lān/) [intrans.] (of an action, charge, or claim) be admissible or sustainable: *judicial review of such a declaratory ruling would have lain in the court of appeals.*
ORIGIN Old English *licgan*, of Germanic origin; related to Dutch *liggen* and German *liegen*, from an Indo-European root shared by Greek *lektron, lekhos* and Latin *lectus* 'bed.'

lie de•tec•tor /'lī di,tektər/
▸ n. an instrument for determining whether a person is telling the truth by testing for physiological changes considered to be associated with lying. Compare with POLYGRAPH.

lien /'lē(ə)n/
▸ n. a right to take or keep possession of property belonging to another person until a debt owed by that person is discharged: *creditor holds a judicial **lien against** the property in the amount of $2,472.01.*
ORIGIN mid 16th cent.: from French, via Old French *loien* from Latin *ligamen* 'bond,' from *ligare* 'to bind.'

life in•ter•est /'līf 'int(ə)rist/
▶ n. a right to property that a person holds for life but cannot dispose of further.

life sen•tence /'līf 'sentns/
▶ n. a criminal punishment of imprisonment for life.

lim•i•ta•tion /ˌlimi'tāsHən/
▶ n. **1** the action of limiting something: *the limitation of local authorities' powers.*
2 (also **limitation period**) a legally specified period beyond which an action may be defeated or a property right is not to continue. See also STATUTE OF LIMITATIONS.
ORIGIN late Middle English: from Latin *limitatio(n-),* from the verb *limitare,* from *limes* 'boundary, frontier.'

liq•ui•date /'likwiˌdāt/
▶ v. [trans.] close the affairs of (a company or firm) by ascertaining liabilities and apportioning assets: *no concluding inventory is necessary until the fiduciary liquidates the business.*
■ [intrans.] (of a company) undergo such a process. ■ convert (assets) into cash: *the plan allows them to liquidate $10,000,000 worth of property over seven years.* ■ pay off (a debt): *this system allows us to wait until recording the expense to liquidate the obligation.*
DERIVATIVES **liq•ui•da•tion** /ˌlikwi'dāsHən/ n.
ORIGIN mid 16th cent. (in the sense 'set out (accounts) clearly'): from medieval Latin *liquidat-* 'made clear,' from the verb *liquidare,* from Latin *liquidus,* from *liquere* 'be liquid.'

lis pen•dens /'lis 'pendenz/
▶ n. a pending legal action: *there is now a lis pendens against the Jones's home.*
■ a formal notice of this.
ORIGIN Latin.

lit•er•ar•y ex•ec•u•tor /ˈlitəˌrerē igˌzekyətər/
▸ **n.** a person entrusted with a dead writer's papers and copyrighted and unpublished works.

lit•i•gant /ˈlitəgənt/
▸ **n.** a person involved in a lawsuit.
▸ **adj.** [postpositive] archaic involved in a lawsuit: *the parties litigant.*
ORIGIN mid 17th cent.: from French, from Latin *litigant-* 'carrying on a lawsuit,' from the verb *litigare* (see LITIGATE).

lit•i•gate /ˈlitəˌgāt/
▸ **v.** [intrans.] go to law; be a party to or subject of a lawsuit: *that issue has been fully litigated.*
■ be counsel to a party to a lawsuit. ■ [trans.] take (a claim or a dispute) to a court of law: *once a taxpayer has litigated a particular year, no other litigation of that year is permitted.*
DERIVATIVES **lit•i•ga•tion** /ˌlitəˈgāsHən/ n.; **lit•i•ga•tive** /ˈlitəˌgātiv/ adj.; **lit•i•ga•tor** /ˈlitəˌgātər/ n.
ORIGIN early 17th cent.: from Latin *litigat-* 'disputed in a lawsuit,' from the verb *litigare*, from *lis, lit-* 'lawsuit.'

li•ti•gious /ləˈtijəs/
▸ **adj.** concerned with lawsuits or litigation: *defense nuclear facilities are increasingly vulnerable to litigious proceedings.*
■ unreasonably prone to go to law to settle disputes. ■ suitable to become the subject of a lawsuit.
DERIVATIVES **li•ti•gious•ly** adv.; **li•ti•gious•ness** n.
ORIGIN late Middle English: from Old French *litigieux* or Latin *litigiosus*, from *litigium* 'litigation,' from *lis, lit-* 'lawsuit.'

liv•ing will /ˈliviNG ˈwil/
▸ **n.** a written statement detailing a person's desires regarding their medical treatment in circumstances in

which they are no longer able to express informed consent, esp. an advance directive.

LLB

▸ **abbr.** Bachelor of Laws, formerly the first degree in law.
ORIGIN from Latin *legum baccalaureus*.

LLD

▸ **abbr.** Doctor of Laws, typically an honorary degree.
ORIGIN from Latin *legum doctor*.

LLM

▸ **abbr.** Master of Laws.
ORIGIN from Latin *legum magister*.

lo•cus /ˈlōkəs/

▸ **n.** (pl. **lo•ci** /ˈlō͵sī; -͵sē; -͵kī; -͵kē/) the place where a particular event, especially a trespass, occurred: *a suspected locus of marijuana dealing*.
ORIGIN early 18th cent.: from Latin, 'place.'

lodge /läj/

▸ **v.** [trans.] present (a complaint, appeal, claim, etc.) formally to the proper authorities: *he has 28 days in which to lodge an appeal*.

loi•ter /ˈloitər/

▸ **v.** [intrans.] stand or wait around idly or without apparent purpose: *report suspicious activity or persons loitering around bike racks to the police*.
DERIVATIVES **loi•ter•er** n.
ORIGIN late Middle English: perhaps from Middle Dutch *loteren* 'wag around.'

loss of con•sor•ti•um /ˈlôs əv kənˈsôrsHəm/

▸ see **CONSORTIUM**.

low•er court /ˈlōər ˈkôrt/
▶ n. a court whose decisions may be overruled by another court on appeal.

lynch /linCH/
▶ v. [trans.] (of a mob) kill (someone), esp. by hanging, for an alleged offense without legal authority: *four of eight suspected thieves were lynched when a mob broke into the Nyaburara subcounty jail.*
DERIVATIVES **lynch•er** n.
ORIGIN mid 19th cent.: from *Lynch's law,* early form of *lynch law*'the practice of killing an alleged criminal by lynching,' named after Capt. William *Lynch,* head of a self-constituted judicial tribunal in Virginia *c.*1780.

M

mag•is•trate /'mæjə,strāt/
▸ n. a civil officer or lay judge who administers the law, esp. one who conducts a court that deals with minor offenses and holds preliminary hearings for more serious ones.
■ in federal courts, a lower judicial officer.
DERIVATIVES **mag•is•tra•ture** /'mæjis,strāCHər; -strə,CHŌŌ(ə)r/ n.
ORIGIN late Middle English: from Latin *magistratus* 'administrator,' from *magister* 'master.'

main•te•nance /'mānt(ə)nəns/
▸ n. the provision of financial support for a person's living expenses, or the support so provided.
■ alimony or child support: *spousal maintenance*.
ORIGIN Middle English (in the sense 'aiding a party in a legal action without lawful cause'): from Old French, from *maintenir*, from Latin *manu tenere* 'hold in the hand.'

ma•jor•i•ty /mə'jôrətē; -'jär-/
▸ n. (pl. **ma•jor•i•ties**) the age when a person is legally considered an adult, in most contexts either 18 or 21: *a minor claimant may wait until her majority to file a claim on her own behalf.*
ORIGIN mid 16th cent. (denoting superiority): from French *majorité*, from medieval Latin *majoritas*, from Latin *major*, comparative of *magnus* 'great.'

mal•fea•sance /mæl'fēzəns/
▸ n. wrongdoing, esp. misconduct in the performance of duty by a public official: *corporate malfeasance*.
DERIVATIVES **mal•fea•sant** /mæl'fēzənt/ n. & adj.

ORIGIN late 17th cent.: from Anglo-Norman French *malfaisance*, from *mal-* 'evil' + Old French *faisance* 'activity.' Compare with MISFEASANCE.

mal•ice /'mælis/
▶ n. wrongful or harmful intention, esp. as increasing the guilt of certain offenses: *petitioner's papers continuously assert that respondent **acted with malice** and in bad faith*.
ORIGIN Middle English: via Old French from Latin *malitia*, from *malus* 'bad.'

mal•ice a•fore•thought /'mælis ə'fôr‚тнôt/
▶ n. a special form of the intention to kill or harm, which is held to distinguish manslaughter from murder.

ma•li•cious /mə'lishəs/
▶ adj. characterized by malice, especially malice aforethought; intending or intended to do harm: *malicious destruction of property*.
DERIVATIVES **ma•li•cious•ly** adv.; **ma•li•cious•ness** n.
ORIGIN Middle English (also in the sense 'wicked'): from Old French *malicios*, from Latin *malitiosus*, from *malitia* (see MALICE).

mal•prac•tice /mæl'præktis/
▶ n. improper, illegal, or negligent professional treatment or activity, esp. by a medical practitioner, lawyer, or public official: *victims of medical malpractice | investigations into malpractices and abuses of power*.

man•da•mus /mæn'dāməs/
▶ n. a judicial writ issued as a command to an inferior court or ordering a person or agency to perform a public or statutory duty: *a writ of mandamus*.
ORIGIN mid 16th cent.: from Latin, literally 'we command.'

man•date /'mæn,dāt/

▸ **n.** an official order or commission to do something: *a mandate to seek the release of political prisoners.*

■ a commission by which a party is entrusted to perform a service, esp. without payment and with indemnity against loss by that party. ■ an order from an appellate court to a lower court to take a specific action. ■ a written authority enabling someone to carry out transactions on another's bank account.

▸ **v.** [trans.] require (something) to be done; make mandatory: *the government began mandating better car safety.*

ORIGIN early 16th cent.: from Latin *mandatum* 'something commanded,' neuter past participle of *mandare*, from *manus* 'hand' + *dare* 'give.'

man•da•to•ry /'mændə,tôrē/

▸ **adj.** required by law or rules; compulsory: *wearing helmets was made mandatory for cyclists.*

DERIVATIVES **man•da•to•ri•ly** /'mændə,tôrəlē/ **adv.**

ORIGIN late 15th cent.: from late Latin *mandatorius*, from Latin *mandatum* 'something commanded.'

man•slaugh•ter /'mæn,slôtər/

▸ **n.** the crime of killing a human being without malice aforethought, or otherwise in circumstances not amounting to murder: *the defendant was convicted of manslaughter.*

ma•re clau•sum /,märā 'klowsəm; 'klôzəm/

▸ **n.** (pl. **ma•ri•a clau•sa** /,märēə 'klowsə; 'klôzə/) a sea or body of navigable water under the jurisdiction of a particular country.

ORIGIN Latin, 'closed sea.'

ma•re li•be•rum /,märā 'lēbə,rŏŏm; 'lībərəm/

▸ **n.** (pl. **ma•ri•a li•be•ra** /,märēə 'lēbərə; 'lībərə/) a sea open to all nations.

ORIGIN Latin, literally 'free sea.'

mar•riage /'mærij; 'mer-/

▸ n. the formal union of a man and a woman, typically recognized by law, by which they become husband and wife.

■ a relationship between married people or the period for which it lasts: *the children from his first marriage.*

PHRASES **by marriage** as a result of a marriage: *a distant cousin by marriage.* **marriage of convenience** a marriage concluded to achieve a practical purpose.

ORIGIN Middle English: from Old French *mariage*, from *marier* 'marry.'

mar•riage li•cense /'mærij ˌlīsəns; 'merij/

▸ n. a document giving official permission, as from a county, to marry.

■ a copy of the record of a legal marriage, with details of names, date, etc.

mar•ry[1] /'mærē; 'merē/

▸ v. (**mar•ries, mar•ried**) [trans.] join in marriage: *I was married in church | the priest who married us*

■ take (someone) as one's wife or husband in marriage: *Eric asked me to marry him.* ■ [intrans.] enter into marriage: *they had no plans to marry.* ■ [intrans.] (**marry into**) become a member of (a family) by marriage. ■ (of a parent or guardian) give (a son or daughter) in marriage, esp. for reasons of expediency: *her parents married her to a wealthy landowner.*

ORIGIN Middle English: from Old French *marier*, from Latin *maritare*, from *maritus*, literally 'married,' (as a noun) 'husband.'

mar•shal /'märsHəl/

▸ n. a federal or municipal law officer, typically with specified duties relating to court functions.

■ the head of a police department. ■ the head of a fire department.

DERIVATIVES **mar•shal•ship** /ˈmärSHəlˌSHip/ **n.**
ORIGIN Middle English (denoting a high-ranking officer of state): from Old French *mareschal* 'blacksmith, commander,' from late Latin *mariscalcus*, from Germanic elements meaning 'horse' and 'servant.'

mar•tial law /ˈmärSHəl ˈlô/
▸ **n.** military government involving the suspension of ordinary law.

mas•ter /ˈmæstər/
▸ **n.** an officer appointed to assist the judge in a court case, as by making special findings.
ORIGIN Old English *mæg(i)ster* (later reinforced by Old French *maistre*), from Latin *magister*; probably related to *magis* 'more' (i.e., 'more important').

ma•te•ri•al /məˈtirēəl/
▸ **adj.** (of evidence or a fact) significant or influential, esp. to the extent of determining a cause or affecting a judgment: *information that could be **material to** a murder inquiry.*
ORIGIN late Middle English (in the sense 'relating to matter'): from late Latin *materialis*, adjective from Latin *materia* 'matter.'

ma•te•ri•al•i•ty /məˌtirēˈælətē/
▸ **n.** (pl. **ma•te•ri•al•i•ties**) the quality of being significant or influential: *the applicant must establish materiality on the balance of probabilities.*

mat•ter /ˈmætər/
▸ **n.** something that is to be tried or proved in court; a case: *the Supreme Court granted certiorari in the matter of the second WorldCom order.*
PHRASES **a matter of record** see RECORD.
ORIGIN Middle English: via Old French from Latin

materia 'timber, substance,' also 'subject of discourse,' from *mater* 'mother.'

may•hem /'mᾱhem/
▶ n. chiefly historical the crime of maliciously injuring or maiming someone, originally so as to render the victim defenseless.
ORIGIN early 16th cent.: from Old French *mahaignier*, from which *maim* is derived.

meas•ure /'mezHər/
▶ n. a legislative bill: *the Senate passed the measure by a 48–30 vote.*
ORIGIN Middle English (as a noun in the senses 'moderation,' 'instrument for measuring,' 'unit of capacity'): from Old French *mesure*, from Latin *mensura*, from *mens-* 'measured,' from the verb *metiri*.

med•i•cal ju•ris•pru•dence /'medikəl ,jŏŏri'sprŏŏdns/
▶ n. forensic medicine.

mens re•a /menz 'rēə/
▶ n. the intention or knowledge of wrongdoing that constitutes part of a crime, as opposed to the action or conduct of the accused. Compare with ACTUS REUS.
ORIGIN mid 19th cent.: Latin, literally 'guilty mind.'

men•tal cru•el•ty /'mentl 'krŏŏəltē/
▶ n. conduct that makes another person, especially one's spouse, suffer but does not involve physical assault: *a divorce on the grounds of mental cruelty.*

merge /mərj/
▶ v. combine or cause to combine to form a single entity, esp. a commercial organization: [intrans.] *the utility companies are cutting costs and **merging with** other companies* | [trans.] *the company plans to **merge** its US oil*

*production operations **with** those of a London-based organization.*

ORIGIN mid 17th cent. (in the sense 'immerse (oneself)'): from Latin *mergere* 'to dip, plunge.' The use in legal contexts is from Anglo-Norman French *merger*.

merg•er /ˈmərjər/
▸ n. a combination of two things, esp. companies, into one: *a **merger between** two supermarket chains | local companies ripe for merger or acquisition.*
■ the incorporation of one right, estate, claim, etc., into another.
ORIGIN early 18th cent.: from Anglo-Norman French *merger* (verb used as a noun): see MERGE.

mer•ger clause /ˈmərjər ˌklôz/
▸ n. in a contract, provision stating that the written agreement constitutes the entire agreement between the parties.

mer•i•to•ri•ous /ˈmeriˌtôrēəs/
▸ adj. (of an action or claim) likely to succeed on the merits of the case: *defendant failed to raise even a hint of a defense that the court considered meritorious.*
DERIVATIVES **mer•i•to•ri•ous•ly** adv.; **mer•i•to•ri•ous•ness** n.
ORIGIN late Middle English (in the sense 'entitling a person to reward'): from late Latin *meritorius* (from *merit-* 'earned,' from the verb *mereri*) + *-ous*.

mer•its /ˈmerits/
▸ n. the intrinsic rights and wrongs of a case, outside of any other considerations, such as jurisdiction: *a plaintiff who has a good arguable case **on the merits**.*
ORIGIN Middle English (originally in the sense 'deserved reward or punishment'): via Old French from Latin *meritum* 'due reward,' from *mereri* 'earn, deserve.'

mesne /mēn/
> **adj.** in the midst of an action; intermediate: *the Escrow Account is not subject to lien, garnishment, attachment, or any other similar process, mesne or final, on the part of the bank.*
ORIGIN late Middle English (as adverb and noun): from legal French, variant of Anglo-Norman French *meen* 'middle.'

mesne prof•its /'mēn ˌpräfits/
> **plural n.** the profits of an estate received by a tenant in wrongful possession and recoverable by the landlord.

mes•suage /'meswij/
> **n.** a dwelling house with outbuildings and land assigned to its use.
ORIGIN late Middle English: from Anglo-Norman French, based on Latin *manere* 'dwell.'

mil•i•tar•y law /'miliˌterē ˌlô/
> **n.** the law governing the armed forces.

min•i•mum wage /'minəməm 'wāj/
> **n.** the lowest wage permitted by law or by a special agreement (such as one with a labor union).

min•is•te•ri•al /ˌminə'stirēəl/
> **adj.** of or relating to the duties of a government official: *ministerial acts.*
DERIVATIVES **min•is•te•ri•al•ly** adv.
ORIGIN mid 16th cent.: from French *ministériel* or late Latin *ministerialis*, from Latin *ministerium* 'ministry.'

Mi•ran•da /mə'rændə/
> **adj.** denoting or relating to the duty of the police to inform a person taken into custody of their right to legal counsel and the right to remain silent under questioning: *the patrolman read Lee his **Miranda rights.***

ORIGIN mid 20th cent.: from *Miranda* v. Arizona (1966), the case that led to this ruling by the US Supreme Court.

mis•car•riage of jus•tice /mis'kærij əv 'jəstis/
▸ n. a failure of a court or judicial system to attain the ends of justice, esp. one that results in the conviction of an innocent person.

mis•chief /'misCHif/
▸ n. harm or trouble caused by someone or something: *criminal mischief.*
ORIGIN late Middle English (denoting misfortune or distress): from Old French *meschief*, from the verb *meschever*, from *mes-* 'adversely' + *chever* 'come to an end' (from *chef* 'head').

mis•de•mean•ant /ˌmisdə'mēnənt/
▸ n. formal a person convicted of a misdemeanor.
◾ a person guilty of misconduct.
ORIGIN early 19th cent.: from archaic *misdemean* 'misbehave' + *-ant.*

mis•de•mean•or /'misdi,mēnər/ (Brit. **mis•de•mean•our**)
▸ n. a crime regarded in the US (and formerly in the UK) as less serious than a felony.

mis•fea•sance /mis'fēzəns/
▸ n. a transgression, esp. the wrongful exercise of lawful authority.
ORIGIN early 17th cent.: from Old French *mesfaisance*, from *mesfaire*, from *mes-* 'wrongly' + *faire* 'do' (from Latin *facere*). Compare with MALFEASANCE, NONFEASANCE.

mis•pri•sion /mis'priZHən/ (also **mis•pri•sion of trea•son** or **fel•o•ny**)
▸ n. chiefly historical the deliberate concealment of one's knowledge of a treasonable act or a felony.

ORIGIN late Middle English: from Old French *mesprision* 'error,' from *mesprendre*, from *mes-* 'wrongly' + *prendre* 'to take.'

mis•rep•re•sen•ta•tion /mis,reprəzən'tāsHən/
▶ n. a false or misleading statement: *persons who suffer from a realtor's misrepresentation may be able to recover their losses.*
■ the legal action to provide a remedy for a false or misleading statement.

mis•tri•al /'mis,trī(ə)l/
▶ n. a trial rendered invalid through an error in the proceedings: *the juvenile court judge disqualified himself because of concerns about his impartiality and **declared a mistrial**.*
■ an inconclusive trial, such as one in which the jury cannot agree on a verdict.

mit•i•ga•tion /,miti'gāsHən/
▶ n. the action of reducing the severity, seriousness, or painfulness of something.
PHRASES **in mitigation** so as to make something, esp. a crime, appear less serious and thus be punished more leniently: *in mitigation she said her client had been deeply depressed.*
DERIVATIVES **mit•i•gate** /'miti,gāt/ v.; **mit•i•gat•ing as adj.**: *mitigating circumstances.*
ORIGIN late Middle English: from Old French, or from Latin *mitigatio(n-)*, from the verb *mitigare* 'alleviate.'

moi•e•ty /'moi-itē/
▶ n. (pl. **moi•e•ties**) formal technical each of two parts into which a thing is or can be divided, especially a joint tenancy.
■ a part or portion, esp. a lesser share.
ORIGIN late Middle English: from Old French *moite*, from Latin *medietas* 'middle,' from *medius* 'mid, middle.'

moot /mo͞ot/

▸**adj.** subject to debate, dispute, or uncertainty, and typically not admitting of a final decision.

▸**n.** a mock trial set up to examine a hypothetical case as an academic exercise.

ORIGIN Old English *mōt* 'assembly or meeting' and *mōtian* 'to converse,' of Germanic origin; related to *meet*. The adjective (originally an attributive noun use: see MOOT COURT) dates from the mid 16th cent.

moot court

▸**n.** a mock court at which law students argue imaginary cases for practice.

mor•a•to•ri•um /ˌmôrəˈtôrēəm; ˌmär-/

▸**n.** (pl. **mor•a•to•ri•ums** or **mor•a•to•ri•a** /ˌmôrəˈtôrēə; ˌmär-/) a legal authorization to debtors to postpone payment.

■ the period of this postponement.

ORIGIN late 19th cent.: modern Latin, neuter (used as a noun) of late Latin *moratorius* 'delaying,' from Latin *morat-* 'delayed,' from the verb *morari*, from *mora* 'delay.'

mort•gage /ˈmôrgij/

▸**n.** the conveyance of real (or personal) property by a debtor to a creditor as security for a debt (esp. one incurred by the debtor in the purchase of the property), on the condition that it shall be returned on payment of the debt within a certain period.

■ a deed effecting such a transaction. ■ a loan obtained through the conveyance of property as security: *I put down a hundred thousand in cash and took out a mortgage for the rest.*

▸**v.** [trans.] (often **be mortgaged**) convey (a property) to a creditor as security on a loan: *the estate was mortgaged up to the hilt.*

DERIVATIVES **mort•gage•a•ble adj.**

ORIGIN late Middle English: from Old French, literally 'dead pledge,' from *mort* (from Latin *mortuus* 'dead') + *gage* 'pledge.'

mort•ga•gee /ˌmôrgəˈjē/
▶ n. the lender in a mortgage, typically a bank.

mort•ga•gor /ˌmôrgiˈjôr; ˈmôrgijər/
▶ n. the borrower in a mortgage, typically a homeowner.

mo•tion /ˈmōSHən/
▶ n. an application for a rule or order of court: *the agency's motion to block the acquisition was denied.*
ORIGIN late Middle English: via Old French from Latin *motio(n-)*, from *movere* 'to move.'

mouth•piece /ˈmowTH,pēs/
▶ n. informal a lawyer.

mov•a•ble /ˈmōovəbəl/ (also **move•a•ble**)
▶ adj. (of property) of the nature of a chattel, as distinct from land or buildings; personal.
▶ n. (usu. **movables**) property or possessions not including land or buildings: *we have not appraised the movables as part of the real estate.*
■ an article of furniture that may be removed from a house, as distinct from a fixture.
ORIGIN late Middle English: from Old French, from *moveir* 'to move.'

mov•ant /ˈmōovənt/
▶ n. a person who applies to or petitions a court or judge for a ruling in his or her favor.
ORIGIN late 19th cent.: from *move* + *-ant*.

move /mōov/
▶ v. [trans.] make a formal request or application to (a court or assembly) for something: *his family **moved** the*

court for adequate "maintenance expenses" to run the household.

ORIGIN Middle English: from Old French *moveir*, from Latin *movere*.

mur•der /ˈmərdər/

▶ n. the unlawful premeditated killing of one human being by another. Compare with MANSLAUGHTER.

▶ v. [trans.] kill (someone) unlawfully and with premeditation.

PHRASES **murder one** (or **two**) informal first-degree (or second-degree) murder.

DERIVATIVES **mur•der•er** n.; **mur•der•ess** /ˈmərdərəs/ n.

ORIGIN Old English *morthor*, of Germanic origin; related to Dutch *moord* and German *Mord*, from an Indo-European root shared by Sanskrit *mará* 'death' and Latin *mors*; reinforced in Middle English by Old French *murdre*.

N

neg•li•gence /'neglijəns/
▶ n. failure to use reasonable care, resulting in damage or injury to another: *manslaughter by negligence.*

neg•li•gent /'neglijənt/
▶ adj. failing to take proper or reasonable care in doing something: *directors have been negligent in the performance of their duties.*
DERIVATIVES **neg•li•gent•ly** adv.
ORIGIN late Middle English: from Old French, or from Latin *negligent-* 'disregarding,' from the verb *negligere* (variant of *neglegere* 'disregard, slight.'

ne•go•ti•a•ble /nə'gōsH(ē)əbəl/
▶ adj. open to discussion or modification: *the price was not negotiable.*
■ (of a document) able to be transferred or assigned to the legal ownership of another person: *negotiable securities.*
DERIVATIVES **ne•go•ti•a•bil•i•ty** /nə,gōsH(ē)ə'bilitē/ n.

ni•si /'nīsī/
▶ adj. [postpositive] (of a decree, order, or rule) taking effect or having validity only after a specified period of time, as long as certain changes of condition have not occurred: *a decree nisi.*
ORIGIN mid 19th cent.: from Latin, literally 'unless.'

no-fault /'nō 'fôlt/
▶ adj. [attrib.] not assigning fault or blame, in particular:
■ denoting an insurance policy that is valid regardless of whether the policyholder was at fault: *no-fault automobile insurance.* ■ denoting an insurance or compensa-

tion plan (esp. one covering medical or industrial accidents) whereby a claimant need not legally prove negligence against any party. ■ of or denoting a form of divorce granted without requiring one party to prove that the other is to blame for the breakdown of the marriage.

no-knock /'nō 'näk/
▶ **adj.** denoting or relating to a search or raid by the police made without warning or identification: *a no-knock raid.*

nol•le pros /ˌnälē 'präs/ (also **nol-pros** /ˌnôl 'präs/) (abbr.: **nol. pros.**)
▶ **v.** (**prossed, pros•sing**) [trans.] abandon or dismiss (a suit) by issuing a nolle prosequi: *all of the bills are marked "fugitive" and were nolle prossed in 1952.*

nol•le pros•e•qui /ˌnälē 'präsiˌkwī/
▶ **n.** a formal notice of abandonment by a plaintiff or prosecutor of all or part of a suit or action.
■ the entry of this in a court record.
ORIGIN late 17th cent.: Latin, literally 'be unwilling to pursue.'

no•lo con•ten•de•re /ˌnōlō kən'tendərē/
▶ **n.** (also **no•lo**) a plea by which a criminal defendant accepts conviction as though a guilty plea had been entered but does not admit guilt: *he pleaded nolo contendere in Providence County Superior Court to a charge of possession of heroin.*
ORIGIN Latin, literally 'I do not wish to contend.'

non•ap•pear•ance /ˌnänə'pirəns/
▶ **n.** failure to appear or be present in a court of law, esp. as a witness, defendant, or plaintiff.

non•cap•i•tal /nän'kæpitl/
▸ adj. (of an offense) not punishable by death.

non•de•liv•er•y /ˌnändi'livərē/
▸ n. failure to deliver property: *nondelivery of merchandise ordered on the Internet.*

non•fea•sance /nän'fēzəns/
▸ n. failure to perform an act that one should perform: *the injury is directly traceable to the Commission's alleged nonfeasance.*

non•ju•ry /nän'joŏrē/
▸ adj. denoting a trial or legal action not involving or requiring a jury.

non•suit /nän'soōt/
▸ v. [trans.] (of a judge or court) subject (a plaintiff) to the stoppage of a suit on the grounds of failure to make a legal case or bring sufficient evidence. *the judge at the circuit nonsuited the plaintiff, then fifth district affirmed.*
▸ n. the stoppage of a suit on such grounds: *a motion for nonsuit.*
ORIGIN late Middle English (as a noun): from Anglo-Norman French, literally 'not pursuing.'

no•ta•rize /'nōtəˌrīz/
▸ v. [trans.] have (a document) legalized by a notary.
■ (of a notary) legalize a document by certifying its authenticity.

no•ta•ry /'nōtərē/ (in full **no•ta•ry pub•lic**)
▸ n. (pl. **no•ta•ries**) a person authorized to perform certain legal formalities, esp. to certify contracts, deeds, and other documents.
DERIVATIVES **no•tar•i•al** /nō'terēəl/ adj.

ORIGIN Middle English (in the sense 'clerk or secretary'): from Latin *notarius* 'secretary,' from *nota* 'mark.'

no•va•tion /nōˈvāsʜən/

▶ **n.** the substitution of a new contract (especially with a substitute debtor) in place of an old one.

DERIVATIVES **no•vate** /ˈnōvāt; nōˈvāt/ **v.**

ORIGIN early 16th cent.: from late Latin *novatio(n-)*, from the verb *novare* 'make new.'

nui•sance /ˈn(y)o͞osəns/

▶ **n.** a person, thing, or circumstance causing inconvenience or annoyance.

■ (also **private nuisance**) an unlawful interference with the use and enjoyment of a person's property. ■ see **PUBLIC NUISANCE.**

ORIGIN late Middle English (in the sense 'injury, hurt'): from Old French, 'hurt,' from the verb *nuire*, from Latin *nocere* 'to harm.'

null /nəl/

▶ **adj.** having no legal or binding force; invalid: *the establishment of a new interim government was declared **null and void**.*

ORIGIN late Middle English: from French *nul*, *nulle*, from Latin *nullus* 'none,' from *ne* 'not' + *ullus* 'any.'

nul•li•ty /ˈnəlitē/

▶ **n.** (pl. **nul•li•ties**) an act or thing that is legally void: *the decision is not a nullity simply because it has been appealed.*

■ the state of being legally void; invalidity, esp. of a marriage.

ORIGIN mid 16th cent.: from French *nullité*, from medieval Latin *nullitas*, from Latin *nullus* 'none.'

nun•cu•pa•tive /ˈnənɢkyə͵pātiv/

▶ **adj.** (of a will or testament) declared orally as opposed to in writing, often by a mortally wounded person: *nuncupative wills are valid only in a minority of states.*

ORIGIN mid 16th cent.: from late Latin *nuncupativus*, from Latin *nuncupat-* 'named, declared,' from the verb *nuncupare*.

O

oath /ōTH/
▸ n. (pl. **oaths** /ōTHs; ōT͟Hz/) a sworn declaration that one will tell the truth, esp. in a court of law.
PHRASES **under oath** having sworn to tell the truth, esp. in a court of law.
ORIGIN Old English *āth*, of Germanic origin; related to Dutch *eed* and German *Eid*.

ob•i•ter dic•tum /'ōbiṯər 'diktəm/
▸ n. (pl. **ob•i•ter dic•ta** /'ōbiṯər 'diktə/) a judge's incidental expression of opinion, not essential to the decision of a case and not establishing precedent.
ORIGIN Latin *obiter* 'in passing' + *dictum* 'something that is said.'

ob•li•ga•tion /ˌäbli'gāsHən/
▸ n. the condition of being morally or legally bound to do something: *a juvenile **under obligation** to pay restitution may petition the court for modification of the restitution order.*
■ a binding agreement committing a person to a payment or other action. ■ a document containing a binding agreement; a written contract or bond.
DERIVATIVES **ob•li•ga•tion•al** /ˌäbli'gāsHənl/ **adj.**
ORIGIN Middle English (in the sense 'formal promise'): via Old French from Latin *obligatio(n-)*, from the verb *obligare*, *ob-* 'toward' + *ligare* ' to bind.'

ob•li•gee /ˌäbli'jē/
▸ n. a person to whom another is bound by contract or other legal procedure. Compare with OBLIGOR.

ob•li•gor /ˌäbli'gôr/
▸ n. a person who is bound to another by contract or other legal procedure. Compare with OBLIGEE.

ob•scene /əbˈsēn/
▶ **adj.** (of the portrayal or description of sexual matters) offensive or disgusting by accepted standards of morality and decency: *obscene literature.*
DERIVATIVES **ob•scene•ly adv.**
ORIGIN late 16th cent.: from French *obscène* or Latin *obscaenus* 'ill-omened or abominable.'

ob•scen•i•ty /əbˈsenitē/
▶ **n.** (pl. **ob•scen•i•ties**) the state or quality of being obscene; obscene behavior, language, or images: *the book was banned for obscenity.*
■ an extremely offensive word or expression: *they muttered obscenities.*
ORIGIN late 16th cent.: from French *obscénité* or Latin *obscaenitas*, from *obscaenus* (see OBSCENE).

ob•struct /əbˈstrəkt; äb-/
▶ **v.** [trans.] commit the offense of intentionally hindering (a legal process): *the defendant knowingly obstructed a federal grand jury investigation.*
DERIVATIVES **ob•struc•tion** /əbˈstrəkSHən; äb-/ n.; **ob•struc•tor** /əbˈstrəktər; äb-/ n.
ORIGIN late 16th cent.: from Latin *obstruct-* 'blocked up,' from the verb *obstruere*, from *ob-* 'against' + *struere* 'build, pile up.'

oc•cu•pan•cy /ˈäkyəpənsē/
▶ **n.** the action or fact of occupying a place: *the right of private occupancy of a room* .

oc•cu•pant /ˈäkyəpənt/
▶ **n.** a person holding property, esp. land, in actual possession.
ORIGIN late 16th cent. (in the legal sense 'person who establishes a title'): from French, or from Latin *occupant-* 'seizing,' from the verb *occupare.*

of•fense /əˈfens/ (Brit. **of•fence**)

▸ n. a breach of a law or rule; an illegal act: *neither offense violates any federal law.*

ORIGIN late Middle English: from Old French *offens* 'misdeed,' from Latin *offensus* 'annoyance,' reinforced by French *offense*, from Latin *offensa* 'a striking against, a hurt, or displeasure'; based on Latin *offendere* 'strike against.'

of•fi•cer /ˈôfisər; ˈäf-/

▸ n. a bailiff.

ORIGIN Middle English: via Anglo-Norman French from medieval Latin *officiarius*, from Latin *officium* 'performance of a task.'

Old Bai•ley /ˌōld ˈbālē/ the central criminal court in London, England.

o•mis•sion /ōˈmisHən/

▸ n. a failure to do something, esp. something that one has a moral or legal obligation to do: *they were fined for a wrongful omission of material information.*

DERIVATIVES **o•mis•sive** /ōˈmisiv/ **adj.**

ORIGIN late Middle English: from late Latin *omissio(n-)*, from the verb *omittere*, from *ob-* 'down' + *mittere* 'let go.'

o•pen•ing /ˈōp(ə)niNG/

▸ n. an attorney's preliminary statement of a case in a court of law: [as adj.] *the defense's opening statement.*

o•pin•ion /əˈpinyən/

▸ n. a formal statement of reasons for a judgment given: *a five-justice majority opinion.*

■ a lawyer's or official's advice on the merits of a case or legalities of an issue.

ORIGIN Middle English: via Old French from Latin *opinio(n-)*, from the stem of *opinari* 'think, believe.'

or•deal /ôr'dēl/
▸ n. historical an ancient test of guilt or innocence by subjection of the accused to severe pain, survival of which was taken as divine proof of innocence.
ORIGIN Old English *ordāl*, *ordēl*, of Germanic origin; related to German *urteilen* 'give judgment,' from a base meaning 'share out.' The word is not found in Middle English (except once in Chaucer's *Troylus*); modern use of this sense began in the late 16th cent.

or•der /'ôrdər/
▸ n. 1 the prescribed or established procedure followed by a meeting, legislative assembly, debate, or court of law: *the meeting was **called to order**.*
2 a written direction of a court or judge: *a judge's order forbidding the reporting of evidence.*
■ a written direction to pay money or deliver property: *a spousal maintenance order.*
▸ v. [reporting verb] give an authoritative direction or instruction to do something: [with clause] *the court ordered that the case should be heard at the end of August* | [trans.] *the judge ordered a retrial.*
PHRASES **by order of** according to directions given by the proper authority: *he was released from prison by order of the court.* **in order** in accordance with the rules of procedure at a meeting, legislative assembly, etc. **Order!** a call for silence or the observance of prescribed procedures by someone in charge of a trial, legislative assembly, etc. **out of order** not according to the rules of a meeting, legislative assembly, etc.
ORIGIN Middle English: from Old French *ordre*, from Latin *ordo*, *ordin-* 'row, series, rank.'

or•di•nance /'ôrdn-əns/
▸ n. 1 a piece of legislation enacted by a municipal authority: *a city ordinance banned smoking in nearly all types of restaurants.*

2 an authoritative order; a decree.

ORIGIN Middle English (also in the sense 'arrangement in ranks'): from Old French *ordenance*, from medieval Latin *ordinantia*, from Latin *ordinare* 'put in order.'

or•di•nar•y /'ôrdn‚erē/

▸ **adj.** (esp. of a judge) exercising authority by virtue of office and not by delegation.

▸ **n.** (pl. **or•di•nar•ies**) Brit. a person, esp. a judge, exercising authority by virtue of office and not by delegation. ■ in some US states, a judge of probate.

ORIGIN late Middle English: the noun partly via Old French; the adjective from Latin *ordinarius* 'orderly' (reinforced by French *ordinaire*), from *ordo*, *ordin-* 'order.'

o•rig•i•nal jur•is•dic•tion /ə'rijənl ‚jo͞oris'dikSHən/

▸ **n.** the authority of a court to hear and decide a matter prior to any other court's review of the matter: *the Supreme Court shall have original jurisdiction of all controversies between two or more states.*

oust /owst/

▸ **v.** [trans.] deprive (someone) of or exclude (someone) from possession of something: *Roberts was in serious jeopardy of being ousted from his apartment.*

ORIGIN late Middle English (as a legal term): from Anglo-Norman French *ouster* 'take away,' from Latin *obstare* 'oppose, hinder.'

oust•er /'owstər/

▸ **n.** ejection from a freehold or other possession; deprivation of an inheritance.

out /owt/

▸ **adv. 1** no longer detained in custody or in jail: *they would be out on bail in no time.*

2 (of a jury) considering its verdict in secrecy: *they set-*

*tled on a confidential basis with one of the defendants while
the jury was out.*
ORIGIN Old English *ūt* (adverb), *ūtian* (verb), of Germanic origin; related to Dutch *uit* and German *aus*.

out•law /'owt,lô/
▶ n. a person who has broken the law, esp. one who remains at large or is a fugitive.
■ a person or group regarded as acting outside accepted norms of behavior: [as adj.] *outlaw nations.* ■ historical a person deprived of the benefit and protection of the law.
▶v. [trans.] ban; make illegal: *Maryland outlawed cheap small-caliber pistols* | [as adj.] (**outlawed**) *the outlawed terrorist group.*
■ historical deprive (someone) of the benefit and protection of the law.
DERIVATIVES **out•law•ry** /'owt,lôrē/ n.
ORIGIN late Old English *ūtlaga* (noun), *ūtlagian* (verb), from Old Norse *útlagi*, noun from *útlagr* 'outlawed or banished.'

out-of-court /'owt əv 'kôrt/
▶ adj. [attrib.] (of a settlement) made or done without a court decision.

P

pack /pæk/

▶ v. [trans.] fill (a jury, committee, etc.) with people likely to support a particular decision or tendency: *his efforts to **pack** the Supreme Court **with** men who shared his ideology are being cricitized.*

ORIGIN early 16th cent. (in the sense 'enter into a private agreement'): probably from the obsolete verb *pact* 'enter into an agreement with,' the final *-t* being interpreted as an inflection of the past tense.

pan•el /'pænl/

▶ n. a list of available jurors or a jury.
■ a group of judges drawn from a larger body to hear a particular matter: *the case went to a three-judge panel.*

par•a•le•gal /ˌpærə'lēgəl/

▶ n. a person trained in subsidiary legal matters but not fully qualified as a lawyer, who typically works as an assistant to a lawyer.
▶ adj. of or relating to auxiliary aspects of the law.

par•don /'pärdn/

▶ n. a remission of the legal consequences of an offense or conviction: *he offered a full pardon to five convicted men.*
▶ v. [trans.] release (an offender) from the legal consequences of an offense or conviction, and often implicitly from blame: *he was pardoned for his treason.*

DERIVATIVES **par•don•a•ble** adj.

ORIGIN Middle English: from Old French *pardun* (noun), *pardoner* (verb), from medieval Latin *perdonare* 'concede, remit,' from *per-* 'completely' + *donare* 'give.'

pa•rens pa•tri•ae /ˌperənz ˈpætri-ē/

▶ n. the government, or any other authority, regarded as the legal protector of citizens unable to protect themselves.

■ the principle that political authority carries with it the responsibility for such protection.

ORIGIN modern Latin, literally 'parent of the country.'

pa•rol /pəˈrōl; ˈpærəl/

▶ adj. given or expressed orally: *the parol evidence.*

■ (of a document) agreed orally, or in writing but not under seal: *there was a parol agreement.*

PHRASES **by parol** by oral declaration.

ORIGIN late 15th cent. (as a noun): from Old French *parole* 'word' (see PAROLE).

pa•role /pəˈrōl/

▶ n. the release of a prisoner temporarily (for a special purpose) or permanently before the completion of a sentence, on the promise of good behavior and under continuing supervision: *he committed a burglary while on parole.*

■ historical a promise or undertaking given by a prisoner of war not to escape or, if released, to return to custody under stated conditions.

▶ v. [trans.] (usu. **be paroled**) release (a prisoner) on parole: *he was paroled after serving nine months of a two-year sentence.*

DERIVATIVES **pa•rol•ee** /pəˌrōˈlē/ n.

ORIGIN late 15th cent.: from Old French, literally 'word,' also 'formal promise,' from ecclesiastical Latin *parabola* 'speech'; compare with PAROL.

par•ri•cide /ˈperəˌsīd; ˈpærə-/

▶ n. the killing of a parent or other near relative.

■ a person who commits parricide.

DERIVATIVES **par•ri•cid•al** /ˌperəˈsīdl; ˌpærə-/ **adj.**

ORIGIN late 16th cent.: from French, from Latin *parri-cidium* 'murder of a parent,' with first element of unknown origin, but long associated with Latin *pater* 'father' and *parens* 'parent.'

pass /pæs/

▸ **v. 1** [intrans.] be transferred from one person or place to another, esp. by inheritance: *if Ann remarried the estate would **pass to** her new husband.*
2 [trans.] (of a legislative or other official body) approve or put into effect (a proposal or law) by voting on it: *the bill was passed despite fierce opposition.*
■ (of a proposal or law) be examined and approved by (a legislative body or process): *bills that passed committees last year.* ■ [intrans.] (of a proposal) be approved: *the bill passed by 164 votes to 107.*
3 [trans.] pronounce (a judgment or judicial sentence): *don't shrink from **passing** judgment **on** this crucial issue | it is now my duty to **pass** sentence **upon** you.*
■ [intrans.] (**pass on/upon**) archaic adjudicate or give a judgment on: *a jury could not be trusted to pass upon the question of Endicott's good faith.*
ORIGIN Middle English: from Old French *passer*, based on Latin *passus* 'pace.'

Pat.

▸ **abbr.** Patent.

pat•ent /'pætnt/

▸ **n.** /'pætnt/ a government authority to an individual or organization conferring a right or title, esp. the sole right to make, use, or sell some invention: *he **took out** a patent for an improved steam hammer.* [ORIGIN: Compare with LETTERS PATENT.]
▸ **v.** [trans.] obtain a patent for (an invention): *an invention is not your own until it is patented.*
DERIVATIVES **pat•ent•a•ble** adj.

ORIGIN late Middle English: from Old French, from Latin *patent-* 'lying open,' from the verb *patere*.

pat•ent•ee /ˌpætn'tē/
▸ n. a person or organization that obtains or holds a patent for something.

pat•ent of•fice /'pætnt ˌôfis; ˌäfis/
▸ n. an office from which patents are issued.

pa•ter•ni•ty /pə'tərnitē/
▸ n. the state of being someone's father: *he refused to admit paternity of the child.*
ORIGIN late Middle English: from Old French *paternité*, from late Latin *paternitas*, from *paternus* 'relating to a father.'

pa•ter•ni•ty suit /pə'tərnitē ˌso͞ot/
▸ n. a legal action to establish formally the identity of a child's father, typically in order to require him to support the child financially.

pat•ri•cide /'pætriˌsīd/
▸ n. the killing of one's father.
■ a person who kills their father.
DERIVATIVES **pat•ri•cid•al** /ˌpætri'sīdl/ **adj.**
ORIGIN early 17th cent.: from late Latin *patricidium*, alteration of Latin *parricidium* (see PARRICIDE).

peace of•fi•cer /'pēs ˌôfisər; ˌäf-/
▸ n. a civil officer appointed to preserve law and order, such as a sheriff or police officer.

pe•nal /'pēnl/
▸ adj. of, relating to, or prescribing the punishment of offenders under the legal system: *she is a champion of penal reform* | *under the Penal Code, this bill would permit certain exempt organizations to conduct raffles.*

■ used or designated as a place of punishment: *a former penal colony.* ■ (of an act or offense) punishable by law.

DERIVATIVES **pe•nal•ly** adv.

ORIGIN late Middle English: from Old French *penal*, from Latin *poenalis*, from *poena* 'pain, penalty.'

pe•nal•ize /'pēnl͵īz; 'pen-/
▶v. [trans.] (often **be penalized**) make or declare (an act or offense) legally punishable: *section twenty penalizes possession of a firearm when trespassing.*

DERIVATIVES **pe•nal•i•za•tion** /͵pēnəli'zāsʜən; ͵pen-/ n.

pen•den•te li•te /pen'dentē 'līt̬ē/
▶adv. during litigation: *a judge may award interim fees pendente lite where the complainant has prevailed on an important allegation.*

ORIGIN Latin, literally 'with the lawsuit pending.'

per cu•ri•am /pər 'kyo͝orēəm/
▶adv. by decision of a court in unanimous agreement: *the court dismissed, per curiam, union petitions for review of two Authority decisions.*

▶n. such a decision: *in only a few cases did the panel publish a per curiam.*

■ an opinion signed by a court as a whole, rather than by an individual judge.

ORIGIN Latin, literally 'by the court.'

per•emp•to•ry /pə'remptərē/
▶adj. not open to appeal or challenge; final: *there has been no disobedience of a peremptory order of the court.*

DERIVATIVES **per•emp•to•ri•ly** /pə'remptərəlē/ adv.; **per•emp•to•ri•ness** n.

ORIGIN late Middle English (as a legal term): via Anglo-Norman French from Latin *peremptorius* 'deadly, decisive,' from *perempt-* 'destroyed, cut off,' from the verb *perimere*, from *per-* 'completely' + *emere* 'take, buy.'

per•emp•to•ry chal•lenge /pə'remptərē CHӕlinj/
▸ n. a defendant's or lawyer's objection to a proposed juror, made without needing to give a reason.

per•fect /pər'fekt/
▸ v. [trans.] satisfy the necessary conditions or requirements for the transfer of (a gift, title, etc.): *equity will not perfect an imperfect gift.*
ORIGIN Middle English: from Old French *perfet,* from Latin *perfectus* 'completed,' from the verb *perficere,* from *per-* 'through, completely' + *facere* 'do.'

per•jure /'pərjər/
▸ v. (**perjure oneself**) willfully tell an untruth when giving evidence to a court; commit perjury: *when a defendant perjures himself on the stand, the court is warranted in enhancing the defendant's offense level.*
DERIVATIVES **per•jur•er** n.
ORIGIN late Middle English (as *perjured* in the sense 'guilty of perjury'): from Old French *parjurer,* from Latin *perjurare* 'swear falsely,' from *per-* 'to ill effect' + *jurare* 'swear.'

per•jured /'pərjərd/
▸ adj. (of evidence) involving willfully told untruths.
■ (of a person) guilty of perjury: *a perjured witness.*

per•ju•ry /'pərjərē/
▸ n. (pl. **per•ju•ries**) the offense of willfully telling an untruth, especially in a court, after having taken an oath or made an affirmation.
DERIVATIVES **per•ju•ri•ous** /pər'jŏŏrēəs/ **adj.**
ORIGIN late Middle English: from Anglo-Norman French *perjurie,* from Latin *perjurium* 'false oath,' from the verb *perjurare* (see PERJURE).

per•mis•sive /pər'misiv/
▸ adj. allowed or optional, but not obligatory: *the Hague Convention was permissive, not mandatory.*

ORIGIN late 15th cent. (in the sense 'tolerated, allowed'): from Old French, or from medieval Latin *permissivus*, from *permiss-* 'allowed,' from the verb *permittere*, from *per-* 'through' + *mittere* 'send, let go.'

per•pe•tu•i•ty /ˌpərpi't(y)ōōitē/
▸ n. (pl. **per•pe•tu•i•ties**) a thing that lasts forever or for an indefinite period, in particular:
■ a restriction making an estate inalienable perpetually or for a period beyond certain limits fixed by law: *the property must be used and maintained as a park or recreation area **in perpetuity**.* ■ an estate so restricted.
ORIGIN late Middle English: from Old French *perpetuite*, from Latin *perpetuitas*, from *perpetuus* 'continuing throughout.'

per•son•al in•ju•ry /'pərs(ə)nl 'injərē/
▸ n. injury inflicted on a person's body or mind, as opposed to damage to property or reputation: [as **adj.**] *personal injury lawyers.*

per•son•al pro•per•ty /'pərs(ə)nl 'präpərtē/
▸ n. all of someone's property except land and those interests in land that pass to their heirs. Compare with REAL PROPERTY.

per•son•al•ty /'pərsənəltē/
▸ n. a person's personal property. The opposite of REALTY.
ORIGIN mid 16th cent. (in the legal phrase *in the personalty* 'for damages'): from Anglo-Norman French *personaltie*, from medieval Latin *personalitas*, from Latin *personalis* 'of a person.'

per•tain /pər'tān/
▸ v. [intrans.] belong to something as a part, appendage, or accessory: *the premises, stock, and all assets **pertaining to** the business.*

ORIGIN late Middle English: from Old French *partenir*, from Latin *pertinere* 'extend to, have reference to,' from *per-* 'through' + *tenere* 'to hold.'

pet•it /'petē/
▸ **adj.** (of a crime) petty: *petit larceny*.
ORIGIN late Middle English (in the sense 'small or insignificant'): from Old French, 'small'; the same word as PETTY, with retention of the French spelling.

pe•ti•tion /pi'tisHən/
▸ **n.** an application to a court for a writ, judicial action in a suit, etc.: *a divorce petition*.
▸ **v.** [trans.] make or present a formal request to (an authority) with respect to a particular cause: *Americans who moved west **petitioned** Congress **for** admission to the Union as states* | [with obj. and infinitive] *leaders petitioned the government to hold free elections soon.*
■ make a formal application to (a court) for a writ, judicial action in a suit, etc.: *the custodial parent **petitioned** the court **for** payment of the arrears* | [intrans.] *the process allows both spouses to jointly **petition for** divorce.*
DERIVATIVES **pe•ti•tion•ar•y** /pitisHə‚nerē/ **adj.**; **pe•ti•tion•er n.**
ORIGIN Middle English: from Latin *petitio(n-)*, from *petit-* 'aimed at, sought, laid claim to,' from the verb *petere.*

pet•it ju•ry /'petē 'jo͞orē/
▸ **n.** see JURY.

pet•ty /'petē/
▸ **adj.** (**pet•ti•er, pet•ti•est**) (of a crime) of lesser importance: *petty theft.* Compare with GRAND).
ORIGIN late Middle English (in the sense 'small in size'): from a phonetic spelling of the pronunciation of French *petit* 'small.' Compare with PETIT.

pet•ty ju•ry /'petē ˌjŏŏrē/
▸ n. see JURY.

pet•ty lar•ce•ny /'petē lärsənē/
▸ n. theft of personal property having a value less than a legally specified amount.

pi•ra•cy /'pīrəsē/
▸ n. the practice of attacking and robbing ships at sea. ■ a similar practice in other contexts, esp. hijacking: *air piracy.* ■ the unauthorized use or reproduction of another's work: *software piracy.*
ORIGIN mid 16th cent.: via medieval Latin from Greek *pirateia,* from *peiratēs,* from *peirein* 'to attempt, attack.'

plain•tiff /'plăntif/
▸ n. a person who brings a case against another in a court of law. Compare with DEFENDANT.
ORIGIN late Middle English: from Old French *plaintif* 'plaintive' (used as a noun). The *-f* ending has come down through Law French; the word was originally the same as *plaintive.*

plea /plē/
▸ n. a formal statement by or on behalf of a defendant or prisoner, stating guilt or innocence in response to a charge, offering an allegation of fact, or claiming that a point of law should apply: *he changed his plea to not guilty.*
ORIGIN Middle English (in the sense 'lawsuit'): from Old French *plait, plaid* 'agreement, discussion,' from Latin *placitum* 'a decree,' neuter past participle of *placere* 'to please.'

plea bar•gain•ing /'plē ˌbärgəniNG/
▸ n. an arrangement between a prosecutor and a criminal defendant whereby the defendant pleads guilty to a

lesser charge in the expectation of leniency from the court.

DERIVATIVES **plea-bar•gain** v.: *he plea-bargained his way out of stealing $20,000 from a client.*; **plea bar•gain** n.

plead /plēd/

▶v. (past and past part. **plead•ed** or **pled** /pled/) [trans.] present and argue for (a position), esp. in court or in another public context: *she's famous for using cheap melodrama to plead her clients' causes.*

■ [intrans.] address a court as an advocate on behalf of a party: *the State Council pleaded on behalf of the Commander for an adjournment.* ■ [no obj., with complement] state formally in court whether one is guilty or not guilty of the offense with which one is charged: *he pleaded guilty to the drug charge.* ■ invoke (a reason or a point of law) as an accusation or defense: *on trial for attempted murder, she pleaded self-defense.*

DERIVATIVES **plead•er** n.

ORIGIN Middle English (in the sense 'to wrangle'): from Old French *plaidier* 'resort to legal action,' from *plaid* 'discussion' (see **PLEA**).

USAGE: In a court of law, a person can **plead guilty** or **plead not guilty**. The phrase **plead innocent**, although commonly found in general use, is not a technical legal term. Note that one *pleads guilty to* (not *of*) a charge, and may be *found guilty of* an offense.

plead•ing /'plēdiNG/

▶n. (usu. **pleadings**) a formal statement of the cause of an action or defense.

pledge /plej/

▶n. a thing that is given as security for the fulfillment of a contract or the payment of a debt and is liable to forfeiture in the event of failure: *the Administrator may accept other forms of security, such as a pledge of revenues.*

▸v. [trans.] give as security on a loan: *the creditor to whom the land is pledged.*

DERIVATIVES **pledg•or** /'plejər/ n.

ORIGIN Middle English (denoting a person acting as surety for another): from Old French *plege*, from medieval Latin *plebium*, perhaps related to the Germanic base of *plight*.

pol•i•cy /'pälisē/

▸n. (pl. **pol•i•cies**) a contract of insurance: *they took out a joint policy.*

ORIGIN mid 16th cent.: from French *police* 'bill of lading, contract of insurance,' from Provençal *poliss(i)a*, probably from medieval Latin *apodissa*, *apodixa*, based on Greek *apodeixis* 'evidence, proof,' from *apodeiknunai* 'demonstrate, show.'

pol•y•graph /'päli,græf/

▸ n. a machine designed to detect and record changes in physiological characteristics, such as a person's pulse and breathing rates, used esp. as a lie detector: *Rhinehart contends that the polygraph is too easily manipulated by both the examiner and the examinee.*

■ a lie-detector test carried out with a machine of this type: *should the polygraph be admissible as evidence?*

DERIVATIVES **pol•y•graph•ic** /,päli'græfik/ adj.

pos•se /'päsē/

▸n. historical a body of men, typically armed, summoned by a sheriff to enforce the law.

■ (also **pos•se co•mi•ta•tus** /'päsē ,kämi'tātəs/) historical the body of men in a county whom the sheriff could summon to enforce the law. [ORIGIN: **comitatus** from medieval Latin, 'of the county.'] ■ informal a gang of youths involved in (usually drug-related) crime.

ORIGIN mid 17th cent.: from medieval Latin, literally 'power,' from Latin *posse* 'be able.'

Pos•se Com•i•ta•tus Act /'päsē ˌkämi'tātəs ˌækt/
▶ a federal statute prohibiting use of the military in civilian law enforcement.
ORIGIN Latin *posse comitatus* 'power of the county.'

pos•sess /pə'zes/
▶ v. [trans.] have possession of as distinct from ownership: *a two-year suspended sentence for possessing cocaine.*
ORIGIN late Middle English: from Old French *possesser*, from Latin *possess-* 'occupied, held,' from the verb *possidere*, from *potis* 'able, capable' + *sedere* 'sit.'

pos•ses•sion /pə'zesHən/
▶ n. 1 visible power or control over something, as distinct from lawful ownership; holding or occupancy: *they were imprisoned for possession of explosives.*
■ informal the state of possessing an illegal drug: *they're charged with possession.*
2 (usu. **possessions**) an item of property; something belonging to one: *his will did not specifically dispose of any possessions.*
ORIGIN Middle English: from Old French, from Latin *possessio(n-)*, from the verb *possidere* (see POSSESS).

pos•ses•sor /pə'zesər/
▶ n. a person who takes, occupies, or holds something without necessarily having ownership, or as distinguished from the owner.
DERIVATIVES **pos•ses•so•ry** /pə'zes(ə)rē/ **adj.**

power of ap•point•ment /'pow(-ə)r əv ə'pointmənt/
▶ n. phrase power to decide the disposal of property, in exercise of a right conferred by the owner.

pow•er of at•tor•ney /ˈpou(-ə)r əv əˈtərnē/
▸ n. the authority to act for another person in specified or all legal or financial matters.
▪ a legal document giving such authority to someone: *the debtor has signed a power of attorney giving the attorney authority to issue consents.*

prac•tice /ˈpræktis/
▸ n. the carrying out or exercise of a profession, especially that of a lawyer or doctor: *her interest in the legal practice began in high school.*
▪ the business or premises of a lawyer or doctor: *the practice of Perry and Erikson has moved to Linwood Park.* ▪ an established method of legal procedure.
▸ v. [trans.] (Brit. **practise**) actively pursue or be engaged in (a particular profession, especially law or medicine): *he began to practice law* | [intrans.] *he practiced as an attorney*
ORIGIN late Middle English: the verb from Old French *practiser* or medieval Latin *practizare*, alteration of *practicare* 'perform, carry out,' from *practica* 'practice,' from Greek *praktikē*, feminine (used as a noun) of *praktikos* 'concerned with action'; the noun from the verb in the earlier spelling *practise*, on the pattern of pairs such as *advise, advice.*

prae•ci•pe /ˈprēsə,pē; ˈpres-/
▸ n. an order requesting a writ or other legal document: *court clerks provide forms for making the request, or a praecipe can be filed.*
▪ historical a writ demanding action or an explanation of nonaction: *a praecipe for discontinuance.*
ORIGIN Latin (the first word of the writ), imperative of *praecipere* 'enjoin, command.'

pre•am•ble /ˈprē,æmbəl/
▸ n. the introductory part of a statute, deed, or other sim-

ilar document, stating its purpose, aims, and justification.

DERIVATIVES **pre•am•bu•lar** /prē'æmbyələr/ **adj.** (formal).

ORIGIN late Middle English: from Old French *preambule*, from medieval Latin *praeambulum*, from late Latin *praeambulus* 'going before.'

prec•a•to•ry /'prekə,tôrē/

▶ **adj.** (in a will) expressing a wish or intention of the testator that is advisory but not binding: *a trust can be left in precatory words.*

ORIGIN mid 17th cent.: from late Latin *precatorius*, from *precat-* 'prayed,' from the verb *precari.*

prec•e•dent

▶ **n.** /'presid(ə)nt/ a previous case or legal decision that may be or (**binding precedent**) must be followed in subsequent similar cases: *the decision* **set a precedent** *for others to be sent to trial in the United States.*

▶ **adj.** /pri'sēd(ə)nt; 'presid(ə)nt/ preceding in time, order, or importance: *a precedent case.*

ORIGIN late Middle English: from Old French, literally 'preceding.'

pre•cept /'prē,sept/

▶ **n.** a writ or warrant: *the Commissioner issued precepts requiring the companies to provide information.*

ORIGIN late Middle English: from Latin *praeceptum*, neuter past participle of *praecipere* 'warn, instruct,' from *prae* 'before' + *capere* 'take.'

pre•empt /prē'empt/

▶ **v.** [trans.] **1** (of a superior authority) take action to prevent an inferior authority from acting: *Congress has preempted the regulation of cigarette advertising.*

2 take (something, esp. public land) for oneself so as to have the right of preemption.
DERIVATIVES **pre•emp•tor** /prē'emptôr; -tər/ n.
ORIGIN mid 19th cent.: back-formation from PREEMP-
TION.

pre•emp•tion /prē'empsHən/
▶n. 1 action by a superior authority that prevents an inferior authority from acting.
2 the purchase of goods or shares by one person or party
before the opportunity is offered to others: *the commission had the right of preemption.*
■ historical the right to purchase public land in this way.
ORIGIN early 17th cent.: from medieval Latin *praeemp-
tio(n-)*, from the verb *praeemere*, from *prae* 'in advance'
+ *emere* 'buy.'

pre•fer /pri'fər/
▶v. (**pre•ferred, pre•fer•ring**) [trans.] submit (a charge or
a piece of information) for consideration: *the police will
prefer charges.*
ORIGIN late Middle English: from Old French *preferer*,
from Latin *praeferre*, from *prae* 'before' + *ferre* 'to bear,
carry.'

pref•er•ence /'pref(ə)rəns/
▶n. a prior right or precedence, esp. in connection with
the payment of debts: *debts owed to the community should
be accorded a preference.*
ORIGIN late Middle English (in the sense 'promotion'):
from Old French, from medieval Latin *praeferentia*, from
Latin *praeferre* 'carry in front' (see PREFER).

prej•u•dice /'prejədis/
▶n. harm or injury that results or may result from some
action or judgment: *prejudice resulting from delay in the
institution of the proceedings.*

▸v. [trans.] **1** give rise to prejudice in (someone); make biased: *the statement might prejudice the jury.*
2 cause harm to (a state of affairs): *delay is likely to prejudice the child's welfare.*
PHRASES **with prejudice** (of a judgment) with binding effect: *the case is dismissed with prejudice.* **without prejudice** without detriment to any existing right or claim: *the payment was made **without any prejudice to** her rights.*
ORIGIN Middle English: from Old French, from Latin *praejudicium*, from *prae* 'in advance' + *judicium* 'judgment.'

prej•u•di•cial /ˌprejəˈdiSHəl/
▸adj. harmful to someone or something; detrimental: *the behavior is **prejudicial to** good order and discipline.*
■ (of evidence) tending to lead to an incorrect decision (and therefore excludable); likely to cause prejudice: *the district court sustained Jones's objection to admission of this evidence as prejudicial.*
DERIVATIVES **prej•u•di•cial•ly** adv.
ORIGIN late Middle English: from Old French *prejudiciel*, from *prejudice* (see PREJUDICE).

pre•med•i•tate /prēˈmediˌtāt/
▸v. [trans.] [usu. as adj.] (**premeditated**) think out or plan (an action, esp. a crime) beforehand: *premeditated murder.*
DERIVATIVES **pre•med•i•ta•tion** /prēˌmedəˈtāSHən/ n.
ORIGIN mid 16th cent.: from Latin *praemeditat-* 'thought out before,' from the verb *praemeditari*, from *prae* 'before' + *meditari* 'meditate.'

prem•is•es /ˈpremisiz/
▸plural n. a house or building, together with its land and outbuildings, occupied by a business or considered in an official context: *business premises* | *supplying alcoholic liquor for consumption **on the premises**.*

pre•nup•tial a•gree•ment /prē'nəpsHəl ə'grēmənt; prē 'nəpCHəl/

▶ n. an agreement made by a couple before they marry concerning the ownership of their respective assets should the marriage fail.

pre•rog•a•tive /p(r)i'rägətiv/

▶ n. a right or privilege exclusive to a particular individual, institution, or class: *the case affirmed the right of the state to overrule a parental prerogative for the welfare of the child.*

■ (also **royal prerogative**) the right of the sovereign, which in British law is theoretically subject to no restriction.

▶adj. [attrib.] Brit. arising from the prerogative of the Crown (usually delegated to the government or the judiciary) and based in common law rather than statutory law: *the monarch retained the formal prerogative power to appoint the Prime Minister.*

ORIGIN late Middle English: via Old French from Latin *praerogativa* '(the verdict of) the political division that was chosen to vote first in the assembly,' feminine (used as noun) of *praerogativus* 'asked first,' from *prae* 'before' + *rogare* 'ask.'

pre•rog•a•tive writ /pri'rägətiv 'rit/

▶ n. an order in exercise of a court's discretionary power: *nine men applied for a prerogative writ of habeas corpus after being in detention since 1994 on aggravated robbery and/or murder charges.*

pre•scrip•tion /pri'skripSHən/

▶ n. (also **positive prescription**) the establishment of a claim founded on the basis of a long or indefinite period of uninterrupted use or of long-standing custom. *Alvey had a 16.5-foot easement by prescription on the western portion of Lot 32.*

ORIGIN late Middle English (as a legal term): via Old French from Latin *praescriptio(n-)*, from the verb *praescribere* 'direct in writing,' from *prae* 'before' + *scribere* 'write.'

pre•scrip•tive /priˈskriptiv/
▸ adj. (of a right, title, or institution) having become legally established or accepted by long usage or the passage of time: *a prescriptive right of way.*
DERIVATIVES **pre•scrip•tive•ly** adv.; **pre•scrip•tive•ness** n.
ORIGIN mid 18th cent.: from late Latin *praescriptivus* 'relating to a legal exception,' from *praescript-* 'directed in writing,' from the verb *praescribere* (see PRESCRIPTION).

pre•sent•ment /priˈzentmənt/
▸ n. chiefly historical a formal presentation of information to a court, esp. by a grand jury regarding an offense or other matter not contained in a bill of indictment it has considered.
ORIGIN Middle English: from Old French *presentement*, from *presenter* 'place before.'

pre•sump•tion /priˈzəmpsHən/
▸ n. an attitude adopted in law or as a matter of policy toward an action or proposal in the absence of acceptable reasons or proof to the contrary: *the **presumption** of guilt has changed to a presumption of innocence.*
ORIGIN Middle English: from Old French *presumpcion*, from Latin *praesumptio(n)* 'anticipation,' from the verb *praesumere* 'anticipate' (in Late Latin 'take for granted'), from *prae* 'before' + *sumere* 'take.'

pre•sump•tive /priˈzəmptiv/
▸ adj. giving grounds for the inference of a fact or of the appropriate interpretation of the law: *the document sets out rules for a finding of presumptive disability or presumptive blindness.*

DERIVATIVES **pre•sump•tive•ly** adv.
ORIGIN late Middle English: from French *présomptif,
-ive,* from late Latin *praesumptivus,* from *praesumpt-*
'taken before,' from the verb *praesumere* (see **PRESUMP-
TION**).

pre•ven•tive de•ten•tion /pri'ventiv di'tenCHən/
▶ n. the imprisonment of a person prior to conviction,
with the aim of preventing them from committing further offenses or of maintaining public order.

pri•ma fa•ci•e /ˌprīmə 'fāSHē(ˌē)/
▶ adj. & adv. based on the first impression; accepted as
correct until proved otherwise: [as adj.] *a prima facie case
of professional misconduct* | [as adv.] *the original lessee prima
facie remains liable for the payment of the rent.*
ORIGIN Latin, from *primus* 'first' + *facies* 'face.'

prin•ci•pal /'prinsəpəl/
▶ n. a person directly responsible for a crime, by committing, instigating, or assisting in it. Compare with
ACCESSORY.
ORIGIN Middle English: via Old French from Latin
principalis 'first, original,' from *princeps, princip-* 'first,
chief.'

pris•on /'prizən/
▶ n. a building or place to which people are legally committed, typically as a punishment for crimes they have
committed: *he died **in prison*** | *both men were **sent to
prison.***
■ confinement in such a building: *prison saves one man
and hardens another.*
ORIGIN late Old English, from Old French *prisun,* from
Latin *prensio(n-),* variant of *prehensio(n-)* 'laying hold
of,' from the verb *prehendere.*

pris•on•er /'priz(ə)nər/
▸ n. a person legally committed to prison as a punishment for crimes they have committed.
■ a person held otherwise by the law, as in jail while awaiting trial. ■ a person captured and kept confined by an enemy, opponent, or criminal: *American citizens were being* **held prisoner** *in Iran* | *200 rebels were* **taken prisoner***.*
ORIGIN late Middle English: from Old French *prisonier*, from *prison* (see PRISON).

pri•vate law /'prīvit 'lô/
▸ n. a branch of the law (such as contract, tort, or property law) that deals with the relations between individuals or institutions, rather than relations between these and the government.

pri•vate prac•tice /'prīvit 'præktis/
▸ n. the work of a professional practitioner, such as a lawyer or doctor, who is self-employed or employed by a firm or group rather than by the government: *there was a preference for judicial nominees who had substantial experience* **in private practice***.*
DERIVATIVES **pri•vate prac•ti•tion•er** /'prīvit præk 'tisHənər/ n.

priv•i•lege /'priv(ə)lij/
▸ n. (also **absolute privilege**) (in a parliamentary context) the right to say or write something without the risk of incurring punishment or legal action for defamation.
■ the right of a person, especially a lawyer or official, to refuse to divulge confidential information, especially at trial.
▸ v. [trans.] formal grant a privilege or privileges to: *English inheritance law privileged the eldest son.*
■ (usu. **be privileged from**) exempt (someone) from a

liability or obligation to which others are subject: *some officers are privileged from obeying any subpoena to testify.* ORIGIN Middle English: via Old French from Latin *privilegium* 'bill or law affecting an individual,' from *privus* 'private' + *lex, leg-* 'law.'

priv•i•leged /ˈpriv(ə)lijd/
▸ adj. (of information) legally protected from being revealed in the legal process or made public: *the intelligence reports are privileged.*

priv•i•ty /ˈprivitē/
▸ n. (pl. **priv•i•ties**) a relation between two parties that is recognized by law, particularly by contract or property interest: *the parties no longer have privity with each other.* ORIGIN Middle English (in the sense 'secrecy, intimacy'): from Old French *privete*, from medieval Latin *privitas*, from Latin *privus* 'private.'

prob•a•ble cause /ˈpräbəbəl ˈkôz/
▸ n. reasonable grounds (for making a search, pressing a charge, etc.): *the government still has to **show probable cause** that the target of the surveillance is a public threat.*

pro•bate /ˈprō,bāt/
▸ n. the official proving of a will: *the will was in probate* | [as adj.] *a probate court.*
■ a verified copy of a will with a certificate as handed to the executors. ■ the processing of the estate of a decedent.
▸ v. [trans.] establish the validity of (a will): *there is no set time frame in which a will must be probated.* ORIGIN late Middle English: from Latin *probatum* 'something proved,' neuter past participle of *probare* 'to test, prove.'

pro•ba•tion /prōˈbāSHən/
▸ n. the release of an offender from detention, subject to

a period of good behavior under supervision: *I went to court and was **put on probation**.*

DERIVATIVES **pro•ba•tion•ar•y** /prōˈbāsHəˌnerē/ adj.

ORIGIN late Middle English (denoting testing, investigation, or examination): from Old French *probacion*, from Latin *probatio(n-)*, from *probare* 'to test, prove' (see PROVE). The legal use dates from the late 19th cent.

pro•ba•tion•er /prōˈbāsHənər/
▸ n. a person who is serving a probationary or trial period in a job or position to which they are newly appointed.
■ an offender on probation.

pro•ba•tion of•fi•cer /prōˈbāsHən ˌôfisər; ˌäfisər/
▸ n. a person appointed to supervise offenders who are on probation.

pro•ba•tive /ˈprōbətiv/
▸ adj. having the quality or function of proving or demonstrating something; affording proof or evidence: *it places the probative burden on the defendant.*
ORIGIN late Middle English (describing something that serves as a test): from Latin *probativus*, from *probat-* 'proved,' from the verb *probare* (see PROVE).

pro•ceed /prəˈsēd; prō-/
▸ v. [intrans.] start a lawsuit against someone: *he may still be able to **proceed against** the contractor under the common law negligence rules.*
ORIGIN late Middle English: from Old French *proceder*, from Latin *procedere*, from *pro-* 'forward' + *cedere* 'go.'

pro•ceed•ings /prəˈsēdiNGz; prō-/
▸ plural n. action taken in a court to enforce a law or settle a dispute: *criminal proceedings were brought against him.*

proc•ess /'präses; -səs; 'prō-/

▶ n. a summons or writ requiring a person to appear in court.

ORIGIN Middle English: from Old French *proces*, from Latin *processus* 'progression, course,' from the verb *procedere*, from *pro-* 'forward' + *cedere* 'go.'

proc•ess serv•er /'präses ,sərvər; 'präsəs; 'prō-/

▶ n. a person, esp. a sheriff or deputy, who serves writs, warrants, subpoenas, etc.

proc•tor /'präktər/

▶ n. an attorney in an admiralty court.

DERIVATIVES **proc•to•ri•al** /präk'tôrēəl/ adj.; **proc•tor•ship** /'präktər,SHip/ n.

ORIGIN late Middle English: contraction of PROCURATOR.

proc•u•ra•tor /'präkyə,rātər/

▶ n. an agent representing others in a court of law in countries retaining Roman civil law.

DERIVATIVES **proc•u•ra•to•ri•al** /,präkyərə'tôrēəl/ adj.; **proc•u•ra•tor•ship** /'präkyə,rātər,SHip/ n.

ORIGIN Middle English (denoting a steward): from Old French *procuratour* or Latin *procurator* 'administrator, agent,' from *procurat-* 'taken care of,' from the verb *procurare* 'take care of, manage,' from *pro-* 'on behalf of' + *curare* 'see to.'

pro•hi•bi•tion /,prō(h)ə'bisHən/

▶ n. 1 the action of forbidding something, esp. by law: *they argue that prohibition of drugs will always fail.*

■ a law or regulation forbidding something: *prohibitions on insider trading.*

2 (**Pro•hi•bi•tion**) the prevention by law of the manufacture and sale of alcoholic beverages, esp. in the US between 1920 and 1933.

DERIVATIVES **pro•hi•bi•tion•ar•y** /,prō(h)ə'bisHə,nerē/ adj.; **Pro•hi•bi•tion•ist** /,prō(h)ə'bisHənist/ n.

ORIGIN late Middle English: from Old French, from Latin *prohibitio(n-)*, from *prohibere* 'keep in check.'

prom•is•ee /ˌpräməˈsē/
▶ n. a person to whom a promise is made.

prom•i•sor /ˈpräməsər; -ˌsôr/
▶ n. a person who makes a promise.

prom•is•so•ry /ˈpräməˌsôrē/
▶ adj. conveying or implying a promise: *statements that are promissory in nature | promissory words.*
ORIGIN late Middle English: from medieval Latin *promissorius*, from *promiss-* 'promised.'

prom•is•so•ry note /ˈpräməˌsôrē ˈnōt/
▶ n. a signed document containing a written promise to pay a stated sum to a specified person or the bearer at a specified date or on demand.

pro•nounce /prəˈnowns/
▶ v. [trans.] declare or announce, typically formally or solemnly: *the legislature tried a second time to craft a congressional plan, but the court pronounced it unconstitutional.*
■ [intrans.] (**pronounce on**) pass judgment or make a decision on: *the secretary of state will shortly pronounce on alternative measures.*
DERIVATIVES **pro•nounce•ment** n.
ORIGIN late Middle English: from Old French *pronuncier*, from Latin *pronuntiare*, from *pro-* 'out, forth' + *nuntiare* 'announce' (from *nuntius* 'messenger').

proof /proōf/
▶ n. the evidence in a trial.
■ the action or process of establishing the truth of a statement: *it shifts the onus of proof in convictions from the police to the public.*
ORIGIN Middle English *preve*, from Old French *proeve*,

from late Latin *proba*, from Latin *probare* 'to test, prove.'
The change of vowel in late Middle English was due to
the influence of PROVE.

prop•er•ty /ˈpräpərtē/

▶ n. (pl. **prop•er•ties**) a thing or things belonging to someone; possessions collectively: *she wanted Oliver and his
property out of her house* | *the stolen property was not re-
covered.*
■ short for REAL PROPERTY. ■ short for PERSONAL PROPERTY.
■ the right to the possession, use, or disposal of something; ownership: *rights of property.*
ORIGIN Middle English: from an Anglo-Norman
French variant of Old French *propriete*, from Latin *pro-
prietas*, from *proprius* 'one's own, particular.'

pros•e•cute /ˈpräsiˌkyo͞ot/

▶ v. [trans.] institute legal, especially criminal, proceedings
against (a person or organization): *they were prosecuted
for obstructing the highway.*
■ institute legal proceedings in respect of (a claim or offense): *the state's attorney's office seemed to decide that this
was a case worth prosecuting* | [intrans.] *the company didn't
prosecute because of his age.* ■ [intrans.] (of a lawyer) conduct the case against the party being accused or sued
in a lawsuit: *Mr. Ryan will be prosecuting this morning.*
DERIVATIVES **pros•e•cut•a•ble** adj.
ORIGIN late Middle English: from Latin *prosecut-* 'pursued, accompanied,' from the verb *prosequi*, from *pro-*
'onward' + *sequi* 'follow.'

pros•e•cu•tion /ˌpräsiˈkyo͞oSHən/

▶ n. the institution and conducting of legal proceedings
against someone in respect of a criminal charge: *Olesky
faces prosecution on charges he spied for Russian intelligence.*
■ (**the prosecution**) [treated as sing. or pl.] the party
(specifically, the government) instituting or conducting

criminal proceedings against someone: *the main witness for the prosecution.*

ORIGIN mid 16th cent.: from Old French, or from late Latin *prosecutio(n-)*, from *prosequi* 'pursue, accompany' (see PROSECUTE).

pros•e•cu•tor /'präsi,kyōōt̬ər/
‣ n. a public official who institutes legal proceedings against someone.
■ a lawyer who conducts the case against a defendant in a criminal court. Also called **prosecuting attorney**.
DERIVATIVES **pros•e•cu•to•ri•al** /,präsikyə'tôrēəl/ **adj.**

pro•test
‣ n. /'prō,test/ a written declaration that a bill has been presented and payment or acceptance refused: *you have 30 days from the date the notice was mailed to* **file a protest**.
‣ v. /prə'test; prō'test; 'prō,test/ [trans.] write or obtain a protest in regard to (a bill).
DERIVATIVES **pro•tes•tor** /'prō,testər; prə'tes-/ **n.**
ORIGIN late Middle English (as a verb in the sense 'make a solemn declaration'): from Old French *protester*, from Latin *protestari*, from *pro-* 'forth, publicly' + *testari* 'assert' (from *testis* 'witness').

pro•tho•no•ta•ry /,prōt̬ə'nōt̬ərē; prō'tänə,terē/ (also **pro•to•no•ta•ry**)
‣ n. (pl. **pro•tho•no•ta•ries**) chiefly historical a chief clerk in some courts of law.
ORIGIN late Middle English: via medieval Latin from late Greek *prōtonotarios*, from *prōtos* 'first' + *notarios* 'notary.'

pro•to•col /'prōt̬ə,kôl; -,käl/
‣ n. 1 the official procedure or system of rules governing affairs of state or diplomatic occasions: *protocol*

*forbids the prince from making any public statement in his
defense.*
2 the original draft of a diplomatic document, esp. of
the terms of a treaty agreed to in conference and signed
by the parties.
■ an amendment or addition to a treaty or convention:
a protocol to the treaty allowed for this Danish referendum.
ORIGIN late Middle English (denoting the original record of an agreement, forming the legal authority for future dealings relating to it): from Old French *prothocole*,
via medieval Latin from Greek *prōtokollon* 'first page, fly-
leaf,' from *prōtos* 'first' + *kolla* 'glue.' Sense 1 derives
from French *protocole*, the collection of set forms of et-
iquette to be observed by the French head of state, and
the name of the government department responsible for
this (in the 19th cent.).

prove /prōov/
▶ **v.** (past part. **proved** or **prov•en** /'prōovən/) [trans.]
demonstrate the truth or existence of (something) by
evidence or argument: *the concept is difficult to prove.*
■ demonstrate by evidence or argument (someone or
something) to be: *innocent until proven guilty.* ■ establish
the genuineness and validity of (a will).
DERIVATIVES **prov•a•bil•i•ty** /,prōovə'bilitē/ n.; **prov•a•
ble** adj.
ORIGIN Middle English: from Old French *prover*, from
Latin *probare* 'test, approve, demonstrate,' from *probus*
'good.'

prov•o•ca•tion /,prävə'kāsHən/
▶ **n.** action or speech held to be likely to prompt physical retaliation: *the assault had taken place **under provo-
cation**.*
ORIGIN late Middle English: from Old French, from
Latin *provocatio(n-)*, from the verb *provocare* 'challenge,'
from *pro-* 'forth' + *vocare* 'to call.'

pub•lic act /'pəblik 'ækt/
▸ n. an act of legislation affecting the public as a whole; public law: *as a state legislator she authored over 50 public acts.*

pub•lic de•fend•er /'pəblik di'fendər/
▸ n. a lawyer employed at public expense in a criminal trial to represent a defendant who is unable to afford legal assistance.

pub•lic do•main /'pəblik dō'mān/
▸ n. the state of belonging or being available to the public as a whole.
■ not subject to copyright: *the photograph had been **in the public domain** for 15 years* | [as adj.] *public-domain software.* ■ public land: *a grazing permit on public domain.*

pub•lic law /'pəblik 'lô/
▸ n. **1** the law of relationships between individuals and the government, such as constitutional, criminal, and administrative law.
2 another term for PUBLIC ACT.

pub•lic nui•sance /'pəblik 'n(y)ōōsəns/
▸ n. an act, condition, or thing that is illegal because it interferes with the rights of the public generally.
■ informal an obnoxious or dangerous person or group of people.

pub•lic pros•e•cu•tor /'pəblik 'präsə,kyōōtər/
▸ n. a law officer who conducts criminal proceedings on behalf of the government or in the public interest.

pub•lish /'pəblisʜ/
▸ v. [trans.] communicate (a defamatory statement) to a third party or to the public: *Nelson alleges that the defen-*

dants caused these false and malicious statements to be published.

ORIGIN Middle English (in the sense 'make generally known'): from the stem of Old French *puplier*, from Latin *publicare* 'make public.'

pu•ni•tive damages /'pyōōnitiv 'dæmijiz/
‣ plural n. damages exceeding simple compensation and awarded to punish the defendant; exemplary damages.

pur•chase /'pərCHəs/
‣ v. [trans.] acquire (something) by paying for it; buy: *all items purchased must be removed the day of the auction.*
‣ n. the acquisition of property by means other than inheritance.
DERIVATIVES **pur•chas•er** n.
ORIGIN Middle English: from Old French *pourchacier* 'seek to obtain or bring about,' the earliest sense also in English, which soon gave rise to the senses 'gain' (hence, in nautical use, the notion of "gaining" one portion of rope after another) and 'buy.'

purge /pərj/
‣ v. [trans.] atone for or wipe out (contempt of court).
ORIGIN Middle English (in the legal sense 'clear oneself of a charge'): from Old French *purgier*, from Latin *purgare* 'purify,' from *purus* 'pure.'

Q

QC
▸ **abbr.** Queen's Counsel.

qual•i•fi•ca•tion /ˌkwäləfiˈkāsHən/
▸ **n.** a condition that must be fulfilled before a right can be acquired; an official requirement: *there is a five-year residency qualification for presidential candidates.*
ORIGIN mid 16th cent.: from medieval Latin *qualificatio(n-)*, from the verb *qualificare*, from Latin *qualis* 'of what kind, of such a kind.'

quan•tum me•ru•it /ˌkwäntəm ˈmerōōit/
▸ **n.** [usu. as adj.] a reasonable sum of money to be paid for services rendered or work done when the amount due is not stipulated in a legally enforceable contract: *plaintiff was entitled to be paid for its contract efforts on an quantum meruit basis.*
ORIGIN Latin, literally 'as much as he has deserved.'

quash /kwôSH; kwäSH/
▸ **v.** [trans.] reject as invalid, esp. by legal procedure: *his conviction was quashed on appeal.*
ORIGIN Middle English: from Old French *quasser* 'annul,' from late Latin *cassare* (medieval Latin also *quassare*), from *cassus* 'null, void.'

qua•si con•tract /ˈkwäzī ˈkäntrækt; ˈkwäzē/ (also **quasi-contract**)
▸ **n.** an obligation of one party to another imposed by law independently of a formal agreement between the parties: *an express contract precludes the existence of a contract implied by law or a quasi contract.*

DERIVATIVES **qua•si-con•trac•tu•al** /'kwäzī kəntræk-CHO͞oəl; 'kwäzē/ **adj.**

Queen's Bench /'kwēnz 'bencH/ (in full **Queen's Bench Division**)
▸ **n.** (in the UK) a division of the High Court of Justice.

Queen's Coun•sel /'kwēnz 'kownsəl/ (abbr.: **QC**)
▸ **n.** a senior barrister appointed on the recommendation of the Lord Chancellor.

ques•tion of fact /'kwescHən əv 'fækt/
▸ **n. phrase** an issue of factual circumstances, decided at trial, usually by a jury, and not appealable: *whether a physician-patient relationship is created is a question of fact.*

ques•tion of law /'kwescHən əv 'lô/
▸ **n. phrase** an issue of the law's application, decided by a judge and appealable: *the military judge properly decided the issue of lawfulness as a question of law in this case.*

qui•et /'kwīət/
▸ **adj.** not interfered with, as by an adverse claim: *quiet enjoyment of land.*
▸ **v.** [trans.] settle or establish the fact of ownership of (a title, etc.): *the court will not quiet title in favor of a foreclosure purchaser.*

quit•claim /'kwit,klām/
▸ **n.** a formal renunciation or relinquishing of a claim.
▸ **v.** [trans.] renounce or relinquish a claim: *Aikins quitclaimed his interest in the three parcels of real estate.*
▸ **adj.** (of a deed) relinquishing all of the grantor's claim to land: *the club executed a quitclaim deed conveying the five lots to the decedant's immediate heirs.*

quo war•ran•to /ˌkwō wə'ræntō/
▸ **n.** [usu. as adj.] a writ or legal action requiring a person

to show by what warrant an office or franchise is held, claimed, or exercised: *the DA argues that he is not subject to a quo warranto proceeding because the plaintiffs have an adequate remedy at law.*

ORIGIN Law Latin, literally 'by what warrant.'

R

r
> ▸ **abbr.** ■ rule: *under r 7.4 (6) the court may hear an application immediately.*

rape /rāp/
> ▸ **n.** the crime, committed by a man, of forcing another person to have sexual intercourse with him without their consent and against their will, esp. by the threat or use of violence against them: *he denied two charges of attempted rape* | *he had committed at least two rapes.* Compare with STAUTORY RAPE.
> ▸ **v.** [trans.] (of a man) force (another person) to have sexual intercourse with him without their consent and against their will, esp. by the threat or use of violence against them: *the woman was raped at knifepoint.*
> ORIGIN late Middle English (originally denoting violent seizure of property, later carrying off a woman by force): from Anglo-Norman French *rap* (noun), *raper* (verb), from Latin *rapere* 'seize.'

rap•ist /'rāpist/
> ▸ **n.** a man who commits rape.

ra•ti•o de•ci•den•di /'rätē,ō ,desi'dendē; 'rætē,ō/
> ▸ **n.** (pl. **ra•ti•o•nes de•ci•den•di** /,rätē'ōnēz ,desi'dendē; ,rætē'ōnēz/) the rule of law on which a judicial decision is based: *the ratio decidendi of the judgment creates a precedent for the future.*
> ORIGIN Latin, literally 'reason for deciding.'

re•al es•tate /'rē(ə)l i,stāt/
> ▸ **n.** another term for REAL PROPERTY.

realm /relm/
> ▸ **n.** a kingdom: *the defense of the realm.*

ORIGIN Middle English *rewme*, from Old French *reaume*, from Latin *regimen* 'government.' The spelling with -*l*- (standard from *c.* 1600) was influenced by Old French *reiel* 'royal.'

re•al prop•er•ty /'rē(ə)l 'präpərtē/
▶ n. property consisting of land, buildings, and other related immovables (e.g., the rights to resources in or on the land). Compare with PERSONAL PROPERTY.

re•al•ty /'rē(ə)ltē/
▶ n. a person's real property. The opposite of PERSONALTY.

re•but•tal /ri'bətl/
▶ n. a refutation or contradiction: *his rebuttal claimed that the health of the defendant was indeed a precipitating factor.*
■ the presenting of one's refutation or contradiction: *normally the court will not grant additional time for rebuttal.* ■ evidence offered in contradiction: *yes, Judge, I've got some rebuttal.*

re•ceiv•er•ship /ri'sēvər,SHip/
▶ n. the state of being dealt with by a court-appointed receiver: *the company went **into receivership** last week.*

re•cit•al /ri'sītl/
▶ n. (usu. **recitals**) the part of a legal document, such as a deed, that explains its purpose and gives factual information: *he trustee's deed may contain recitals of compliance with the following requirements.*

re•cog•ni•zance /ri'kä(g)nəzəns/
▶ n. a bond by which a person undertakes before a court or magistrate to observe some condition, esp. to appear when summoned: *he was released **on his own recognizance**.*

ORIGIN Middle English: from Old French *reconnissance*, from *reconnaistre* 'recognize.'

re•com•mit /ˌrēkə'mit/
▸ v. (**re•com•mit•ted, re•com•mit•ting**) [trans.] commit again.
■ return (a motion, proposal, or legislative bill) to a committee for further consideration: *the entire bill has been recommitted* | [intrans.] *a motion to recommit.*
DERIVATIVES **re•com•mit•ment** n.; **re•com•mit•tal** /ˌrē-kə'miṯl/ n.

rec•ord
▸ n. /'rekərd/ **1** (also **court record**) an official report of the proceedings and judgment in a court.
2 short for CRIMINAL RECORD.
▸ v. /ri'kôrd/ [trans.] set down in writing or some other permanent form for later reference, esp. officially: *they were asked to keep a diary and record everything they observed* | [as adj.] (**recorded**) *levels of recorded crime.*
■ state or express publicly or officially; make an official record of: *the coroner recorded a verdict of accidental death.*
PHRASES **a matter of record** a thing that is established as a fact through being officially recorded: *the circumstances of his death are now a matter of record.* **off the record** not made as an official or attributable statement: *anything I may tell you is strictly off the record.* **on record** (also **on the record**) used in reference to the making of an official or public statement: *Ives was unwilling to go on record when the discussion turned to gun control.* **set** (or **put**) **the record straight** give the true version of events that have been reported incorrectly; correct a misapprehension.
DERIVATIVES **re•cord•a•ble** /ri'kôrdəbəl; rē-/ adj.
ORIGIN Middle English: from Old French *record* 'remembrance,' from *recorder* 'bring to remembrance,' from Latin *recordari* 'remember,' based on *cor, cord-*

'heart.' The noun was earliest used in law to denote the fact of being written down as evidence. The verb originally meant 'narrate orally or in writing,' also 'repeat so as to commit to memory.'

re•cov•er /ri'kəvər/
▶ v. [trans.] find or regain possession of (something stolen or lost): *police recovered a stolen video.*
■ regain or secure (compensation) by means of a legal process or subsequent profits: *many companies recovered their costs within six months.*
ORIGIN Middle English (originally with reference to health): from Anglo-Norman French *recoverer*, from Latin *recuperare* 'get again.'

re•cov•er•y /ri'kəv(ə)rē/
▶ n. (pl. **re•cov•er•ies**) the action or process of regaining possession or control of something stolen or lost.
■ the action of regaining or securing compensation or money lost or spent by means of a legal process or subsequent profits: *debt recovery.* ■ an object or amount of money recovered: *the recoveries included gold jewelry.*
ORIGIN late Middle English (denoting a means of restoration): from Anglo-Norman French *recoverie*, from *recovrer* 'get back.'

re•cuse /ri'kyo͞oz/
▶ v. [trans.] (**recuse oneself**) (of a judge) excuse oneself from a case because of a possible conflict of interest or lack of impartiality: *the Justice Department demanded that he recuse himself from the case.*
DERIVATIVES **re•cus•al** /ri'kyo͞ozəl/ n.
ORIGIN late Middle English: from Latin *recusare* 'to refuse,' from *re-* (expressing opposition) + *causa* 'a cause.' The sense 'excuse (oneself from a case)' dates from the early 19th cent.

re•dress /ri'dres; 're͵dres/
▶ v. [trans.] remedy or set right (an undesirable or unfair situation): *the power to redress the grievances of our citizens.*
▶ n. remedy or compensation for a wrong or grievance: *those seeking redress for an infringement of public law rights.*
ORIGIN Middle English: the verb from Old French *redresser*; the noun via Anglo-Norman French *redresse*.

re•en•act /͵rēə'nækt/
▶ v. [trans.] bring (a law) into effect again when the original statute has been repealed: *chapter forty-eight of said code shall be amended and reenacted.*
DERIVATIVES **re•en•act•ment** n.

re•en•try /rē'entrē/
▶ n. (pl. **re•en•tries**) the action of retaking or repossession of property that had been let or granted: *reentry may be allowed if the buyer defaults.*

re•ex•am•ine /͵rē-ig'zæmin/
▶ v. [trans.] examine again or further: *I will have the body reexamined.*
■ examine (a witness) again, after cross-examination by the opposing counsel; submit a witness to redirect examination: *the prosecuting lawyer may reexamine the witness.*
DERIVATIVES **re•ex•am•i•na•tion** /͵rēig͵zæmə'nāsHən/ n.

Re•gi•na /rə'jīnə/
▶ n. (in the UK) the reigning queen (used following a name or in the titles of lawsuits, e.g., *Regina v. Jones*, the Crown versus Jones).
ORIGIN Latin, literally 'queen.'

reg•is•trar /'reji,strär/

▸ **n.** an official responsible for keeping a register or official records: *the registrar of births and deaths.*
ORIGIN late 17th cent.: from medieval Latin *registrarius*, from *registrum*, singular of Late Latin *regesta* 'things recorded,' from *regerere* 'enter, record.'

re•hear /rē'hir/

▸ **v.** (past and past part. **re•heard** /rē'hərd/) [trans.] hear (a case or plaintiff) in a court again: [as n.] (**rehearing**) *the parents produced fresh evidence and won a rehearing.*

re•la•tor /ri'lāṯər/

▸ **n.** a person who brings a public lawsuit, typically in the name of the attorney general, regarding the abuse of an office or franchise: *if the government declines to intervene, the relator may go forward with the lawsuit.*

re•lease /ri'lēs/

▸ **v.** [trans.] **1** allow or enable to escape from confinement; set free: *the government announced that the prisoners would be released.*
2 remit or discharge (a debt): *releasing a debt is merely dealing with symptoms.*
■ surrender (a right): *the New York Power Authority released rights to land at Hyde Park Golf Course.* ■ make over (property or money) to another: *the sum of $8,000 has been released to the nephew's account.*
▸ **n. 1** the action or process of releasing or being released: *upon her release, Wanda returned to the streets.*
2 the action of releasing property, money, or a right to another: *the father consented to the release of his parental rights.*
■ a document effecting this: *signing this release allows Dayco the commercial use of your poem* | [as adj.] *a release form.*

DERIVATIVES **re•leas•ee** /ri͵lē'sē/ n.; **re•leas•or** /ri 'lēsôr/ n.
ORIGIN Middle English: from Old French *reles* (noun), *relesser* (verb), from Latin *relaxare* 'stretch out again, slacken.'

rel•e•vant /'reləvənt/
▸ adj. (of evidence or a fact) pertinent; closely connected or appropriate to the matter at hand, especially to the extent of proving or disproving the matter: *evidence which is not relevant is not admissible.*
DERIVATIVES **rel•e•vance** n.; **rel•e•van•cy** /-vənsē/ n.
ORIGIN early 16th cent. (as a Scots legal term meaning 'legally pertinent'): from medieval Latin *relevant-* 'raising up,' from Latin *relevare.*

re•lief /ri'lēf/
▸ n. the redress of a hardship or grievance: *debt relief.*
ORIGIN late Middle English: from Old French, from *relever* 'raise up, relieve,' from Latin *relevare* 'raise again, alleviate.'

re•main•der /ri'māndər/
▸ n. an interest in an estate that becomes effective in possession only when a prior interest (devised at the same time) ends: *after all other bequests and expenses of the estate are met, the remainder is your charitable gift.*
ORIGIN late Middle English: from Anglo-Norman French, from Latin *remanere*, from *re-* (expressing intensive force) + *manere* 'to stay.'

re•mand /ri'mænd/
▸ v. [trans.] place (a defendant) on bail or in custody, esp. when a trial is adjourned: *I had a seventeen-year-old son remanded to a drug-addiction program.*
■ return (a case) to a lower court for reconsideration: *the Supreme Court summarily vacated the opinion and remanded the matter back to the California Court of Appeal.*

▸**n.** a committal to custody.

ORIGIN late Middle English (as a verb in the sense 'send back again'): from late Latin *remandare*, from *re-* 'back' + *mandare* 'commit.' The noun dates from the late 18th cent.

rem•e•dy /ˈremədē/

▸**n.** (pl. **rem•e•dies**) a means of legal reparation: *the doctrine took away their only **remedy against** merchants who refused to honor their contracts.*

ORIGIN Middle English: from Anglo-Norman French *remedie*, from Latin *remedium*, from *re-* 'back' (also expressing intensive force) + *mederi* 'heal.'

re•mis•sion /riˈmiSHən/

▸**n.** the cancellation of a debt, charge, or penalty: *the plan allows for the partial remission of tuition fees.*

ORIGIN Middle English: from Old French, or from Latin *remissio(n-)*, from *remittere* 'send back, restore' (see REMIT).

re•mit

▸**v.** /riˈmit/ (**re•mit•ted, re•mit•ting**) [trans.] **1** cancel or refrain from exacting or inflicting (a debt or punishment): *the excess of the sentence over 12 months was remitted.*

2 send back (a case) to a lower court: *the case should be remitted back to the Commissioners for further findings of fact.*

■ send (someone) from one tribunal to another for a trial or hearing.

▸**n.** /riˈmit; ˈrēˌmit/ **1** the task or area of activity officially assigned to an individual or organization: *the committee was becoming caught up in issues that did not fall within its remit.*

2 an item referred to someone for consideration.

DERIVATIVES **re•mit•ta•ble** adj.; **re•mit•tal** /riˈmitl/ n.; **re•mit•ter** n.

ORIGIN late Middle English: from Latin *remittere* 'send back, restore,' from *re-* 'back' + *mittere* 'send.' The noun dates from the early 20th cent.

re•nounce /ri'nowns/

▸ v. [trans.] formally declare one's abandonment of (a claim, right, or possession): *we renounce our right to Israeli citizenship.*
■ [intrans.] refuse or resign a right or position, esp. one as an heir or trustee: *there will be forms enabling the allottee to renounce.*
DERIVATIVES **re•nounce•a•ble** adj.; **re•nounce•ment** n.; **re•nounc•er** n.
ORIGIN late Middle English: from Old French *renoncer*, from Latin *renuntiare* 'protest against,' from *re-* (expressing reversal) + *nuntiare* 'announce.'

re•nun•ci•a•tion /ri,nənsē'āsHən/

▸ n. the formal rejection of something, typically a belief, claim, or course of action: *the heirs have ten years to retract their renunciation of the succession.*
■ a document expressing renunciation.
DERIVATIVES **re•nun•ci•ant** /ri'nənsēənt/ n. & adj.
ORIGIN late Middle English: from late Latin *renuntiatio(n-)*, from Latin *renuntiare* 'protest against' (see RE-NOUNCE).

re•peal /ri'pēl/

▸ v. [trans.] revoke or annul (a law or congressional act): *the legislation was repealed five months later.*
▸ n. the action of revoking or annulling a law or congressional act: *the House voted in favor of repeal.*
DERIVATIVES **re•peal•a•ble** adj.
ORIGIN late Middle English: from Anglo-Norman French *repeler*, from Old French *re-* (expressing reversal) + *apeler* 'to call, appeal.'

re•plev•in /ri'plevən/

▸ n. a procedure whereby goods wrongfully taken or detained may be provisionally restored to their owner pending the outcome of an action to determine the rights of the parties concerned: *an attorney filed a complaint for replevin on his own behalf* | [as adj.] *the creditor may seek a determination of ownership rights as a part of a replevin action.*

■ an action arising from such a process.

ORIGIN late Middle English: from Anglo-Norman French, from Old French *replevir* 'recover' (see REPLEVY).

re•plev•y /ri'plevē/

▸ v. (**re•plev•ies, re•plev•ied**) [trans.] recover (goods taken or detained) by replevin: *a defendant who replevies the property is not required to account for the revenue of the property* | [as adj.] *all of the replevied cattle were sold at Bassett or Burwell.*

ORIGIN mid 16th cent.: from Old French *replevir* 'recover'; apparently related to PLEDGE.

re•ply /ri'plī/

▸ n. (pl. **re•plies**) a plaintiff's response to the defendant's plea.

DERIVATIVES **re•pli•er** n.

ORIGIN late Middle English (as a verb): from Old French *replier*, from Latin *replicare* 'repeat,' later 'make a reply.'

re•port /ri'pôrt/

▸ v. [trans.] (of a legislative committee) formally announce that the committee has dealt with (a bill): *the chairman shall report the bill to the House.*

▸ n. a detailed formal account of a case heard in a court, giving the main points in the judgment, esp. as prepared for publication.

PHRASES **on report** (esp. of a prisoner or member of the armed forces) on a disciplinary charge: *the first time you step out of line, you'll be on report.*

▶**report a bill out** (of a committee of Congress) return a bill to the legislative body for action: *if the committee chooses to report a bill out they must choose whether or not to incorporate amendments.*

ORIGIN late Middle English: from Old French *reporter* (verb), *report* (noun), from Latin *reportare* 'bring back,' from *re-* 'back' + *portare* 'carry.'

rep•re•sent /ˌrepriˈzent/

▶ v. [trans.] **1** be entitled or appointed to act or speak for (someone), esp. in an official capacity, as a lawyer for a client: *for purposes of litigation, an infant can and must be represented by an adult.*

■ be an elected member of a legislature for (a particular constituency, party, or group): *she became the first woman to represent her district.*

2 [with clause] allege; claim: *the vendors have represented that such information is accurate.*

ORIGIN late Middle English: from Old French *representer* or Latin *repraesentare*, from *re-* (expressing intensive force) + *praesentare* 'to present.'

re•pu•di•ate /riˈpyo͞odēˌāt/

▶ v. [trans.] refuse to fulfill or discharge (an agreement, obligation, or debt): *breach of a condition by one party gives the other party the right to repudiate a contract.*

DERIVATIVES **re•pu•di•a•tion** /riˌpyo͞odēˈāsHən/ n.; **re•pu•di•a•tor** /riˈpyo͞odēˌātər/ n.

ORIGIN late Middle English (originally an adjective in the sense 'divorced'): from Latin *repudiatus* 'divorced, cast off,' from *repudium* 'divorce.'

res•er•va•tion /ˌrezərˈvāsHən/

▶ n. a right or interest retained in an estate being conveyed: *the agreement does not contain a specific reservation of appellee's right to seek appointment as co-executrix of the estate.*

ORIGIN late Middle English (denoting the pope's right of nomination to a benefice): from Old French, or from late Latin *reservatio(n-)*, from *reservare* 'keep back.'

res ges•tae /'rāz 'gestī; 'rēz 'jestē/
▸ plural n. the events, circumstances, remarks, etc., that relate to a particular case, esp. as constituting admissible evidence in a court of law: *these declarations were admissible as part of the res gestae* | [as adj.] *the court held that the officers were not res gestae witnesses because they arrived at the scene after the crime allegedly took place.*

ORIGIN Latin, literally 'things done.'

re•sid•u•ar•y /ri'zijo͞o,erē/
▸ adj. of or relating to the residue of an estate: *a residuary legatee.*

res•i•due /'rezə,d(y)o͞o/
▸ n. the part of an estate that is left after the payment of charges, debts, and bequests: *this bequest directs that either all or a percentage of your estate's residue be paid to the San Jose Cathedral Foundation.*

ORIGIN late Middle English: from Old French *residu*, from Latin *residuum* 'something remaining.'

res ip•sa lo•qui•tur /,rāz ,ipsə 'läkwiṭər; 'lōkwə,to͞or/
▸ n. the principle that the occurrence of an accident implies negligence if circumstances were such that it would not ordinarily otherwise have happened: *the court said res ipsa loquitur did not apply when the anesthesiologist introduced evidence that broken teeth are a normal risk of a laryngoscopic procedure.*

ORIGIN Latin, literally 'the matter speaks for itself.'

res ju•di•ca•ta /ˌräz ˌjo͞odi'kätə/

▶ n. (pl. **res ju•di•ca•tae** /'räz ˌjo͞odi'kätē; -'kätī/) a matter that has been adjudicated by a competent court and may not be pursued further by the same parties: *res judicata also bars subsequent actions on claims that should have been—but were not—raised in the first proceeding.*

ORIGIN Latin, literally 'judged matter.'

re•spond•ent /ri'spändənt/

▶ n. a defendant in a lawsuit, esp. one in an appeal or in a divorce case: *the respondent is a telecommunications corporation.*

▶ adj. [attrib.] in the position of defendant in a lawsuit: *the plaintiff says he has worked for the respondent party for many years.*

ORIGIN from Latin *respondent-* 'answering, offering in return.'

rest /rest/

▶ v. [intrans.] conclude the case for the prosecution or the defense in a law case: *the prosecution rests.* See also **rest one's case** below.

PHRASES **rest one's case** conclude one's presentation of evidence and arguments in a lawsuit.

ORIGIN Old English *ræst, rest* (noun), *ræstan, restan* (verb), of Germanic origin, from a root meaning 'league' or 'mile' (referring to a distance after which one rests).

res•ti•tu•tion /ˌrestə't(y)o͞osHən/

▶ n. return of a benefit received: *he was ordered to pay $6,000 in restitution.*

■ the restoring of both parties to their original position after recission of a contract.

DERIVATIVES **res•ti•tu•tive** /'restə,t(y)o͞otiv/ **adj.**

ORIGIN Middle English: from Old French, or from Latin *restitutio(n-)*, from *restituere* 'restore,' from *re-* 'again' + *statuere* 'establish.'

re•straint of trade /ri'strānt əv 'trād/
▶ n. action that interferes with free competition in a market.

re•stric•tive cov•e•nant /ri'striktiv 'kəvənənt/
▶ n. a covenant imposing a restriction on the occupancy or use of land, typically so that the value and enjoyment of adjoining land will be preserved.
■ a covenant in an employment contract that forbids the employee from working for a competitor if he or she leaves the first employer.

re•tain /ri'tān/
▶ v. [trans.] secure the services of (a person, esp. an attorney) with a preliminary payment: *retain an attorney to handle the client's business.*
ORIGIN late Middle English: via Anglo-Norman French from Old French *retenir*, from Latin *retinere*, from *re-* 'back' + *tenere* 'hold.'

re•tain•er /ri'tānər/
▶ n. a fee paid in advance to an attorney in order to secure or keep their services when required.

re•tri•al /rē'trīəl; 'rē,trīəl/
▶ n. a second or further trial.

ret•ro•ac•tive /,retrō'æktiv/
▶ adj. (esp. of legislation) taking effect from a date in the past: *a big retroactive tax increase.*
DERIVATIVES **ret•ro•ac•tion** /,retrō'ækSHən/ n.; **ret•ro•ac•tive•ly** adv.; **ret•ro•ac•tiv•i•ty** /,retrōæk'tivətē/ n.

ret•ro•spec•tive /,retrə'spektiv/
▶ adj. (of a statute or legal decision) taking effect from a date in the past; retroactive: *retrospective pay awards.*

re•try /rē'trī/
> ▸ v. (**re•tries, re•tried**) [trans.] try (a defendant or case) again: *the state of Alabama then retried one of the accused, and once again convicted him.*

re•turn /ri'tərn/
> ▸ v. [trans.] (of a judge or jury) state or present (a verdict) in response to a formal request: *the jury of nine women and three men returned the verdict within hours.*
> ▸ n. an endorsement or report by a court officer or sheriff on a writ: *the officer shall promptly make a return of the facts to the court.*
> ORIGIN Middle English: the verb from Old French *returner,* from Latin *re-* 'back' + *tornare* 'to turn'; the noun via Anglo-Norman French.

re•turn date /'ritərn ˌdāt/
> ▸ n. the day on which process is due or an order is to be answered. Also called **return day**: *Stevens failed to appear in court on the return date.*

re•ver•sal /ri'vərsəl/
> ▸ n. an annulment of a judgment, sentence, or decree made by a lower court or authority: *the Court has upheld the appellate justices in their reversal of the trial court judgment.*
> ORIGIN late 15th cent. (as a legal term): from the verb REVERSE + *-al.*

re•verse /ri'vərs/
> ▸ v. [trans.] revoke or annul (a judgment, sentence, or decree made by a lower court or authority): *the court reversed his conviction.*
> ORIGIN Middle English: from Old French *revers, reverse* (nouns), *reverser* (verb), from Latin *reversus* 'turned back,' past participle of *revertere,* from *re-* 'back' + *vertere* 'to turn.'

re•ver•sion /ri'vərᴢʜən/

▸ n. the right, esp. of the original owner or their heirs, to possess or succeed to property on the death of the present possessor or at the end of a lease: *the reversion of property.*

■ a property to which someone has such a right.

DERIVATIVES **re•ver•sion•ar•y** /ti'vərᴢʜə,nerē/ **adj.**

ORIGIN late Middle English (denoting the action of returning to or from a place): from Old French, or from Latin *reversio(n-)*, from *revertere* 'turn back' (see RE-VERSE).

re•ver•sion•er /ri'vərᴢʜənər/

▸ n. a person who possesses the reversion to a property or privilege.

re•vert /ri'vərt/

▸ v. [intrans.] (**revert to**) (of property) return or pass to (the original owner) by reversion: *the title to the property shall revert to and be vested in the state of Mississippi.*

DERIVATIVES **re•vert•er** n.

ORIGIN Middle English: from Old French *revertir* or Latin *revertere* 'turn back.' Early senses included 'recover consciousness,' 'return to a position,' and 'return to a person (after estrangement).'

re•view /ri'vyōō/

▸ n. a reconsideration of a judgment, sentence, etc., by a higher court or authority: *a review of her sentence* | *his case comes up for review in January.* Compare with JUDICIAL REVIEW.

▸ v. [trans.] (of a higher court or authority) reconsider (the action of a lower court or authority): *the attorney general asked the court to review the sentence.*

ORIGIN late Middle English (as a noun denoting a formal inspection of military or naval forces): from obsolete French *reveue*, from *revoir* 'see again.'

Rex /reks/

▶ n. (in the UK) the reigning king (used following a name or in the titles of lawsuits, e.g., *Rex v. Jones*: the Crown versus Jones).

ORIGIN Latin, literally 'king.'

RICO /'rēkō/

▶ abbr. (in the US) Racketeer Influenced and Corrupt Organizations Act.

rid•er /'rīdər/

▶ n. an addition or amendment to a document, esp. a piece of legislation or a contract: *the rules of Congress make it difficult to attach a rider to an appropriations bill* | *a rider to an eligible life insurance policy.*

ORIGIN late Old English *rīdere* 'mounted warrior, knight.'

right /rīt/

▶ n. a moral or legal entitlement to have or obtain something or to act in a certain way: [with infinitive] *you're quite* ***within your rights*** *to ask for your money back* | *there is no* ***right of*** *appeal against the decision.*

■ (**rights**) one's civil liberties. ■ (**rights**) the authority to perform, publish, film, or televise a particular work, event, etc.: *they sold the paperback rights.*

PHRASES **be in the right** be morally or legally justified in one's views, actions, or decisions. (**as**) **of right** (or **by right**) as a result of having a moral or legal claim or entitlement: *the state will be obliged to provide health care and education as of right.*

ORIGIN Old English *riht* (adjective and noun), *rihtan* (verb), *rihte* (adverb), of Germanic origin; related to Latin *rectus* 'ruled,' from an Indo-European root denoting movement in a straight line.

right of way /'rīt əv 'wā/ (also **right-of-way**)

▶ n. 1 the legal right, established by usage or grant, to

pass along a specific route through grounds or property belonging to another.

■ a path or thoroughfare subject to such a right.

2 the legal right of a pedestrian, rider, or driver to proceed with precedence over other road users at a particular point: *he waves on other drivers, even when it's not their right of way.*

■ the right of a ship, boat, or aircraft to proceed with precedence over others in a particular situation.

3 the right to build and operate a railroad line, road, or utility on land belonging to another.

■ the land on which a railroad line, road, or utility is built: *the right of way of the South Penn Railroad was a section that ran between Harrisburg and Pittsburgh.*

Ri•ot Act /ˈrīət ˌækt/ a law passed by the British government in 1715 and repealed in 1967, designed to prevent civil disorder. The act made it a felony for an assembly of more than twelve people to refuse to disperse after being ordered to do so and having been read a specified portion of the act by lawful authority.

ri•par•i•an /rəˈperēən; rī-/

▶ **adj.** of, relating to, or situated on the banks of a river: *all the riparian states must sign an agreement.*

PHRASES **riparian rights** legal entitlement to use of flowing water.

ORIGIN mid 19th cent.: from Latin *riparius* (from *ripa* 'bank') + *-an.*

rise /rīz/

▶ **v.** (past **rose** /rōz/; past part. **ris•en** /ˈrizən/) [intrans.] chiefly Brit. (of a meeting or a session of a court) adjourn: *the judge's remark heralded the signal for the court to rise.*

ORIGIN Old English *rīsan* 'make an attack,' 'wake, get out of bed,' of Germanic origin; related to Dutch *rijzen* and German *reisen.*

rob /räb/

▸ v. (**robbed, rob•bing**) [trans.] take property unlawfully from (a person or place) by force or threat of force: *he tried, with three others, to rob a bank* | *she was **robbed of** her handbag* | [intrans.] *he was convicted of assault with intent to rob.*

ORIGIN Middle English: from Old French *rober*, of Germanic origin; related to the verb *reave.*

USAGE: In law, to **rob** is to take something from someone by causing fear of harm, whether or not actual harm occurs. The term is widely, but incorrectly, used to mean **theft**: *our house was robbed while we were away.* Technically, the more correct statement would be *our house was burglarized while we were away.*

rob•ber /'räbər/

▸ n. a person who commits robbery.

ORIGIN Middle English: from Anglo-Norman French and Old French *robere*, from the verb *rober* (see ROB).

rob•ber•y /'räb(ə)rē/

▸ n. (pl. **rob•ber•ies**) the action of robbing a person or place: *he was involved in drugs, violence, extortion, and robbery* | *an armed robbery.*

■ the felonious taking of personal property from someone using force or the threat of force.

ORIGIN Middle English: from Anglo-Norman French and Old French *roberie*, from the verb *rober* (see ROB).

Ro•man law /'rōmən 'lô/

▸ n. the law code of the ancient Romans, which forms the basis of civil law in many countries today.

rule /rool/

▸ n. **1** a regulation or principle of law.

2 ■ an order made by a judge or court with reference to a particular case only.

▶**v.** [with clause] pronounce authoritatively and legally to be the case: *a federal court ruled that he was unfairly dismissed from his job.*

PHRASES **rule of law** the restriction of the arbitrary exercise of power by subordinating it to well-defined and established laws.■ a doctrine or precedent applied to the facts of a case under consideration: *what rule of law applies, given these facts?*

ORIGIN Middle English: from Old French *reule* (noun), *reuler* (verb), from late Latin *regulare*, from Latin *regula* 'straight stick.'

rule of the road /'rool əv THə 'rōd/
▶**n.** (usu. **rules of the road**) a custom or law regulating the direction in which two vehicles (or riders or ships) should move to pass one another on meeting, or which should yield to the other, so as to avoid collision.

S

s
> ▸ abbr. ◼ section (of an act).

safe con•duct /'sāf 'kän,dəkt/
> ▸ n. immunity from arrest or harm when passing through an area: *the article provides safe conduct at sea for medical equipment intended for wounded and sick members of the armed forces.*
> ◼ a document securing such a privilege.

sal•vage /'sælvij/ (also **salvage payment**)
> ▸ n. payment made or due to a person who has saved a ship or its cargo.
> ORIGIN mid 17th cent.: from French, from medieval Latin *salvagium*, from Latin *salvare* 'to save.'

sanc•tion /'sæNG(k)sHən/
> ▸ n. 1 a penalty for disobeying a law or rule: *a range of sanctions aimed at deterring insider abuse.*
> 2 official confirmation or ratification of a law.
> ◼ historical a law or decree, esp. an ecclesiastical decree.
> ▸ v. [trans.] 1 impose a sanction or penalty on: *the client is hereby sanctioned.*
> 2 officially confirm; uphold as legal: *in* Plessy v. Ferguson, *the court sanctioned segregation in public facilities.*
> DERIVATIVES **sanc•tion•a•ble** adj.
> ORIGIN late Middle English (as a noun denoting an ecclesiastical decree): from French, from Latin *sanctio(n-)*, from *sancire* 'ratify.' The verb dates from the late 18th cent.

sanc•tu•ar•y /'sæNG(k)CHŌŌ,erē/
> ▸ n. (pl. **sanc•tu•ar•ies**) immunity from arrest: *he has been given sanctuary in the US Embassy in Beijing.*

ORIGIN from Old French *sanctuaire*, from Latin *sanctuarium*, from *sanctus* 'holy.' The early sense 'a church or other sacred place where a fugitive was immune, by the law of the medieval church, from arrest' gave rise to the sense 'immunity from arrest.'

sat•is•fac•tion /ˌsætisˈfækSHən/
▶n. the payment of a debt or fulfillment of an obligation or claim: *in full and final satisfaction of the claim.*
ORIGIN Middle English: from Old French, or from Latin *satisfactio(n-)*, from *satisfacere* 'satisfy, content.'

sav•ing /ˈsāviNG/
▶n. a reservation; an exception.

sav•ing clause /ˈsāviNG ˌklôz/
▶n. an exception in a statute preserving prior law from repeal: *section 8 includes a saving clause intended to make clear that the copyright protection of a private work is not affected if the work is published by the government.*
■ a clause in a contract or agreement containing an exemption from one or more of its conditions.

seal /sēl/
▶n. a piece of wax, lead, or other material with an individual design stamped into it, attached to a document to show that it has come from the person who claims to have issued it.
■ a design embossed in paper for this purpose. ■ an engraved device used for stamping a design that authenticates a document.
▶v. [trans.] fix a piece of wax or lead stamped with a design to (a document) to authenticate it.
PHRASES **under seal** under legal protection of secrecy: *the judge ordered that the videotape be kept under seal.*
ORIGIN Middle English: from Old French *seel* (noun), *seeler* (verb), from Latin *sigillum* 'small picture,' diminutive of *signum* 'a sign.'

search war•rant /'sərCH ,wôrənt; ,wärənt/
▸ n. a legal document authorizing a police officer or other official to enter and search premises.

sec•ond-de•gree /'sekən(d) də,grē/
▸ adj. [attrib.] denoting a category of a crime, esp. murder, that is less serious than a first-degree crime: *the jury returned a verdict of second-degree murder.*

se•di•tion /si'disHən/
▸ n. conduct or speech inciting people to rebel against the authority of a state or monarch.
ORIGIN late Middle English (in the sense 'violent strife'): from Old French, or from Latin *seditio(n-)*, from *sed-* 'apart' + *itio(n-)* 'going' (from the verb *ire*).

se•di•tious /si'disHəs/
▸ adj. inciting or causing people to rebel against the authority of a state or monarch: *the letter was declared seditious.*
DERIVATIVES **se•di•tious•ly** adv.
ORIGIN late Middle English: from Old French *seditieux* or Latin *seditiosus*, from *seditio* 'mutinous separation' (see SEDITION).

se•di•tious li•bel /si'disHəs 'lībəl/
▸ n. a published statement that is seditious: *Zenger was charged with publishing seditious libel.*
■ the action or crime of publishing such a statement: *the doctrine of seditious libel was upheld in the American colonies.*

sei•sin /'sēzin/ (also **sei•zin**)
▸ n. possession of land by freehold.
■ Brit., historical possession, esp. of land: *Richard Fitzhugh did not take **seisin of** his lands until 1480.*

ORIGIN Middle English: from Old French *seisine*, from *saisir* 'seize.'

seize /sēz/

▶v. [trans.] **1** (of the police or another authority) take possession of (something) by warrant or legal right; confiscate; impound: *police have seized 726 lb of cocaine.*
2 (also **seise**) (**be seized of**) English Law be in legal possession of: *the court is currently seized of custody applications.*
■ historical have or receive freehold possession of (property): *any person who is seized of land has a protected interest in that land.*
ORIGIN Middle English: from Old French *seizir* 'give seisin,' from medieval Latin *sacire*, in the phrase *ad proprium sacire* 'claim as one's own,' from a Germanic base meaning 'procedure.'

self-de•fense /'self di'fens/

▶n. the defense of one's person or interests, esp. through the use of physical force, which is permitted in certain cases as an answer to a charge of violent crime or a tort: *he claimed self-defense in the attempted murder charge* | [as adj.] *self-defense classes.*
DERIVATIVES **self-de•fen•sive adj.**

self-prov•ing /'self 'prōōviNG/

▶adj. (of a will) accompanied by a witnesses' affidavit for which no oral testimony is needed to be admitted to probate: *we recommend that all wills be self-proving.*
■ of or relating to an affidavit that makes a will self-proving: *attached to the will offered for probate was a self-proving affidavit and certificate executed by the testatrix, the two witnesses to the will, and a notary public.*

sen•a•tor /'senəṭər/

▶n. a member of a senate.

DERIVATIVES **sen•a•to•ri•al** /ˌsenəˈtôrēəl/ **adj.; sen•a•tor•ship** /ˈsenətərˌsHip/ **n.**

ORIGIN Middle English (denoting a member of the ancient Roman senate): from Old French *senateur*, from Latin *senator*.

sen•tence /ˈsent(ə)ns/
▶ **n.** the punishment assigned to a defendant found guilty by a court: *her husband is **serving** a three-year **sentence** for fraud.*
■ the punishment fixed by law for a particular offense: *slander of an official carried an eight-year prison sentence.*
▶ **v.** [trans.] declare the punishment decided for (an offender): *ten army officers were **sentenced to** death.*
PHRASES **under sentence of** having been condemned to: *he was under sentence of death.*
ORIGIN Middle English (in the senses 'way of thinking, opinion,' 'court's declaration of punishment,' and 'gist (of a piece of writing)'): via Old French from Latin *sententia* 'opinion,' from *sentire* 'feel, be of the opinion.'

sep•a•ra•tion /ˌsepəˈrāsHən/
▶ **n.** the state in which a husband and wife remain married but live apart: *legal grounds for divorce or separation* | *she and her husband have agreed to a **trial separation**.* See also LEGAL SEPARATION (sense 1).
ORIGIN late Middle English: via Old French from Latin *separatio(n-)*, from *separare* 'disjoin, divide.'

sep•a•ra•tion of pow•ers /ˌsepəˈrāsHən əv ˈpowərz/
▶ **n. phrase** the vesting of the legislative, executive, and judicial powers of government in separate bodies: *the separation of powers insures that the authority of the president may not encroach upon that of the Congress or the Supreme Court.*

se•ques•ter /si'kwestər/
▶ v. [trans.] **1** isolate (a jury) from outside influences during a trial: *the jurors had been sequestered since Monday.* **2** take legal possession of (assets) until a debt has been paid or other claims have been met: *the power of courts to sequester the assets of unions.*
■ legally place (the property of a bankrupt) in the hands of a trustee for division among the creditors: [as adj.] (**sequestered**) *a trustee in a sequestered estate.* ■ declare (someone) bankrupt: *two more poll tax rebels were sequestered.*
ORIGIN late Middle English: from Old French *sequestrer* or late Latin *sequestrare* 'commit for safekeeping,' from Latin *sequester* 'trustee.'

se•ques•trate /'sēkwi,strāt; 'sek-; si'kwestrāt/
▶ v. [trans.] another term for SEQUESTER (sense 2).
DERIVATIVES **se•ques•tra•ble** /si'kwestrəbəl/ **adj.**
ORIGIN late Middle English (in the sense 'separate from general access'): from late Latin *sequestrat-* 'given up for safekeeping,' from the verb *sequestrare* (see SEQUESTER).

se•ques•tra•tion /,sēkwi'strāsHən; ,sek-/
▶ n. **1** the action of taking legal possession of assets until a debt has been paid or other claims have been met: *if such court injunctions are ignored, sequestration of trade union assets will follow.*
■ an act of declaring someone bankrupt. **2** the action of isolating a jury during a trial: *either party may move for sequestration of the jury.*

ser•geant-at-arms /'särjənt æt 'ärmz; ət/ (Brit. **ser•jeant-at-arms**)
▶ n. (pl. **sergeants-at-arms**) an official of a legislative or other assembly whose duty includes maintaining order and security.

serve /sərv/

▶ v. [trans.] **1** spend (a period) in jail or prison: *he is serving a ten-year jail sentence.*

2 deliver (a document such as a summons or writ) in a formal manner to the person to whom it is addressed: *a warrant was **served on** Jack Sherman.*

■ deliver a document to (someone) in such a way: *they were just about to **serve** him **with** a writ.*

PHRASES **serve one's time** (also **serve time**) spend time in jail or prison.

ORIGIN Middle English: from Old French *servir*, from Latin *servire*, from *servus* 'slave.'

serv•ice /'sərvis/

▶ n. the formal delivery of a document such as a writ or summons.

ser•vi•tude /'sərvi,t(y)ood/

▶ n. the subjection of property to an easement or other restriction: *the deed of easement granted a public forest servitude to the state.*

ORIGIN late Middle English: via Old French from Latin *servitudo*, from *servus* 'slave.'

set a•side /'set ə'sīd/

▶ phrasal verb overrule or annul (a legal decision or process): *the Supreme Court has set aside the order in its entirety.*

set•off /'set ,ôf/

▶ n. a counterbalancing debt pleaded by the defendant in an action to recover money due *the set-off may diminish or entirely cancel the claim of the plaintiff.*

set•tle /'setl/

▶ v. end (a legal dispute) by mutual agreement: *the matter was settled out of court* | [intrans.] *he sued for libel and then settled out of court.*

PHRASES **settle one's affairs** (or **estate**) make any necessary arrangements, such as writing a will, before one's death.
ORIGIN Old English *setlan* 'to seat, place.'

set•tle•ment /'setlmənt/
▸ **n. 1** a formal arrangement made between the parties to a lawsuit in order to resolve it, esp. out of court: *the owner reached an out-of-court settlement with the plaintiffs.* **2** an arrangement whereby property passes to a person or succession of people as dictated by the settlor.
■ the amount or property given: *a generous settlement.*

set•tlor /'setl-ər; 'setlər/
▸ **n.** a person who makes a settlement, esp. of property.

sev•er•al /'sev(ə)rəl/
▸ **adj.** applied or regarded separately. Often contrasted with JOINT.
DERIVATIVES **sev•er•al•ly** adv.
ORIGIN late Middle English: from Anglo-Norman French, from medieval Latin *separalis*, from Latin *separ* 'separate, different.'

sev•er•al•ty /'sev(ə)rəltē/
▸ **n.** the tenure of land held by an individual, not jointly or in common with another.
■ the condition of land so held: *the Dawes Severalty Act provides for the allotment of lands* **in severalty** *to Indians on the various reservations* ■ a piece of land so held.
ORIGIN late Middle English: from Anglo-Norman French *severalte*, from *several* (see SEVERAL).

sev•er•ance /'sev(ə)rəns/
▸ **n.** the action of ending a connection or relationship, especially a property interest among co-owners: *a portion of the property may be sold through a severance.*

ORIGIN late Middle English: from Anglo-Norman French, based on Latin *separare* 'disjoin, divide.'

sex crime /'seks ˌkrīm/
▶ n. informal a crime involving sexual assault or having a sexual motive.

sex dis•crim•i•na•tion /'seks disˌkrimǝˌnāsHǝn/ (also **sexual discrimination**)
▶ n. discrimination in employment and opportunity against a person (typically a woman) on grounds of sex.

sex•u•al ha•rass•ment /'seksHo͞oǝl hǝ'ræsmǝnt/
▶ n. harassment (typically of a woman) in a workplace, or other professional situation, usually involving the making of unwanted sexual advances or obscene remarks.

SG
▶ abbr. solicitor general.

sher•iff /'sHerif/
▶ n. (in the US) an elected officer in a county who is responsible for law enforcement and judicial administration.
■ (also **high sheriff**) (in England and Wales) the chief executive officer of the Crown in a county, having various administrative and judicial functions. ■ an honorary officer elected annually in some English towns. ■ (in Scotland) a judge.
DERIVATIVES **sher•iff•dom** /'sHerifdǝm/ n.
ORIGIN Old English *scīrgerēfa* (see SHIRE, REEVE[1]).

shop•lift•ing /'sHäpˌliftiNG/
▶ n. the criminal action of stealing goods from a store while pretending to be a customer.
DERIVATIVES **shop•lift** v.; **shop•lift•er** /-ˌliftǝr/ n.

side•bar /'sīd,bär/ (also **sidebar conference**)
▸ n. (in a court of law) a discussion between the lawyers and the judge held out of earshot of the jury.

silk /silk/
▸ n. Brit., informal a Queen's (or King's) Counsel. [ORIGIN: so named because of the right accorded to wear a gown made of this cloth.]

si•ne di•e /'sīnə 'dī,ē; 'sēnā 'dē,ā/
▸ adv. (with reference to business or proceedings that have been adjourned) with no appointed date for resumption: *the case was adjourned sine die.*
ORIGIN Latin, literally 'without a day.'

si•tus /'sītəs; 'sē-/
▸ n. the place to which, for purposes of legal jurisdiction or taxation, an act occurred or a property belongs: *finally, the court held that the situs of these ferries was Norfolk, where the company had its principal place of business.* | *a vehicle has situs for taxation in the City if it is garaged, parked, or stored in the City.*

slan•der /'slændər/
▸ n. the tortious act of making a false spoken statement damaging to a person's reputation: *he is suing the TV network for slander.* Compare with LIBEL.
▸ v. [trans.] make false and damaging statements about (someone): *they were accused of slandering the head of state.*
DERIVATIVES **slan•der•er** n.; **slan•der•ous** /'slændərəs/ adj.; **slan•der•ous•ly** /'slændərəslē/ adv.
ORIGIN Middle English: from Old French *esclandre*, alteration of *escandle*, from late Latin *scandalum* 'cause of offense,' from Greek *skandalon* 'snare, stumbling block.'

small-claims court /ˈsmôl ˈklāmz ˌkôrt/
▸ n. a local court in which claims for small sums of money can be heard and decided quickly and cheaply, without legal representation.

so•lic•it /səˈlisit/
▸ v. (**so•lic•it•ed, so•lic•it•ing**) [intrans.] incite or persuade (a person) to commit an illegal or insubordinate act.
■ accost someone and offer one's or someone else's services as a prostitute: [as n.] (**soliciting**) *although prostitution was not itself an offense, soliciting was.*
DERIVATIVES **so•lic•i•ta•tion** /sə,lisiˈtāSHən/ n.
ORIGIN late Middle English: from Old French *solliciter*, from Latin *sollicitare* 'agitate,' from *sollicitus* 'anxious,' from *sollus* 'entire' + *citus* (past participle of *ciere* 'set in motion').

so•lic•i•tor /səˈlisitər/
▸ n. the chief law officer of a city, town, or government department.
■ Brit. a member of the legal profession qualified to deal with conveyancing, the drawing up of wills, and other legal matters. Compare with BARRISTER.
ORIGIN late Middle English (denoting an agent or deputy): from Old French *solliciteur*, from *solliciter* (see SOLICIT).

so•lic•i•tor gen•er•al /səˈlisitər ˈjen(ə)rəl/
▸ n. (pl. **so•lic•i•tors gen•er•al**) in the US Department of Justice, the law officer responsible for arguing cases before the US Supreme Court.

spe•cial ver•dict /ˈspeSHəl ˈvərdikt/
▸ n. a verdict that states facts as proved but leaves the court to draw conclusions from them in order to render judgment.

spe•cie /'spēsнē; -sē/

▸ n. (as **in specie**) in the real, precise, or actual form specified: *the plaintiff could not be sure of recovering his goods in specie.*

ORIGIN mid 16th cent.: from Latin, ablative of *species* 'form, kind,' in the phrase *in specie* 'in the actual form.'

spe•cif•ic per•for•mance /spə'sifik pər'fôrmens/

▸ n. the performance of a contractual duty, as ordered in cases where damages would not be adequate remedy: *a decree for specific performance may include any terms and conditions as to payment of the rent, damages, or other relief that the court deems just.*

speed lim•it /'spēd ‚limit/

▸ n. the maximum speed at which a vehicle may legally travel on a particular stretch of road.

speed•y tri•al /'spēdē 'trīəl/

▸ n. a criminal trial held after minimal delay, as a citizen's constitutional right.

split de•ci•sion /'split di'sizнən/

▸ n. a decision based on a majority verdict rather than on a unanimous one: *a split decision has been reached in the malpractice trial filed by a Rockville woman.*

spo•li•a•tion /‚spōlē'āsнən/

▸ n. **1** the action of destroying, mutilating, or altering a document (e.g., a will) or evidence unfavorable to oneself: *the plaintiff's alleged spoliation of evidence.*
2 the action of taking goods or property from somewhere by illegal or unethical means: *the spoliation of the Church.*

ORIGIN late Middle English (denoting pillaging): from Latin *spoliatio(n-)*, from the verb *spoliare* 'strip, deprive.'

spous•al /'spowzəl/
▶ adj. [attrib.] of or relating to marriage or to a husband or wife: *the spousal benefits of married couples.*

stale /stāl/
▶ adj. (**stal•er, stal•est**) (of a check or legal claim) invalid because not acted on within a reasonable time: *nonpayment of a stale claim is not actionable.*
ORIGIN Middle English (describing beer in the sense 'clear from long standing, strong'): probably from Anglo-Norman French and Old French, from *estaler* 'to halt.'

stand /stænd/
▶ n. (**the stand**) a witness stand: *Sergeant Harris took the stand.*
▶ v. [trans.] undergo or submit to, as in **stand trial** (see below).
PHRASES **stand trial** be tried in a court of law: *one of the suspects died before standing trial.*
▶ **stand down** (of a witness) leave the witness stand after giving evidence: *the witness may stand down.*
ORIGIN Old English *standan* (verb), *stand* (noun), of Germanic origin, from an Indo-European root shared by Latin *stare* and Greek *histanai*, also by the noun *stead.*

Star Cham•ber /'stär 'CHămbər/ an English court of civil and criminal jurisdiction that developed in the late 15th century, trying esp. those cases affecting the interests of the Crown. It was noted for its arbitrary and oppressive judgments and was abolished in 1641.

sta•re de•ci•sis /'sterē də'sīsis/
▶ n. the legal principle that courts should abide by precedent.
ORIGIN Latin, literally 'stand by things decided.'

state /stāt/
▶ **n. 1** the particular condition that someone or something is in at a specific time: *the state of the company's finances* | *we're worried about her* **state of mind**.
2 the civil government of a country: *services provided by the state* | [in combination] *state-owned companies.*
▶ **adj.** [attrib.] of, provided by, or concerned with the civil government of a country: *the future of state education* | *a state secret.*
▶ **v.** [trans.] specify the facts of (a case) for consideration: *judges must give both sides an equal opportunity to state their case.*
ORIGIN Middle English (as a noun): partly a shortening of ESTATE, partly from Latin *status* 'manner of standing, condition.'

state•ment /ˈstātmənt/
▶ **n.** a formal account of events given by a witness, defendant, or other party to the police or in a court of law: *she* **made a statement** *to the police.*

state's at•tor•ney /ˈstāts əˈtərnē/
▶ **n.** a lawyer representing a state in court.

state's ev•i•dence /ˈstāts ˈevidns/
▶ **n.** evidence for the prosecution given by a participant in or accomplice to the crime being tried.
PHRASES **turn state's evidence** give such evidence: *persuading one-time gang members to turn state's evidence.*

stat•ute /ˈstæCHo͞ot/
▶ **n.** a written law passed by a legislative body: *violation of the hate crimes statute* | *the tax is not specifically disallowed* **by statute**.
ORIGIN Middle English: from Old French *statut*, from late Latin *statutum*, neuter past participle of Latin *statuere* 'set up,' from *status* 'standing.'

stat•ute book /'stæcH͞o͞ot ˌbo͝ok/
▸ n. a book in which laws are written.

stat•ute law /'stæcH͞o͞ot ˌlô/
▸ n. the body of principles and rules of law laid down in statutes. Compare with COMMON LAW, CASE LAW.

stat•ute of lim•i•ta•tions /'stæcH͞o͞ot əv ˌlimi'tāsHənz/
▸ n. a statute prescribing a period of time limitation for the bringing of certain kinds of legal action: *California's statute of limitations in personal injury cases is one year.*

stat•utes at large /'stæcH͞o͞ots æt 'lärj; ət/
▸ plural n. a country's statutes in their original version, regardless of later modifications or codification.

stat•u•to•ry /'stæcHəˌtôrē/
▸ adj. required, permitted, or enacted by statute: *the courts did award statutory damages to each of the plaintiffs.* ■ (of a criminal offense) defined by, or carrying a penalty prescribed by, statute: *statutory theft.* ■ of or relating to statutes: *constitutional and statutory interpretation.*
DERIVATIVES **stat•u•to•ri•ly** /'stacHəˌtôrəlē/ **adv.**

stat•u•to•ry rape /'stæcHəˌtôrē 'rāp/
▸ n. sexual intercourse with a person under the age of consent.

stay /stā/
▸ v. [trans.] stop, delay, or prevent (something), in particular suspend or postpone (judicial proceedings or a particular procedure) or refrain from pressing (charges): *their appeal will not stay proceedings.*
▸ n. a suspension or postponement of judicial proceedings or a particular procedure: *a stay of prosecution.*
PHRASES **a stay of execution** a delay in carrying out a court order.

strict con•struc•tion /'strikt kən'strəkSHən/
▸ n. a literal interpretation of a statute or document (e.g., a constitution) by a court.
DERIVATIVES **strict con•struc•tion•ist** n.

strict li•a•bil•i•ty /'strikt ˌlīə'bilitē/
▸ n. liability that arises from certain actions without a showing of actual negligence or intent to harm: *this is a classic dog-bite case that turns on whether there is strict liability for violating a leash law.*

strike /strīk/
▸ v. (past and past part. **struck** /strək/; past part. **stricken** 'strikən) [trans.] cancel, remove, or cross out with or as if with a pen, particularly testimony or remarks in court: *strike his name from the list | these remarks will be stricken from the record.*
▪ (**strike down**) abolish or invalidate (a law or regulation) by judicial decision: *the law was struck down by the Supreme Court.*
ORIGIN Old English *strīcan* 'go, flow' and 'rub lightly,' of West Germanic origin; related to German *streichen* 'to stroke.'

sub ju•di•ce /ˌso͞ob 'yo͞odiˌkā; ˌsəb 'jo͞odiˌsē/
▸ adj. under judicial consideration and therefore prohibited from public discussion elsewhere: *the cases were still sub judice.*
ORIGIN Latin, literally 'under a judge.'

sub•lease
▸ n. /'səbˌlēs/ a lease of a property by a tenant to a subtenant.
▸ v. /ˌsəb'lēs/ another term for SUBLET.

sub•les•see /ˌsəble'sē/
▸ n. a person who holds a sublease.

sub•les•sor /ˌsəble'sôr/
▸ n. a person who grants a sublease.

sub•let
▸ v. /ˌsəb'let/ (**sub•let•ting**; past and past part. **sub•let**) [trans.] lease (a property) to a subtenant: *I quit my job and sublet my apartment.*
▸ n. /'səbˌlet/ another term for SUBLEASE.
■ informal a property that has been subleased.

sub•mis•sion /səb'misHən/
▸ n. a proposition or argument presented by a lawyer to a judge or jury: *the defense lawyer for murder suspect P. D. Jones will make her last submission before the jury.*
ORIGIN late Middle English: from Old French, or from Latin *submissio(n-)*, from the verb *submittere* (see SUBMIT).

sub•mit /səb'mit/
▸ v. (**sub•mit•ted, sub•mit•ting**) [trans.] present (a proposal, application, or other document) to a person or body for consideration or judgment: *the panel's report was **submitted to** a parliamentary committee.*
■ [with clause] (esp. in judicial contexts) suggest; argue: *he submitted that such measures were justified.*
DERIVATIVES **sub•mit•ter** n.
ORIGIN late Middle English: from Latin *submittere*, from *sub-* 'under' + *mittere* 'send, put.' The sense 'present for judgment' dates from the mid 16th cent.

sub•orn /sə'bôrn/
▸ v. [trans.] bribe or otherwise induce (someone) to commit an unlawful act such as perjury: *he was accused of conspiring to suborn witnesses.*
■ obtain (perjury or another unlawful act) by such inducement: *I thought it was a ludicrous suggestion that I*

*had urged someone to lie or tried to suborn perjury in other
ways.*
DERIVATIVES **sub•or•na•tion** /ˌsəbôr'nāsHən/ **n.; sub•
orn•er n.**
ORIGIN mid 16th cent.: from Latin *subornare* 'incite secretly,' from *sub-* 'secretly' + *ornare* 'equip.'

sub•poe•na /sə'pēnə/

▸**n.** (in full **subpoena ad testificandum**) a writ ordering a person to attend a court: *a subpoena may be issued
to compel their attendance* | *they were all **under subpoena**
to appear.*
▸**v.** (**sub•poe•nas, sub•poe•naed** /sə'pēnəd/, **sub•poe•
na•ing** /sə'pēnəˌiNG/) [trans.] summon (someone) with a
subpoena: *the Queen is above the law and cannot be sub-
poenaed.*
■ require (a document or other evidence) to be submitted to a court of law: *the decision to subpoena government records.*
ORIGIN late Middle English (as a noun): from Latin *sub
poena* 'under penalty' (the first words of the writ). Use
as a verb dates from the mid 17th cent.

sub•poe•na du•ces te•cum /sə'pēnə 'doŌsēz 'tēkəm/

▸**n.** a writ ordering a person to attend a court and bring
relevant documents.
ORIGIN Latin, literally 'under penalty you shall bring
with you.'

sub•ro•ga•tion /ˌsəbrə'gāsHən/

▸**n.** the substitution of one person or group by another
in respect of a debt or insurance claim, accompanied by
the transfer of any associated rights and duties: *the right
of subrogation entitles a surety to step into the shoes of any
party whose obligations it assumed.*
DERIVATIVES **sub•ro•gate** /'səbrəˌgāt/ **v.**

ORIGIN late Middle English (in the general sense 'substitution'): from late Latin *subrogatio(n-)*, from *subrogare* 'choose as substitute,' from *sub-* 'in place of another' + *rogare* 'ask.'

sub•stan•tive /'səbstəntiv/
▸ **adj.** defining rights and duties as opposed to giving the rules by which such things are established.
DERIVATIVES **sub•stan•ti•val** /ˌsəbstən'tīvəl/ **adj.**; **sub•stan•tive•ly adv.**
ORIGIN late Middle English (in the sense 'having an independent existence'): from Old French *substantif, -ive* or late Latin *substantivus*, from *substantia* 'essence.'

sub•sti•tute /'səbstiˌt(y)o͞ot/
▸ **n.** (in litagation) a party who acts or serves in place of another.
▸ **v.** [trans.] (in litagation) replace one party with another.
DERIVATIVES **sub•sti•tut•a•bil•i•ty** /ˌsəbstəˌt(y)o͞otə'bilite/ **n.**; **sub•sti•tut•a•ble adj.**; **sub•sti•tu•tive** /'səbstiˌt(y)o͞otiv/ **adj.**
ORIGIN late Middle English (denoting a deputy or delegate): from Latin *substitutus* 'put in place of,' past participle of *substituere*, based on *statuere* 'set up.'

suc•ces•sion /sək'sesHən/
▸ **n.** the action or process of inheriting a title, office, property, etc.
■ the right or sequence of inheriting a position, title, etc.: *the succession to the vice presidency was disputed.*
■ the body of law dealing with inheritance.
PHRASES **in succession to** inheriting or elected to the place of: *he is not first in succession to the presidency.* **settle the succession** determine who shall succeed someone.
DERIVATIVES **suc•ces•sion•al** /sək'sesHənl/ **adj.**
ORIGIN Middle English (denoting legal transmission of

an estate or the throne to another, also in the sense 'successors, heirs'): from Old French, or from Latin *successio(n-)*, from the verb *succedere* 'come close after,' from *sub-* 'close to' + *cedere* 'go.'

sue /soo/
▸ v. (**sues, sued, su•ing**) [trans.] institute legal proceedings against (a person or institution), typically for redress: *she is to sue the baby's father* | [intrans.] *I sued for breach of contract.*
DERIVATIVES **su•er** /'sooər/ n.
ORIGIN Middle English: from Anglo-Norman French *suer*, based on Latin *sequi* 'follow.' Early senses were very similar to those of the verb *follow*.

suf•fer•ance /'səf(ə)rəns/
▸ n. the condition of the holder of an estate who continues to hold it after the title has ceased, without the express permission of the owner: *an estate at sufferance.*

su•i ju•ris /ˌsoo,ī 'jooris; ˌsoo,ē/
▸ adj. of full age and capacity; independent: *the beneficiaries are all sui juris.*
ORIGIN Latin, literally 'of one's own right.'

suit /soot/
▸ n. short for LAWSUIT.

sum•ma•ry /'səmərē/
▸ adj. (of a judicial process) conducted without the customary legal formalities: *summary arrest.*
■ (of a conviction or judgment) made by a judge or magistrate without a trial.
PHRASES **summary judgment** judgment of the court prior to trial, because the law is clear and the case presents no genuine issues of material fact.
DERIVATIVES **sum•mar•i•ly** /sə'merəlē; 'səmərəlē/ adv.

ORIGIN late Middle English (as an adjective): from Latin *summarius*, from *summa* 'sum total' (see SUM).

sum•ma•tion /sə'māsHən/
▸ n. an attorney's closing speech at the conclusion of the giving of evidence: *the state was allowed a rebuttal to the defense summation.*

sum•mon /'səmən/
▸ v. [trans.] authoritatively or urgently call on (someone) to be present, esp. as a defendant or witness in a court of law: *the victim's ex-wife has been summoned to appear in court on Thursday.*
DERIVATIVES **sum•mon•a•ble** adj.; **sum•mon•er** n.
ORIGIN Middle English: from Old French *somondre*, from Latin *summonere* 'give a hint,' later 'call, summon,' from *sub-* 'secretly' + *monere* 'warn.'

sum•mons /'səmənz/
▸ n. (pl. **sum•mons•es**) an order to appear before a judge or magistrate, or the writ containing it: *a summons for nonpayment of a parking ticket.*
▸ v. [trans.] serve (someone) with a summons: [with obj. and infinitive] *he has been summonsed to appear in court next month.*
ORIGIN Middle English: from Old French *sumunse*, from an alteration of Latin *summonita*, feminine past participle of *summonere* (see SUMMON).

sum up /ˌsəm 'əp/
▸ v. (**summed up, sum•ming up**) (of a judge) review the evidence at the end of a case, and direct the jury regarding points of law.
▪ give a brief summary of something: *Gerard will open the debate and I will sum up.*
DERIVATIVES **sum•ming-up** /'səmiNG 'əp/ n.
ORIGIN Middle English: via Old French from Latin

summa 'main part, sum total,' feminine of *summus* 'highest.'

sun•set law /'sənset ˌlô/
▶ n. a law that automatically terminates a regulatory agency, board, or function of government on a certain date, unless renewed: *in accordance with the state sunset law, the act sets the expiration date for the committee three years after the date of its creation.*

sun•shine law /'sənˌSHīn ˌlô/
▶ n. a law requiring certain proceedings of government agencies to be open or available to the public.

su•pe•ri•or court /sə'pirēər/
▶ n. **1** (in many states of the US) a court of appeals or a court of general (original) jurisdiction.
2 a court with general jurisdiction over other courts; a higher court.

Su•preme Court /sə'prēm 'kôrt; sŏŏ-/
▶ n. the highest judicial court in most US states.
■ a court of original jurisdiction in some states, including New York. ■ (in full **US Supreme Court**) the highest federal court in the US, consisting of nine justices and having appellate jurisdiction over all cases involving questions of federal law.

sur•e•ty /'SHŏŏritē/
▶ n. (pl. **sur•e•ties**) a person who takes responsibility for another's performance of an undertaking, for example their appearing in court or the payment of a debt.
■ money given to support an undertaking that someone will perform a duty, pay their debts, etc.; a guarantee: *the judge granted bail with a surety of $500.*
DERIVATIVES **sur•e•ty•ship** /'SHŏŏritēˌSHip/ n.
ORIGIN Middle English (in the sense 'something given

to support an undertaking that someone will fulfill an obligation'): from Old French *surte*, from Latin *securitas*, from *securus* 'free from care.'

sur•ren•der /sə'rendər/
▶ v. [intrans.] cease resistance to an enemy or opponent and submit to their authority: *three of the suspects surrendered to the authorities.*
■ [trans.] give up or hand over (a person, right, or possession), typically on compulsion or demand: *we have never ceded or surrendered title to our lands, rights to our resources, or the power to make decisions within our territory.*
▶ n. the action of surrendering.
■ the action of surrendering a life insurance policy.
ORIGIN late Middle English (chiefly in legal use): from Anglo-Norman French.

sur•ro•gate /'sərəgit; -ˌgāt/
▶ n. a substitute, esp. a person deputizing for another in a specific role or office: *she was regarded as the **surrogate for** the governor during his final illness.*
■ in many states, a public official with responsibility for administration of estates. ■ a judge in charge of probate, inheritance, and guardianship.
ORIGIN early 17th cent.: from Latin *surrogatus*, past participle of *surrogare* 'elect as a substitute,' from *super-* 'over' + *rogare* 'ask.'

sur•vi•vor /sər'vīvər/
▶ n. a joint tenant who has the right to the whole estate on the other's death: *making substantial gifts to children reduces estate taxes on the survivor's estate.*

sur•vi•vor•ship /sər'vīvərˌSHip/
▶ n. a right depending on survival, esp. the right of a survivor of holders of a joint interest to take the whole on the death of the others: *in some states the survivorship*

position is created automatically when the property is acquired by two or more people.

sus•pend /sə'spend/

▸ v. [trans.] (usu. **be suspended**) prevent from continuing or being in force or effect, in particular:
■ officially prohibit (someone) from holding their usual post or carrying out their usual role for a particular length of time: *two officers were **suspended from** duty pending the outcome of the investigation.* ■ defer or delay (an action, event, or judgment): *the judge suspended judgment until January 15.* ■ (of a judge or court) cause (an imposed sentence) to be unenforced as long as no further offense is committed within a specified period: *the sentence was suspended for six months* | [as adj.] (**suspended**) *a suspended jail sentence.*
ORIGIN Middle English: from Old French *suspendre* or Latin *suspendere*, from *sub-* 'from below' + *pendere* 'hang.'

sus•tain /sə'stān/

▸ v. [trans.] uphold, affirm, or confirm the justice or validity of (especially an objection to the introduction of evidence in court): *the allegations of discrimination were sustained.*
ORIGIN Middle English: from Old French *soustenir*, from Latin *sustinere*, from *sub-* 'from below' + *tenere* 'hold.'

swear /swer/

▸ v. (past **swore** /swôr/; past part. **sworn** /swôrn/) [trans.] take a solemn oath as to the truth of (a statement): *I asked him if he would swear a statement to this effect.* Compare with AFFIRM.
■ [trans.] (**swear someone in**) admit someone to a particular office or position by directing them to take a formal oath: *he was sworn in as a witness.*
▸**swear something out** obtain the issue of (a warrant

for arrest) by making a charge on oath: *if the police don't make an arrest, you may swear out a warrant.*
DERIVATIVES **swear•er** n.
ORIGIN Old English *swerian*, of Germanic origin; related to Dutch *zweren*, German *schwören*, also to *answer*.

syl•la•bus /ˈsiləbəs/
▸ n. (pl. **syllabuses** or **syllabi** /ˈsiləˌbī/) a summary of the opinion of a court.
ORIGIN mid 17th cent. (in the sense 'concise table of headings of a discourse'): modern Latin, originally a misreading of Latin *sittybas*, accusative plural of *sittyba*, from Greek *sittuba* 'title slip, label.'

T

tar•iff /'tærif; 'ter-/
▶ n. a tax or duty to be paid on a particular class of imports or exports.
■ a list of these taxes. ■ a table of the fixed charges made by a business, esp. in a hotel or restaurant.
▶ v. [trans.] fix the price of (something) according to a tariff: *these services are tariffed by volume.*
ORIGIN late 16th cent. (also denoting an arithmetical table): via French from Italian *tariffa*, based on Arabic '*arrafa* 'notify.'

tax /tæks/
▶ n. a compulsory contribution to federal, state, or municipal revenue, levied by the government on income and business profits or added to the cost of some goods, services, and transactions.
▶ v. [trans.] **1** impose a tax on (someone or something): *hardware and software is taxed at 7.5 percent.*
2 examine and assess (the costs of a case).
DERIVATIVES **tax•a•ble adj.**
ORIGIN Middle English (also in the sense 'estimate or determine the amount of a penalty or damages,' surviving in sense 2): from Old French *taxer*, from Latin *taxare* 'to censure, charge, compute,' perhaps from Greek *tassein* 'fix.'

tax a•void•ance /'tæks ə,voidns/
▶ n. the arrangement of one's financial affairs to minimize tax liability within the law. Compare with TAX EVASION.

tax e•va•sion /'tæks i,vāzнən/
▶ n. the illegal nonpayment or underpayment of tax. Compare with TAX AVOIDANCE.

tech•ni•cal /'teknikəl/
▸ **adj.** according to a strict application or interpretation of the law or rules: *the arrest was a technical violation of the treaty.*

tech•ni•cal•i•ty /ˌtekni'kælitē/
▸ **n.** (pl. **tech•ni•cal•i•ties**) a precise, usually procedural point of law or a small detail of a set of rules: *their convictions were overturned **on a technicality**.*

ten•an•cy /'tenənsē/
▸ **n.** (pl. **ten•an•cies**) possession of land or property as a tenant: *Holding took over the tenancy of the farm.*
■ the state, condition, or period of being a tenant: *tenancy was for less than one year.*

ten•an•cy in com•mon /'tenənsē in 'kämən/
▸ **n.** a shared tenancy in which each holder has a distinct, separately transferable interest.

ten•ant /'tenənt/
▸ **n.** a person who occupies land or property rented from a landlord.
■ a person holding real property by private ownership.
▸ **v.** [trans.] (usu. **be tenanted**) occupy (property) as a tenant: [as adj.] *some insurance companies will cover the loss or damage of contents in your tenanted properties.*
DERIVATIVES **ten•ant•a•ble adj.** (formal); **ten•ant•less adj.**
ORIGIN Middle English: from Old French, literally 'holding,' present participle of *tenir*, from Latin *tenere*.

ten•ant at will /'tenənt æt 'wil/
▸ **n.** (pl. **ten•ants at will**) a tenant who has no stated lease term and can be evicted, or can vacate, at any time, provided statutory notice requirements are met.

ten•ure /ˈtenyər/
▸ n. 1 the conditions under which land or buildings are held or occupied: *our focus is on agricultural land use and land tenure within the city.*
2 the holding of an office: *his tenure of the premiership would be threatened.*
▪ a period for which an office is held.
3 guaranteed permanent employment, esp. as a teacher or professor, after a probationary period.
▸v. [trans.] give (someone) a permanent post, esp. as a teacher or professor: *I had recently been tenured and then promoted to full professor.*
▪ [as adj.] (**tenured**) having or denoting such a post: *a tenured faculty member.*
ORIGIN late Middle English: from Old French, from *tenir* 'to hold,' from Latin *tenere.*

term /tərm/
▸ n. 1 (also **term for years** or Brit. **term of years**) a tenancy of a fixed period.
2 (**terms**) conditions under which an action may be undertaken or agreement reached; stipulated or agreed-upon requirements: *the union and the company agreed upon the contract's terms.*
ORIGIN Middle English (denoting a limit in space or time, or (in the plural) limiting conditions): from Old French *terme,* from Latin *terminus* 'end, boundary, limit.'

ter•ri•to•ri•al /ˌteriˈtôrēəl/
▸adj. 1 of or relating to the ownership of an area of land or sea: *territorial disputes.*
2 of or relating to a particular territory, district, or locality: *territorial public health departments*
DERIVATIVES **ter•ri•to•ri•al•i•ty** /ˌteriˌtôrēˈælitē/ n.; **ter•ri•to•ri•al•ly** adv.

ORIGIN early 17th cent.: from late Latin *territorialis*, from Latin *territorium* (see TERRITORY).

ter•ri•to•ri•al wa•ters /ˌteri'tôrēəl 'wôtərz; 'wätərz/
▸ plural n. the waters under the jurisdiction of a state, esp. the part of the sea within a stated distance of the shore (traditionally three miles from low-water mark, but extended in the 20th century by most countries).

ter•ri•to•ry /'terə,tôrē/
▸ n. (pl. **ter•ri•to•ries**) an area of land under the jurisdiction of a ruler or state: *the government was prepared to give up the nuclear weapons on its territory.*
ORIGIN late Middle English: from Latin *territorium*, from *terra* 'land.' The word originally denoted the district surrounding and under the jurisdiction of a town or city, specifically a Roman or provincial city.

tes•ta•ment /'testəmənt/
▸ n. a person's will, esp. the part relating to personal property: *the testament said that the ex-wives get nothing and his children get enough money to just pay off all of their debts.*
ORIGIN Middle English: from Latin *testamentum* 'a will' (from *testari* 'testify'), in Christian Latin also translating Greek *diathēkē* 'covenant.'

tes•ta•men•ta•ry /ˌtestə'men(t)ərē/
▸ adj. of, relating to, or bequeathed or appointed through a will: *a testamentary gift to your alma mater.*
ORIGIN late Middle English: from Latin *testamentarius*, from *testamentum* 'a will,' from *testari* 'testify.'

tes•tate /'testāt/
▸ adj. [predic.] having made a valid will before one dies: *Marjorie died testate and in her will she named her son as the personal representative.*

■ denoting property settled by will: *if a will has been left, you will be dealing with a testate estate.*
▸n. a person who has died leaving such a will: *it is incumbent upon the executor and the court to honor the testate's wishes.*
ORIGIN late Middle English (as a noun): from Latin *testatus* 'testified, witnessed,' past participle of *testari*, from *testis* 'a witness.'

tes•ta•tion /teˈstāsHən/
▸n. the disposal of property by will: *restrictions on testation.*

tes•ta•tor /ˈtesˌtātər/
▸n. a person who has made a will.
ORIGIN Middle English: from Anglo-Norman French *testatour*, from Latin *testator*, from the verb *testari* 'testify.'

test case /ˈtest ˌkās/
▸n. a case initiated to set a precedent for other cases involving similar questions of law: *civil servant wins test case to stop wearing necktie.*

tes•ti•fy /ˈtestəˌfī/
▸v. (**tes•ti•fies, tes•ti•fied**) [intrans.] give evidence as a witness in a law court: *he testified against his own commander* | [with clause] *he testified that he had supplied Barry with crack.*
DERIVATIVES **tes•ti•fi•er** n.
ORIGIN late Middle English: from Latin *testificari*, from *testis* 'a witness.'

tes•ti•mo•ny /ˈtestəˌmōnē/
▸n. (pl. **tes•ti•mo•nies**) a formal written or spoken statement, esp. one given in a court of law.
ORIGIN Middle English: from Latin *testimonium*, from *testis* 'a witness.'

theft /ᴛнeft/
▶ n. the action or crime of stealing: *he was convicted of theft* | *the latest theft happened at a garage.*
ORIGIN Old English *thīefth, thēofth,* of Germanic origin; related to ᴛнιᴇf.

USAGE: See **usage** at ʀᴏʙ.

thief /ᴛнēf/
▶ n. (pl. **thieves** /ᴛнēvz/) a person who steals another person's property, esp. by stealth and without using force or violence.
ORIGIN Old English *thīof, thēof,* of Germanic origin; related to Dutch *dief* and German *Dieb,* also to ᴛнᴇfᴛ.

thieve /ᴛнēv/
▶ v. [intrans.] be a thief; steal something: *they began thieving again.*
ORIGIN Old English *thēofian,* from *thēof* 'thief.' Transitive uses began in the late 17th cent.

thiev•er•y /'ᴛнēv(ə)rē/
▶ n. the action of stealing another person's property: *livestock thievery is still afoot in the state.*

third-de•gree /'ᴛнərd di'grē/
▶ n. (**the third degree**) long and harsh questioning, esp. by police, to obtain information or a confession: *Officer Lee observed Lieutenant Billings giving the suspect the third degree.*

third par•ty /'ᴛнərd 'pärtē/
▶ n. a person or group besides the two primarily involved in a situation, esp. a dispute or contract.
▶ adj. [attrib.] of or relating to a person or group besides the two primarily involved in a situation: *third-party suppliers.*

third per•son /'THərd 'pərsən/
> ▸ n. a third party.

threat /THret/
> ▸ n. **1** a statement of an intention to inflict pain, injury, damage, or other hostile action on someone in retribution for something done or not done: *members of her family have received death threats*.
> **2** a person or thing likely to cause damage or danger.
> ORIGIN Old English *thrēat* 'oppression,' of Germanic origin; related to Dutch *verdrieten* 'grieve,' German *verdriessen* 'irritate.'

three strikes /'THrē 'strīks/
> ▸ n. [usu. as adj.] (**three-strikes**) legislation providing that an offender's third felony is punishable by life imprisonment or another severe sentence: [as adj.] *they are in favor of limiting the three-strikes law to only violent and serious offenders*.
> ORIGIN 1990s: from the phrase *three strikes and you're out* (with allusion to baseball).

tip•staff /'tip‚stæf/
> ▸ n. a bailiff.
> ORIGIN mid 16th cent. (first denoting a metal-tipped staff): contraction of *tipped staff* (carried by a bailiff).

ti•tle /'tītl/
> ▸ n. a right or claim to the ownership of property or to a rank or throne: *a local family had **title to** the property* | *the buyer acquires a good title to the merchandise*.
> ▪ short for TITLE DEED.
> ORIGIN Old English *titul*, reinforced by Old French *title*, both from Latin *titulus* 'inscription, title.' The word originally denoted a placard or inscription placed on an object, giving information about it, hence a descriptive heading in a book or other composition.

ti•tle deed /'tītl ˌdēd/
▶ n. a legal deed or document constituting evidence of a right, esp. to ownership of property.

Tor•rens sys•tem /'tôrənz ˌsistəm; 'tär-/
▶ n. a system of land title registration, adopted originally in Australia and later in some states of the US, under which a judicial decree and registration obviate the need for title insurance.
ORIGIN mid 19th cent.: named after Sir Robert *Torrens* (1814-84), first premier of South Australia.

tort /tôrt/
▶ n. a noncriminal breach of a duty imposed by law (rather than by contract) that gives the right of action for damages: *the common-law torts of assault and trespass.*
ORIGIN Middle English (in the general sense 'wrong, injury'): from Old French, from medieval Latin *tortum* 'wrong, injustice,' neuter past participle of Latin *torquere* 'to twist.'

tort•fea•sor /'tôrtˌfēzər; -zôr/
▶ n. a person who commits a tort.
ORIGIN mid 17th cent.: from Old French *tort-fesor*, from *tort* 'wrong' and *fesor* 'doer.'

tor•tious /'tôrsHəs/
▶ adj. constituting or pertaining to a tort: *tortious breach of contract.*
DERIVATIVES **tor•tious•ly** adv.
ORIGIN late Middle English: from Anglo-Norman French *torcious*, from the stem of *torcion* 'extortion, violence,' from late Latin *tortio(n-)* 'twisting, torture,' from Latin *torquere* 'to twist.' The original sense was 'injurious.'

trade•mark /'trād,märk/
▶ n. a symbol, device, or words legally registered or established by use as representing a company or product.
▶ v. [trans.] [usu. as adj.] (**trademarked**) provide with a trademark: *they are counterfeiting trademarked goods.*

trans•fer
▶ v. /træns'fər; 'træns,fər/ (**trans•ferred, trans•fer•ring**) [trans.] make over the possession of (property, a right, or a responsibility) to someone else: *more than 400 acres of unspoiled forest was transferred to the Conservancy.*
▶ n. /'træns,fər/ a conveyance of property, esp. stocks, from one person to another: *the transfer of ownership is legal and binding.*
DERIVATIVES **trans•fer•ee** /,trænsfə'rē/ n.; **trans•fer•or** /træns'fərər; 'træns,fərər/ n.
ORIGIN late Middle English (as a verb): from French *transférer* or Latin *transferre*, from *trans-* 'across' + *ferre* 'to bear.' The earliest use of the noun (late 17th cent.) was as a legal term in the sense 'conveyance of property.'

trav•erse /trə'vərs/
▶ v. [trans.] deny (an allegation) in pleading: *the defendant might have traversed the plaintiff's allegation that he was a citizen of the State of Missouri.*
DERIVATIVES **tra•vers•a•ble** adj.
ORIGIN Middle English: from Old French *traverser*, from late Latin *traversare*; the noun is from Old French *travers* (masculine), *traverse* (feminine), partly based on *traverser*.

trea•son /'trēzən/
▶ n. (also **high treason**) the crime of betraying one's country, esp. by attempting to kill the sovereign or overthrow the government: *they were convicted of treason.*

◼ **(petty treason)** historical the crime of murdering someone to whom the murderer owed allegiance, such as a
master or husband.
DERIVATIVES **trea•son•ous** /ˈtrēzənəs/ **adj.**
ORIGIN Middle English: from Anglo-Norman French
treisoun, from Latin *traditio(n-)* 'handing over,' from the
verb *tradere.*

USAGE: In British law, there were formerly two types of
crime to which the term **treason** was applied: **petty
treason** (the crime of murdering one's master or husband) and **high treason** (the crime of betraying one's
country). As a classification of offense, the crime of
petty treason was abolished in 1828. In modern use,
the term **high treason** is now often simply called **treason.** In American law, **treason** is defined in Article 3,
Section 3, of the US Constitution.

treas•ure trove /ˈtrezHər ˌtrōv/
▶ **n.** valuables of unknown ownership that are found hid-
den, in some cases declared the property of the finder.
ORIGIN late Middle English: from Anglo-Norman
French *tresor trové,* literally 'found treasure.'

trea•ty /ˈtrētē/
▶ **n.** (pl. **trea•ties**) a formally concluded and ratified
agreement between countries.
ORIGIN late Middle English: from Old French *traite,*
from Latin *tractatus* 'treatise.'

tres•pass /ˈtrespəs; -ˌpæs/
▶ **v.** [intrans.] enter the owner's land or property without
permission: *there is no excuse for **trespassing on** railroad
property.*
▶ **n.** entry to a person's land or property without their
permission: *the defendants were guilty of trespass | a mass
trespass on the hills.*

■ an unlawful act deliberately committed against the person or property of another.

DERIVATIVES **tres•pass•er** n.

ORIGIN from Old French *trespasser* 'pass over, trespass,' *trespas* 'passing across.'

tri•a•ble /ˈtrīəbəl/
▸ **adj.** able to be tried in court; liable to trial.
■ (of a case or issue) able to be investigated and decided judicially: *a triable issue of fact.*

ORIGIN late Middle English: from Anglo-Norman French, from Old French *trier* 'sift' (see TRY).

tri•al /ˈtrī(ə)l/
▸ **n.** a formal examination of evidence by a judge or tribunal, especially a jury, in order to determine the facts in criminal or civil proceedings: *the newspaper accounts of the trial.*

PHRASES **on trial** being tried in a court of law: *this is the first time the Church of Scientology itself and its recruitment methods have gone on trial.* **stand trial** see STAND.

ORIGIN late Middle English: from Anglo-Norman French, or from medieval Latin *triallum.*

tri•al court /ˈtrīəl ˌkôrt/
▸ **n.** a court of law where cases are tried in the first place, as distinguished from an appeals court.

tri•al law•yer /ˈtrīəl ˌloiər; ˌlôyər/
▸ **n.** a lawyer who practices in a trial court.

tri•bu•nal /trīˈbyo͞onl; trə-/
▸ **n.** a court of justice: *an international war crimes tribunal.*
■ a seat or bench for a judge or judges.

ORIGIN late Middle English (denoting a seat for judges): from Old French, or from Latin *tribunal* 'raised platform provided for magistrates' seats,' from *tribunus*, literally 'head of a tribe.'

tri•er /'trīər/
> ▶ n. a person or body responsible for investigating and deciding a case judicially: *the jury is the **trier** of fact*.

-trix /triks/
> ▶ suffix (pl. **-tri•ces** /'trīsēz/ or **-trix•es**) forming feminine agent nouns corresponding to masculine nouns ending in *-tor* (such as *executrix* corresponding to *executor*).
> ORIGIN from Latin.

true bill /'troo 'bil/
> ▶ n. a bill of indictment found by a grand jury to be supported by sufficient evidence to justify the hearing of a case.

trust /trəst/
> ▶ n. **1** an arrangement whereby one person is the nominal owner of property that is to be held or used for the benefit of one or more others: *a trust was set up* | *the property is to be **held in trust** for his son*.
> **2** a body of trustees.
> ▨ an organization or company managed by trustees: *a charitable trust* | [in names] *the National Trust for Historic Preservation*. ▨ dated a large company that has or attempts to gain monopolistic control of a market.
> ORIGIN Middle English: from Old Norse *traust*, from *traustr* 'strong'; the verb from Old Norse *treysta*, assimilated to the noun.

trust com•pa•ny /'trəst ˌkəmpənē/
> ▶ n. a company formed to act as a trustee or to deal with trusts.

trust deed /'trəst ˌdēd/
> ▶ n. a deed of conveyance creating and setting out the conditions of a trust.

■ (in certain states) the equivalent of a mortgage. Also called DEED OF TRUST.

trust•ee /ˌtrəsˈtē/
▶ **n.** an individual person or member of a board given control or powers of administration of property in trust with a legal obligation to administer it solely for the purposes specified.
DERIVATIVES **trust•ee•ship** /ˌtrəsˈtē, SHip/ **n.**

trust•ee in bank•rupt•cy /ˌtrəsˈtē ˈbæNGkrəp(t)sē/
▶ **n.** a person taking administrative responsibility for the financial affairs of a bankrupt and the distribution of assets to creditors.

try /trī/
▶ **v.** (**tries, tried**) [trans.] (usu. **be tried**) subject (someone) to trial: *he was arrested and tried for the murder.*
■ investigate and decide (a case or issue) in a formal trial: *the most serious criminal cases must be tried by a jury.*
ORIGIN Middle English: from Old French *trier* 'sift,' of unknown origin.

U

ul•tra vi•res /ˌəltrə ˈvīrēz/
▸ **adj. & adv.** beyond one's (typically, a corporation's) legal power or authority: [as adj.] *jurisdictional errors render the decision ultra vires.*
ORIGIN Latin, literally 'beyond the powers.'

un•al•ien•a•ble /ˌənˈālyənəbəl; -ˈālēə-/
▸ **adj.** another term for INALIENABLE.

un•ap•peal•a•ble /ˌənəˈpēləbəl/
▸ **adj.** (of a case or ruling) not able to be referred to a higher court for review: *the jury verdict in a recent tobacco case may be unappealable.*

un•charged /ˌənˈCHärjd/
▸ **adj.** not accused of an offense under the law: *she was released uncharged.*

un•cor•rob•o•rat•ed /ˌənkəˈräbəˌrātid/
▸ **adj.** not confirmed or supported by other evidence or information: *the unreliability of uncorroborated confessions.*

un•de•fend•ed /ˌəndiˈfendid/
▸ **adj.** not defended: *legal aid for undefended divorces.*

un•der•sher•iff /ˈəndərˌsherif/
▸ **n.** a deputy sheriff.

un•der the in•flu•ence /ˈəndər THē ˈinflo͞oəns/
▸ **adverbial phrase** informal affected by alcoholic drink or other intoxicants: *he was charged with driving under the influence.*

un•due in•flu•ence /ˈən₁d(y)o͞o ˈinflo͞oəns/

▸ **n.** influence by which a person is induced to act subject to coercion or without adequate attention to the consequences: *it shall be presumed that the transfer of property by the dependent elderly owner was the result of undue influence.*

un•en•cum•bered /₁ənenˈkəmbərd/

▸ **adj.** not having any burden or impediment: *the land was unencumbered by mortgages.*

■ free of debt or other financial liability: *the objective is to start their working lives unencumbered by debt.*

un•en•force•a•ble /₁ənenˈfôrsəbəl/

▸ **adj.** (esp. of an obligation or law) impossible to enforce: *such contracts may be declared unenforceable by the courts.*

u•ni•cam•er•al /₁yo͞oniˈkæm(ə)rəl/

▸ **adj.** (of a legislative body) having a single legislative chamber: *the unicameral system favors rule by the majority.*

ORIGIN mid 19th cent.: from *uni-*'one' + Latin *camera* 'chamber' + *-al.*

un•law•ful /₁ənˈlawfəl/

▸ **adj.** not conforming to, permitted by, or recognized by law or rules: *the use of unlawful violence | they claimed the ban was unlawful.*

DERIVATIVES **un•law•ful•ly** /ənˈlôfəlē/ adv.; **un•law•ful•ness** n.

un•liq•ui•dat•ed /₁ənˈlikwi₁dātid/

▸ **adj.** (of a debt) not cleared or paid off.

■ not calculated precisely: *unliquidated damages.*

un•served /₁ənˈsərvd/

▸ **adj.** (of a writ or summons) not officially delivered to a person: *there is no point in leaving a writ unserved.*

un•sworn /ˌən'swôrn/
▸ **adj.** (of testimony or evidence) not given under oath: *unsworn statements in criminal trials.*

un•tried /ˌən'trīd/
▸ **adj.** (of an accused person) not yet subjected to a trial in court: *untried suspects.*

un•writ•ten /ˌən'ritn/
▸ **adj.** (esp. of a law) resting originally on custom or judicial decision rather than on statute: *an unwritten constitution.*

us•er /'yo͞ozər/
▸ **n.** the continued use or enjoyment of a right.

u•su•rer /'yo͞ozHərər/
▸ **n.** a person who lends money at unreasonably high rates of interest.
ORIGIN Middle English: from Anglo-Norman French, from Old French *usure*, from Latin *usura* (see USURY).

u•su•ri•ous /yo͞o'zHo͝orēəs/
▸ **adj.** of or relating to the practice of usury: *they lend money at usurious rates.*
DERIVATIVES **u•su•ri•ous•ly adv.**

u•su•ry /'yo͞ozH(ə)rē/
▸ **n.** the illegal action or practice of lending money at unreasonably high rates of interest.
◼ archaic interest at such rates.
ORIGIN Middle English: from Anglo-Norman French *usurie*, or from medieval Latin *usuria*, from Latin *usura*, from *usus* 'a use' (see USE).

ut•ter /ˈətər/

▶ v. [trans.] put (forged money) into circulation: *he knowingly uttered and possessed counterfeit securities beyond a reasonable doubt.*

ORIGIN late Middle English: from Middle Dutch *ūteren* 'speak, make known, give currency to (coins).'

V

v.
▶ **abbr.** versus.

va•cant /'vākənt/
▶ **adj.** (of premises) having no fixtures, furniture or inhabitants; empty: *a vacant warehouse.*
ORIGIN Middle English: from Old French, or from Latin *vacant-* 'remaining empty,' from the verb *vacare.*

va•cate /'vākāt/
▶ **v.** [trans.] **1** leave (a place that one previously occupied): *the Ludds will vacate the premises before March 15.*
2 cancel or annul (a judgment, contract, or charge): *the administrator argues that the judge's decision should be vacated.*
ORIGIN mid 17th cent.: from Latin *vacat-* 'left empty,' from the verb *vacare.*

val•id /'vælid/
▶ **adj.** legally binding due to having been executed in compliance with the law: *a valid contract.*
■ legally acceptable: *the visas are valid for thirty days.*
DERIVATIVES **va•lid•i•ty** /və'liditē/ **n.; val•id•ly adv.**
ORIGIN late 16th cent.: from French *valide* or Latin *validus* 'strong,' from *valere* 'be strong.'

val•u•a•ble con•sid•er•a•tion /'væy(ŏŏ)əbəl kən͵sidə'rā-SHən/
▶ **n.** legal consideration having some economic value, in order to make a contract enforceable: *the airline prohibits the sale or auction of travel-related documents for cash or other valuable consideration.*

var•i•ance /'verēəns/
▶ **n.** a discrepancy between two statements or documents.
▪ an official dispensation from a rule or regulation, typically a building regulation.
ORIGIN Middle English: via Old French from Latin *variantia* 'difference.'

vend /vend/
▶ **v.** [trans.] sell (something): *bottled water will be vended throughout the event.*
DERIVATIVES **vend•i•ble** (also **vend•a•ble**) adj.
ORIGIN early 17th cent. (in the sense 'be sold'): from French *vendre* or Latin *vendere* 'sell,' from *venum* 'something for sale' + a variant of *dare* 'give.'

ven•dor /'vendər; -dôr/ (also **vend•er**)
▶ **n.** the seller in a sale, esp. of property.
ORIGIN late 16th cent.: from Anglo-Norman French *vendour* (see VEND).

ven•ue /'venyōo/
▶ **n.** the county or district within which a criminal or civil case must be heard: *the public defender is not seeking a jury trial and has not asked for a change of venue.*
ORIGIN late 16th cent. (denoting a thrust or bout in fencing; also in the Law sense): from Old French, literally 'a coming,' feminine past participle of *venir* 'come,' from Latin *venire*.

ver•dict /'vərdikt/
▶ **n.** the jury's decision on a disputed issue in a civil or criminal case or an inquest: *the jury returned a verdict of 'not guilty.'*
ORIGIN Middle English: from Anglo-Norman French *verdit*, from Old French *veir* 'true' (from Latin *verus*) + *dit* (from Latin *dictum* 'saying').

ver•sus /'vərsəs; -səz/ (abbr.: **v.** or **vs.**)
▶ **prep.** against: *the State of Pennsylvania versus Jefferson-King Industries.*
ORIGIN late Middle English: from a medieval Latin use of Latin *versus* 'toward.'

vest•ed in•ter•est /'vestid 'int(ə)rist/
▶ **n.** [usu. in sing.] an interest (usually in land or money held in trust) recognized as belonging to a particular person: *the unmarried minor child held a vested interest in the income and capital.*

ve•to /'vētō/
▶ **n.** (pl. **ve•toes**) a constitutional right to reject a decision or proposal made by a lawmaking body: *Congress can override the president's veto.*
■ such a rejection.
▶ **v.** (**ve•toes, ve•toed**) [trans.] exercise a veto against (a decision or proposal made by a lawmaking body): *the president vetoed the bill.*
DERIVATIVES **ve•to•er** n.
ORIGIN early 17th cent.: from Latin, literally 'I forbid,' used by Roman tribunes of the people when opposing measures of the Senate.

vex•a•tious /vek'sāSHəs/
▶ **adj.** denoting an action or the bringer of an action that is brought without sufficient grounds for winning, purely to cause annoyance to the defendant: *there was no vexatious action by either party* | *a vexatious litigant.*
DERIVATIVES **vex•a•tious•ly** adv.; **vex•a•tious•ness** n.

vice chan•cel•lor /ˌvīs 'CHæns(ə)lər/
▶ **n. 1** a deputy chancellor, esp. one of a British university who discharges most of its administrative duties.
2 a judge appointed to assist a chancellor, esp. in chancery court or court of equity.

vic•i•nage /'visənij/

▸ n. the area from which cases may be brought to a court: *he has been the assignment judge for the Morris/Sussex vicinage for 17 years.*

ORIGIN Middle English: from Old French *vis(e)nage*, from an alteration of Latin *vicinus* 'neighbor.'

view /vyo͞o/

▸ n. (in court proceedings) a formal inspection by the judge and jury of the scene of a crime or property mentioned in evidence: *if you are going to have a view, it is desirable you do it together with the control and cooperation of the court.*

PHRASES **in plain view** capable of being seen on open inspection: *officers may seize property that they find in plain view, if they have probable cause to believe it is evidence of a crime.*

ORIGIN Middle English: from Anglo-Norman French *vieue*, feminine past participle of *veoir* 'see,' from Latin *videre.*

vi•o•lence /'vī(ə)ləns/

▸ n. the unlawful exercise of physical force.

PHRASES **do violence to** damage or adversely affect: *he used visitation and custody issues to harass and do violence to her.*

ORIGIN Middle English: via Old French from Latin *violentia*, from *violent-* 'vehement, violent' (see VIOLENT).

vi•o•lent /'vī(ə)lənt/

▸ adj. involving an unlawful exercise of force: *violent behavior* | *violent crimes.*

DERIVATIVES **vi•o•lent•ly** adv.

ORIGIN Middle English (in the sense 'having a marked or powerful effect'): via Old French from Latin *violent-* 'vehement, violent.'

vis•it•a•tion /ˌviziˈtāsHən/

▸ n. a person's right to spend time with their children who are in the custody of the other parent, a foster parent, or other legal guardian.

ORIGIN Middle English: from Old French, or from late Latin *visitatio(n-)*, from the verb *visitare* 'go to see.'

void /void/

▸ adj. not valid or legally binding: *the contract was void.*
▸ v. [trans.] declare that (something) is not valid or legally binding: *the Supreme court voided the statute.*

DERIVATIVES **void•a•ble** adj.

ORIGIN Middle English (in the sense 'unoccupied'): from a dialect variant of Old French *vuide*; related to Latin *vacare* 'vacate'; the verb partly a shortening of *avoid*, reinforced by Old French *voider.*

voir dire /ˈvwär ˈdir/

▸ n. a preliminary examination of a witness or a juror by a judge or counsel: *was there bias on the part of the juror who concealed information on voir dire?* | [as adj.] *the voir dire session is not meant to intrude on your privacy.*
■ an oath taken by such a witness.

ORIGIN Law French, from Old French *voir* 'true' + *dire* 'say.'

vouch•er /ˈvowCHər/

▸ n. a small printed piece of paper that entitles the holder to a discount or that may be exchanged for goods or services.

W

waiv•er /'wāvər/
▶ n. an act or instance of knowingly relinquishing a right or claim: *waiver of landlord's claim to annexed fixtures.*
■ a document recording such waiving of a right or claim: *participants are asked to sign a waiver on all Sierra Club outings.*

ward /wôrd/
▶ n. **1** a person, usually a minor, under the care and control of a guardian appointed by their parents or a court. **2** one of the divisions of a prison.
PHRASES **ward of the court** a person, usually a minor or of unsound mind, for whom a guardian has been appointed by a court or who has become directly subject to the authority of that court.
DERIVATIVES **ward•ship** /'wôrd,SHip/ n.
ORIGIN Old English *weard*, *weardian* 'keep safe, guard,' of Germanic origin; reinforced in Middle English by Old Northern French *warde* (noun), *warder* (verb) 'guard.'

war•rant /'wôrənt; 'wä-/
▶ n. a document issued by a legal or government official authorizing the police or some other body to make an arrest, search premises, or carry out some other action relating to the administration of justice: *magistrates issued a warrant for his arrest* | *an extradition warrant.*
■ a document that entitles the holder to receive goods, money, or services: *we'll issue you with a travel warrant.*
DERIVATIVES **war•rant•er** n.
ORIGIN from variants of Old French *guarant* (noun), *guarantir* (verb), of Germanic origin.

war•ran•tee /ˌwôrən'tē; ˌwä-/
▸ n. a person to whom a warranty is given.

USAGE: **Warrantee** means 'person to whom a warranty is made'; it is not a spelling variant of **warranty**.

war•ran•tor /'wôrəntôr; 'wä-/
▸ n. a person or company that provides a warranty.

war•ran•ty /'wôrəntē; 'wä-/
▸ n. (pl. **war•ran•ties**) a written guarantee, issued to the purchaser of an article by its manufacturer, promising to repair or replace it if necessary within a specified period of time: *the car comes with a three-year warranty | as your machine is under warranty, I suggest getting it checked.*
■ (in contract law) a promise that something in furtherance of the contract is guaranteed by one of the contractors, esp. the seller's promise that the thing being sold is as promised or represented. ■ (in an insurance contract) an engagement by the insured party that certain statements are true or that certain conditions shall be fulfilled, the breach of it invalidating the policy. ■ (in property law) a covenant by which the seller binds themselves and their heirs to secure to the buyer the estate conveyed in the deed.
ORIGIN Middle English: from Anglo-Norman French *warantie*, variant of *garantie* . Early use was as a legal term denoting a covenant annexed to a conveyance of property, in which the vendor affirmed the security of the title.

USAGE: See **usage** at GUARANTEE and WARRANTEE.

waste /wāst/
▸ n. damage to an estate caused by an act or by neglect, esp. by a life-tenant.

■ damage to the value of assets being held or managed, as by a trustee.
ORIGIN Middle English: from Old Northern French *wast(e)* (noun), *waster* (verb), based on Latin *vastus* 'unoccupied, uncultivated.'

where•as /(h)wer'æz/
▸**conj.** (esp. in legal preambles) taking into consideration the fact that: *whereas, under the right conditions, community service offers great benefits to both the service providers and recipients.*

will /wil/
▸**n.** a legal document containing instructions as to what should be done with one's property and to provide for one's minor children after one's death.
▸**v.** [trans.] (**will something to**) bequeath something to (someone) by the terms of one's will.
■ [with clause] leave specified instructions in one's will: *he willed that his body be given to the hospital.*
PHRASES **at will** subject to termination at any time: *employment at will* | *tenancy at will* | *contract at will.*
ORIGIN Old English *willa* (noun), *willian* (verb), of Germanic origin; related to Dutch *wil*, German *Wille* (nouns), also to the modal verb *will* and the adverb *well.*

wit•ness /'witnis/
▸**n. 1** a person who sees an event, typically a crime or accident, take place: *police are appealing for **witnesses** to the accident.*
■ a person giving sworn testimony to a court of law or the police. See also EXPERT WITNESS. ■ a person who is present at the signing of a document and who also signs it to confirm this.
2 used to refer to confirmation or evidence given by sig-

nature, under oath, or otherwise: *in witness thereof, the parties sign this document.*

▸v. [trans.] see (an event, typically a crime or accident) take place: *a bartender who witnessed the murder.*

■ be present as someone signs (a document) or gives (their signature) to a document and sign it oneself to confirm this: *the clerk witnessed her signature.*

wit•ness stand /'witnis ˌstænd/ (Brit. **wit•ness box**)
  ▸n. the place in a court from which a witness gives evidence.

writ /rit/
  ▸n. a form of written command in the name of a court or other legal authority to act, or abstain from acting, in some way.

■ **(one's writ)** one's power to enforce compliance or submission; one's authority: *you have business here which is out of my writ and competence.*

ORIGIN Old English, as a general term denoting written matter, from the Germanic base of *write.*

writ of cer•ti•o•ra•ri /'rit əv ˌsərsH(ē)ə'rärē/
  ▸n. see CERTIORARI.

writ of ex•e•cu•tion /'rit əv ˌeksi'kyo͞osHən/
  ▸n. a judicial order that a judgment be enforced: *applicant requests the court issue a writ of execution against the property of the following person.*

wrong /rôNG/
  ▸n. a breach, by commission or omission, of one's legal duty: *environmental wrongs.*

■ an invasion of a right to the damage or prejudice of another: *the women and children in this pseudo-religious community suffered numerous wrongs.*

ORIGIN late Old English *wrang*, from Old Norse *rangr* 'awry, unjust.'

wrong•ful /'rôNGfəl/
▶ **adj.** constituting a wrong; not fair, just, or legal: *an action for wrongful death.*
■ not entitled to a position or claimed standing: *the wrongful heir.*
DERIVATIVES **wrong•ful•ly** adv.; **wrong•ful•ness** n.

Resources

Legal Aid Organizations

Alabama

Alabama Legal Services Programs
http://www.alabamalegalservices.org
  info@alsp.org

Offices:
Legal Services Corporation of
  Alabama, Inc.
500 Bell Building
207 Montgomery Street
Montgomery, AL 36104

Legal Services of Metro
  Birmingham, Inc.
1820 Seventh Avenue North
P.O. Box 11765
Birmingham, AL 35202

Legal Services of North-Central
  Alabama, Inc.
2000-C Vernon Street
P. O. Box 2465
Huntsville, AL 35804

Alaska

Alaska Legal Services Corporation
http://www.alsc-law.org

Offices:
1016 West Sixth Avenue, Suite 200
Anchorage, AK 99501
(907) 272-9431; (800) 478-9431
anchorage3@alsc-law.org

P.O. Box 248
Bethel, AK 99559-0248
(907) 543-2237; (800) 478-2230
alscbthl@unicom-alaska.com

P.O. Box 176
Dillingham, AK 99576-0176
(907) 842-1452; (888) 391-1475
dillingham@alsc-law.org

P.O. Box 1429
Nome, AK 99762-1429
(907) 443-2230 *or* (888) 495-6663
nome@alsc-law.org

1648 Cushman, Suite 300
Fairbanks, AK 99701-6202
(907) 452-5181; (800) 478-5401
fairbanks@alsc-law.org

416 6th Street, Suite 322
Juneau, AK 99801-1096
(907) 586-6425; (800) 789-6426
alscjno@alaska.net
306 Main Street #218
Ketchikan, AK 99901-6483
(907) 225-6420
alscket@ptialaska.net

P.O. Box 526
Kotzebue, AK 99752-0526
(907) 442-3500; (887) 622-9797
alsckotz@yahoo.com

Arizona

DNA–Legal People's Services, Inc.
[Provides free legal services in civil matters to qualified low-income residents on and near the Navajo Nation.]
http://www.dnalegalservices.org/
information@dnalegalservices.org

William E. Morris Institute for Justice
http://www.azji.org/

Offices:
305 South Second Avenue
Phoenix, AZ 85001
(602) 252-3432

100 North Stone, Suite 305
Tucson, AZ 85701
(520) 740-1207

Arkansas

Arkansas Legal Services Programs
http://www.arlegalservices.org/

Offices:
Center for Arkansas Legal Services
303 West Capital, Suite 200
Little Rock, AR 72201
(501) 376-3423

Legal Aid of Arkansas
4083 North Shiloh Drive, Suite 3
Fayetteville, AR 72703
(479) 442-0600

California

Bay Area Legal Aid
http://www.baylegal.org/
405 14th Street, 9th Floor
Oakland, CA 94612
(510) 663-4755; (510) 663-4744;
  (800) 551-5554

Bet Tzedek Legal Services
http://www.bettzedek.org

Offices:
145 South Fairfax Avenue
Suite 200
Los Angeles, CA 90036
(323) 939-0506

12821 Victory Boulevard
North Hollywood, CA 91606
(818) 769-0136

California Indian Legal Services, Inc.
[Services for Native Americans and Indian Tribes in California]
http://www.calindian.org
510 16th Street, Fourth Floor
Oakland, CA 94612
(510) 835-0284; (800) 829-0284

787 North Main Street, Suite D
Bishop, CA 93514
(760) 873-3581; (800) 736-3582

609 S. Escondido Boulevard
Escondido, CA 92025
(760) 746-8941; (800) 743-8941

324 F Street
Eureka, CA 95501
(707) 443-8397; (800) 347-2402

510 16th Street, Fourth Floor
Oakland, CA 94612
(510) 835-0284; (800)829-0284

37 Old Courthouse Square
Suite 207
Santa Rosa, CA 95404
(707) 573-8016

California Rural Legal Assistance,
  Inc.
631 Howard Street, Suite 300
San Francisco, CA 94105-3907
(415) 777-2752

Central California Legal Services
http://www.las.org/

Offices:
1999 Tuolumne St.
Suite 700
Fresno, CA 93721
(559) 570-1200

357 W. Main St.
Suite 201
Merced, CA 95340
(209) 723-5466

208 W. Main St.
Suite U-1
Visalia, CA 93291
(559) 733-8770; (800) 350-3654

Greater Bakersfield Legal Assistance, Inc.
615 California Avenue
Bakersfield, CA 93304
(661) 325-5943

Inland Counties Legal Services,
  Inc.
http://www.iellaaid.org/pages/
  icls_link.html
1737 Atlanta Avenue, Suite H-3
Riverside, CA 92507
(909) 368-2531; (909) 368-2555

Legal Aid Foundation of Los
  Angeles
http://www.lafla.org
1102 South Crenshaw Boulevard
Los Angeles, CA 90019-3111
(323) 801-7990; (800) 399-4529

Legal Aid Society of Orange
  County, Inc.
902 North Main Street
Santa Ana, CA 92701
(714) 571-5233; (800) 834-5001

Legal Aid Society of San Diego,
  Inc.
110 South Euclid Avenue
San Diego, CA 92114
(619) 471-2620, (619) 262-0896

Legal Services of Northern
  California
http://www.lsnc.net/
517 12th Street
Sacramento, CA 95814
(916) 551-2150

Napa County Legal Assistance
  Agency
1227 Coombs St.
Napa, CA 94559
(707) 255-4933

Neighborhood Legal Services of
 Los Angeles County
http://www.nls-la.org
13327 Van Nuys Boulevard
Pacoima, CA 91331-3099
(818) 834-7590; (818) 896-5211

Colorado

Colorado Legal Services
1905 Sherman Street
Suite 400
Denver, CO 80203
(303) 837-1313; (303) 837-1321

Connecticut

Statewide Legal Services of Connecticut, Inc.
http://www.slsct.org
425 Main Street, 4th Floor
Middletown, CT 06457
(860) 344-8096; (800) 453-3320

Delaware

Legal Services Corporation of
 Delaware, Inc.
http://www.lscd.com
100 West 10th Street
Suite 203
Wilmington, DE 19801
(302) 575-0408

District of Columbia

Neighborhood Legal Services Program of the District of Columbia
http://www.nlsp.org
701 Fourth Street, N.W.
Washington, DC 20001
(202) 682-2720

Florida

Bay Area Legal Services, Inc.
http://www.bals.org
Riverbrook Center, 2nd Floor
829 W. Dr. Martin Luther King
Tampa, FL 33603
(813) 232-1343

Central Florida Legal Services, Inc.
http://www.cfls.org
128-A Orange Avenue
Daytona Beach, FL 32114-4310
(386) 255-6573

Florida Rural Legal Services, Inc.
http://www.frls.org
963 East Memorial Boulevard
P.O. Box 24688
Lakeland, FL 33802-4688
(863) 688-7376; (800) 277-7680

Greater Orlando Area Legal Services, Inc.
1036 West Amelia Street
Orlando, FL 32805
(407) 841-7777

Gulfcoast Legal Services, Inc.
http://www.gulfcoastlegal.org
641 First Street South
St. Petersburg, FL 33701-5003
(727) 821-0726; (800) 230-5920

Jacksonville Area Legal Aid, Inc.
http://www.jaxlegalaid.org
126 West Adams Street
Jacksonville, FL 32202-3849
(904) 356-8371

Legal Aid Service of Broward
County
609 Southwest First Avenue
Fort Lauderdale, FL 33301
(954) 765-8957; (954) 765-8950

Legal Services of Greater
Miami, Inc.
http://www.lsgmi.org
3000 Biscayne Boulevard, Suite
500
Miami, FL 33137-4129
(305) 576-0080

Legal Services of North
Florida, Inc.
2119 Delta Boulevard
Tallahassee, FL 32303-4209
(850) 385-9007

Northwest Florida Legal
Services, Inc.
701 South J Street
P.O. Box 1551
Pensacola, FL 32597-1551
(850) 432-1750; (850) 432-2336

Three Rivers Legal Services, Inc.
http://www.trls.org
214 W. University Avenue
Primrose Square, Suite A
Gainesville, FL 32601
(352) 372-0519

Withlacoochee Area Legal
Services, Inc.
222 S.W. Broadway Street
Ocala, FL 34474-4151
(352) 629-0105

Georgia

Atlanta Legal Aid Society, Inc.
151 Spring Street, N.W.
Atlanta, GA 30303-2097
(404) 614-3990; (404) 524-5811

Georgia Legal Services Program
http://www.glsp.org
1100 Spring Street, Suite 200A
Atlanta, GA 30309-2848
(404) 206-5175; (800) 498-9469

Guam

Guam Legal Services Corporation
113 Bradley Place
Hagatna, GU 96910-4911
(671) 477-9811

Hawaii

Legal Aid Society of Hawaii
924 Bethel Street
P.O. Box 37375
Honolulu, HI 96837-0375
(808) 536-4302

Native Hawaiian Legal Corporation
*[Serving Native Americans in
Hawaii]*
1164 Bishop Street, Suite 1205
Honolulu, HI 96813-2826
(808) 521-2302

Idaho

Idaho Legal Aid Services, Inc.
http://www.idaholegalaid.org
310 North Fifth Street
P.O. Box 913
Boise, ID 83701-0913
(208) 336-8980; (208) 345-0106

Illinois

Land of Lincoln Legal Assistance
  Foundation, Inc.
http://www.lollaf.org
2420 Bloomer Drive
Alton, IL 62002-4809
(618) 462-0036

Legal Assistance Foundation of
  Metropolitan Chicago
http://www.lafchicago.org
111 W. Jackson Boulevard
  Suite 300
Chicago, IL 60604-3502
(312) 341-1070

Prairie State Legal Services, Inc.
975 North Main Street
Rockford, IL 61103-7064
(815) 965-2134

Indiana

Indiana Legal Services, Inc.
http://www.indianajustice.org
Market Square Ctr., Suite 1640
151 North Delaware Street
Indianapolis, IN 46204-2517
(317) 631-9410; (800) 869-0212

Iowa

Legal Services Corporation of Iowa
1111 Ninth Street, Suite 230
Des Moines, IA 50314-2527
(515) 243-2151; (800) 532-1275

Legal Aid Society of Polk County
Human Services Campus
1111 Ninth Street, Suite 380
Des Moines, IA 50314-2527
(515) 243-1193

Kansas

Kansas Legal Services, Inc.
712 S. Kansas Ave., Ste. 200
Topeka, KS 66603
(785) 233-2068; (800) 723-6953

Kentucky

Appalachian Research and Defense
  Fund of Kentucky
120 North Front Avenue
Prestonsburg, KY 41653
(606) 886-3876; (800) 556-3876

Cumberland Trace Legal Services,
  Inc.
http://www.klaid.org
KLAid@KLAid.org
520 East Main Street
P.O. Box 1776
Bowling Green, KY 42102-1776
(270) 782-1924; (866) 452-9243;
  (800) 782-1924

Central Kentucky Legal Services
  Inc.
498 Georgetown Street
P.O. Box 12947
Lexington, KY 40583-2947
(800) 928-4556

Legal Aid of the Blue Grass
302 Greenup Street
Covington, KY 41011-1740
(859) 431-8200

Legal Aid Society
http://www.laslou.org
425 West Muhammad Ali Blvd
Louisville, KY 40202-2353
(502) 584-1254; (800) 292-1862

Louisiana

Acadiana Legal Service Corporation
http://www.la-law.org
1020 Surrey Street
P.O. Box 4823
Lafayette, LA 70502-4823
(337) 237-4320; (800) 256-1175

Capital Area Legal Services Corporation
http://www.calscla.org
calsc@calscla.org
200 Third Street
P.O. Box 3273
Baton Rouge, LA 70821
(225) 338-9797; (800) 256-1900

Kisatchie Legal Services Corporation
134 St. Denis Street
P.O. Drawer 1189
Natchitoches, LA 71458-1189
(800) 960-9109

Legal Services of North Louisiana, Inc.
http://www.lsnl.org
720 Travis Street
Shreveport, LA 71101
(318) 222-7186; (800) 826-9265

New Orleans Legal Assistance Corporation
http://www.nolac.org/
144 Elk Place Suite 1000
New Orleans, LA 70112-2635
(504) 529-1000

North Louisiana Legal Assistance Corporation
200 Washington Street

P.O. Box 3325
Monroe, LA 71210-3325
(800) 256-1262

Northwest Louisiana Legal Services Inc.
720 Travis Street
Shreveport, LA 71101
(800) 826-9265

Southeast Louisiana Legal Services Corporation
1200 Derek Drive Suite 100
P. O. Drawer 2867
Hammond, LA 70404-2867
(985) 345-2130; (800) 349-0886

Southwest Louisiana Legal Services Society Inc.
1011 Lakeshore Drive Suite 402
P.O. Box 3002
Lake Charles, LA 70602-3002
(800) 256-1955

Maine

Pine Tree Legal Assistance, Inc.
http://www.ptla.org
88 Federal Street
P.O. Box 547
Portland, ME 04112-0547
(207) 774-4753; (207) 774-8211

Maryland

Legal Aid Bureau, Inc.
http://www.mdlab.org
500 East Lexington Street
Baltimore, MD 21202
(410) 539-5340

Massachusetts

Legal Services for Cape Cod and
  Islands, Inc.
http://www.lscci.org
460 West Main Street
Hyannis, MA 02601-3695
(508) 775-7020; (800) 742-4107

Massachusetts Justice Project, Inc.
57 Suffolk Street
Suite 401
Holyoke, MA 01040
(413) 533-2660; (800) 639-1209

Merrimack Valley Legal
  Services, Inc.
http://www.mvlegal.org
35 John Street, Suite 302
Lowell, MA 01852-1101
(978) 458-1465

New Center for Legal Advocacy,
  Inc.
257 Union Street
New Bedford, MA 02740
(508) 979-7160; (800) 244-9023

South Middlesex Legal Services,
  Inc.
http://www.smlegal.org
354 Waverly Street
Framingham, MA 01702
(508) 620-1830; (800) 696-1501

Volunteer Lawyers Project of the
  Boston Bar Association
http://www.vlpnet.org
29 Temple Place
Boston, MA 02111
(617) 423-0648

Michigan

Center for Civil Justice
320 S. Washington (2nd floor)
Saginaw, MI 48607
(517) 755-3120; (800) 724-7441

Lakeshore Legal Aid
Robert A. Verkuilen Building
21885 Dunham Road, Suite 4
Clinton Twp., MI 48036
(586) 469-5185

Legal Aid and Defender Association, Inc.
http://www.ladadetroit.org
645 Griswold
Suite 3466
Detroit, MI 48226-4216
(313) 965-4553; (313) 965-9419

Legal Services of South Central
  Michigan, Inc.
420 North Fourth Avenue
Ann Arbor, MI 48104-1197
(734) 665-6181

Legal Services of Eastern Michigan
http://www.lsem-mi.org
436 South Saginaw Street
Flint, MI 48502
(810) 234-2621; (800) 339-9513

Legal Services of Northern Michigan, Inc.
1349 S. Otsego Avenue Unit 7B
Parkside Mini-Mall
Gaylord, MI 49735
(989) 705-1067; (888) 645-9993

Michigan Indian Legal Services,
   Inc.
*[Provides legal aid to low-income Indi-
   an individuals and tribes]*
814 South Garfield Avenue
Suite A
Traverse City, MI 49686-3430
(231) 947-0122; (800) 968-6877

Michigan Legal Services
220 Bagley Avenue, Suite 900
Detroit, Michigan 48226
(313) 964-4130; (800) 875-4130

Oakland Livingston Legal Aid
35 West Huron Street, 5th Floor
Pontiac, MI 48342-2125
(248) 456-8861; (248) 456-8888

Western Michigan Legal Services
Cornerstone Bldg., Suite 400
89 Ionia Avenue,N.W.
Grand Rapids, MI 49503
(616) 774-0672; (800) 442-2777

Minnesota

Central Minnesota Legal Services,
   Inc.
430 First Avenue North
Suite 359
Minneapolis, MN 55401-1780
(612) 332-8151; (612) 783-4970

Judicare of Anoka County, Inc.
1201 89th Avenue, N.E., Suite 310
Blaine, MN 55434
(763) 783-4970; (612) 783-4970

Legal Aid Service of Northeastern
   Minnesota
http://www.lasnem.org
302 Ordean Building
424 West Superior Street
Duluth, MN 55802
(218) 726-4800; (800) 622-7266

Legal Services of Northwest
   Minnesota Corporation
1015 7th Avenue North
P.O. Box 838
Moorhead, MN 56561-0838
(218) 233-8585; (800) 450-8585

Southern Minnesota Regional
   Legal Services, Inc.
http://www.smrls.org
700 Minnesota Building
46 East Fourth Street
St. Paul, MN 55101-1112
(651) 228-9823

Mississippi

Central Mississippi Legal Services
   Corporation
414 South State St., 3rd Floor
P.O. Box 951
Jackson, MS 39205-0951
(601) 948-6752; (800) 959-6752

North Mississippi Rural Legal Services, Inc.
http://www.nmrls.com
2134 West Jackson Avenue
P.O. Box 767
Oxford, MS 38655-0767
(662) 234-8731; (800) 959-6752

Southeast Mississippi Legal
Services Corporation
111 East Front Street
P.O. Drawer 1728
Hattiesburg, MS 39403-1728
(601) 545-2950

South Mississippi Legal Services
Corporation
203 Fountain Square Building
P.O. Box 1386
Biloxi, MS 39533-1386
(228) 374-4160

Southwest Mississippi Legal
Services Corporation
P. O. Box 1242
221 Main Street
McComb, MS 39649-1242
(601) 684-0578

Micronesia

Micronesian Legal Services, Inc.
Chalon Kanoa Village, Dist. #2
P.O. Box 500269
Saipan, MP 96950-0269
(670) 234-6471; (670) 234-6243

Missouri

Legal Aid of Western Missouri
http://www.lawmo.org
1125 Grand Avenue, Suite 1900
Kansas City, MO 64106
(816) 474-6750; (816) 474-6750

Legal Services of Eastern Missouri,
Inc.
http://www.lsem.org
info@lsem.org
4232 Forest Park Avenue

St. Louis, MO 63108
(314) 534-4200; (800) 444-0514

Legal Services of Southern
Missouri
http://www.lsosm.org
la@lsosm.org
2872 South Meadowbrook Avenue
Springfield, MO 65807
(417) 881-1397; (800) 444-4863

Mid-Missouri Legal Services
Corporation
legalaid@mmls.org
205 East Forest Avenue
Columbia, MO 65203
(573) 442-0116; (800) 568-4931

Montana

Montana Legal Services
Association
http://www.montanalegalservices.com
616 Helena Ave., Suite 100
Helena, MT 59601
(406) 442-9830; (800) 666-6124

Nebraska

Nebraska Legal Services
http://www.nebls.com
500 South 18th St.
Suite 300, The Law Bldg.
Omaha, NE 68102-2533
(402) 348-1069; (402) 348-1060

Nevada

Nevada Legal Services, Inc.
530 South 6th Street
Las Vegas, NV 89101
(702) 386-0404

New Hampshire

Legal Advice & Referral Center, Inc.
http://www.larcnh.org
33 North Main St., 2nd Floor
P.O. Box 4147
Concord, NH 03302-4147
(603) 224-5723; (800) 639-5290

New Jersey

Bergen County Legal Services
61 Kansas Street
Hackensack, NJ 07601
(201) 487-2166

Camden Regional Legal Services Inc.
745 Market Street
Camden, NJ 08102-1117
(609) 964-2010

Cape-Atlantic Legal Services, Inc.
26 So. Pennsylvania Ave.
Atlantic City, NJ 08401
(800) 870-7547

Central New Jersey Legal Services
http://www.lsnj.org
78 New Street, 3rd Floor
New Brunswick, NJ 08901-2584
(732) 249-7600

Essex-Newark Legal Services Project, Inc.
http://www.lsnj.org
5 Commerce Street, 2nd Floor
Newark, NJ 07102
(973) 624-4500

Hudson County Legal Services Corporation
574 Summit Avenue
Jersey City, NJ 07306-2797
(201) 792-6363

Hunterdon County Legal Service Corporation
82 Park Avenue
Flemington, NJ 08822-1170
(908) 782-7979

Legal Aid Society of Mercer County
198 West State Street
Trenton, NJ 08608-1103
(609) 695-6249

Legal Aid Society of Morris County
30 Schuyler Place 2nd Floor
P.O. Box 900
Morristown, NJ 07963-0900
(973) 285-6911

Legal Services of New Jersey
http://www.lsnj.org
P.O. Box 1357
Edison, NJ 08818-1357
732-572-9100

Legal Services of Northwest Jersey
http://www.lsnj.org
91 Front Street
P.O. Box 65
Belvidere, NJ 07823-0065
(908) 475-2010

Middlesex County Legal Services Corporation
78 New Street 3rd Floor
New Brunswick, NJ 08901-2584
(732) 249-7600

Northeast New Jersey Legal
  Services Corporation
http://www.lsnj.org
574 Summit Avenue
Jersey City, NJ 07306-2797
(201) 792-6363

Ocean-Monmouth Legal
  Services, Inc.
http://www.lsnj.org
9 Robbins Street, Suite 2A
Toms River, NJ 08753
(732) 866-0020; (732) 341-2727

Passaic County Legal Aid Society
175 Market Street 4th Floor
Paterson, NJ 07505
(973) 345-7171

Somerset-Sussex Legal Services
  Corporation
78 Grove Street
Somerville, NJ 08876
(908) 231-0840

South Jersey Legal Services
http://www.lsnj.org
745 Market Street
Camden, NJ 08102-1117
(856) 964-2010

Union County Legal Services
  Corporation
60 Prince Street
Elizabeth, NJ 07208
(908) 354-4340

Warren County Legal Services Inc.
91 Front Street
P.O. Box 65
Belvidere, NJ 07823-0065
(908) 475-2010

New Mexico

Community and Indian Legal
  Services Inc.
805 Early Street Building F
P.O. Box 5175
Santa Fe, NM 87502-5175
(800) 373-9881

Legal Aid Society of Albuquerque
  Inc.
121 Tijeras Ave. NE Suite 3100
P.O. Box 25486
Albuquerque, NM 87125-5486
(505) 243-7871

New Mexico Legal Aid
500 Cooper NW Suite 300
P.O. Box 25486
Albuquerque, NM 87125-5486
(505) 243-7871

Southern New Mexico Legal
  Services Inc.
300 North Downtown Mall
Las Cruces, NM 88001-1216
(800) 376-5727

New York

Chemung County Neighborhood
  Legal Services, Inc.
215 E. Church Street, Suite 301
Elmira, NY 14901-2889
(607) 734-1647

Legal Aid for Broome and
  Chenango
http://www.wnylc.net
30 Fayette Street
Binghamton, NY 13901
(607) 723-7966

Legal Aid Society of Mid-New
   York, Inc.
255 Genesee Street, 2nd Floor
Utica, NY 13501
(315) 732-2131

Legal Aid Society of Northeastern
   New York, Inc.
55 Colvin Avenue
Albany, NY 12206
(518) 462-6765; (800) 462-2922

Legal Aid Society of Rockland
   County, Inc.
http://www.wnylc.net
2 Congers Road
New City, NY 10956-0314
(845) 634-3627

Legal Services for New York City
http://www.legalsupport.org
350 Broadway, 6th Floor
New York, NY 10013-9998
(212) 431-7200

Legal Services of Central New
   York, Inc.
http://www.wnylc.net
472 South Salina Street, #300
Syracuse, NY 13202
(315) 475-3127

Monroe County Legal Assistance
   Corporation
http://www.wnylc.net
80 St. Paul Street, Suite 700
Rochester, NY 14604-1350
(716) 325-2520

Nassau/Suffolk Law Services
   Committee, Inc.
http://www.wnylc.net
One Helen Keller Way
5th Floor
Hempstead, NY 11550
(516) 292-8100

Neighborhood Legal Services, Inc.
http://www.nls.org
Ellicott Square Building
295 Main Street, Room 495
Buffalo, NY 14203-2473
(716) 847-0650

Niagara County Legal Aid Society,
   Inc.
http://www.wnylc.net
775 Third Street
P.O. Box 844
Niagara Falls, NY 14302-0844
(716) 284-8831

North Country Legal Services, Inc.
http://www.wnylc.net
100 Court Street
P.O. Box 989
Plattsburgh, NY 12901-0989
(518) 563-4022; (800) 722-7380

Southern Tier Legal Services
http://www.wnylc.net
104 East Steuben Street
Bath, NY 14810
(607) 776-4126

Westchester/Putnam Legal
   Services, Inc.
http:///www.wpls.org
4 Cromwell Place
White Plains, NY 10601
(914) 949-1305

North Carolina

Legal Aid of North Carolina, Inc.
http://www.legalaidnc.org
224 South Dawson St.
Raleigh, NC 27611-6087
(919) 856-2130

Legal Aid Society of Northwest
  North Carolina Inc.
Patten Building
216 West Fourth Street
Winston-Salem, NC 27101-2824
(800) 660-6663

Legal Services of Southern
  Piedmont Inc.
1431 Elizabeth Avenue
Charlotte, NC 28204
(704) 376-1600

North Central Legal Assistance
  Program Inc.
212 North Mangum Street
P.O. Box 2101
Durham, NC 27702-2101
(800) 331-7594

North Dakota

Legal Assistance of North Dakota,
  Inc.
http://www.legalassist.org
1025 Third Street North
P.O. Box 1893
Bismarck, ND 58502-1893
(701) 222-2110; (800) 634-5263

North Dakota Legal Services Inc.
Main Street
P.O. Box 217
New Town, ND 58763-0217
(701) 627-4719

Ohio

Community Legal Aid Services,
  Inc.
http://www.communitylegalaid.org
The Rose Building, 3rd Floor
265 South Main Street
Akron, OH 44308
(330) 535-4191; (866) 584-2350

Legal Aid Society of Greater
  Cincinnati
http://www.lascinti.org
215 East Ninth Street
Suite 200
Cincinnati, OH 45202
(513) 241-9400; (800) 582-2682

The Legal Aid Society of Cleveland
http://www.lasclev.org
1223 West Sixth St., 4th Floor
Cleveland, OH 44113-1301
(216) 687-1900

The Legal Aid Society of Columbus
http://www.columbuslegalaid.org
40 West Gay Street
Columbus, OH 43215-2896
(614) 737-0135; (614) 224-8374

Legal Services of Northwest Ohio,
  Inc.
640 Spitzer Building
520 Madison Avenue
Toledo, OH 43604-1371
(419) 724-0030; (877) 894-4599

Ohio State Legal Services
http://www.oslsa.org
555 Buttles Avenue
Columbus, OH 43215-1137
(614) 221-7201; (800) 589-5888

Western Ohio Legal Services
Association
http://www.wolsaoh.org
311 East Market St., Suite 307
Lima, OH 45801-4565
(419) 224-9070

Oklahoma

Oklahoma Indian Legal Services,
Inc.
*[Providing legal services to Native
Americans in Oklahoma]*
http://www.oilsonline.org
4200 Perimeter Center Drive
Suite 222
Oklahoma City, OK 73112
(405) 943-6457; (800) 658-1497

Legal Aid Services of Oklahoma,
Inc.
http://www.legalaidok.org
2915 North Classen Boulevard
Suite 110
Oklahoma City, OK 73106
(405) 557-0020; (800) 421-1641

Legal Services of Eastern Oklahoma
Inc.
http://www.lseo.org/
115 West Third St., Suite 701
Tulsa, OK 74103-3403
(800) 299-3338

Oregon

Lane County Legal Aid Service
Inc.
http://www.lanecountylegalservices.org
376 East 11th Avenue
Eugene, OR 97401-3246
(541) 342-6056

Legal Aid Services of Oregon
700 S.W. Taylor St., Suite 310
Portland, OR 97205
(503) 224-4094

Marion-Polk Legal Aid Service Inc.
http://www.mplas.org
1655 State Street
Salem, OR 97301-4258
(800) 359-1845

Pennsylvania

Laurel Legal Services, Inc.
306 South Pennsylvania Avenue
Greensburg, PA 15601-3066
(724) 836-2211; (800) 253-9558

Legal Aid of Southeastern
Pennsylvania
http://www.lasp.org
317 Swede Street
Norristown, PA 19401-4801
(610) 275-5400

MidPenn Legal Services, Inc.
http://www.midpenn.org
3540 North Progress Avenue
Suite 102
Harrisburg, PA 17110
(717) 541-8141; (717) 232-0581

Montgomery County Legal Aid
Service
317 Swede Street
Norristown, PA 19401-4801
(610) 275-5400

Neighborhood Legal Services
Association
928 Penn Avenue
Pittsburgh, PA 15222-3799
(412) 644-7450; (412) 255-6700

North Penn Legal Services, Inc.
http://www.northpennlegal.org
65 E. Elizabeth Ave, STE 903
Bethlehem, PA 18018
(610) 317-5312; (800) 982-4387

Northwestern Legal Services
http://www.nwls.org
Renaissance Center, Suite 1200
1001 State Street
Erie, PA 16501-1833
(814) 452-6949; (800) 665-6957

Philadelphia Legal Assistance
  Center
http://www.philalegal.org
1424 Chestnut Street
2nd Floor
Philadelphia, PA 19102
(215) 981-3808; (215) 981-3800

Southwestern Pennsylvania Legal
  Services, Inc.
10 West Cherry Avenue
Washington, PA 15301
(724) 225-6170; (800) 846-0871

Puerto Rico

Community Law Office, Inc.
170 Calle Federico Costa
Box 194735
San Juan, PR 00919-4735
(787) 751-1600

Puerto Rico Legal Services, Inc.
http://www.servicioslegales.org
1859 Ave. Ponce de León-Pda 26
Apartado 9134
San Juan, PR 00908-9134
(787) 728-9561; (800) 981-5342

Rhode Island

Rhode Island Legal Services, Inc.
http://www.rils.org
56 Pine Street, 4th Floor
Providence, RI 02903
(401) 274-2652; (800) 662-5034

South Carolina

Carolina Regional Legal Services
  Corporation
http://www.sclegalservicespro-
  grams.org/crls/index.html
279 West Evans Street
P.O. Box 479
Florence, SC 29503-0479
(803) 667-1896

Legal Services Agency of Western
  Carolina Inc.
http://www.sclegalservicespro-
  grams.org/lsawc/index.html
1 Pendleton Street
Greenville, SC 29601
(864) 467-3232

Neighborhood Legal Assistance
  Program Inc.
http://www.sclegalservicespro-
  grams.org/programs.html
438 King Street
Charleston, SC 29403-6283
(803) 722-0107

Palmetto Legal Services
http://www.netside.com/~plslex/
  index2.html
2109 Bull Street
P.O. Box 2267
Columbia, SC 29202-2267
(800) 273-1200

Piedmont Legal Services Inc.
http://www.sclegalservicespro-
  grams.org/plsinc/index.html
148 East Main Street
Spartanburg, SC 29306
(800) 922-8176

The South Carolina Centers for
  Equal Justice
1 Pendleton Street
Greenville, SC 29601
(864) 679-3232

South Dakota

Black Hills Legal Services Inc.
528 Kansas City Street
P.O. Box 1500
Rapid City, SD 57709
(800) 742-8602

Dakota Plains Legal Services, Inc.
160 Second Street
P.O. Box 727
Mission, SD 57555-0727
(605) 856-4444; (800) 658-2297

East River Legal Services
335 North Main Ave., Suite 300
Sioux Falls, SD 57104
(605) 336-9230; (800) 952-3015

Tennessee

Knoxville Legal Aid Society Inc.
http://korrnet.org/klas/
502 South Gay Street Suite 404
Knoxville, TN 37902-1502
(423) 637-0484

Legal Aid of East Tennessee
http://www.laet.org
502 South Gay St.
Suite 404
Knoxville, TN 37902-1502
(865) 637-0484

Legal Aid Society of Middle Tennessee and the Cumberlands
211 Union Street, Suite 800
Nashville, TN 37201-1504
(615) 780-7123; (615) 244-6610

Legal Services of South Central
  Tennessee Inc.
104 West Seventh Street
P.O. Box 1256
Columbia, TN 38402-1256
(931) 381-5533

Legal Services of Upper East Tennessee Inc.
311 West Walnut Street
P.O. Box 360
Johnson City, TN 37605-0360
(423) 928-8311

Memphis Area Legal Services, Inc.
Claridge House, Suite 200
109 North Main Street
Memphis, TN 38103-5013
(901) 523-8822

Rural Legal Services of Tennessee
  Inc.
226 Broadway Jackson Square
P.O. Box 5209
Oak Ridge, TN 37831-5209
(423) 483-8454

West Tennessee Legal Services, Inc.
http://www.wtls.org
210 West Main Street
P.O. Box 2066
Jackson, TN 38302-2066
(731) 426-1311; (800) 372-8346

Texas

Bexar County Legal Aid
  Association Inc.
http://www.barrera.atfreeweb.com/
434 South Main Ave. Suite 300
San Antonio, TX 78204
(210) 227-0111

Coastal Bend Legal Services
102 Pueblo Street
Corpus Christi, TX 78405
(800) 840-3379

East Texas Legal Services Inc.
http://www.etls.org/
414 East Pillar Street
P.O. Box 631070
Nacogdoches, TX 75963-1070
(800) 354-1889

El Paso Legal Assistance Society
1301 N. Oregon
El Paso, TX 79902
(800) 373-9028

Gulf Coast Legal Foundation
http://www.gclf.org/
1415 Fannin Avenue 3rd Floor
Houston, TX 77002
(800) 733-8394

Legal Aid of Central Texas
http://www.lact.org/
2201 Post Road, Suite 104
Austin, TX 78704
(800) 369-9270

Legal Aid of NorthWest Texas
600 East Weatherford Street
Fort Worth, TX 76102
(817) 877-0609; (800) 955-3959

Legal Services of North Texas
http://www.lsnt.org/
1515 Main Street
Dallas, TX 75201-4803
(214) 748-1234

Lone Star Legal Aid
414 East Pilar Street
P.O. Box 631070
Nacogdoches, TX 75963-1070
(936) 560-1455; (800) 354-1889

Texas Rural Legal Aid, Inc.
http://www.trla.org
300 South Texas Boulevard
Weslaco, TX 78596
(956) 968-6574; (800) 968-8823

West Texas Legal Services, Inc.
600 East Weatherford Street
Fort Worth, TX 76102
(800) 955-3959

Utah

Utah Legal Services, Inc.
http://www.andjusticeforall.org
205 North 400 West
Salt Lake City, UT 84103-1125
(801) 328-8891; (800) 662-4245

Vermont

Legal Services Law Line of
  Vermont, Inc.
http://www.lawlinevt.org
30 Elmwood Avenue
Burlington, VT 05401
(802) 863-7153; (800) 639-8857

Vermont Legal Aid
(800) 889-2047

Offices:
264 North Winooski Avenue
Burlington, VT 05402

7 Court Street
Montpelier, VT 05601

1111 Main Street, Suite B
St. Johnsbury, VT 05819

57 North Main Street
Rutland, VT 05701

56 Main Street, Suite 301
Springfield, VT 05156

Virginia

Blue Ridge Legal Services, Inc.
http://www.brls.org
204 North High Street
P.O. Box 551
Harrisonburg, VA 22803
(540) 433-1830; (800) 237-0141

Central Virginia Legal Aid
  Society, Inc.
http://www.cvlas.org
101 West Broad St., Suite 101
P.O. Box 12206
Richmond, VA 23241-2206
(804) 648-1012; (800) 868-1012

Legal Services of Eastern Virginia,
  Inc.
http://www.legalaidva.org
2017 Cunningham Dr., Suite 300
P.O. Box 7502
Hampton, VA 23666
(757) 827-0350; (800) 944-6624

Legal Services of Northern Virginia
  Inc.
http://members.aol.com/lsnvmain/
6400 Arlington Blvd. Suite 630
Falls Church, VA 22042
(703) 534-4343

Potomac Legal Aid Society, Inc.
allstaff@potomaclegalaid.org
6400 Arlington Blvd
Suite 600
Falls Church, VA 22042
(703) 538-3975

Potomac Legal Aid Society, Inc.
allstaff@potomaclegalaid.org
6400 Arlington Blvd
Suite 600
Falls Church, VA 22042
(703) 538-3975

Southwest Virginia Legal Aid
  Society, Inc.
http://www.svlas.org
227 West Cherry Street
Marion, VA 24354
(276) 783-6576; (800) 277-6754

Tidewater Legal Aid Society
125 St. Paul's Blvd.
Suite 400
Norfolk, VA 23510
(757) 627-5423

Virginia Legal Aid Society, Inc.
http://www.vlas.org
513 Church Street
P.O. Box 6058
Lynchburg, VA 24505-6058
(434) 528-4722; (888) 528-8527

Virgin Islands

Legal Services of the Virgin Islands, Inc.
3017 Orange Grove
Christiansted
St. Croix, VI 00820-4375
(340) 773-2626

Washington

Northwest Justice Project
http://www.nwjustice.org
401 Second Avenue South
Suite 407
Seattle, WA 98104
(888) 201-1014; (206) 464-1519

West Virginia

Appalachian Legal Services, Inc.
922 Quarrier Street, 4th Floor
Charleston, WV 25301
(304) 343-4481

Legal Aid of West Virginia, Inc.
http://www.wvlegalservices.org
922 Quarrier Street, 4th Floor
Charleston, WV 25301
(800) 642-8279; (304) 342-6814

Wisconsin

Legal Action of Wisconsin, Inc.
http://www.legalaction.org
230 West Wells St., Room 800
Milwaukee, WI 53203-1866
(414) 278-7722; (414) 278-7777

Legal Services of Northeastern Wisconsin Inc.
201 W. Walnut Street
Suite 203
Green Bay, WI 54303
(800) 236-1127

Western Wisconsin Legal Services Inc.
http://www.mhtc.net/~wwlsdvo/
205 5th Avenue, Suite 300
P.O. Box 2617
La Crosse, WI 54602-2617
(608) 785-2809; (800) 873-0927

Wisconsin Judicare, Inc.
http://www.judicare.org
300 Third Street, Suite 210
P.O. Box 6100
Wausau, WI 54402-6100
(800) 472-1638; (715) 842-1681

Wyoming

Wyoming Legal Services, Inc.
P.O. Box 1160
1017 East Main Street
Lander, WY 82520
(800) 442-6170; (307) 332-6626

Further Reading

A short list, by no means comprehensive, of interesting and informative books about American law and lawyers.

General Books About the Law

Abraham, H.J. *The Judicial Process,* 6th ed. Oxford University Press, 1993.

Bogus, Carl T. *Why Lawsuits are Good for America: Disciplined Democracy, Big Business, and the Common Law.* New York University Press, 2001.

Farnsworth, E. Allan. *An Introduction to the Legal System of the United States,* 2nd ed. Oceana, 1996.

Feinman, Jay M. *Law 101: Everything You Need To Know About the American Legal System.* Oxford University Press, 2000.

Hall, Kermit L. *Oxford Companion to American Law.* Oxford University Press, 2002.

Hall, Kermit L., James W. Ely, and Joel B. Grossman (eds.). *The Oxford Companion to the Supreme Court of the United States.* Oxford University Press, 1992.

Jasanoff, Sheila. *Science at the Bar: Law, Science, and Technology in America.* Harvard University Press, 1996.

Kairys, D., (ed). *The Politics of Law.* 3rd ed. Pantheon Books, 1998.

Lazarus, Edward. *Closed Chambers: The Rise, Fall, and Future of the Modern Supreme Court.* Penguin, 1999.

Levi, Edward H. *An Introduction to Legal Reasoning.* University of Chicago Press, 1962.

Rehnquist, William H. *The Supreme Court.* Vintage Books, 2002.

Schwartz, Bernard. *Decision: How the Supreme Court Decides Cases.* Oxford University Press, 1996.

Tarr, G. Alan. *Judicial Process and Judicial Policymaking.* Wadsworth, 2002.

Wice, P. *Judges and Lawyers.* HarperCollins, 1991.

History of the Law

Auerbach, Jerold S. *Unequal Justice—Lawyers and Social Change in Modern America.* Oxford University Press, 1976.

Brophy, Alfred L. and Randall Kennedy. *Reconstructing the Dreamland: The Tulsa Race Riot of 1921, Race Reparations, and Reconciliation.* Oxford University Press, 2003.

Friedman, Lawrence M. *American Law in the Twentieth Century.* Yale University Press, 2002.

Friedman, Lawrence M. *A History of American Law,* 2nd ed. Touchstone, 1985.

Horwitz, Morton J. *The Transformation of American Law, 1870-1960.* Oxford University Press, 1992.

Levy, Leonard Williams. *Origins of the Bill of Rights.* Yale University Press, 2001.

Patterson, James T. *Brown vs Board of Education: A Civil Rights Milestone and Its Troubled Legacy.* Oxford University Press, 2001.

Schwartz, Bernard. *A Book of Legal Lists.* Oxford University Press, 1997.

Schwartz, Bernard. *A History of the Supreme Court.* Oxford University Press, 1995.

Semonche, John E. *Keeping the Faith: A Cultural History of the U.S. Supreme Court.* Rowman and Littlefield, 1998.

Simon, James F. *What Kind of Nation: Thomas Jefferson, John Marshall, and the Epic Struggle to Create a United States.* Simon and Schuster, 2002.

White, G. Edward. *Tort Law in America,* 2nd ed. Oxford University Press, 2003.

Lawyers and the Legal Profession

Abel, R. *American Lawyers.* Oxford University Press, 1989.

Arron, Deborah. *Running From the Law: Why Good Lawyers Are Getting Out of the Legal Profession.* Niche Press, 1997.

Dershowitz, Alan M. *Letters to a Young Lawyer*. Basic Books, 2001.

Glendon, Mary Ann. *A Nation Under Lawyers: How the Crisis in the Legal Profession Is Transforming American Society*. Harvard University Press, 1996.

Hagan, J., and F. Kay. *Gender in Practice*. Oxford University Press, 1995.

Kronman, Anthony T. *The Lost Lawyer: Failing Ideas of the Legal Profession*. Harvard University Press, 1995.

Margolick, David. *At the Bar: The Passions and Peccadilloes of American Lawyers*. Touchstone Books, 1995.

Linowitz, Sol M., and Martin Mayer. *The Betrayed Profession: Lawyering at the End of the Twentieth Century*. Johns Hopkins University Press, 1996.

Nader, Ralph and Wesley J. Smith. *No Contest: Corporate Lawyers and the Perversion of Justice in America*. Random House, 1999.

Rhode, Deborah. *In the Interests of Justice: Refining the Legal Profession*. Oxford University Press, 2001.

Rosenthal, D.E. *Lawyer and Client*. Russell Sage Foundation, 1974.

Selles, Benjamin. *The Soul of the Law: Understanding Lawyers and the Law*. Vega Books, 2002.

Simenoff, Mark (ed.). *My First Year As a Lawyer*. Signet, 1996.

Zitrin, Richard A. and Carol M. Langford. *The Moral Compass of the American Lawyer: Truth, Justice, Power, and Greed*. Ballantine Books, 2000.

Biographies

Gunther, Gerald. *Learned Hand: The Man and the Judge*. Belknap Press, 1995.

Harbaugh, William H. *Lawyer's Lawyer: The Life of John W. Davis*. Oxford University Press, 1985.

Holmes, Jr. Oliver Wendell, and Richard A. Posner. *The Essential Holmes: Selections from the Letters, Speeches, Judicial Opinions, and Other Writings of Oliver Wendell Holmes, Jr*. University of Chicago Press, 1996.

Kalman, Laura. *Abe Fortas: A Biography.* Yale University Press, 1990.

Newman, Roger K. *Hugo Black: A Biography.* Fordham University Press, 1997.

Polenberg, Richard. *The World of Benjamin Cardozo: Personal Values and the Judicial Process.* Harvard University Press, 1999.

Weinberg, Arthur, William O. Douglas, and Clarence Darrow. *Attorney for the Damned: Clarence Darrow in the Courtroom.* University of Chicago Press, 1989.

White, G. Edward. *The American Judicial Tradition: Profiles of Leading American Judges.* Oxford University Press, 1998.

White, G. Edward. *Oliver Wendell Holmes: Sage of the Supreme Court.* Oxford University Press, 1999.

Williams, Juan. *Thurgood Marshall: American Revolutionary.* Random House, 2000.

Interesting Cases

Black, Roy. *Black's Law: A Criminal Lawyer Reveals His Defense Strategies in Four Cliffhanger Cases.* Simon and Schuster, 1999.

Harr, Jonathan. *A Civil Action.* Vintage Books, 1996.

Jones, Rodney R. *Disorderly Conduct: Verbatim Excerpts from Actual Cases.* W.W. Norton, 1999.

Lewis, Anthony. *Gideon's Trumpet.* Vintage Books, 1989.

McLynn, Frank. *Famous Trials: Cases That Made History.* Reader's Digest, 1995.

Sayer, John William. *Ghost Dancing the Law: The Wounded Knee Trials.* Harvard University Press, 1997.

Stern, Gerald M. *The Buffalo Creek Disaster.* Knopf, 1977.

Werth, Barry. *Damages: One Family's Legal Struggles in the World of Medicine.* Simon and Schuster, 1998.

International Law

Arend, Anthony Clark. *Legal Rules and International Society.* Oxford University Press 1999

Brownlie, Ian. *Principles of Public International Law.* Oxford University Press, 1998.

Steiner, Henry J, and Philip Alston. *International Human Rights in Context.* Oxford University Press, 2000.

Theory of the Law

Bobbit, Philip. *Constitutional Fate : Theory of the Constitution.* Oxford University Press, 1984.

Duxbury, Neil. *Patterns of American Jurisprudence.* Oxford University Press, 1995.

Epstein, Richard A. *Simple Rules for a Complex World.* Harvard University Press, 1997.

Kennedy, Duncan. *A Critique of Adjudication (fin de siecle).* Harvard University Press, 1997.

Llewellyn, Karl N. *Bramble Bush: On Our Law and Its Study.* Oceana Publications, 1981.

Minda, Gary. *Postmodern Legal Movements.* New York University Press, 1995.

Patterson, Dennis. *Companion to Philosophy of Law and Legal Theory.* Blackwell, 1999.

Posner, Richard A. *Overcoming Law.* Harvard University Press, 1996.

Schlag, Pierre. *Laying Down the Law: Mysticism, Fetishism, and the American Legal Mind.* New York University Press, 1998.

Sunstein, Cass R. *Legal Reasoning and Political Conflict.* Oxford University Press, 1998.

Tushnet, Mark V. *Taking the Constitution Away From the Courts.* Princeton University Press, 2000.

Tushnet, Mark V. *The New Constitutional Order.* Princeton University Press, 2002.

White, Jefferson and Dennis Patterson. *Introduction to the Philosophy of Law.* Oxford University Press, 1998.

Criminal Law

Humes, Edward. *No Matter How Loud I Shout: A Year in the Life of Juvenile Court.* Touchstone Books, 1997.

Morris, Norval and David Rothman (eds.). *Oxford History of the Prison: The Practice of Punishment in Western Society.* Oxford University Press, 1997.

Morris, Norval. *The Brothel Boy and Other Parables of the Law.* American Philological Association, 1992.

Prejean, Helen. *Dead Man Walking: An Eyewitness Account of the Death Penalty in the United States.* Vintage Books, 1996.

Tonry, Michael. Handbook of Crime and Punishment. Oxford University Press, 2001.

Zimring, Franklin. *The Contradictions of American Capital Punishment.* Oxford University Press, 2003.

Law School

Osborn, John J. *The Paper Chase.* Whitson Publishing Company, 2003.

Turow, Scott. *One L: The Turbulent True Story of a First Year at Harvard Law School.* Warner Books, 1977.

Stevens, Robert B. *Law School: Legal Education in America from the 1850s to the 1980s.* University of North Carolina Press, 1990

Practical Law Advice

Brill, Steven. *The Court TV Cradle-to-Grave Legal Survival Guide.* Little, Brown, 1995.

Irving, Shae, and Kathleen Michon. *Nolo's Encyclopedia of Everyday Law.* Nolo Press, 2002.

The Declaration of Independence

Action of Second Continental Congress, July 4, 1776
The unanimous Declaration of the thirteen United States of
America

WHEN in the Course of human Events,

it becomes necessary for one People to dissolve the Political
Bands which have connected them with another, and to assume
among the Powers of the Earth, the separate and equal Station
to which the Laws of Nature and of Nature's God entitle them,
a decent Respect to the Opinions of Mankind requires that they
should declare the causes which impel them to the Separation.

WE hold these Truths to be self-evident, that all Men are created equal, that they are endowed by their Creator with certain
unalienable Rights, that among these are Life, Liberty and the
Pursuit of Happiness — That to secure these Rights, Governments are instituted among Men, deriving their just Powers
from the Consent of the Governed, that whenever any Form of
Government becomes destructive of these Ends, it is the Right
of the People to alter or to abolish it, and to institute new Government, laying its Powers on such Principles, and organizing its Powers in such Form, as to them shall seem most likely
to effect their Safety and Happiness. Prudence, indeed, will dic-
tate that Governments long established should not be changed
for light and transient Causes; and accordingly all Experience
hath shewn, that Mankind are more disposed to suffer, while
Evils are sufferable, than to right themselves by abolishing the
Forms to which they are accustomed. But when a long Train of
Abuses and Usurpations, pursuing invariably the same Object,
evinces a Design to reduce them under absolute Despotism, it
is their Right, it is their Duty, to throw off such Government,

and to provide new Guards for their future Security. Such has been the patient Sufferance of these Colonies; and such is now the Necessity which constrains them to alter their former Systems of Government. The History of the present King of Great-Britain is a History of repeated Injuries and Usurpations, all having in direct Object the Establishment of an absolute Tyranny over these States. To prove this, let Facts be submitted to a candid World.

HE has refused his Assent to Laws, the most wholesome and necessary for the public Good.

HE has forbidden his Governors to pass Laws of immediate and pressing Importance, unless suspended in their Operation till his Assent should be obtained; and when so suspended, he has utterly neglected to attend to them.

HE has refused to pass other Laws for the Accommodation of large Districts of People, unless those People would relinquish the Right of Representation in the Legislature, a Right inestimable to them, and formidable to Tyrants only.

HE has called together Legislative Bodies at Places unusual, uncomfortable, and distant from the Depository of their public Records, for the sole Purpose of fatiguing them into Compliance with his Measures.

HE has dissolved Representative Houses repeatedly, for opposing with manly Firmness his Invasions on the Rights of the People.

HE has refused for a long Time, after such Dissolutions, to cause others to be elected; whereby the Legislative Powers, incapable of the Annihilation, have returned to the People at large for their exercise; the State remaining in the mean time exposed to all the Dangers of Invasion from without, and Convulsions within.

HE has endeavoured to prevent the Population of these States; for that Purpose obstructing the Laws for Naturalization of Foreigners; refusing to pass others to encourage their Migrations hither, and raising the Conditions of new Appropriations of Lands.

HE has obstructed the Administration of Justice, by refusing his Assent to Laws for establishing Judiciary Powers.

HE has made Judges dependent on his Will alone, for the Tenure of their Offices, and the Amount and Payment of their Salaries.

HE has erected a Multitude of new Offices, and sent hither Swarms of Officers to harrass our People, and eat out their Substance.

HE has kept among us, in Times of Peace, Standing Armies, without the consent of our Legislatures.

HE has affected to render the Military independent of and superior to the Civil Power.

HE has combined with others to subject us to a Jurisdiction foreign to our Constitution, and unacknowledged by our Laws; giving his Assent to their Acts of pretended Legislation:

FOR quartering large Bodies of Armed Troops among us;

FOR protecting them, by a mock Trial, from Punishment for any Murders which they should commit on the Inhabitants of these States:

FOR cutting off our Trade with all Parts of the World:

FOR imposing Taxes on us without our Consent:

FOR depriving us, in many Cases, of the Benefits of Trial by Jury:

FOR transporting us beyond Seas to be tried for pretended Offences:

FOR abolishing the free System of English Laws in a neighbouring Province, establishing therein an arbitrary Government, and enlarging its Boundaries, so as to render it at once an Example and fit Instrument for introducing the same absolute Rules into these Colonies:

FOR taking away our Charters, abolishing our most valuable Laws, and altering fundamentally the Forms of our Governments:

FOR suspending our own Legislatures, and declaring themselves invested with Power to legislate for us in all Cases whatsoever.

HE has abdicated Government here, by declaring us out of his Protection and waging War against us.

HE has plundered our Seas, ravaged our Coasts, burnt our Towns, and destroyed the Lives of our People.

HE is, at this Time, transporting large Armies of foreign Mercenaries to compleat the Works of Death, Desolation, and Tyranny, already begun with circumstances of Cruelty and Perfidy, scarcely paralleled in the most barbarous Ages, and totally unworthy the Head of a civilized Nation.

HE has constrained our fellow Citizens taken Captive on the high Seas to bear Arms against their Country, to become the Executioners of their Friends and Brethren, or to fall themselves by their Hands.

HE has excited domestic Insurrections amongst us, and has endeavoured to bring on the Inhabitants of our Frontiers, the merciless Indian Savages, whose known Rule of Warfare, is an undistinguished Destruction, of all Ages, Sexes and Conditions.

IN every stage of these Oppressions we have Petitioned for Redress in the most humble Terms: Our repeated Petitions have been answered only by repeated Injury. A Prince, whose Character is thus marked by every act which may define a Tyrant, is unfit to be the Ruler of a free People.

NOR have we been wanting in Attentions to our British Brethren. We have warned them from Time to Time of Attempts by their Legislature to extend an unwarrantable Jurisdiction over us. We have reminded them of the Circumstances of our Emigration and Settlement here. We have appealed to their native Justice and Magnanimity, and we have conjured them by the Ties of our common Kindred to disavow these Usurpations, which, would inevitably interrupt our Connections and Correspondence. They too have been deaf to the Voice of Justice and of Consanguinity. We must, therefore, acquiesce in the Necessity, which denounces our Separation, and hold them, as we hold the rest of Mankind, Enemies in War, in Peace, Friends.

WE, therefore, the Representatives of the UNITED STATES OF AMERICA, in GENERAL CONGRESS, Assembled, appealing to the Supreme Judge of the World for the Rectitude of our Intentions, do, in the Name, and by Authority of the good People of these Colonies, solemnly Publish and Declare, That these United Colonies are, and of Right ought to be, FREE AND INDEPENDENT STATES; that they are absolved from all Allegiance to the British Crown, and that all political Connection between them and the State of Great-Britain, is and ought to be totally dissolved; and that as FREE AND INDEPENDENT STATES, they have full Power to levy War, conclude Peace, contract Alliances, establish Commerce, and to do all other Acts and Things which INDEPENDENT STATES may of right do. And for the support of this Declaration, with a firm Reliance on the Protection of divine Providence, we mutually pledge to each other our Lives, our Fortunes, and our sacred Honor.

Signed by ORDER AND IN BEHALF of the CONGRESS,
    JOHN HANCOCK, President.
  Attest:
    CHARLES THOMSON, Secretary.

SIGNERS:

JOHN HANCOCK

New-Hampshire:
   Josiah Bartlett
   Wm. Whipple,
   Matthew Thornton

Massachusetts-Bay:
   Saml. Adams
   John Adams
   Robt. Treat Paine
   Elbridge Gerry

Rhode-Island and
Providence, &c.:
>   Step. Hopkins
>   William Ellery

Connecticut:
>   Roger Sherman
>   Saml. Huntington
>   Wm. Williams
>   Oliver Wolcott

New-York:
>   Wm. Floyd
>   Phil. Livingston
>   Frans. Lewis
>   Lewis Morris

New-Jersey:
>   Richd. Stockton
>   Jno. Witherspoon
>   Fras. Hopkinson
>   John Hart
>   Abra. Clark

Pennsylvania:
>   Robt. Morris
>   Benjamin Rush
>   Benja. Franklin
>   John Morton
>   Geo. Clymer
>   Jas. Smith
>   Geo. Taylor
>   James Wilson
>   Geo. Ross

Delaware:
>   Caesar Rodney
>   Geo. Read
>   Tho. McKean

Maryland:
>   Samuel Chase
>   Wm. Paca
>   Thos. Stone
>   Charles Carroll, of Carrollton

Virginia:
>   George Wythe
>   Richard Henry Lee
>   Ths. Jefferson
>   Benja. Harrison
>   Thos. Nelson, Jr.
>   Francis Lightfoot Lee
>   Carter Braxton

North-Carolina:
>   Wm. Hooper
>   Joseph Hewes
>   John Penn

South-Carolina:
>   Edward Rutledge
>   Thos. Heyward, Jr.
>   Thomas Lynch, Jr.
>   Arthur Middleton

Georgia:
>   Button Gwinnett
>   Lyman Hall
>   Geo. Walton

Constitution of the United States

PREAMBLE.

We the People of the United States, in Order to form a more perfect Union, establish Justice, insure domestic Tranquility, provide for the common defense, promote the general Welfare, and secure the Blessings of Liberty to ourselves and our Posterity, do ordain and establish this Constitution for the United States of America.

Article I.

Section 1.

All legislative Powers herein granted shall be vested in a Congress of the United States, which shall consist of a Senate and House of Representatives.

Section. 2.

Clause 1:
The House of Representatives shall be composed of Members chosen every second Year by the People of the several States, and the Electors in each State shall have the Qualifications requisite for Electors of the most numerous Branch of the State Legislature.

Clause 2:
No Person shall be a Representative who shall not have attained to the Age of twenty five Years, and been seven Years a Citizen of the United States, and who shall not, when elected, be an Inhabitant of that State in which he shall be chosen.

Clause 3:
[Representatives and direct Taxes shall be apportioned among the several States which may be included within this Union, according to their respective Numbers, which shall be determined by adding to the whole Number of free Persons, including those bound to Service for a Term of Years, and excluding Indians not taxed, *three fifths of all other Persons.*][1] The actual Enumeration shall be made within three Years after the first Meeting of the Congress of the United States, and within every subsequent Term of ten Years, in such Manner as they shall by Law direct. The Number of Representatives shall not exceed one for every thirty Thousand, but each State shall have at Least one Representative; and until such enumeration shall be made, the State of New Hampshire shall be entitled to chuse three, Massachusetts eight, Rhode-Island and Providence Plantations one, Connecticut five, New-York six, New Jersey four, Pennsylvania eight, Delaware one, Maryland six, Virginia ten, North Carolina five, South Carolina five, and Georgia three.

Clause 4:
When vacancies happen in the Representation from any State, the Executive Authority thereof shall issue Writs of Election to fill such Vacancies.

Clause 5:
The House of Representatives shall chuse their Speaker and other Officers; and shall have the sole Power of Impeachment.

Section. 3.

Clause 1:
The Senate of the United States shall be composed of two Senators from each State, [*chosen by the Legislature thereof,*][2] for six Years; and each Senator shall have one Vote.

---

[1] Changed in Section 2, Amendment XIV.
[2] Changed in Section 1, Amendment XVII.

Clause 2:

Immediately after they shall be assembled in Consequence of the first Election, they shall be divided as equally as may be into three Classes. The Seats of the Senators of the first Class shall be vacated at the Expiration of the second Year, of the second Class at the Expiration of the fourth Year, and of the third Class at the Expiration of the sixth Year, so that one third may be chosen every second Year; [*and if Vacancies happen by Resignation, or otherwise, during the Recess of the Legislature of any State, the Executive thereof may make temporary Appointments until the next Meeting of the Legislature, which shall then fill such Vacancies.*][3]

Clause 3:

No Person shall be a Senator who shall not have attained to the Age of thirty Years, and been nine Years a Citizen of the United States, and who shall not, when elected, be an Inhabitant of that State for which he shall be chosen.

Clause 4:

The Vice President of the United States shall be President of the Senate, but shall have no Vote, unless they be equally divided.

Clause 5:

The Senate shall chuse their other Officers, and also a President pro tempore, in the Absence of the Vice President, or when he shall exercise the Office of President of the United States.

Clause 6:

The Senate shall have the sole Power to try all Impeachments. When sitting for that Purpose, they shall be on Oath or Affirmation. When the President of the United States is tried, the Chief Justice shall preside: And no Person shall be convicted without the Concurrence of two thirds of the Members present.

---

[3] Changed in Section 2, Amendment XX.

Clause 7:
Judgment in Cases of Impeachment shall not extend further than to removal from Office, and disqualification to hold and enjoy any Office of honor, Trust or Profit under the United States: but the Party convicted shall nevertheless be liable and subject to Indictment, Trial, Judgment and Punishment, according to Law.

Section. 4.

Clause 1:
The Times, Places and Manner of holding Elections for Senators and Representatives, shall be prescribed in each State by the Legislature thereof; but the Congress may at any time by Law make or alter such Regulations, except as to the Places of chusing Senators.

Clause 2:
The Congress shall assemble at least once in every Year, and such Meeting [shall be on the first Monday in December][4], unless they shall by Law appoint a different Day.

Section. 5.

Clause 1:
Each House shall be the Judge of the Elections, Returns and Qualifications of its own Members, and a Majority of each shall constitute a Quorum to do Business; but a smaller Number may adjourn from day to day, and may be authorized to compel the Attendance of absent Members, in such Manner, and under such Penalties as each House may provide.

Clause 2:
Each House may determine the Rules of its Proceedings, punish its Members for disorderly Behaviour, and, with the Concurrence of two thirds, expel a Member.

---

[4] Changed in Section 2, Amendment XX.

Clause 3:

Each House shall keep a Journal of its Proceedings, and from time to time publish the same, excepting such Parts as may in their Judgment require Secrecy; and the Yeas and Nays of the Members of either House on any question shall, at the Desire of one fifth of those Present, be entered on the Journal.

Clause 4:

Neither House, during the Session of Congress, shall, without the Consent of the other, adjourn for more than three days, nor to any other Place than that in which the two Houses shall be sitting.

Section. 6.

Clause 1:

The Senators and Representatives shall receive a Compensation for their Services, to be ascertained by Law, and paid out of the Treasury of the United States. They shall in all Cases, except Treason, Felony and Breach of the Peace, be privileged from Arrest during their Attendance at the Session of their respective Houses, and in going to and returning from the same; and for any Speech or Debate in either House, they shall not be questioned in any other Place.

Clause 2:

No Senator or Representative shall, during the Time for which he was elected, be appointed to any civil Office under the Authority of the United States, which shall have been created, or the Emoluments whereof shall have been increased during such time; and no Person holding any Office under the United States, shall be a Member of either House during his Continuance in Office.

Section. 7.

Clause 1:

All Bills for raising Revenue shall originate in the House of Representatives; but the Senate may propose or concur with Amendments as on other Bills.

Clause 2:

Every Bill which shall have passed the House of Representatives and the Senate, shall, before it become a Law, be presented to the President of the United States; If he approve he shall sign it, but if not he shall return it, with his Objections to that House in which it shall have originated, who shall enter the Objections at large on their Journal, and proceed to reconsider it. If after such Reconsideration two thirds of that House shall agree to pass the Bill, it shall be sent, together with the Objections, to the other House, by which it shall likewise be reconsidered, and if approved by two thirds of that House, it shall become a Law. But in all such Cases the Votes of both Houses shall be determined by yeas and Nays, and the Names of the Persons voting for and against the Bill shall be entered on the Journal of each House respectively. If any Bill shall not be returned by the President within ten Days (Sundays excepted) after it shall have been presented to him, the Same shall be a Law, in like Manner as if he had signed it, unless the Congress by their Adjournment prevent its Return, in which Case it shall not be a Law.

Clause 3:

Every Order, Resolution, or Vote to which the Concurrence of the Senate and House of Representatives may be necessary (except on a question of Adjournment) shall be presented to the President of the United States; and before the Same shall take Effect, shall be approved by him, or being disapproved by him, shall be repassed by two thirds of the Senate and House of Representatives, according to the Rules and Limitations prescribed in the Case of a Bill.

Section. 8.

Clause 1:

The Congress shall have Power To lay and collect Taxes, Duties, Imposts and Excises, to pay the Debts and provide for the common Defence and general Welfare of the United States; but all Duties, Imposts and Excises shall be uniform throughout the United States;

Clause 2:
To borrow Money on the credit of the United States;

Clause 3:
To regulate Commerce with foreign Nations, and among the several States, and with the Indian Tribes;

Clause 4:
To establish a uniform Rule of Naturalization, and uniform Laws on the subject of Bankruptcies throughout the United States;

Clause 5:
To coin Money, regulate the Value thereof, and of foreign Coin, and fix the Standard of Weights and Measures;

Clause 6:
To provide for the Punishment of counterfeiting the Securities and current Coin of the United States;

Clause 7:
To establish Post Offices and post Roads;

Clause 8:
To promote the Progress of Science and useful Arts, by securing for limited Times to Authors and Inventors the exclusive Right to their respective Writings and Discoveries;

Clause 9:
To constitute Tribunals inferior to the supreme Court;

Clause 10:
To define and punish Piracies and Felonies committed on the high Seas, and Offences against the Law of Nations;

Clause 11:
To declare War, grant Letters of Marque and Reprisal, and make Rules concerning Captures on Land and Water;

Clause 12:
To raise and support Armies, but no Appropriation of Money to that Use shall be for a longer Term than two Years;

Clause 13:
To provide and maintain a Navy;

Clause 14:
To make Rules for the Government and Regulation of the land and naval Forces;

Clause 15:
To provide for calling forth the Militia to execute the Laws of the Union, suppress Insurrections and repel Invasions;

Clause 16:
To provide for organizing, arming, and disciplining, the Militia, and for governing such Part of them as may be employed in the Service of the United States, reserving to the States respectively, the Appointment of the Officers, and the Authority of training the Militia according to the discipline prescribed by Congress;

Clause 17:
To exercise exclusive Legislation in all Cases whatsoever, over such District (not exceeding ten Miles square) as may, by Cession of particular States, and the Acceptance of Congress, become the Seat of the Government of the United States, and to exercise like Authority over all Places purchased by the Consent of the Legislature of the State in which the Same shall be, for the Erection of Forts, Magazines, Arsenals, dock-Yards, and other needful Buildings;—And

Clause 18:
To make all Laws which shall be necessary and proper for carrying into Execution the foregoing Powers, and all other Powers vested by this Constitution in the Government of the United States, or in any Department or Officer thereof.

Section. 9.

Clause 1:
The Migration or Importation of such Persons as any of the States now existing shall think proper to admit, shall not be prohibited by the Congress prior to the Year one thousand eight hundred and eight, but a Tax or duty may be imposed on such Importation, not exceeding ten dollars for each Person.

Clause 2:
The Privilege of the Writ of Habeas Corpus shall not be suspended, unless when in Cases of Rebellion or Invasion the public Safety may require it.

Clause 3:
No Bill of Attainder or ex post facto Law shall be passed.

Clause 4:
No Capitation, or other direct, Tax shall be laid, unless in Proportion to the Census or Enumeration herein before directed to be taken.

Clause 5:
No Tax or Duty shall be laid on Articles exported from any State.

Clause 6:
No Preference shall be given by any Regulation of Commerce or Revenue to the Ports of one State over those of another: nor shall Vessels bound to, or from, one State, be obliged to enter, clear, or pay Duties in another.

Clause 7:
No Money shall be drawn from the Treasury, but in Consequence of Appropriations made by Law; and a regular Statement and Account of the Receipts and Expenditures of all public Money shall be published from time to time.

Clause 8:
No Title of Nobility shall be granted by the United States: And no Person holding any Office of Profit or Trust under

them, shall, without the Consent of the Congress, accept of any present, Emolument, Office, or Title, of any kind whatever, from any King, Prince, or foreign State.

Section. 10.

Clause 1:
No State shall enter into any Treaty, Alliance, or Confederation; grant Letters of Marque and Reprisal; coin Money; emit Bills of Credit; make any Thing but gold and silver Coin a Tender in Payment of Debts; pass any Bill of Attainder, ex post facto Law, or Law impairing the Obligation of Contracts, or grant any Title of Nobility.

Clause 2:
No State shall, without the Consent of the Congress, lay any Imposts or Duties on Imports or Exports, except what may be absolutely necessary for executing its inspection Laws: and the net Produce of all Duties and Imposts, laid by any State on Imports or Exports, shall be for the Use of the Treasury of the United States; and all such Laws shall be subject to the Revision and Controul of the Congress.

Clause 3:
No State shall, without the Consent of Congress, lay any Duty of Tonnage, keep Troops, or Ships of War in time of Peace, enter into any Agreement or Compact with another State, or with a foreign Power, or engage in War, unless actually invaded, or in such imminent Danger as will not admit of delay.

Article II.

Section. 1.

Clause 1:
The executive Power shall be vested in a President of the United States of America. *He shall hold his Office during the Term of four Years,* and, together with the Vice President, chosen for the same Term, be elected, as follows:

Clause 2:

Each State shall appoint, in such Manner as the Legislature thereof may direct, a Number of Electors, equal to the whole Number of Senators and Representatives to which the State may be entitled in the Congress: but no Senator or Representative, or Person holding an Office of Trust or Profit under the United States, shall be appointed an Elector.

Clause 3:

[*The Electors shall meet in their respective States, and vote by Ballot for two Persons, of whom one at least shall not be an Inhabitant of the same State with themselves. And they shall make a List of all the Persons voted for, and of the Number of Votes for each; which List they shall sign and certify, and transmit sealed to the Seat of the Government of the United States, directed to the President of the Senate. The President of the Senate shall, in the Presence of the Senate and House of Representatives, open all the Certificates, and the Votes shall then be counted. The Person having the greatest Number of Votes shall be the President, if such Number be a Majority of the whole Number of Electors appointed; and if there be more than one who have such Majority, and have an equal Number of Votes, then the House of Representatives shall immediately chuse by Ballot one of them for President; and if no Person have a Majority, then from the five highest on the List the said House shall in like Manner chuse the President. But in chusing the President, the Votes shall be taken by States, the Representation from each State having one Vote; A quorum for this Purpose shall consist of a Member or Members from two thirds of the States, and a Majority of all the States shall be necessary to a Choice. In every Case, after the Choice of the President, the Person having the greatest Number of Votes of the Electors shall be the Vice President. But if there should remain two or more who have equal Votes, the Senate shall chuse from them by Ballot the Vice President.*][1]

Clause 4:

The Congress may determine the Time of choosing the Electors, and the Day on which they shall give their Votes; which Day shall be the same throughout the United States.

---

[1] Superseded by Amendment XII.

Clause 5:

No Person except a natural born Citizen, or a Citizen of the United States, at the time of the Adoption of this Constitution, shall be eligible to the Office of President; neither shall any Person be eligible to that Office who shall not have attained to the Age of thirty five Years, and been fourteen Years a Resident within the United States.

Clause 6:

In Case of the Removal of the President from Office, or of his Death, Resignation, or Inability to discharge the Powers and Duties of the said Office, the Same shall devolve on the Vice President, and the Congress may by Law provide for the Case of Removal, Death, Resignation or Inability, both of the President and Vice President, declaring what Officer shall then act as President, and such Officer shall act accordingly, until the Disability be removed, or a President shall be elected.

Clause 7:

The President shall, at stated Times, receive for his Services, a Compensation, which shall neither be encreased nor diminished during the Period for which he shall have been elected, and he shall not receive within that Period any other Emolument from the United States, or any of them.

Clause 8:

Before he enter on the Execution of his Office, he shall take the following Oath or Affirmation:—"I do solemnly swear (or affirm) that I will faithfully execute the Office of President of the United States, and will to the best of my Ability, preserve, protect and defend the Constitution of the United States."

Section. 2.

Clause 1:

The President shall be Commander in Chief of the Army and Navy of the United States, and of the Militia of the several States, when called into the actual Service of the United States; he may require the Opinion, in writing, of the principal Officer in each of the executive Departments, upon any

Subject relating to the Duties of their respective Offices, and he shall have Power to grant Reprieves and Pardons for Offences against the United States, except in Cases of Impeachment.

Clause 2:
He shall have Power, by and with the Advice and Consent of the Senate, to make Treaties, provided two thirds of the Senators present concur; and he shall nominate, and by and with the Advice and Consent of the Senate, shall appoint Ambassadors, other public Ministers and Consuls, Judges of the supreme Court, and all other Officers of the United States, whose Appointments are not herein otherwise provided for, and which shall be established by Law: but the Congress may by Law vest the Appointment of such inferior Officers, as they think proper, in the President alone, in the Courts of Law, or in the Heads of Departments.

Clause 3:
The President shall have Power to fill up all Vacancies that may happen during the Recess of the Senate, by granting Commissions which shall expire at the End of their next Session.

Section. 3.

He shall from time to time give to the Congress Information of the State of the Union, and recommend to their Consideration such Measures as he shall judge necessary and expedient; he may, on extraordinary Occasions, convene both Houses, or either of them, and in Case of Disagreement between them, with Respect to the Time of Adjournment, he may adjourn them to such Time as he shall think proper; he shall receive Ambassadors and other public Ministers; he shall take Care that the Laws be faithfully executed, and shall Commission all the Officers of the United States.

Section. 4.

The President, Vice President and all civil Officers of the United States, shall be removed from Office on Impeachment for, and Conviction of, Treason, Bribery, or other high Crimes and Misdemeanors.

Article III.

Section. 1.

The judicial Power of the United States, shall be vested in one supreme Court, and in such inferior Courts as the Congress may from time to time ordain and establish. The Judges, both of the supreme and inferior Courts, shall hold their Offices during good Behaviour, and shall, at stated Times, receive for their Services, a Compensation, which shall not be diminished during their Continuance in Office.

Section. 2.

Clause 1:
The judicial Power shall extend to all Cases, in Law and Equity, arising under this Constitution, the Laws of the United States, and Treaties made, or which shall be made, under their Author-ity;—to all Cases affecting Ambassadors, other public Ministers and Consuls;—to all Cases of admiralty and maritime Jurisdiction;—to Controversies to which the United States shall be a Party;—to Controversies between two or more States;[—between *a State and Citizens of another State;*—][1] between Citizens of different States,—between Citizens of the same State claiming Lands under Grants of different States, and *between a State, or the Citizens thereof, and foreign States, Citizens or Subjects.*

Clause 2:
In all Cases affecting Ambassadors, other public Ministers

---

[1] Clause affected by Amendment XI.

and Consuls, and those in which a State shall be Party, the supreme Court shall have original Jurisdiction. In all the other Cases before mentioned, the supreme Court shall have appellate Jurisdiction, both as to Law and Fact, with such Exceptions, and under such Regulations as the Congress shall make.

Clause 3:
The Trial of all Crimes, except in Cases of Impeachment, shall be by Jury; and such Trial shall be held in the State where the said Crimes shall have been committed; but when not committed within any State, the Trial shall be at such Place or Places as the Congress may by Law have directed.

Section. 3.

Clause 1:
Treason against the United States, shall consist only in levying War against them, or in adhering to their Enemies, giving them Aid and Comfort. No Person shall be convicted of Treason unless on the Testimony of two Witnesses to the same overt Act, or on Confession in open Court.

Clause 2:
The Congress shall have Power to declare the Punishment of Treason, but no Attainder of Treason shall work Corruption of Blood, or Forfeiture except during the Life of the Person attainted.

Article IV.

Section. 1.

Full Faith and Credit shall be given in each State to the public Acts, Records, and judicial Proceedings of every other State. And the Congress may by general Laws prescribe the Manner in which such Acts, Records and Proceedings shall be proved, and the Effect thereof.

Section. 2.

Clause 1:
The Citizens of each State shall be entitled to all Privileges and Immunities of Citizens in the several States.

Clause 2:
A Person charged in any State with Treason, Felony, or other Crime, who shall flee from Justice, and be found in another State, shall on Demand of the executive Authority of the State from which he fled, be delivered up, to be removed to the State having Jurisdiction of the Crime.

Clause 3:
[*No Person held to Service or Labour in one State, under the Laws thereof, escaping into another, shall, in Consequence of any Law or Regulation therein, be discharged from such Service or Labour, but shall be delivered up on Claim of the Party to whom such Service or Labour may be due.*][1]

Section. 3.

Clause 1:
New States may be admitted by the Congress into this Union; but no new State shall be formed or erected within the Jurisdiction of any other State; nor any State be formed by the Junction of two or more States, or Parts of States, without the Consent of the Legislatures of the States concerned as well as of the Congress.

Clause 2:
The Congress shall have Power to dispose of and make all needful Rules and Regulations respecting the Territory or other Property belonging to the United States; and nothing in this Constitution shall be so construed as to Prejudice any Claims of the United States, or of any particular State.

---

[1] Superseded by Amendment XIII.

Section. 4.

The United States shall guarantee to every State in this Union a Republican Form of Government, and shall protect each of them against Invasion; and on Application of the Legislature, or of the Executive (when the Legislature cannot be convened) against domestic Violence.

Article V.

The Congress, whenever two thirds of both Houses shall deem it necessary, shall propose Amendments to this Constitution, or, on the Application of the Legislatures of two thirds of the several States, shall call a Convention for proposing Amendments, which, in either Case, shall be valid to all Intents and Purposes, as Part of this Constitution, when ratified by the Legislatures of three fourths of the several States, or by Conventions in three fourths thereof, as the one or the other Mode of Ratification may be proposed by the Congress; Provided that no Amendment which may be made prior to the Year One thousand eight hundred and eight shall in any Manner affect the first and fourth Clauses in the Ninth Section of the first Article; and that no State, without its Consent, shall be deprived of its equal Suffrage in the Senate.

Article VI.

Clause 1:
All Debts contracted and Engagements entered into, before the Adoption of this Constitution, shall be as valid against the United States under this Constitution, as under the Confederation.

Clause 2:
This Constitution, and the Laws of the United States which shall be made in Pursuance thereof; and all Treaties made, or which shall be made, under the Authority of the United States, shall be the supreme Law of the Land; and the Judges in every State shall be bound thereby, any Thing in the Constitution or Laws of any State to the Contrary notwithstanding.

Clause 3:
The Senators and Representatives before mentioned, and the Members of the several State Legislatures, and all executive and judicial Officers, both of the United States and of the several States, shall be bound by Oath or Affirmation, to support this Constitution; but no religious Test shall ever be required as a Qualification to any Office or public Trust under the United States.

Article VII.

The Ratification of the Conventions of nine States, shall be sufficient for the Establishment of this Constitution between the States so ratifying the Same.

Done in Convention by the Unanimous Consent of the States present the Seventeenth Day of September in the Year of our Lord one thousand seven hundred and Eighty seven and of the Independence of the United States of America the Twelfth In witness whereof We have hereunto subscribed our Names,

GEORGE WASHINGTON—
Presidt. and deputy from Virginia

New Hampshire
John Langdon
Nicholas Gilman

Delaware
Geo: Read
Gunning Bedford, Junior
John Dickinson
Richard Bassett
Jaco: Broom

Massachusetts
Nathaniel Gorham
Rufus King

Maryland
James McHenry
Dan: of St. Thos. Jenifer
Danl Carroll

Connecticut
Wm. Saml. Johnson
Roger Sherman

Virginia
John Blair—
James Madison, Junior

New York
Alexander Hamilton

New Jersey
Wil: Livingston
David Brearley.
Wm. Paterson.
Jona: Dayton

North Carolina
Wm. Blount
Richd. Dobbs Spaight
Hugh Williamson

Pennsylvania
Benjamin Franklin
Thomas Mifflin
Robt. Morris
Geo. Clymer
Thos. FitzSimons
Jared Ingersoll
James Wilson
Gouverneur Morris

South Carolina
J. Rutledge
Charles Cotesworth Pinckney
Charles Pinckney
Pierce Butler

Georgia
William Few
Abr Baldwin

Attest: William Jackson,
    Secretary

Amendments to the Constitution

CONSTITUTION OF THE UNITED STATES ARTICLES IN ADDITION TO, AND AMENDMENT OF, THE CONSTITUTION OF THE UNITED STATES OF AMERICA, PROPOSED BY CONGRESS, AND RATIFIED BY THE LEGISLATURES OF THE SEVERAL STATES, PURSUANT TO THE FIFTH ARTICLE OF THE ORIGINAL CONSTITUTION

Article I.

Congress shall make no law respecting an establishment of religion, or prohibiting the free exercise thereof; or abridging the freedom of speech, or of the press; or the right of the people peaceably to assemble, and to petition the Government for a redress of grievances.

Article II.

A well regulated Militia, being necessary to the security of a free State, the right of the people to keep and bear Arms, shall not be infringed.

Article III.

No Soldier shall, in time of peace be quartered in any house, without the consent of the Owner, nor in time of war, but in a manner to be prescribed by law.

Article IV.

The right of the people to be secure in their persons, houses, papers, and effects, against unreasonable searches and seizures, shall not be violated, and no Warrants shall issue, but upon probable cause, supported by Oath or affirmation, and particularly describing the place to be searched, and the persons or things to be seized.

Article V.

No person shall be held to answer for a capital, or otherwise infamous crime, unless on a presentment or indictment of a Grand Jury, except in cases arising in the land or naval forces, or in the Militia, when in actual service in time of War or public danger; nor shall any person be subject for the same offence to be twice put in jeopardy of life or limb; nor shall be compelled in any criminal case to be a witness against himself, nor be deprived of life, liberty, or property, without due process of law; nor shall private property be taken for public use, without just compensation.

Article VI.

In all criminal prosecutions, the accused shall enjoy the right to a speedy and public trial, by an impartial jury of the State and district wherein the crime shall have been committed, which district shall have been previously ascertained by law, and to be informed of the nature and cause of the accusation; to be confronted with the witnesses against him; to have compulsory process for obtaining witnesses in his favor, and to have the Assistance of Counsel for his defence.

Article VII.

In Suits at common law, where the value in controversy shall exceed twenty dollars, the right of trial by jury shall be preserved, and no fact tried by a jury, shall be otherwise re-examined in any Court of the United States, than according to the rules of the common law.

Article VIII.

Excessive bail shall not be required, nor excessive fines imposed, nor cruel and unusual punishments inflicted.

Article IX.

The enumeration in the Constitution, of certain rights, shall not be construed to deny or disparage others retained by the people.

Article X.

The powers not delegated to the United States by the Constitution, nor prohibited by it to the States, are reserved to the States respectively, or to the people.

Article XI.

The Judicial power of the United States shall not be construed to extend to any suit in law or equity, commenced or prosecuted against one of the United States by Citizens of another State, or by Citizens or Subjects of any Foreign State.

Proposal and Ratification

The eleventh amendment to the Constitution of the United States was proposed to the legislatures of the several States by the Third Congress, on the 4th of March 1794; and was declared in a message from the President to Congress, dated the 8th of January, 1798, to have been ratified by the legislatures of three-fourths of the States. The dates of ratification were: New York, March 27, 1794; Rhode Island, March 31, 1794; Connecticut, May 8, 1794; New Hampshire, June 16, 1794; Massachusetts, June 26, 1794; Ver-

mont, between October 9, 1794 and November 9, 1794; Virginia, November 18, 1794; Georgia, November 29, 1794; Kentucky, December 7, 1794; Maryland, December 26, 1794; Delaware, January 23, 1795; North Carolina, February 7, 1795.

Ratification was completed on February 7, 1795.

The amendment was subsequently ratified by South Carolina on December 4, 1797. New Jersey and Pennsylvania did not take action on the amendment.

Article XII.

The Electors shall meet in their respective states, and vote by ballot for President and Vice-President, one of whom, at least, shall not be an inhabitant of the same state with themselves; they shall name in their ballots the person voted for as President, and in distinct ballots the person voted for as Vice-President, and they shall make distinct lists of all persons voted for as President, and of all persons voted for as Vice-President, and of the number of votes for each, which lists they shall sign and certify, and transmit sealed to the seat of the government of the United States, directed to the President of the Senate;—The President of the Senate shall, in the presence of the Senate and House of Representatives, open all the certificates and the votes shall then be counted;—The person having the greatest number of votes for President, shall be the President, if such number be a majority of the whole number of Electors appointed; and if no person have such majority, then from the persons having the highest numbers not exceeding three on the list of those voted for as President, the House of Representatives shall choose immediately, by ballot, the President. But in choosing the President, the votes shall be taken by states, the representation from each state having one vote; a quorum for this purpose shall consist of a member or members from two-thirds of the states, and a majority of all the states shall be necessary to a choice. And if the House of Representatives shall not choose a President whenever the right of choice shall devolve upon them, before *the fourth day of March next following, then the Vice-President shall act as President, as in the case of the death or other constitutional disability of the President.*—The person having the greatest number of votes as Vice-President, shall be the Vice-President, if such number be a majority of the whole number of Electors appointed, and if no person have a majority, then from the two highest numbers on the list, the Senate shall choose the Vice-President; a quorum for the purpose shall consist of twothirds of the whole number of Senators, and a majority of the whole number shall be necessary to a choice. But no person constitutionally ineligible to the office of President shall be eligible to that of Vice-President of the United States.

Proposal and Ratification

The twelfth amendment to the Constitution of the United States was proposed to the legislatures of the several States by the Eighth Congress, on the 9th of December, 1803, in lieu of the original third paragraph of the first section of the second article; and was declared in a proclamation of the Secretary of State, dated the 25th of September, 1804, to have been ratified by the legislatures of 13 of the 17 States. The dates of ratification were: North Carolina, December 21, 1803; Maryland, December 24, 1803; Kentucky, December 27, 1803; Ohio, December 30, 1803; Pennsylvania, January 5, 1804; Vermont, January 30, 1804; Virginia, February 3, 1804; New York, February 10, 1804; New Jersey, February 22, 1804; Rhode Island, March 12, 1804; South Carolina, May 15, 1804; Georgia, May 19, 1804; New Hampshire, June 15, 1804.

Ratification was completed on June 15, 1804. The amendment was subsequently ratified by Tennessee, July 27, 1804. The amendment was rejected by Delaware, January 18, 1804; Massachusetts, February 3, 1804; Connecticut, at its session begun May 10, 1804.

Article XIII.

Section 1.

Neither slavery nor involuntary servitude, except as a punishment for crime whereof the party shall have been duly convicted, shall exist within the United States, or any place subject to their jurisdiction.

Section 2.

Congress shall have power to enforce this article by appropriate legislation.

Proposal and Ratification

The thirteenth amendment to the Constitution of the United States was proposed to the legislatures of the several States by the Thirty-eighth Congress, on the 31st day of January, 1865, and was declared, in a proclamation of the Secretary of State, dated the 18th of December, 1865, to have been ratified by the legislatures of twenty-seven of the thirty-six States. The dates of ratification were: Illinois, February 1, 1865; Rhode Island, February 2, 1865; Michigan, February 2, 1865; Maryland, February 3, 1865; New York, February 3, 1865; Pennsylvania, February 3, 1865; West Virginia, February 3, 1865; Missouri, February 6, 1865; Maine, February 7, 1865; Kansas, February 7, 1865; Massachusetts, February 7, 1865; Virginia, February 9, 1865; Ohio, February 10, 1865; Indiana, February 13, 1865; Nevada, February 16, 1865; Louisiana, February 17, 1865; Minnesota, February 23, 1865; Wisconsin, February 24, 1865; Vermont, March 9, 1865; Tennessee, April 7, 1865; Arkansas, April 14, 1865; Connecticut, May 4, 1865; New Hampshire, July 1, 1865; South Carolina, November 13, 1865; Alabama, December 2, 1865; North Carolina, December 4, 1865; Georgia, December 6, 1865.

Ratification was completed on December 6, 1865. The amendment was subsequently ratified by Oregon, December 8, 1865; California, December 19, 1865; Florida, December 28, 1865 (Florida again ratified on June 9, 1868, upon its adoption of a new constitution); Iowa, January 15, 1866; New Jersey, January 23, 1866 (after having rejected the amendment on March 16, 1865); Texas, February 18, 1870; Delaware, February 12, 1901 (after having rejected the amendment on February 8, 1865); Kentucky, March 18, 1976 (after having rejected it on February 24, 1865). The amendment was rejected (and not subsequently ratified) by Mississippi, December 4, 1865.

Article XIV.

Section 1.

All persons born or naturalized in the United States, and subject to the jurisdiction thereof, are citizens of the United States and of the State wherein they reside. No State shall make or enforce any law which shall abridge the privileges or immunities of citizens of the United States; nor shall any State deprive any person of life, liberty, or property, without due process of law; nor deny to any person within its jurisdiction the equal protection of the laws.

Section 2.

Representatives shall be apportioned among the several States according to their respective numbers, counting the whole number of persons in each State, excluding Indians not taxed. But when the right to vote at any election for the choice of electors for President and Vice President of the United States, Representatives in Congress, the Executive and Judicial officers of a State, or the members of the Legislature thereof, is denied to any of the male inhabitants of such State, being twenty-one years of age, and citizens of the United States, or in any way abridged, except for participation in rebellion, or other crime, the basis of representation therein shall be reduced in the proportion which the number of such male citizens shall bear to the whole number of male citizens twenty-one years of age in such State.

Section 3.

No person shall be a Senator or Representative in Congress, or elector of President and Vice President, or hold any office, civil or military, under the United States, or under any State, who, having previously taken an oath, as a member of Congress, or as an officer of the United States, or as a member of any State legislature, or as an executive or judicial officer of any State, to support the Constitution of the United States, shall have engaged in insurrection or rebellion against the same, or given aid or comfort to the enemies thereof. But Congress may by a vote of two-thirds of each House, remove such disability.

Section 4.

The validity of the public debt of the United States, authorized by law, including debts incurred for payment of pensions and bounties for services in suppressing insurrection or rebellion, shall not be questioned. But neither the United States nor any State shall assume or pay any debt or obligation incurred in aid of insurrection or rebellion against the United States, or any claim for the loss or emancipation of any slave; but all such debts, obligations and claims shall be held illegal and void.

Section 5.

The Congress shall have power to enforce, by appropriate legislation, the provisions of this article.

Proposal and Ratification

The fourteenth amendment to the Constitution of the United States was proposed to the legislatures of the several States by the Thirty-ninth Congress, on the 13th of June, 1866. It was declared, in a certificate of the Secretary of State dated July 28, 1868 to have been ratified by the legislatures of 28 of the 37 States. The dates of ratification were: Connecticut, June 25, 1866; New Hampshire, July 6, 1866; Tennessee, July 19, 1866; New Jersey, September 11, 1866 (subsequently the legislature rescinded its ratification, and on March 24, 1868, readopted its resolution of rescission over the Governor's veto, and on Nov. 12, 1980, expressed support for the amendment); Oregon, September 19, 1866 (and rescinded its ratification on October 15, 1868); Vermont, October 30, 1866; Ohio, January 4, 1867 (and rescinded its ratification on January 15, 1868); New York, January 10, 1867; Kansas, January 11, 1867; Illinois, January 15, 1867; West Virginia, January 16, 1867; Michigan, January 16, 1867; Minnesota, January 16, 1867; Maine, January 19, 1867; Nevada, January 22, 1867; Indiana,

January 23, 1867; Missouri, January 25, 1867; Rhode Island, February 7, 1867; Wisconsin, February 7, 1867; Pennsylvania, February 12, 1867; Massachusetts, March 20, 1867; Nebraska, June 15, 1867; Iowa, March 16, 1868; Arkansas, April 6, 1868; Florida, June 9, 1868; North Carolina, July 4, 1868 (after having rejected it on December 14, 1866); Louisiana, July 9, 1868 (after having rejected it on February 6, 1867); South Carolina, July 9, 1868 (after having rejected it on December 20, 1866).

Ratification was completed on July 9, 1868.

The amendment was subsequently ratified by Alabama, July 13, 1868; Georgia, July 21, 1868 (after having rejected it on November 9, 1866); Virginia, October 8, 1869 (after having rejected it on January 9, 1867); Mississippi, January 17, 1870; Texas, February 18, 1870 (after having rejected it on October 27, 1866); Delaware, February 12, 1901 (after having rejected it on February 8, 1867); Maryland, April 4, 1959 (after having rejected it on March 23, 1867); California, May 6, 1959; Kentucky, March 18, 1976 (after having rejected it on January 8, 1867).

Article XV.
Section 1.

The right of citizens of the United States to vote shall not be denied or abridged by the United States or by any State on account of race, color, or previous condition of servitude.

Section 2.

The Congress shall have power to enforce this article by appropriate legislation.

Proposal and Ratification

The fifteenth amendment to the Constitution of the United States was proposed to the legislatures of the several States by the Fortieth Congress, on the 26th of February, 1869, and was declared, in a proclamation of the Secretary of State, dated March 30, 1870, to have been ratified by the legislatures of twenty-nine of the thirty-seven States. The dates of ratification were: Nevada, March 1,

1869; West Virginia, March 3, 1869; Illinois, March 5, 1869; Louisiana, March 5, 1869; North Carolina, March 5, 1869; Michigan, March 8, 1869; Wisconsin, March 9, 1869; Maine, March 11, 1869; Massachusetts, March 12, 1869; Arkansas, March 15, 1869; South Carolina, March 15, 1869; Pennsylvania, March 25, 1869; New York, April 14, 1869 (and the legislature of the same State passed a resolution January 5, 1870, to withdraw its consent to it, which action it rescinded on March 30, 1970); Indiana, May 14, 1869; Connecticut, May 19, 1869; Florida, June 14, 1869; New Hampshire, July 1, 1869; Virginia, October 8, 1869; Vermont, October 20, 1869; Missouri, January 7, 1870; Minnesota, January 13, 1870; Mississippi, January 17, 1870; Rhode Island, January 18, 1870; Kansas, January 19, 1870; Ohio, January 27, 1870 (after having rejected it on April 30, 1869); Georgia, February 2, 1870; Iowa, February 3, 1870.

Ratification was completed on February 3, 1870, unless the withdrawal of ratification by New York was effective; in which event ratification was completed on February 17, 1870, when Nebraska ratified.

The amendment was subsequently ratified by Texas, February 18, 1870; New Jersey, February 15, 1871 (after having rejected it on February 7, 1870); Delaware, February 12, 1901 (after having rejected it on March 18, 1869); Oregon, February 24, 1959; California, April 3, 1962 (after having rejected it on January 28, 1870); Kentucky, March 18, 1976 (after having rejected it on March 12, 1869). The amendment was approved by the Governor of Maryland, May 7, 1973; Maryland having previously rejected it on February 26, 1870. The amendment was rejected (and not subsequently ratified) by Tennessee, November 16, 1869.

Article XVI.

The Congress shall have power to lay and collect taxes on incomes, from whatever source derived, without apportionment among the several States, and without regard to any census or enumeration.

Proposal and Ratification

The sixteenth amendment to the Constitution of the United States was proposed to the legislatures of the several States by the Sixty-

*first Congress on the 12th of July, 1909, and was declared, in a
proclamation of the Secretary of State, dated the 25th of February,
1913, to have been ratified by 36 of the 48 States. The dates of ratification were: Alabama, August 10, 1909; Kentucky, February 8,
1910; South Carolina, February 19, 1910; Illinois, March 1,
1910; Mississippi, March 7, 1910; Oklahoma, March 10, 1910;
Maryland, April 8, 1910; Georgia, August 3, 1910; Texas, August
16, 1910; Ohio, January 19, 1911; Idaho, January 20, 1911;
Oregon, January 23, 1911; Washington, January 26, 1911; Montana, January 30, 1911; Indiana, January 30, 1911; California,
January 31, 1911; Nevada, January 31, 1911; South Dakota,
February 3, 1911; Nebraska, February 9, 1911; North Carolina,
February 11, 1911; Colorado, February 15, 1911; North Dakota,
February 17, 1911; Kansas, February 18, 1911; Michigan, Feb-
ruary 23, 1911; Iowa, February 24, 1911; Missouri, March 16,
1911; Maine, March 31, 1911; Tennessee, April 7, 1911;
Arkansas, April 22, 1911 (after having rejected it earlier); Wis-
consin, May 26, 1911; New York, July 12, 1911; Arizona, April 6,
1912; Minnesota, June 11, 1912; Louisiana, June 28, 1912; West
Virginia, January 31, 1913; New Mexico, February 3, 1913.*

*Ratification was completed on February 3, 1913. The amend-
ment was subsequently ratified by Massachusetts, March 4, 1913;
New Hampshire, March 7, 1913 (after having rejected it on
March 2, 1911).*

*The amendment was rejected (and not subsequently ratified) by
Connecticut, Rhode Island, and Utah.*

Article XVII.

The Senate of the United States shall be composed of two Senators from each State, elected by the people thereof, for six
years; and each Senator shall have one vote. The electors in each
State shall have the qualifications requisite for electors of the
most numerous branch of the State legislatures.

When vacancies happen in the representation of any State in
the Senate, the executive authority of such State shall issue writs
of election to fill such vacancies: *Provided,* That the legislature of
any State may empower the executive thereof to make temporary appointments until the people fill the vacancies by election
as the legislature may direct.

This amendment shall not be so construed as to affect the election or term of any Senator chosen before it becomes valid as part of the Constitution.

Proposal and Ratification

The seventeenth amendment to the Constitution of the United States was proposed to the legislatures of the several States by the Sixty-second Congress on the 13th of May, 1912, and was declared, in a proclamation of the Secretary of State, dated the 31st of May, 1913, to have been ratified by the legislatures of 36 of the 48 States. The dates of ratification were: Massachusetts, May 22, 1912; Arizona, June 3, 1912; Minnesota, June 10, 1912; New York, January 15, 1913; Kansas, January 17, 1913; Oregon, January 23, 1913; North Carolina, January 25, 1913; California, January 28, 1913; Michigan, January 28, 1913; Iowa, January 30, 1913; Montana, January 30, 1913; Idaho, January 31, 1913; West Virginia, February 4, 1913; Colorado, February 5, 1913; Nevada, February 6, 1913; Texas, February 7, 1913; Washington, February 7, 1913; Wyoming, February 8, 1913; Arkansas, February 11, 1913; Maine, February 11, 1913; Illinois, February 13, 1913; North Dakota, February 14, 1913; Wisconsin, February 18, 1913; Indiana, February 19, 1913; New Hampshire, February 19, 1913; Vermont, February 19, 1913; South Dakota, February 19, 1913; Oklahoma, February 24, 1913; Ohio, February 25, 1913; Missouri, March 7, 1913; New Mexico, March 13, 1913; Nebraska, March 14, 1913; New Jersey, March 17, 1913; Tennessee, April 1, 1913; Pennsylvania, April 2, 1913; Connecticut, April 8, 1913.

Ratification was completed on April 8, 1913. The amendment was subsequently ratified by Louisiana, June 11, 1914. The amendment was rejected by Utah (and not subsequently ratified) on February 26, 1913.

Article XVIII.

Section 1.

After one year from the ratification of this article the manufacture, sale, or transportation of intoxicating liquors within, the importation thereof into, or the exportation thereof from the United States and all territory subject to the jurisdiction thereof for beverage purposes is hereby prohibited.

Section 2.

The Congress and the several States shall have concurrent power to enforce this article by appropriate legislation.

Section 3.

This article shall be inoperative unless it shall have been ratified as an amendment to the Constitution by the legislatures of the several States, as provided in the Constitution, within seven years from the date of the submission hereof to the States by the Congress.

Proposal and Ratification

The eighteenth amendment to the Constitution of the United States was proposed to the legislatures of the several States by the Sixty-fifth Congress, on the 18th of December, 1917, and was declared, in a proclamation of the Secretary of State, dated the 29th of January, 1919, to have been ratified by the legislatures of 36 of the 48 States. The dates of ratification were: Mississippi, January 8, 1918; Virginia, January 11, 1918; Kentucky, January 14, 1918; North Dakota, January 25, 1918; South Carolina, January 29, 1918; Maryland, February 13, 1918; Montana, February 19, 1918; Texas, March 4, 1918; Delaware, March 18, 1918; South Dakota, March 20, 1918; Massachusetts, April 2, 1918; Arizona, May 24, 1918; Georgia, June 26, 1918; Louisiana, August 3, 1918; Florida, December 3, 1918; Michigan, January 2, 1919; Ohio, January 7, 1919; Oklahoma, January 7, 1919; Idaho, January 8, 1919; Maine, January 8, 1919; West Virginia, January 9, 1919; California, January 13, 1919; Tennessee, January 13, 1919; Washington, January 13, 1919; Arkansas, January 14, 1919; Kansas, January 14, 1919; Alabama, January 15, 1919; Colorado, January 15, 1919; Iowa, January 15, 1919; New Hampshire, January 15, 1919; Oregon, January 15, 1919;

Nebraska, January 16, 1919; North Carolina, January 16, 1919; Utah, January 16, 1919; Missouri, January 16, 1919; Wyoming, January 16, 1919.

*Ratification was completed on January 16, 1919. See **Dillon v. Gloss,** 256 U.S. 368, 376 (1921).*

The amendment was subsequently ratified by Minnesota on January 17, 1919; Wisconsin, January 17, 1919; New Mexico, January 20, 1919; Nevada, January 21, 1919; New York, January 29, 1919; Vermont, January 29, 1919; Pennsylvania, February 25, 1919; Connecticut, May 6, 1919; and New Jersey, March 9, 1922. The amendment was rejected (and not subsequently ratified) by Rhode Island.

Article XIX.

The right of citizens of the United States to vote shall not be denied or abridged by the United States or by any State on account of sex.

Congress shall have power to enforce this article by appropriate legislation.

Proposal and Ratification

The nineteenth amendment to the Constitution of the United States was proposed to the legislatures of the several States by the Sixty-sixth Congress, on the 4th of June, 1919, and was declared, in a proclamation of the Secretary of State, dated the 26th of August, 1920, to have been ratified by the legislatures of 36 of the 48 States. The dates of ratification were: Illinois, June 10, 1919 (and that State readopted its resolution of ratification June 17, 1919); Michigan, June 10, 1919; Wisconsin, June 10, 1919; Kansas, June 16, 1919; New York, June 16, 1919; Ohio, June 16, 1919; Pennsylvania, June 24, 1919; Massachusetts, June 25, 1919; Texas, June 28, 1919; Iowa, July 2, 1919; Missouri, July 3, 1919; Arkansas, July 28, 1919; Montana, August 2, 1919; Nebraska, August 2, 1919; Minnesota, September 8, 1919; New Hampshire, September 10, 1919; Utah, October 2, 1919; California, November 1, 1919; Maine, November 5, 1919; North Dakota, December 1, 1919; South Dakota, December 4, 1919; Colorado, December 15, 1919; Kentucky, January 6, 1920; Rhode Island, January 6,

1920; Oregon, January 13, 1920; Indiana, January 16, 1920; Wyoming, January 27, 1920; Nevada, February 7, 1920; New Jersey, February 9, 1920; Idaho, February 11, 1920; Arizona, February 12, 1920; New Mexico, February 21, 1920; Oklahoma, February 28, 1920; West Virginia, March 10, 1920; Washington, March 22, 1920; Tennessee, August 18, 1920.

Ratification was completed on August 18, 1920. The amendment was subsequently ratified by Connecticut on September 14, 1920 (and that State reaffirmed on September 21, 1920); Vermont, February 8, 1921; Delaware, March 6, 1923 (after having rejected it on June 2, 1920); Maryland, March 29, 1941 (after having rejected it on February 24, 1920, ratification certified on February 25, 1958); Virginia, February 21, 1952 (after having rejected it on February 12, 1920); Alabama, September 8, 1953 (after having rejected it on September 22, 1919); Florida, May 13, 1969; South Carolina, July 1, 1969 (after having rejected it on January 28, 1920, ratification certified on August 22, 1973); Georgia, February 20, 1970 (after having rejected it on July 24, 1919); Louisiana, June 11, 1970 (after having rejected it on July 1, 1920); North Carolina, May 6, 1971; Mississippi, March 22, 1984 (after having rejected it on March 29, 1920).

Article XX.

Section 1.

The terms of the President and Vice President shall end at noon on the 20th day of January, and the terms of Senators and Representatives at noon on the 3d day of January, of the years in which such terms would have ended if this article had not been ratified; and the terms of their successors shall then begin.

Section 2.

The Congress shall assemble at least once in every year, and such meeting shall begin at noon on the 3d day of January, unless they shall by law appoint a different day.

Section 3.

If, at the time fixed for the beginning of the term of the President, the President elect shall have died, the Vice President elect shall become President. If a President shall not have been chosen before the time fixed for the beginning of his term, or if the President elect shall have failed to qualify, then the Vice President elect shall act as President until a President shall have qualified; and the Congress may by law provide for the case wherein neither a President elect nor a Vice President elect shall have qualified, declaring who shall then act as President, or the manner in which one who is to act shall be selected, and such person shall act accordingly until a President or Vice President shall have qualified.

Section 4.

The Congress may by law provide for the case of the death of any of the persons from whom the House of Representatives may choose a President whenever the right of choice shall have devolved upon them, and for the case of the death of any of the persons from whom the Senate may choose a Vice President whenever the right of choice shall have devolved upon them.

Section 5.

Sections 1 and 2 shall take effect on the 15th day of October following the ratification of this article.

Section 6.

This article shall be inoperative unless it shall have been ratified as an amendment to the Constitution by the legislatures of three-fourths of the several States within seven years from the date of its submission.

Proposal and Ratification

The twentieth amendment to the Constitution was proposed to the legislatures of the several states by the Seventy-Second Congress, on the 2d day of March, 1932, and was declared, in a proclamation by the Secretary of State, dated on the 6th day of February, 1933, to have been ratified by the legislatures of 36 of the 48 States. The dates of ratification were: Virginia, March 4, 1932; New York, March 11, 1932; Mississippi, March 16, 1932; Arkansas, March 17, 1932; Kentucky, March 17, 1932; New Jersey, March 21, 1932; South Carolina, March 25, 1932; Michigan, March 31, 1932; Maine, April 1, 1932; Rhode Island, April 14, 1932; Illinois, April 21, 1932; Louisiana, June 22, 1932; West Virginia, July 30, 1932; Pennsylvania, August 11, 1932; Indiana, August 15, 1932; Texas, September 7, 1932; Alabama, September 13, 1932; California, January 4, 1933; North Carolina, January 5, 1933; North Dakota, January 9, 1933; Minnesota, January 12, 1933; Arizona, January 13, 1933; Montana, January 13, 1933; Nebraska, January 13, 1933; Oklahoma, January 13, 1933; Kansas, January 16, 1933; Oregon, January 16, 1933; Delaware, January 19, 1933; Washington, January 19, 1933; Wyoming, January 19, 1933; Iowa, January 20, 1933; South Dakota, January 20, 1933; Tennessee, January 20, 1933; Idaho, January 21, 1933; New Mexico, January 21, 1933; Georgia, January 23, 1933; Missouri, January 23, 1933; Ohio, January 23, 1933; Utah, January 23, 1933.

Ratification was completed on January 23, 1933. The amendment was subsequently ratified by Massachusetts on January 24, 1933; Wisconsin, January 24, 1933; Colorado, January 24, 1933; Nevada, January 26, 1933; Connecticut, January 27, 1933; New Hampshire, January 31, 1933; Vermont, February 2, 1933; Maryland, March 24, 1933; Florida, April 26, 1933.

Article XXI.

Section 1.

The eighteenth article of amendment to the Constitution of the United States is hereby repealed.

Section 2.

The transportation or importation into any State, Territory, or possession of the United States for delivery or use therein of intoxicating liquors, in violation of the laws thereof, is hereby prohibited.

Section 3.

This article shall be inoperative unless it shall have been ratified as an amendment to the Constitution by conventions in the several States, as provided in the Constitution, within seven years from the date of the submission hereof to the States by the Congress.

Proposal and Ratification

The twenty-first amendment to the Constitution was proposed to the several states by the Seventy-Second Congress, on the 20th day of February, 1933, and was declared, in a proclamation by the Secretary of State, dated on the 5th day of December, 1933, to have been ratified by 36 of the 48 States. The dates of ratification were: Michigan, April 10, 1933; Wisconsin, April 25, 1933; Rhode Island, May 8, 1933; Wyoming, May 25, 1933; New Jersey, June 1, 1933; Delaware, June 24, 1933; Indiana, June 26, 1933; Massachusetts, June 26, 1933; New York, June 27, 1933; Illinois, July 10, 1933; Iowa, July 10, 1933; Connecticut, July 11, 1933; New Hampshire, July 11, 1933; California, July 24, 1933; West Virginia, July 25, 1933; Arkansas, August 1, 1933; Oregon, August 7, 1933; Alabama, August 8, 1933; Tennessee, August 11, 1933; Missouri, August 29, 1933; Arizona, September 5, 1933; Nevada, September 5, 1933; Vermont, September 23, 1933; Colorado, September 26, 1933; Washington, October 3, 1933; Minnesota, October 10, 1933; Idaho, October 17, 1933; Maryland, October 18, 1933; Virginia, October 25, 1933; New Mexico, November 2, 1933; Florida, November 14, 1933; Texas, November 24, 1933; Kentucky, November 27, 1933; Ohio, December 5, 1933; Pennsylvania, December 5, 1933; Utah, December 5, 1933.

Ratification was completed on December 5, 1933. The amendment was subsequently ratified by Maine, on December 6, 1933,

*and by Montana, on August 6, 1934. The amendment was reject-
ed (and not subsequently ratified) by South Carolina, on December 4, 1933.*

Article XXII.

Section 1.

No person shall be elected to the office of the President more
than twice, and no person who has held the office of President,
or acted as President, for more than two years of a term to
which some other person was elected President shall be elected
to the office of the President more than once. But this Article
shall not apply to any person holding the office of President
when this Article was proposed by the Congress, and shall not
prevent any person who may be holding the office of President,
or acting as President, during the term within which this Article
becomes operative from holding the office of President or acting as President during the remainder of such term.

Section 2.

This article shall be inoperative unless it shall have been ratified
as an amendment to the Constitution by the legislatures of
three-fourths of the several States within seven years from the
date of its submission to the States by the Congress.

Proposal and Ratification

*This amendment was proposed to the legislatures of the several
States by the Eightieth Congress on Mar. 21, 1947 by House Joint
Res. No. 27, and was declared by the Administrator of General
Services, on Mar. 1, 1951, to have been ratified by the legislatures
of 36 of the 48 States. The dates of ratification were: Maine, March
31, 1947; Michigan, March 31, 1947; Iowa, April 1, 1947;
Kansas, April 1, 1947; New Hampshire, April 1, 1947; Delaware,
April 2, 1947; Illinois, April 3, 1947; Oregon, April 3, 1947; Col-
orado, April 12, 1947; California, April 15, 1947; New Jersey,*

April 15, 1947; Vermont, April 15, 1947; Ohio, April 16, 1947; Wisconsin, April 16, 1947; Pennsylvania, April 29, 1947; Connecticut, May 21, 1947; Missouri, May 22, 1947; Nebraska, May 23, 1947; Virginia, January 28, 1948; Mississippi, February 12, 1948; New York, March 9, 1948; South Dakota, January 21, 1949; North Dakota, February 25, 1949; Louisiana, May 17, 1950; Montana, January 25, 1951; Indiana, January 29, 1951; Idaho, January 30, 1951; New Mexico, February 12, 1951; Wyoming, February 12, 1951; Arkansas, February 15, 1951; Georgia, February 17, 1951; Tennessee, February 20, 1951; Texas, February 22, 1951; Nevada, February 26, 1951; Utah, February 26, 1951; Minnesota, February 27, 1951.

Ratification was completed on February 27, 1951. The amendment was subsequently ratified by North Carolina on February 28, 1951; South Carolina, March 13, 1951; Maryland, March 14, 1951; Florida, April 16, 1951; Alabama, May 4, 1951. The amendment was rejected (and not subsequently ratified) by Oklahoma in June 1947, and Massachusetts on June 9, 1949.

Certification of Validity

Publication of the certifying statement of the Administrator of General Services that the amendment had become valid was made on Mar. 1, 1951, F.R. Doc. 51 092940, 16 F.R. 2019.

Article XXIII.

Section 1.

The District constituting the seat of Government of the United States shall appoint in such manner as the Congress may direct:

A number of electors of President and Vice President equal to the whole number of Senators and Representatives in Congress to which the District would be entitled if it were a State, but in no event more than the least populous State; they shall be in addition to those appointed by the States, but they shall be considered, for the purposes of the election of President and Vice President, to be electors appointed by a

State; and they shall meet in the District and perform such duties as provided by the twelfth article of amendment.

Section 2.

The Congress shall have power to enforce this article by appropriate legislation.

Proposal and Ratification

This amendment was proposed by the Eighty-sixth Congress on June 17, 1960 and was declared by the Administrator of General Services on Apr. 3, 1961, to have been ratified by 38 of the 50 States. The dates of ratification were: Hawaii, June 23, 1960 (and that State made a technical correction to its resolution on June 30, 1960); Massachusetts, August 22, 1960; New Jersey, December 19, 1960; New York, January 17, 1961; California, January 19, 1961; Oregon, January 27, 1961; Maryland, January 30, 1961; Idaho, January 31, 1961; Maine, January 31, 1961; Minnesota, January 31, 1961; New Mexico, February 1, 1961; Nevada, February 2, 1961; Montana, February 6, 1961; South Dakota, February 6, 1961; Colorado, February 8, 1961; Washington, February 9, 1961; West Virginia, February 9, 1961; Alaska, February 10, 1961; Wyoming, February 13, 1961; Delaware, February 20, 1961; Utah, February 21, 1961; Wisconsin, February 21, 1961; Pennsylvania, February 28, 1961; Indiana, March 3, 1961; North Dakota, March 3, 1961; Tennessee, March 6, 1961; Michigan, March 8, 1961; Connecticut, March 9, 1961; Arizona, March 10, 1961; Illinois, March 14, 1961; Nebraska, March 15, 1961; Vermont, March 15, 1961; Iowa, March 16, 1961; Missouri, March 20, 1961; Oklahoma, March 21, 1961; Rhode Island, March 22, 1961; Kansas, March 29, 1961; Ohio, March 29, 1961.

Ratification was completed on March 29, 1961. The amendment was subsequently ratified by New Hampshire on March 30, 1961 (when that State annulled and then repeated its ratification of March 29, 1961). The amendment was rejected (and not subsequently ratified) by Arkansas on January 24, 1961.

Certification of Validity

Publication of the certifying statement of the Administrator of General Services that the amendment had become valid was made on Apr. 3, 1961, F.R. Doc. 61 093017, 26 F.R. 2808.

Article XXIV.

Section 1.

The right of citizens of the United States to vote in any primary or other election for President or Vice President, for electors for President or Vice President, or for Senator or Representative in Congress, shall not be denied or abridged by the United States or any State by reason of failure to pay any poll tax or other tax.

Section 2.

The Congress shall have power to enforce this article by appropriate legislation.

Proposal and Ratification

This amendment was proposed by the Eighty-seventh Congress by Senate Joint Resolution No. 29, which was approved by the Senate on Mar. 27, 1962, and by the House of Representatives on Aug. 27, 1962. It was declared by the Administrator of General Services on Feb. 4, 1964, to have been ratified by the legislatures of 38 of the 50 States. This amendment was ratified by the following States: Illinois, November 14, 1962; New Jersey, December 3, 1962; Oregon, January 25, 1963; Montana, January 28, 1963; West Virginia, February 1, 1963; New York, February 4, 1963; Maryland, February 6, 1963; California, February 7, 1963; Alaska, February 11, 1963; Rhode Island, February 14, 1963; Indiana, February 19, 1963; Utah, February 20, 1963; Michigan, February 20, 1963; Colorado, February 21, 1963; Ohio, February 27, 1963; Minnesota, February 27, 1963; New Mexico, March 5, 1963; Hawaii, March 6, 1963; North Dakota, March 7, 1963; Idaho,

March 8, 1963; Washington, March 14, 1963; Vermont, March 15, 1963; Nevada, March 19, 1963; Connecticut, March 20, 1963; Tennessee, March 21, 1963; Pennsylvania, March 25, 1963; Wisconsin, March 26, 1963; Kansas, March 28, 1963; Massachusetts, March 28, 1963; Nebraska, April 4, 1963; Florida, April 18, 1963; Iowa, April 24, 1963; Delaware, May 1, 1963; Missouri, May 13, 1963; New Hampshire, June 12, 1963; Kentucky, June 27, 1963; Maine, January 16, 1964; South Dakota, January 23, 1964; Virginia, February 25, 1977.

Ratification was completed on January 23, 1964. The amendment was subsequently ratified by North Carolina on May 3, 1989. The amendment was rejected by Mississippi (and not subsequently ratified) on December 20, 1962. Certification of Validity Publication of the certifying statement of the Administrator of General Services that the amendment had become valid was made on Feb. 5, 1964, F.R. Doc. 64 091229, 29 F.R. 1715.

Article XXV.

Section 1.

In case of the removal of the President from office or of his death or resignation, the Vice President shall become President.

Section 2.

Whenever there is a vacancy in the office of the Vice President, the President shall nominate a Vice President who shall take office upon confirmation by a majority vote of both Houses of Congress.

Section 3.

Whenever the President transmits to the President pro tempore of the Senate and the Speaker of the House of Representatives his written declaration that he is unable to discharge the powers and duties of his office, and until he transmits to them a written declaration to the contrary, such powers and duties shall be discharged by the Vice President as Acting President.

Section 4.

Whenever the Vice President and a majority of either the principal officers of the executive departments or of such other body as Congress may by law provide, transmit to the President pro tempore of the Senate and the Speaker of the House of Representatives their written declaration that the President is unable to discharge the powers and duties of his office, the Vice President shall immediately assume the powers and duties of the office as Acting President.

Thereafter, when the President transmits to the President pro tempore of the Senate and the Speaker of the House of Representatives his written declaration that no inability exists, he shall resume the powers and duties of his office unless the Vice President and a majority of either the principal officers of the executive department or of such other body as Congress may by law provide, transmit within four days to the President pro tempore of the Senate and the Speaker of the House of Representatives their written declaration that the President is unable to discharge the powers and duties of his office. Thereupon Congress shall decide the issue, assembling within forty-eight hours for that purpose if not in session. If the Congress, within twenty-one days after receipt of the latter written declaration, or, if Congress is not in session, within twenty-one days after Congress is required to assemble, determines by two-thirds vote of both Houses that the President is unable to discharge the powers and duties of his office, the Vice President shall continue to discharge the same as Acting President; otherwise, the President shall resume the powers and duties of his office.

Proposal and Ratification

This amendment was proposed by the Eighty-ninth Congress by Senate Joint Resolution No. 1, which was approved by the Senate on Feb. 19, 1965, and by the House of Representatives, in amended form, on Apr. 13, 1965. The House of Representatives agreed to a Conference Report on June 30, 1965, and the Senate agreed to the Conference Report on July 6, 1965. It was declared by the Administrator of General Services, on Feb. 23, 1967, to have been ratified by the legislatures of 39 of the 50 States. This amendment was ratified by the following States: Nebraska, July 12, 1965; Wisconsin, July 13, 1965; Oklahoma, July 16, 1965; Massachusetts, August 9, 1965; Pennsylvania, August 18, 1965; Kentucky, September 15, 1965; Arizona, September 22, 1965; Michigan, October 5, 1965; Indiana, October 20, 1965; California, October 21, 1965; Arkansas, November 4, 1965; New Jersey, November 29, 1965; Delaware, December 7, 1965; Utah, January 17, 1966; West Virginia, January 20, 1966; Maine, January 24, 1966; Rhode Island, January 28, 1966; Colorado, February 3, 1966; New Mexico, February 3, 1966; Kansas, February 8, 1966; Vermont, February 10, 1966; Alaska, February 18, 1966; Idaho, March 2, 1966; Hawaii, March 3, 1966; Virginia, March 8, 1966; Mississippi, March 10, 1966; New York, March 14, 1966; Maryland, March 23, 1966; Missouri, March 30, 1966; New Hampshire, June 13, 1966; Louisiana, July 5, 1966; Tennessee, January 12, 1967; Wyoming, January 25, 1967; Washington, January 26, 1967; Iowa, January 26, 1967; Oregon, February 2, 1967; Minnesota, February 10, 1967; Nevada, February 10, 1967.

Ratification was completed on February 10, 1967. The amendment was subsequently ratified by Connecticut, February 14, 1967; Montana, February 15, 1967; South Dakota, March 6, 1967; Ohio, March 7, 1967; Alabama, March 14, 1967; North Carolina, March 22, 1967; Illinois, March 22, 1967; Texas, April 25, 1967; Florida, May 25, 1967.

Certification of Validity

Publication of the certifying statement of the Administrator of General Services that the amendment had become valid was made on Feb. 25, 1967, F.R. Doc. 67 092208, 32 F.R. 3287.

Article XXVI.

Section 1.

The right of citizens of the United States, who are eighteen years of age or older, to vote shall not be denied or abridged by the United States or by any State on account of age.

Section 2.

The Congress shall have power to enforce this article by appropriate legislation.

Proposal and Ratification

This amendment was proposed by the Ninety-second Congress by Senate Joint Resolution No. 7, which was approved by the Senate on Mar. 10, 1971, and by the House of Representatives on Mar. 23, 1971. It was declared by the Administrator of General Services on July 5, 1971, to have been ratified by the legislatures of 39 of the 50 States. This amendment was ratified by the following States: Connecticut, March 23, 1971; Delaware, March 23, 1971; Minnesota, March 23, 1971; Tennessee, March 23, 1971; Washington, March 23, 1971; Hawaii, March 24, 1971; Massachusetts, March 24, 1971; Montana, March 29, 1971; Arkansas, March 30, 1971; Idaho, March 30, 1971; Iowa, March 30, 1971; Nebraska, April 2, 1971; New Jersey, April 3, 1971; Kansas, April 7, 1971; Michigan, April 7, 1971; Alaska, April 8, 1971; Maryland, April 8, 1971; Indiana, April 8, 1971; Maine, April 9, 1971; Vermont, April 16, 1971; Louisiana, April 17, 1971; California, April 19, 1971; Colorado, April 27, 1971; Pennsylvania, April 27, 1971; Texas, April 27, 1971; South Carolina, April 28, 1971; West Virginia, April 28, 1971; New Hampshire, May 13, 1971; Arizona, May 14, 1971; Rhode Island, May 27, 1971; New York, June 2, 1971; Oregon, June 4, 1971; Missouri, June 14, 1971; Wisconsin, June 22, 1971; Illinois, June 29, 1971; Alabama, June 30, 1971; Ohio, June 30, 1971; North Carolina, July 1, 1971; Oklahoma, July 1, 1971.

Ratification was completed on July 1, 1971. The amendment was subsequently ratified by Virginia, July 8, 1971; Wyoming, July 8, 1971; Georgia, October 4, 1971.

Certification of Validity

Publication of the certifying statement of the Administrator of General Services that the amendment had become valid was made on July 7, 1971, F.R. Doc. 71 099691, 36 F.R. 12725.

Article XXVII.

No law, varying the compensation for the services of the Senators and Representatives, shall take effect, until an election of Representatives shall have intervened.

Proposal and Ratification

This amendment, being the second of twelve articles proposed by the First Congress on Sept. 25, 1789, was declared by the Archivist of the United States on May 18, 1992, to have been ratified by the legislatures of 40 of the 50 States. This amendment was ratified by the following States: Maryland, December 19, 1789; North Carolina, December 22, 1789; South Carolina, January 19, 1790; Delaware, January 28, 1790; Vermont, November 3, 1791; Virginia, December 15, 1791; Ohio, May 6, 1873; Wyoming, March 6, 1978; Maine, April 27, 1983; Colorado, April 22, 1984; South Dakota, February 21, 1985; New Hampshire, March 7, 1985; Arizona, April 3, 1985; Tennessee, May 23, 1985; Oklahoma, July 10, 1985; New Mexico, February 14, 1986; Indiana, February 24, 1986; Utah, February 25, 1986; Arkansas, March 6, 1987; Montana, March 17, 1987; Connecticut, May 13, 1987; Wisconsin, July 15, 1987; Georgia, February 2, 1988; West Virginia, March 10, 1988; Louisiana, July 7, 1988; Iowa, February 9, 1989; Idaho, March 23, 1989; Nevada, April 26, 1989; Alaska, May 6, 1989; Oregon, May 19, 1989; Minnesota, May 22, 1989; Texas, May 25, 1989; Kansas, April 5, 1990; Florida, May 31, 1990; North Dakota, March 25, 1991; Alabama, May 5, 1992; Missouri, May 5, 1992; Michigan, May 7, 1992; New Jersey, May 7, 1992.

Ratification was completed on May 7, 1992. The amendment was subsequently ratified by Illinois on May 12, 1992.

Certification of Validity

Publication of the certifying statement of the Archivist of the United States that the amendment had become valid was made on May 18, 1992, F.R. Doc. 92 0911951, 57 F.R. 21187.

[Explanatory material courtesy MacMillan Law Library, Emory University.]

[*Editorial note:* There is some conflict as to the exact dates of ratification of the amendments by the several States. In some cases, the resolutions of ratification were signed by the officers of the legislatures on dates subsequent to that on which the second house had acted. In other cases, the Governors of several of the States "approved" the resolutions (on a subsequent date), although action by the Governor is not contemplated by article V, which required ratification by the legislatures (or conventions) only. In a number of cases, the journals of the State legislatures are not available. The dates set out in this document are based upon the best information available.]

BERKLEY OXFORD

The first name—and the last word—in reference

BERKLEY OXFORD

THE WORLD TURNS TO OXFORD FOR ANSWERS.

THE OXFORD BUSINESS SPANISH DICTIONARY
0-425-19095-1

THE OXFORD ESSENTIAL DICTIONARY OF
ABBREVIATIONS
0-425-19704-2

THE OXFORD ESSENTIAL DICTIONARY OF
LEGAL WORDS
0-425-19706-9

THE OXFORD ESSENTIAL OFFICE HANDBOOK
0-425-19703-4